THE ROA
A Tale of High Treason

By
Richard Unwin

The third book of Laurence the Armourer

Fond impious man, think'st thou yon sanguine cloud,
Raised by thy breath, has quenched the orb of day?
Tomorrow he repairs the golden flood,
And warms the nation with redoubled ray.
Enough for me: with joy I see
The different dooms our fates assign.
Be thine despair and sceptred care;
To triumph, and to die, are mine.
He spoke, and headlong from the mountain's height
Deep in the roaring tide he plunged to endless night.

Thomas Grey.

Other books by the same author

On Summer Seas (Book 1 of Laurence the Armourer)

A Wilderness of Sea (Book 2 of Laurence the Armourer)

Who Wrote Marlowe? The Mystery of Christopher Marlowe

Ironmaster (The Life and Times of John Wilkinson)

WEB SITE: www.quoadultra.net

THE ROARING TIDE

1 – Poor Painted Queen

The crowd fell silent as they appeared. First came the daughters, five of them, sanctimoniously clutching their books of hours. Elizabeth of York, the eldest, came out first and alone, followed by the other four walking in pairs. The great abbey of Westminster from which they emerged, massive and impassive, diminished them. Dressed in their best finery they moved slowly, the morning air motionless with only the fluid movements of their young bodies swirling the pale blue silk and white voile that floated around them. There was some small rumbling in the throats of the crowd, but little in the way of hostility. In truth, most were glad that the impossible situation with the daughters of the late King Edward the Fourth and his queen was at last resolved and they were to come out of sanctuary. Elizabeth, her mother's true daughter, had her head high, neither looking to the right or left, but straight ahead, disdaining the crowd. Her sisters were less confident. They walked with downcast eyes in the order of their birth and in fear of the crowd: Cecily named for the king's mother beside Anne, then Catherine and Bridget, these two holding hands.

They made their way between the king's soldiers that were standing with their halberds ready should there be any hostility, though it soon became apparent what the crowd were waiting for was the emergence of the Wydville woman, now named Dame Elizabeth Grey, onetime queen of England. The princesses climbed into a covered wagon, aided by gentlemen of the king's household, and were swiftly taken off towards the river, where a barge would convey them to their new residence, arranged for them by King Richard.

Silence fell as if a giant hand had struck the people dumb. All eyes were turned towards the west door of the abbey, open like a gaping mouth where, any moment, the defunct queen would emerge. The world held breath as a small glimmer of light was discerned in the deep black throat of the abbey interior. Slowly the image drew nearer only to provoke a growl of disappointment as it was perceived that this was a procession of the abbey clergy, dressed in white robes and carrying lighted candles. Two dozen of them processed into the daylight, twelve each side. They stopped and turned to face each other before stepping back, making a passage between them.

Laurence the armourer stood with the rest, in spite of himself with bated breath. He had come to see the final solution to the problem that had bedevilled King Richard ever since he took the throne. Having the former Queen of England and her daughters living in sanctuary allegedly in fear of him was politically disconcerting. He cast a fearful eye at the sky, where the clouds, despite the stillness below, were chasing one another in dark fury. It was not raining, but the uncertainty of the moment was written there in a confusion of light and dark along with the promise of a storm to come. He touched the scar on his face, feeling it tight in the dampness of the cold morning air. A small, fair haired woman stood beside him, noting his gesture and remembering that it was in the defence of the sons of Elizabeth Wydville that Laurence de la Halle had come by that mark. She noted a few grey hairs among the dominant black of the short, neatly trimmed beard he wore, and thought that they could not be the result of age, he being but three and thirty years. Perhaps they were the visible product of those scars within that otherwise could only be seen in his eyes, and then only by one who cared for him enough to notice what lay in their depths. The pair turned their full attention to the west door of the abbey.

Soon she would come, she who had conjured up the magical mist at the battle of Barnet and whose witch of a mother, for all anyone knew, had caused the three suns to rise above the army of Edward earl of March before the battle of Mortimer's Cross then shortly after emblazoned on his banner showing the *Sunne in Splendour* at the Battle of Towton where he first won his crown. She who had turned the Lancastrian lords against each other at the battle of Tewksbury, bringing her king Edward of the House of York his greatest victory. She who had brought a royal prince, the king's brother Clarence to his doom, was now about to emerge once more into the world.

She came almost, it seemed, as if she had materialised from the depths of the abbey, her disembodied pale white face and neck the first parts of her to come into sight. As she moved out onto the steps of the abbey they could see she was dressed in a black gown decorated with light fawn embroidered collar and cuffs. She wore her hair as she always had, severely swept back from a face that, even yet, could be described as beautiful, though Laurence noticed that she had drawn the sheer veil so that any fine detail in her features would be smoothed away. Her headdress was a black hennin with a delicate trim to match her collar and truncated in the English style. A simple gold carcanet was at her throat, its centre containing a single red ruby, while hanging down the front of her gown was a jewelled pendant from which three pearls depended. As her daughters, she too carried a book of hours, based on her private psalter. Was this a show of false piety, he wondered? His thoughts drifted darkly to an image of the lady Margaret Stanley, another who used her piety as a weapon and to protect her from the consequences of her black scheming.

Dame Elizabeth Grey stopped at the top of the steps that led down from the abbey and waited quietly. The hush of expectation became palpable. Laurence fingered the silver reliquary at his neck and muttered a paternoster under his breath. The reliquary contained metal filings from the nail that had fixed the feet of Christ to the cross and was a powerful talisman. His female companion crossed herself, as she gazed at the former queen, no less in awe of her power than Laurence. She moved closer to Laurence suddenly feeling the need for protection. He looked down at her and smiled comfortingly. She was Anna, the wife of his father-in-law Cornelius Quirke. The apothecary was laid up on his sickbed though he would be waiting anxiously for a report from the pair when they returned to his shop near the Cripplegate.

There was a further stir within the abbey as a man, dressed as a herald, stepped out and after bowing gracefully to dame Grey, turned to the crowd and unrolled a parchment. Looking around to ensure he had their full attention he began to read:

"*A proclamation of the high and mighty Richard the Third, by the grace of God King of England, France and Lord of Ireland,*" he paused dramatically and looked around the crowd before continuing. "*I promise and swear that if the daughters of Elizabeth Grey, late calling herself queen of England should come to me out of sanctuary in Westminster Abbey and be guided and ruled by me, then I shall see that they be sure of their lives, suffer no hurt, nor be imprisoned, but I shall put them into honest places of good name and arrange good marriages for them to gentlemen of good family born. They shall have all the things that they require as my kinswomen. Also I shall give them lands and property to the value of two hundred marks for the terms of their lives. . .*"

"The king is over generous, I think," whispered Laurence to Anna Quirke.

"Your recent assurances to her regarding the young prince, Richard of York have worked, it would seem," she returned. He stroked at his beard and thought on this. It was true that he had been the one to arrange the secret removal of the young prince from the

9

Tower of London, and to secure him a safe haven abroad. The Lancastrian faction, headed by Margaret Stanley, countess of Richmond, had been desperate to get at the boy and she was incandescent when she suspected he was no longer in the Tower. She and the traitorous duke of Buckingham had spread rumours that the two princes, Edward and his brother Richard had been murdered in the Tower on the order of their uncle, the king. It had been a ruse to get King Richard to disprove the rumour by declaring their whereabouts. This he had refused to do, realising that the knowledge there was a Plantagenet prince somewhere in the world would be a constant threat to Lady Stanley's plans to put her own son on the English throne. The king knew that the young prince Richard, his nephew whose sacred duty of guardianship had been placed upon him by his brother King Edward, once discovered would not live long. In order to establish some credence for Henry Tudor, the descendant of a dubious line of bastard Beauforts and Tudors, the two sons of Edward the fourth had to be dead, having a better claim than Henry. One of them, the elder prince Edward was indeed dead, but the other was free and just a few in the land knew where he was, Laurence de la Halle being one. Now, after a secret meeting with the king's armourer, Elizabeth Wydville, now called by the name of her first husband John Grey, also knew the truth regarding the fate of her sons, which was why she had decided it was safe to come out of sanctuary.

". . .*Furthermore I shall place dame Elizabeth Grey into the protection of my servant John Nesfield, squire of my body, giving him the administration of an allowance of seven hundred marks each year to keep her during her natural life. Furthermore, I shall give no faith nor credence to any evil pertaining to dame Grey or her daughters, nor put them to any manner of punishment . . .*"

"Dame Grey has done better than she might have expected," murmured Laurence.

"I wonder if she sees it that way," whispered Anna. "A woman of her ambition must be seething at the loss of her lands and those of her family."

"His grace the king is ever generous in his treatment of women," said Laurence. "I saw Elizabeth Shore the other day with her new husband. Any other king would have had her hanged, or burned as a witch; she very nearly was, but after a short penance she is free and well married."

Anna snorted disdainfully. She had no desire to see the Shore woman put to death but she could not entirely approve of the former paramour of King Edward the Fourth escaping punishment so readily. The woman had done her share of mischief in those days last year when all was in confusion and Richard of Gloucester took the Crown of England. She considered briefly that perhaps her feelings were simply those of jealousy as she looked up at the tall dark man beside her. They had been lovers once and had a son together. Their true relationship had never been revealed, though her husband, Cornelius, had some idea of their past. Elizabeth Shore had won some happiness with her new man and, she conceded with a sigh, good luck to her.

There was a stirring in the crowd as the court herald finished reading the king's proclamation. Everyone looked skywards as a distant rumble of thunder was heard. It was this that prompted dame Grey to quickly walk between the lines of clergy rather than pretend to be unhurried, as she would have preferred.

"Today is Monday - Monday thunder," said Laurence leaning down to speak into Anna's ear. "That means the death of women. I wonder not that the dame must needs to be away from here quickly." Both signed themselves at the thought.

Dame Grey was confronted by an elegant man robed *déguisée*, that is, in the latest fashion, who stood by a covered chariot ready to convey her to meet with the king at court, which at the moment was nearby at Westminster.

"Who is that man," asked Anna as she watched him install dame Grey in the conveyance with a good deal of polite bowing and genuflecting.

"It is he I told you of, John Nesfield. He it was who arranged my audience with dame Grey. I am sure you will be meeting him yourself before long. He is an agent of your husband, and now while Cornelius is sick, is helping out with his more *particular* business."

Before she could reply a spot of rain fell, followed closely by another. The crowd was dispersing fast as the month of March, having pretended a lamb for some days, was now about to display its legendary leonine attributes as the wind began to rise. The rows of clergy scuttled back into the abbey, the flames of their candles extinguished in the consequential draught of their rapid dispersal.

Anna and Laurence pulled up the hoods of their mantles and moved towards the palace of Westminster where they knew dame Grey was taken. Laurence had been commanded to attend upon the king and Anna would wait close by there rather than go back alone to the apothecary's shop in the city. The king's armourer was well known to the Sergeant at Arms at the palace gate and he passed easily through into the great hall accompanied by Anna. The place was alive with chatter and colour. He pushed a way for them through the press of courtiers, merchants, lawyers and others who were there to consult with the king. He knew that King Richard preferred to conduct his private business in an ante-chamber and this was where he headed. Two halberdiers guarded the stout oak door and even the king's armourer, though recognised by the guards, would not gain entry until conducted within by royal command.

Laurence looked about him, wondering where to deposit Anna while he attended upon the king. Lord Stanley was hovering around and when he saw Laurence he beckoned him over. He was dressed in black doublet and hose covered over with a mantle of red velvet trimmed with sable. His beard, jutting out from his chin like a weapon, was his dominant feature. His attitude was habitually avuncular and he looked benignly on Anna.

"Is this your lady?" he asked innocently. Lord Thomas Stanley was a powerful magnate and even though his wife, the lady Margaret was the chief conspirator of the land, yet King Richard could hardly ignore his power. He owned most of the northwest of England and the Isle of Man. His brother, William, who Laurence had good reason to steer well clear of, owned vast estates in Cheshire. Laurence swept him a low bow of obeisance while Anna sank respectfully before him. "Please arise my dear," he intoned gracefully. Anna got to her feet and stood there, head bowed, hardly knowing how to conduct herself. She was of low birth and had never ever been so close before to a man of lord Stanley's rank. She was petrified and Laurence took her arm to calm her. He had first met her in an alehouse where she worked under her stepfather, a cruel bully. Laurence had got her away from there but she had never been in a situation greater than a tavern or a servants' hall. As the wife of Cornelius Quirke, a prosperous apothecary, she had some local status, but this was not nearly enough to sustain her at court.

"May I present mistress Anna Quirke," said Laurence gallantly. "She is the wife of my father-in-law and I have brought her with me to witness the coming out of sanctuary of dame Grey." Anna bobbed him a further curtsey.

"How kind of you," replied lord Stanley. "I think, master armourer, you are to attend upon his grace the king . . .?"

"That is so, my lord."

"Then allow me to see that mistress Quirke is entertained while you are with his grace." With that he beckoned over a lady who had been standing nearby. "Lady Staunton, would you please take mistress Quirke into your care. She is a stranger at court and in need of some small comfort."

"As it pleases your lordship," said the lady who spoke with a northern brogue and therefore probably hailed from the northern estates of lord Stanley. She took Anna by the elbow and led her to the side of the hall where there were seats. He watched as they walked away and lady Staunton conducted Anna to a bench that was occupied by two ladies. Lady Staunton it seemed had some authority and she waved them away and directed Anna to sit alone with her. Laurence was swept with a sense of unease as he observed this performance, but there was nothing he could do about it for the moment and at least he was free to devote his attention to the king when called upon.

"The king has some strange ways, don't you find?" said lord Stanley.

"Kings are different to other men," Laurence replied non-committally, wondering what the lord was driving at.

"I mean here you are, his armourer, commanded to attend upon his grace while at the same time he entertains the Wydville woman."

"I suppose dame Grey will be conducted to the chamber of Queen Anne. I have no more idea than you have, my lord except his armour is, at present being gilded and I believe he wants some work done on the harness of his prince, the lord Edward. No doubt the king wishes to know when the work will be finished."

"I have heard that the young prince is unwell up at Middleham castle. If you go into Wensleydale now, you will find yourself in the company of nursemaids, physicians and astrologers."

"I fear that is so, my lord, and therefore the young prince will be pleased with any diversion I can bring him."

"Well, we speculate. Here is that Nesfield fellow, the Wydville's shadow. It seems you are required." Lord Stanley turned and strolled off to be immediately surrounded by other courtiers anxious to associate with the powerful magnate. The door to the king's privy chamber had opened and John Nesfield was indeed beckoning to Laurence to come to him.

Laurence already had some dealing with the man and was yet to make up his mind about him. King Richard had appointed him to have particular charge of Elizabeth while she was in sanctuary. At first glance he appeared as any number of courtiers, dressed in the latest fashion commensurate with his status as one of King Richard's captains of the fleet. Today he was wearing green doublet and yellow hose with fashionable pointed toed slippers. His mantle was black wool lined with *foynes*, stone-marten fur. His manners were obsequious when in the presence of a noble but tinged with arrogance when associating with those of lesser rank. Standing something just under six feet, he was muscular with a face that was broad with high cheekbones and framed by long, carefully combed brown hair. He sported a short forked beard. His demeanour with Laurence had previously been as that of an equal and so it was now, bordering on familiarity, though the two hardly knew each other well.

"Give you fair greeting," he said sweeping a courtly bow. "The king is asking for you, if you would come with me?" Laurence returned his bow and followed him through the door into the king's privy chamber.

King Richard the Third was seated at one end of the chamber on a low dais behind which was hung the cloth of state embroidered with the royal arms of England. His chair was draped with gold cloth and the king sat, his chin resting on his right hand as he looked down at the woman kneeling at his feet. The similar chair beside his was empty so Queen Anne was not to be privy to their meeting. Long tables were arranged either side of the chamber and Laurence briefly noted the presence of John Kendall, the king's secretary before he and Nesfield knelt and turned their faces up to the king. Lesser nobles expected a bowed head, but Laurence knew that a king did not take kindly to such an attitude; it smacked of guile and a monarch wanted to see plainly what was written in the faces of his courtiers.

The king ignored them for the moment while he stood and, smiling benignly, put his hands out towards the woman, dame Elizabeth Grey. She rose and took his hands in hers.

"Our heart is gladdened now that our misunderstandings are put behind us," he told her kindly. "For once we may engage our minds in a common cause, with the help of these gentlemen." With that he looked directly at Laurence and John Nesfield. He released her hands and indicated they should stand. As they did so dame Elizabeth turned to face them. Laurence had spoken privately with her some weeks ago and then found himself slightly shocked by her appearance. Previously he had only ever seen her at the court of King Edward, and with the rest had marvelled at her beauty, though at some distance. Today she was showing her years and the signs of the stress she had suffered while in sanctuary. The veil she had worn on the steps of the abbey had been put back over her hennin. Her face was painted thickly in an attempt to hide her wrinkles, though nothing could disguise the fullness beneath her eyes and the severe lines each side of her mouth.

On reflection he considered that was not really surprising. She had borne twelve children in all, ten of them to King Edward, and at forty-six years no woman could expect to preserve her good looks as a consequence. Her eyes were deep and dark brown, he noticed as she scrutinised his face coldly, but with interest, an improvement from the disdain she had regarded him with when last they met. He recalled how Edward had lost interest in her during the final few months of his life, declaring that his greatest love was his paramour Elizabeth Shore, not Elizabeth his queen. At the end Edward took from her the guardianship of their two sons and placed them into the care of his brother, Richard of Gloucester. From that point, when Edward died suddenly, her fortune had declined spectacularly. She, along with her brothers, had moved to deprive the duke of Gloucester of his guardianship of the two princes and failing, she was lucky indeed that she still lived or, at best, was not confined to a convent for life. Her eldest brother, earl Anthony Rivers and one of her sons, Richard, from her first marriage to Sir John Grey had, after all, lost *their* heads. Of course, that had been her only true marriage as her alliance with King Edward had been shown to be bigamous, thus void and the children of the union declared bastard; hence she was now known as dame Grey, the name of her first husband, which she seemed to prefer over her maiden name of Wydville.

All this Laurence knew well and he prudently let the remembrance of it scatter to ashes in the depths of his brain as he swept her an elegant bow.

"We meet again, good sir," intoned Elizabeth. Her voice had lost none of its regal tone. "This time in happier circumstances, I am led to believe." Laurence had the feeling her remark was couched for the benefit of the king, tinged as it was with residual doubt. King Richard's eyes flickered almost imperceptibly with annoyance but instantly regained their kindly gaze.

"I am sure the whole realm is glad to have you back in the world, my lady."

Elizabeth gave a toss of her head indicating she cared little for the opinions of the people. "I wish to learn what is to be done with my sons. One is beyond our earthly help, I know, but the other lives you have assured me." Was her declaration that it had been the king's armourer who had given this assurance another snipe at the king? He had better be careful here otherwise he might find himself in deep trouble.

"His grace the king has commanded me to secure the life of the lord bastard Richard and that I have done. Be assured he is, and will remain, safe and well."

King Richard presented Elizabeth with a solemn smile. "Edward, my brother's son, lies to the north within a plain but decent tomb. After we have dealt properly with our enemies then he shall be given a new one fit for his rank. At the moment the world is unaware he is dead and it must remain so for the sake of the living boy. The Lancastrians are looking for two princes and though they might suspect neither is in the Tower of London, they can do nothing without knowledge of what actually happened and that will not be forthcoming. We have managed to sow confusion, which is our best security."

"My lord king," interrupted John Nesfield, "I think it might be appropriate at this point to discuss the situation regarding the Tudor?"

"Yes, John, I believe you are right," said the king. "It concerns your son, the marques of Dorset, madam."

Laurence was intrigued. The marques of Dorset, Thomas Grey, was the lady's eldest son by her first marriage and had fled to Brittany and the Tudor after the failure of the duke of Buckingham's rebellion. Elizabeth Wydville, plotting from her sanctuary in Westminster Abbey, along with Margaret Beaufort had encouraged the duke in his attempt to overthrow King Richard and help put Henry Tudor on the throne, believing at the time that the king had murdered her two boys in the Tower of London. If the marques had been caught, he would have lost his head as Buckingham had, thus both her legitimate sons would be gone at the hands of King Richard. Now she was aware of the true fate of the two princes she bore to Edward, she no longer had an interest in promoting the Tudor, in fact, along with his mother Margaret Stanley, the Tudor was a dire threat to the life of the surviving boy. What, he wondered, was the king up to? Richard nodded to John Nesfield clearly intending that he should be the one to state what was afoot.

"Since the Tudor's last ignominious attempt at invading the king's realm of England," he began, "and the defeat of Buckingham, it is possible he might be discouraged to try again. Henry Tudor, however, is a constant annoyance even though in exile. His mother, Margaret Beaufort, the countess of Richmond still entertains the hope he will come over once again and take the throne of England from its rightful king. That is why, by order of the king, she is confined to her house under the authority of her husband, lord

Stanley. We are aware that her plotting continues in spite of this and will only stop when her hopes are finally extinguished. Furthermore, the Council of Regency in France and Duke Francis in Brittany are using the Tudor as a counter in the dispute between their two countries. Duke Francis is threatening to send him to France unless King Richard sends him military aid. It is therefore my lord king's intention to encourage Henry Tudor to invade again when he can be brought to battle and defeated once and for all."

"How is that to be done?" asked Laurence. He understood that France wanted to invade and incorporate Brittany into her own territory and, as a Breton himself, wished to prevent that. King Louis the Eleventh had died just last year and his son, Charles the eighth, was a mere boy. A council of regency had been formed in France to serve during his minority.

"To start with, by undermining his support amongst his fellow exiles," replied Nesfield. "There is much discontent there, even though most of them are committed Lancastrians. While in Brittany they are impotent and they have lost lands here in England. Some already acknowledge that the crown of England is secure and might be persuaded to make their peace with our king, in spite of their dynastic differences, and hope to be restored. His grace wishes to tempt them with that possibility, at least for some of them." King Richard held up a hand at this point to stop Nesfield's narrative.

"You might wonder why I am so lenient in this regard," he said pointedly. "It is because I desire peace for my realm and this will not happen until old differences are healed. The Tudor is an impediment and when he is removed there is no other to make a challenge that will disturb us. The marques of Dorset is central to my plan. He was prominent at court during the rule of my brother Edward. He is no Lancastrian and thus a valuable potential ally. I wish him to be informed that there is no bar to his returning to England, indeed reward is all that will follow; it will be in his best interests to do so." He looked directly at Elizabeth as he spoke.

Laurence could see the process of logic chasing across her face in spite of the fact that, as a former queen, she should be practised in anonymity of facial expression. At the moment the Wydvilles were powerless, but with her eldest son returned she might yet retrieve something from the shambles she and her family had created. *And her little prince lived, with a better claim to the throne than Henry Tudor!*

"I shall write to my son the marques telling him of your grace's intention," was her decisive reply. In fact there could have been no other. Her alternative was to retire into a convent and she had twice in her life tasted the boredom of sanctuary; besides, Elizabeth Wydville was not of that stamp, not while there was some advantage to play for, and she yet had a son, and girls to marry off. "Have you the means of getting word to him secretly?"

"We believe so," said the king, turning to Laurence as he spoke.

Laurence's stomach dropped upon his bowels at the sudden turn of events. He had walked into this situation in complete innocence, stupid perhaps, but there it was.

"My lord king . . .? " was all he could utter.

"You once made harness for Dorset's uncle Anthony Wydville, did you not?"

"That is so, your grace. I made his battle harness and maintained his jousting armour."

"Master Laurence, we find you perfectly placed for this agency," intoned the king superciliously. "As a native Breton you may enter Brittany and move amongst the Lancastrian exiles there with some ease. You are liegeman to duke Francis of Brittany, to whom we are not well disposed at the moment. Duke Francis has disturbed us, once his best ally, but he fears France. All this means you can give a credible reason why you have come out of England. It will not be the first time you have gone there on the business of the English court, so, unless you can come up with another more suitable candidate . . . ?" King Richard spread his arms and laughed. Laurence felt it prudent not to mention that the last time he had been in Brittany, on the business of King Edward, he ended up spending three months in a St Malo goal. Nevertheless, in this instance he was the only man for the job, and he knew it.

* * *

Rain lashed the river turning the surface to froth as they sat in the small boat, huddled within their mantles, hoods down and feeling the wet soak through. The waterman was oblivious to the weather, clad in an oiled coat with a hat of similar kind on his head and tied securely under his chin. He pulled for the city shore, expertly dodging the larger craft plying the river that were careless of any smaller vessels. Laurence was pleased they had decided to come to Westminster by water rather than on horseback. The trip up river had been relatively pleasant, and now it was raining, the return journey, aided by the flow of the River Thames was at least speedy. He had not relished the plod on horseback along the Strand to

Westminster and back again. They huddled down further as the small craft rounded the bend in the river while the wind, sweeping across Lambeth Moor drove the rain into their faces. Finally, the waterman landed them near the outlet of the Fleet River and after some haggling, brought about by a demand for more money due to the weather conditions, Laurence paid him off and they began the tramp towards St Paul's, massive and grey, its upper pinnacles obscured in the louring clouds.

Traversing St Paul's churchyard, they made their way across Watling Street and soon were hurrying, as bravely as they could, through the mire that was Wood Street towards the Cripplegate. Just before the massive gate they turned down a side lane and flung themselves through a doorway above which hung a sign inscribed with a pestle and mortar. The room they entered, though unheated was at least dry. A youth was sitting behind a table with a candle illuminating a paper on which he was writing. An inkhorn was propped by a clay bowl and a couple of spare quills lay beside it along with a small sharp knife. He looked up as they came in.

"Good e'en, mother," he said, his face breaking into a smile. "We were hoping you would make it home before the curfew."

"I see you are practising your letters, Philip," Anna replied fondly.

"I am," he said and presented the page to her. She handed it to Laurence, being unable to comment on what was written there other than observe her sons neatness of line.

"This is a description of the humours of the body," stated Laurence as he scrutinised the paper. "You have them all here: blood, yellow bile, black bile and phlegm. Very good; I suppose you have been in the company of Dr. Maddison again?" The physician was a friend of Cornelius, whose recipes were the only ones the apothecary made up without altering them.

"Dr Maddison is with grandfather now," replied Philip. "He has prescribed a concoction of lungwort to ease the phlegm off his chest." The boy was acutely interested in the details of simples and other medicines used for healing and remembered exactly how each was used. Laurence looked at Anna. They had already spoken together regarding Philip's future and, seeing that he had a clear penchant for medicine, and encouraged by Dr Maddison's interest in the boy, they were wondering if he should be sent away to university. Of course, the final decision was with her husband, Cornelius Quirke. Philip was Laurence's natural son with Anna, although they had kept this secret even from the boy, who believed his father to have been Barrat Thorne, Anna's first husband. The apothecary had been ailing for some months now and the good doctor had been a regular caller both professionally and as a friend. They would raise the matter of Philip's education now that Cornelius and Dr Maddison were conveniently together.

"Let us get out of these wet clothes," said Anna. "We need to speak to Cornelius seeing as you are to go into Brittany." The two of them left Philip to his letters and made their way through to the interior of the house where the apothecary lived and had his workroom. They passed by a niche where the floor was covered in straw. This was the lair of a great wolfhound, named simply Beast, as nobody had thought of a proper name for the animal. The creature was nowhere to be seen and they expected it would be loose in the garden of the house, especially if Mother Malkin was tending the medicinal herbs that grew there. The massive animal followed the old crone around like a lapdog, though if an intruder should be foolish enough to enter the house or garden he would find himself in danger of being torn to pieces. Laurence was wary of the beldam, thinking her to have powers not entirely approved of by Holy Church and he was not sure if Beast had become her familiar – most witches had one. He was careful to keep these thoughts to himself when Anna was around. She was fiercely defensive of the old woman. He contented himself by touching his own charm, the reliquary hanging around his neck, whenever the old woman entered the house.

Both Laurence and Anna knew Mother Malkin from the days when they first met, on the Great March when King Edward the Fourth won his crown back after returning from exile in 1471. She was a cunning woman who tended the hurts, illnesses and wounds of the soldiers in Edward's army. Having been cast out to starve in London from her later position in the household of the duke of Clarence, Laurence had found her and brought her to his wife Joan. The beldam had some information locked away in her confused brain, which they needed in order to effect the rescue of the lady Anne Neville from the duke of Clarence's clutches and take her to Richard of Gloucester. Having told them what she knew, Anne was discovered and having later married Richard of Gloucester, was now queen of England. Mother Malkin was taken into the home of the apothecary due to her extensive knowledge of herbal and other more practical healing skills.

Laurence quickly changed into dry clothes. When in London he stayed with the apothecary using the same chamber he had once shared with his wife, Joan. Before leaving the room, he patted the lid of the great chest where Joan had kept her clothes; empty now they had been sold, being of good quality. He had brought them to London from their home in Gloucester then made sure not to have been in the house when they were taken away. Joan would have hated the idea of them not being used when there were those in the town who would benefit from them. Somewhat more comfortable now he was dry again, he left the chamber, gently pulling the door shut, as if to bang it would disturb Joan's spirit and went down to join Dr Maddison and the apothecary.

The room where the apothecary lived and worked was spacious with a large workbench in its centre covered in a proliferation of bowls, jars and other paraphernalia used by Cornelius in his trade. Around the walls were shelves and cupboards containing mysterious ingredients and objects of which only those who practised the arts of healing knew the properties. A variety of dried animal parts hung from the rafters including the wings of bats, ravens, a peacock tail; skeletons of mammals and birds, even the horn of a unicorn. Dr Maddison was sitting by Cornelius who was slumped in a chair by the fireside with a woollen blanket around his shoulders. The physician stood and greeted Laurence with a friendly smile. He was a short, rotund man who liked to dress in the finest clothes. As a physician he had become a wealthy man, a fact not lost on Laurence who was beginning to consider the benefit of such a career for Philip. Of course, the decision on that was in the hands of Cornelius as Anna's husband and thereby in *loco parentis* as it were. It had been prudent for Laurence not to acknowledge the boy as his bastard son, but at least he might still have a measure of control over the boy's future. He bowed politely to the doctor just as Anna came into the room. Dr Maddison swept her a gallant bow, his attention diverted from Laurence for the moment.

"I see you have Philip at his letters?" said Anna gaily, as a way of opening the conversation regarding Philip's education.

"He writes down everything I tell him, as if he were constructing a learned text," said Dr Maddison with a nod of his head. "I tried him with some Greek the other day and although he struggled mightily with the meaning, he soon mastered the little I gave him."

"The boy needs to go where he can get himself some proper learning," muttered Cornelius, in a voice thick due to his chest ailment.

That is true," agreed the doctor. "Cambridge would be the best place for him. I studied there myself. He will need to master Latin,

Greek, astrology, logic and rhetoric before he can enter a medical faculty."

"We have some unpleasant memories of Cambridge," said Anna interrupting him and looking towards Laurence. The armourer felt at his throat, recalling the incident she was referring to when he was part hanged. That was on the road back from Cambridge to London, though, at Duxford.

"I cannot think that Oxford would be any less violent than the colleges at Cambridge," he mused. "Both universities breed opinion that leads to all sorts of trouble and students are always ready to fight."

"Yes," agreed Dr Maddison, "and not only amongst themselves; there is the abiding detestation between town and gown, a sort of running warfare."

"Worse at Cambridge, being the newer of the two universities and having a history of conflict with the townspeople."

"Philip will have to make his way no matter which university he attends," declared Cornelius.

"I would be pleased to contribute to Philip's support while he is a scholar," said Laurence, looking around at the assembly. Cornelius gazed at him quizzically while Anna smiled fondly at him.

"I might make the necessary enquiries with the Proctor at Queens," offered Dr Maddison beaming in his usual avuncular manner. "It is one of the newer colleges?"

"If you would do that," replied Cornelius, "it would be well if we get working on the preliminaries and then consider the cost of it all."

"I will write to the Proctor at Queens right away." The doctor reached for his mantle, which was draped over a chair, and enveloped himself in it. "I must hurry; the curfew will be ringing soon and I don't want to get taken up by the Watch," he chuckled, only half in jest.

Once the doctor had left they assembled together at the fireside with Cornelius, to discuss the day's events. The room had a proper stone fireplace, a necessity for the apothecary who needed a good fire to make up some of his potions. Laurence told him what the king had said. The apothecary had his agents on the continent and Laurence would need the names of contacts there if he were to prosecute the king's instructions.

"I understand well the king's strategy," wheezed Cornelius Quirke. "Now that the Wydville's five daughters are out of sanctuary they are available to be married off and that must have the Tudor wetting himself with frustration."

"Yes," said Anna who was ladling out a bowl of potage for him from a cauldron suspended over the fire. "And also Margaret Beaufort his mother. Her plan is for him to marry one of them, in fact, I have heard he has declared his intention of taking the eldest, Elizabeth of York to wife despite the fact of her illegitimacy."

"Which he expects to ignore if he ever wins the crown of England, and that is unlikely," snorted Cornelius. "His mother spent a considerable time trying to get King Edward to allow her son to return to England and marry one of his daughters. Edward pretended to fall in with her plan, wishing to get hold of Henry Tudor, but Henry, advised no doubt by his uncle Jasper, was having none of it and remained in Brittany, except for his abortive invasion last year."

"Yet if Laurence manages to get the marquis of Dorset to return to the fold, then others will almost certainly follow and all except his most ardent supporters are bound to waver in their commitment to his cause." She handed the wooden bowl to her husband along with a carved spoon. After slowly stirring the contents, he began spooning some of the pottage into his mouth.

Laurence, who had been leaning against the apothecary's workbench, pushed himself off to stand upright. "It could be that the problem with Henry Tudor will fade if we can degrade his support sufficiently. In that case he will never try an invasion and it is unlikely either duke Francis or the French court will want to finance him then. The wonder is he has managed to maintain his pretence to the throne for so long."

"That is due to the efforts of his mother," said Anna. "I believe that if she had died when he was born, which she very nearly did, her son would never had thought to pursue such a course."

"That is why the king is pushing him hard," said Laurence. "If his plan works, the Tudor must invade quickly or lose all future chances. The advantage is that he will have less time to gather meaningful support and thus any invasion force would be relatively small and easy to defeat."

Cornelius nodded in silent agreement. Laurence had no further comment to make as his mind had drifted on to something else.

"What did lady Staunton talk to you of while I was with the king?" he asked Anna.

"She was inquisitive, to say the least," replied Anna, "mostly with regard to you."

"Don't tell me she wants a suit of harness?" he joked.

23

Anna laughed. "No, but she seemed to know of your family and in particular Robert's position with the duke of Norfolk."

Laurence dropped his chin onto his chest and began to pace the room. She knew what he was thinking and left him alone for a few moments while his mind cleared. His wife, Joan, the only daughter of Cornelius, had died of the sweating sickness less than two years hence at their home in Gloucester where he had his forge and armoury. His two daughters, one a baby and the other but four years had died too. His son Robert, being ten years at the time had been speedily removed away from the forge and into the care of John Fisher, his steward at Gloucester and fellow armourer. Thus Robert had escaped the contagion. Afterwards, Robert had been found a place as a page in the household of John Howard, the duke of Norfolk where he hoped to rise and become a man-at-arms in the duke's service.

"Do we know anything of this lady Staunton?" he asked Cornelius. The apothecary thought for a moment then tugged at his beard.

"She is of the Stanley household. I know nothing of her except that. I think we must consider her as being close to lady Margaret, unless lord Stanley has suddenly taken a paramour – but the whole court would know if that were the case."

"Is it possible lady Margaret knows something as to how Robert helped free the lord bastard Richard from the Tower?" A worried frown creased Laurence's brows as he considered the possibility. "He was seen quite clearly with me at the Tower, though nobody at the time could possibly suspect how we actually freed the boy, indeed it did not become apparent the two boys were no longer there for some days. There had been much going to and fro at the Garden Tower afterwards to deliberately give the impression the two princes were still there."

"Very few know of the escape," returned Cornelius.

"Well dame Grey knows, for sure," replied Laurence. "By the king's order I told her myself what had happened with her sons. Until then she had believed the rumours, spread by Margaret Stanley herself, that King Richard had murdered the boys. The two women had been in regular communication which, after I made my disclosure, will have stopped, or at least changed in tone. Perhaps the fact that dame Grey suddenly became reconciled to the king and has come out of sanctuary along with her daughters, alerted Margaret Beaufort to the probability that the former queen now knows what really happened?"

"Yes," mused Cornelius. "Lady Margaret will have demanded detailed reports from her spies at the Tower along with a list of everyone who visited them. You and Robert are bound to be on such a list, no matter how innocent it appeared at the time."

"Perhaps she believes the boys are in the household of John Howard," suggested Anna. "The duke of Norfolk is a trusted and loyal friend of the king. She may think him the one most likely to have the boys in hiding."

"That might be a deceit worth pursuing," said Cornelius with a crafty smile. In spite of his illness it seemed his dissembling faculties as an agent of the king were still in working order. He delighted in disseminating false information to put his adversaries off the scent.

Anna busied herself tugging the blanket closer around Cornelius. "I wonder if she has worked out that one of the boys is dead?"

"Highly unlikely," snapped Laurence. "Just as the common mass of people, that woman will have her mind fixed on murder. The idea that one of the boys might die of natural causes, being in poor health before he even went into the Tower will not occur to her and that is all to the good. Her spies will be looking for two boys, which serves to confuse the issue." Cornelius nodded in agreement.

Anna laughed suddenly at a thought that occurred to her: "If we were to spread a rumour that Edward had died as truly happened, lady Stanley would immediately suspect it as a ploy to hide his whereabouts!"

"Yes, believing it merely a subterfuge to stop her spies searching for him," chuckled Laurence. "The woman will never feel herself or her son safe until she has two identifiable dead bodies in view and until then she will keep searching." They all laughed together imagining the countess of Richmond, that dark and sinister woman, prayer book in one hand and condemnation ever at her lips, sending her spies ranging all over England searching for a phantom.

Cornelius looked up at Laurence. "I think that your planned agency to Brittany might provide her with another false alley to chase up."

"No doubt I shall be followed, which might prejudice my mission?"

"The best I can do is get you aboard ship and out of England without being detected. I think we can count on your being discovered soon after you land on the other side of the narrow seas. You must move fast. My advice is to get to the marquis of Dorset, give him the letter from his mother, dame Grey and convince him that his interests will be better served should he return to England. If successful, then move away to give him the freedom to do just that."

"I will, if I can escape detection for long enough. My best advantage is that Lady Stanley will have no idea where I am going and hopefully it will not occur to her I will be headed for Thomas Grey, a fellow exile of her son Henry Tudor. With any luck I can complete my mission and be clear of him before my trail is picked up."

"Afterwards she will have more to worry about than chasing you," said Cornelius. "If the marquis deserts Henry Tudor the chances are others may follow and all her plans put in severe jeopardy."

Outside the light was fading fast and soon Mother Malkin came shuffling into the house, the great dog with her. She carried a basket of herbs and placed these on the table and began sorting them into separate piles. Robert, too, came in having locked the front door of the shop and lit a couple of candles to supplement the light from the fireplace. Laurence fingered his reliquary, aware of the presence of the old woman who was muttering to herself as she sorted the herbs. It seemed she was naming them as she worked, but he could not be sure whether or not she was casting some sort of enchantment over them. He caught Anna's eye on him. She was looking at him askance having noticed his action and he rapidly took his fingers away from the silver phial. Anna gave a slight shake of her head and went over to the old woman to help her with her task. Cornelius let his head fall forward and began to doze. Robert was given the job of feeding the dog with reserved scraps. Laurence gazed longingly at the pottage pot and supposed he would have to look for his own bread and serve himself if he wanted to eat this evening.

2 – The Chase

"I can't seem to shake off the feeling I am standing on a shore of shifting sand," grumbled Laurence as he pulled his travelling cloak around him. "The king is away to Nottingham, Robert is at Framlingham with the duke of Norfolk, Philip will soon be away as a scholar and Cornelius is in poor health. Now I am to go into Brittany and who knows what the situation there will be."

"At least the king has a measure of control," responded Anna as she stood looking up at him. "From Nottingham Castle he can move quickly to almost any point in the kingdom. He is working hard to travel around and make himself visible to the people." They were standing outside the apothecary's shop. A local man was loading the last of Laurence's belongings on to a handcart ready to convey them to Smithfield, where he had arranged to join with a convenient band of merchants who were travelling to Gloucester. He would attend to his business before leaving for Brittany. He had orders for arms and harness that would keep his men there in employment while he was away. Hopefully, it would serve to confound any spies that might be trailing him.

It was entirely natural for him to go to Gloucester and his home forge, moreover there were some decided advantages regarding his present agency for the king. For one thing, if it were suspected he knew something of the whereabouts of the lord bastard Richard, he would be drawing anyone watching him in the wrong direction. After a day or so, from Gloucester he would take a quick trip down the River Severn to Bristol where Cornelius had arranged passage for him in a ship to Brittany. His sudden departure, designed to shake off any local pursuit, would alert Margaret Beaufort's spies to the probability that something was afoot. Once in Bristol and aboard ship it would be impossible for anyone to know where he was bound. In Brittany from that point on he would have to watch his back. Tudor spies would eventually pick up his trail, if alerted to look for him, but that would take several days at the worst and a couple of weeks at best. In any case, he had made the journey many times as his family were at Nantes, so his arrival in Brittany should not incur any particular suspicion.

He took Anna's hands in his and looked at her, strangely disturbed by the disquiet that his departure was bringing him. "Hopefully I shall soon be back in England," he said as if to comfort her. It was almost, he thought, as if he were saying his farewells to a wife rather than one who could only ever be a friend. The stillness that had suddenly descended between them was broken as Philip came up leading Laurence's horse, having fed and watered the animal ready for the road.

"Farewell, sir," he chirped gaily being taken up with the idea that Laurence was off on some sort of adventure. Laurence patted him on the shoulder.

"Take good care of your mother and master Cornelius." With that, he gave the man with the handcart a nod and they walked off together towards Smithfield and the party of merchants who would travel together for safety on the road.

As he tramped behind the cart leading his horse, Laurence pondered upon the situation he found himself in. For the moment, his loyalty to his liege lord, Duke Francis the Second of Brittany was in abeyance, seeing as how the duke had fallen into a bout of insanity and his chief minister, Pierre Landais seemed to be in control of events there. Relations between his homeland and the England of King Richard the Third were at low ebb. Breton pirates had been raiding the English coast and the duke had financed the recent abortive invasion of Henry Tudor. Laurence understood this was due to the threat from France. Louis the eleventh had died last year, but his ambition to subsume Brittany into his realm had been taken up by his daughter, Ann of Beaujeu with equal determination. True, the government of France was in turmoil due to the minority of her king, Charles the Eighth so Ann was acting as regent and she was beginning to show some ability. For the moment, however, neither the government of Duke Francis, nor that of France was in a position to support Tudor ambition, so now was the best time for King Richard to seek to undermine it.

Although Laurence, as a Breton, had originally entered England with no particular loyalty to any of her nobles, and with an instruction to get close to those who most influenced policy with regard to Brittany, he had become firmly attached to the duke of Gloucester, who was now the new king. His father-in-law, Cornelius Quirke, though ostensibly neutral, also favoured Richard.

He wondered how he was to present himself in Brittany; he could hardly describe himself as an envoy of King Richard if he wanted to get close to the Tudor exiles. Cornelius, an experienced spymaster, had discussed this with him. They had considered that the present discontent between the English king and Brittany was useful. He would explain he had come as an agent of Elizabeth

Wydville. Just because she was now out of sanctuary, there was no reason why the exiles should not think her remaining ill disposed towards the king. Margaret Beaufort's malicious lies regarding the supposed murder of the two princes in the Tower could be used to advantage. There was a kind of justice in that, the turning of her own lies against her cause. That particular subterfuge would not sustain him long. The probability was that lady Margaret had already realised the Wydville woman was vacillating and warming in her attitude to King Richard and would get word of this to her son Henry – the question was, how long would it take for the Tudors in exile to catch up on events in England?

* * *

The inn at the Sign of the Bell on Southgate Street was lively, its customers coldly indifferent to the tolling of the passing bells ringing from every church in Gloucester. What did they care if Edward of Middleham, the king's son and heir was dead? Each of them had suffered similar loss, not least Laurence the armourer. He, however, did feel keenly the death of the Prince of Wales. It had been at Gloucester where his wife and two daughters had succumbed to the sweating sickness. They lay just by the corner of Southgate Street, in the churchyard of St Michael the Archangel and it was almost as if he felt their presence, being so close. The news of the prince's death had brought back his own buried grief in a sudden rush. He imagined and felt something of the deep anguish King Richard and Queen Anne must be suffering. They were doting parents who cared deeply for their only child now languishing in purgatory until prayer passed him through to heaven. "*Sancte Michael, consolator animarum in purgatorio languentium, ora pro nobis,*" he muttered and crossed himself.

In one sense he felt himself fortunate he was here in Gloucester and not anywhere near the court. He could not bear the idea of looking upon the grief of the royal couple, or stand among the mass of courtiers and self-seekers whose doleful mien would be nothing more than a mask. Already some would be discussing the succession in secret whispers around dark corners. Here was another young death, another prince taken by sickness and nothing to be done about it. He considered how differently people had reacted when it was rumoured that the two sons of King Edward had been murdered. That stirred some people to anger and provoked cries for vengeance, yet death by disease had little claim on their

29

sensibilities. Here, in spite of the sound of the mournful passing bells there was hardly any diminution in their casual chatter.

"I suppose, it's because it's futile to rail at God. A king, being the next best thing and here with us in the world, becomes a substitute target for all the frustration and agony the death of a loved one brings us." The speaker was John Fisher, a fellow armourer and Laurence's forge master. Laurence's prayer, unconsciously spoken aloud, encouraged his response.

"I have often considered that an armourer is something akin to a priest," Laurence replied flippantly in an attempt to shake off his sadness. "We are intimate with the bodily secrets of our customers and always disguise any oddities so they may present themselves as perfect specimens of manhood. Just as with the secrets of the confessional, we never betray those secrets. Perhaps, like scribes, we should take holy orders?"

John Fisher laughed. "That would endow us with Benefit of Clergy. Then we could commit any number of misdemeanours and escape a hanging."

"Then we must propose it to our guild so that it becomes a tenet of our charter."

Their banter had served to lighten the mood and Laurence was now able to consider further his purpose. John had asked him what he knew of the fate of the two princes he believed were still in the Tower of London. Of course, he could not disclose what he knew, and contented himself by saying the boys would be fine, their uncle being committed to their care. He told him something of the Tudor threat to the boys, telling him this was why they were being kept out of sight. John, who could not but be infected by virulent rumours of murder was not entirely satisfied with this explanation, but realising that Laurence was close to King Richard, and with regard to their recent conversation, knew better than to probe further.

"You have spoken to nobody about my journey away from here?" he whispered. For safety he had not told John he was bound for Brittany. They were seated in a far corner of the tavern and the noise of the others in the room tended to mask what they were saying, but you never could tell. A crowded tavern was ideal for a spy and he was quite sure there would be at least one of Margaret Beaufort's men here watching his every move.

"There is a trow leaving the quay tomorrow at dawn. It is a regular trip downriver taking goods from the forge to Bristol. There is just one man and a boy in charge of it. They don't know it yet, but they will have a passenger tomorrow. The water is high at the moment and the tide is on the ebb then. You should have a fast trip and be well away before any steps can be taken to follow you."

Laurence was not so sure about that. There were several parts along the river that were too shallow to pass at low water. They would depend upon the hire of bowhauliers to attach ropes to the flat-bottomed trow and manually pull it over the shallows. This was a regular problem for anyone navigating the River Severn. The trow men tended to be piratical, attacking and robbing any other craft they suspected of taking away their trade. The bowhauliers were worse, being outright felons and were blight on the districts where they lived, usually near a low alehouse. He often hired a couple of men with crossbows to ensure the security of his goods when moving valuable weapons and harness by trow down to Bristol. He could hardly risk doing that tomorrow. Hopefully the water would be high enough for them to pass without hindrance.

"I will stay here tonight. Send someone to the stable and let it be known I wish to have my horse ready in the morning for a journey to Tewksbury. That might cause the stables to be watched and also the road out of town rather than the quay. I just need to get clear of Gloucester. It will not be difficult to work out afterwards that I have gone downriver but once in Bristol I will have disappeared into one of many vessels there. With any luck a pursuer will only be able to watch them as they sail away and wonder which one I am in."

Just then a rough looking fellow came by, seated himself close and leaned casually against the wall. He appeared to have no interest in them, seemingly besotted. He stared vacantly into his wine cup, swilling the dregs around the bottom.

"The road to Tewksbury is mired, I am told," said John in a voice just loud enough to carry to the fellow. "You will have to step carefully and make sure your horse is well shod. Mud is notorious for pulling off iron shoes."

"I will send to have it attended to," replied Laurence as he raised his cup indicating to one of the tavern wenches he wanted a refill. It was the hostess who came to him. She was a well-made woman of moderate height, her once youthful prettiness now turned to a mature and pleasant mien. She was dressed in good linen and wore a snow-white apron. Dark hair showed beneath a woollen coif.

"More wine, master Laurence? You are drinking well tonight it seems." She poured wine from a flask into his cup and then served John.

"Thank you Gurden," he replied saluting her, pretending to be slightly intoxicated. The rough fellow hunched his shoulders, a gesture that unintentionally moved him closer to them. Gurden smiled benignly. John was her man. He had not actually made an honest woman of her, but he lived at The Bell and she went by his name, Gurden Fisher. She had something of an unfortunate past and it had been Laurence who had saved her from freezing to death in a Gloucester lane, and John who had found her a place at this tavern. She had taken up with the landlord here, and when he drowned after falling drunk into a ditch, John provided the financial means for her to run the place. The arrangement was working very well and what with his income from the forge, and the profits she generated at the inn, they were becoming quite well off.

"You two must marry, I think," he declared suddenly. In fact he had been intending to broach the subject to John for some time. For one thing it would permanently tie John to Gloucester and assure his services at the forge while Laurence was about his extended business.

Gurden looked at John questioningly. He wriggled uncomfortably. He had spent most of his life, when not at the forge, in the alehouse or tavern. Here at Gloucester, working in Laurence's interests he had become somewhat settled, but his old habit of taking a woman and keeping to her only as long as he remained in a town still had a sentimental hold over him.

"I will think on it," he murmured as if to himself.

"Well the woman has your name, given to her freely by you," said Laurence. "And what would she do if anything happened to you? She will lose this place unless she is your wife." John looked at her fondly. It seemed that thought had not occurred to him and now that it was mentioned he knew he must consider it. Gurden said nothing, which was unusual for her. She put the wine flask down on a nearby table and leaned casually against a roof post, a soft and patient expression in her eyes.

"I will think on it," he repeated.

Laurence clambered to his feet. This act of being in his cups had provided him with an excuse to progress the matter. "Good masters," he called out. The whole tavern went quiet. "Our host here seems to be in a quandary. Should he take our hostess, our dear Gurden to wife or not?" Everyone shouted a resounding yes. "Then let us go to it right now!" The whole place became a cacophony of cheering and encouragement. John sank down into his seat, overwhelmed for the moment, but not, it seemed, overly disturbed by the prospect of marriage to Gurden.

Laurence took John by the arm and drew him to the centre of the tavern where the denizens moved back to clear a space. He beckoned Gurden over and she came to him, her eyes damp, never taking them off John. For some reason she took on a glow that seemed to light the room. John had never seen her like this and he wondered why he had never noticed this beauty in her before. In spite of himself he found he was unable to take his eyes from her. They stood facing each other. The room fell into a hush where even the timbers of the place dare not creak.

"Say the words, John," said Laurence quietly. John swallowed, his throat moving to betray his nervousness.

"I take thee, Gurden to be my lawful wedded wife."

Gurden smiled at him, clearly struggling to get out her own words.

"I take thee, John to be my lawful wedded husband."

With that, a cheer broke out and everyone started to clamour for more wine. Laurence raised his hand for silence. "There is one thing more," he declared. "John must kiss his bride, and seeing that their union is already consummated," a great cheer arose at this, "and they have made their declaration in front of all you as witnesses, in law, he is now bound to Gurden for life. This calls for a drink all round, I believe?"

John and Gurden were swept up in a whirl of well-wishers and it was some time before the two managed to break free and come to Laurence, who was responsible for the whole thing.

"I have no idea how that happened," spluttered John, who had already disposed of several cups, but I suppose I would never have done it by myself."

"I know your mind better than you do," returned Laurence. "You need Gurden to keep you in hand. Your wandering days are over my friend."

"I thank you, master Laurence," said Gurden, hardly less intoxicated than her new husband. "Be assured, he will be well looked after, you can depend upon it. I have two reasons now to be grateful to you."

John winked at him. "We must be early abed this night. We both have a long ride ahead of us, you to Tewkesbury and I . . ."

"That is quite enough, husband," said Gurden, already warming to the disciplinary duty that came with a good wife. The denizens of the tavern broke into a raucous cheer. Laurence looked around and was just in time to see the rough fellow previously noted ease himself out of the door, seemingly quite sober.

* * *

The quay at Gloucester was no place to wander alone at dawn, especially when a light mist drifted among the barrels, sacks and general trade goods standing ready for loading into the trows that ranged along the water front. A stench of rotting offal came from the far end of the quay, which was used by the butchers of the town to clean animal carcasses. A dark brown travelling mantle with a hood covered his black leather doublet, which was cut in the Italian style. The English style was stuffed with too much bombast and tended to inhibit his movements. Brown hose and calf-length leather boots completed his attire and rendered him somewhat anonymous. He had a baldric across his chest with a short sword, or murderer in a scabbard on his left side. Laurence made sure he wore his mantle open and thrown back to expose the scabbard and making it instantly accessible. Over his left shoulder he carried a leather sack containing the few belongings he needed for the journey. Hidden under his mantle was a purse with enough money to pay his way in Brittany. It wouldn't do to be robbed even before he set off on his journey.

He arrived at the quay just as the bells for matins sounded from the religious houses and churches in this part of the town. John had shown him out of the tavern by a back way and he believed he had not been observed. There were a few churls there already, loading goods into the trows. He walked along, examining the names on the vessels until he found the one he was looking for. Perhaps John had chosen this one for its name: Joan. It was tied to the quay and looked to be already loaded. A tall mast tapered upwards to disappear into the mist. The sail was furled but ready to hoist. The vessel was broad in the beam and long, with a short second mast stepped aft behind the main. Laurence had sailed in these craft before and knew they could carry a surprising amount of sail. Once well downstream of Gloucester and past any of the shallows that might slow them, they should make a fast passage. A young churl was untying the mooring ropes ready to slip and be away. In the stern he could just make out the shadowy form of the trow master. A mangy dog trotted up and down by the side of the trow, sniffing at the rubbish for any scraps. As he approached, it turned and bared its teeth, snarling a warning. The churl snapped a command and the dog jumped off the quay and into the trow.

"Are you master Quince?" he called to the man at the stern.

"Aye, master de la Halle. You are just in time," he said gruffly. "I but wait upon the matins bell, then shove off." It seemed he recognised the armourer and Laurence too thought he appeared familiar. "Are you coming with us this trip? There is a price to pay if you are."

"That I am," he replied, stepping across a short plank and into the vessel, while he and the dog kept a wary eye on each other. "You shall not lose by taking me along."

"I often carry the finished iron goods from your forge," Quince informed him. "But today's cargo is wool bound for Bristol. I've seen you often here on the quay, but this is the first time you've sailed with us. I hope you are handy?"

"I shall help if required," he replied, somewhat put out by the fellow's manner. He had not considered being part of the crew. The churl showed him to a locker where he could secure his belongings. As he closed the lid, the dog came sniffing around the bales of wool cargo, then gave a cough and settled down on the deck, its head on its paws and its eyes wide open.

"'E be looking for rats," said Quince. "That's what I keep 'im for, in spite of the risk o' plague. Never been troubled wi' plague on the river."

"I think it is just the stray dogs and cats that bring the plague," replied Laurence. "In London and Gloucester too, all the strays are regularly rounded up and killed. There are more rats now, of course, but that is better than plague."

"Plague still 'appens even after we've cleared out all the cats and dogs, an' no man knows where it'll strike next. It's a judgement on us."

Quince looked up at the main mast, where the top was just appearing as the morning mist began to blow clear in a light wind and the sun tried to break through. "Let go," he called to the churl, who right away drew the bow painter into the vessel and curled it around a post. Quince did the same at the stern then took hold of the tiller. The churl unhitched the jib sheets and hauled on the halyards to get the two jib sails aloft. The vessel moved off from the quay and into the river where the wind took the sails and drew the vessel into the channel. "You can help us haul the main aloft," said Quince as the trow began to make way. "Might as well take advantage of an extra body."

The churl handed Laurence the main halyard, which extended to the stern where Quince, leaning against the tiller to keep the trow steady, took it up. All three of them hauled the halyard to the sound of squealing blocks. The sail shot up the mast and snapped taught as the wind caught it. Quince tied off the halyard and trimmed the great sail with the main sheet. Already the mist had cleared and they were suddenly out into the river where the low morning sun was rising behind the walls of the castle. Quince hauled at the tiller to put them in the middle of the channel. Now with steerage-way, and helped by the river current they began to glide swiftly in the stream. Soon they came to *The Naight*, where the river parted both sides of the small island made up of mud-banks. Quince took the right channel. Just beyond the *Naight* they had to trim the sails as the river turned at this point thus altering the wind direction.

The river was a muddy brown colour and slick eddies could be seen here and there as the water passed over hidden shoals. Quince would know where all the dangerous ones were, yet even so Laurence found it hard to relax. The trow needed a lot of sail trimming to keep it in the safe channel, which kept him and the churl busy. Apparently, Quince was the only one enjoying the sail. Laurence suspected he was taking advantage of him, letting him do the work the trow owner would otherwise have to do. Certainly the vessel could not be sailed by a single man alone. At one point they had to haul two long baulks of timber over the side and lash them beneath the water line. This was to help prevent the trow moving sideways when pointing into the wind.

"Gloucester is to have a new charter, I hear," said Quince while they sailed along a quiet stretch of the river.

"Yes," replied Laurence. "King Richard has granted such. Gloucester may now elect its own Mayor."

"Makes no difference to the likes o' we," snorted the trow owner, prodding the thumb of his right hand against his chest. "The township hurls abuse at us, yet they need us to get their goods along the river. Precious little profit we get for our trouble." *Aye, thought Laurence, and what profit you do get ends up in the alehouse.*

"I see we are not alone on the river," he said, nodding upstream. Already another trow was away and following them downstream. Quince looked back then turned to face the bow with a puzzled frown on his face.

"That be Dick Button," he growled. "Late yester e'en he had but half a load. He musta picked summat up at the Mug Inn." Laurence knew that the Mug Inn was where the trow owners sealed their business over a mug of ale, a ceremony that served them as a kind of bond. Immediately he took an interest in the craft as it followed. There was nothing particularly suspicious about its close pursuit, having to keep to the same channel as the Joan. No doubt there would be other trows on the river now there was enough daylight to navigate by. It occurred to him, however, that perhaps the quay had been watched after all, in spite of his attempt to throw any spies off the scent. Hopefully they would reach Bristol ahead of the other trow and he could disappear before anyone interested in following him could land.

The river traffic became busier as the morning wore on. They passed by trows and other vessels plying their way upriver on their way to Gloucester and beyond, the river being navigable, with help from the bowhauliers, as far as Lower Mitton at the confluence of the Severn and Stour rivers. Several trows were sailing downriver, but that of Dick Button remained closest to the Joan. Presently the river widened and the resultant shallows exposed mud-banks here and there. Laurence noted gangs of men congregating on the river's banks. These were bowhauliers waiting for the chance of business. At the moment the river seemed high enough for the Joan to pass the shoals but some vessels would inevitably need help. They passed one such, a trow going upstream where the bowhauliers had a rope attached to the top of the mast. A team of men on the bank were heaving at it, physically dragging the vessel over the shallows it had become trapped in. Once or twice the Joan gave a tremble as the keel scraped the river bottom, but so far they had managed to get clear. Around noon it seemed they had cleared the worst of the shallows and now they were entering the further reaches of the tidal estuary. Quince raised the mizzen sail and the trow dipped as the wind took her and the bow wave began to plough into the small waves of the river.

Laurence looked back uneasily at their companion and thought it was closer than it had been. If there was someone on board who had guessed he was heading for Bristol, then perhaps, if his pursuer got there first, he would be waiting for him, the easier to watch and discover where he was headed. Dick Button had raised all sail too and was slowly gaining on them.

"It looks as if Dick Button wants to get ahead of us," he said to Quince.

"Well, he be lightly loaded, I expect," was the reply.

"How about a wager?" suggested Laurence. Quince sat up, his eyes alight with interest. "Four groats was the price we settled on for the trip to Bristol. I'll make it six if you can get there ahead of Dick Button, but three if you don't."

Quince, who had overcharged him in the first place considered he had nothing to lose. "Agreed," he snapped, grinning with excitement. "I can usually outsail Dick Button – it depends on his load whether he can get ahead or not." Quince looked to the trim of his sails and barked a few orders to the churl stationed in the bows. The two jib sails were trimmed while Quince reset the main sail and mizzen. The vessel heeled over just a little more but seemed to pick up speed.

"We have the tide against us," shouted Quince above the sound of the water rushing past the hull and the wind in the rigging, "but the rising water means fewer shoals."

Laurence knew that the dark brown estuary waters had numerous mud flats at low tide, many of which were covered at high water. The tidal range here was enormous, rising as much as forty-nine feet. Sailing as they were, down the estuary into a rising tide, meant strong currents to combat, but plenty of water under the keel. The Severn trow masters knew the estuary and mostly passed without mishap, though the vagaries of Sabrina, the ancient name of the river, like a woman, were unpredictable and sometimes caught out even the most experienced trow masters. On occasion, he had seen the animal force of the tide, pushing as if by a giant hand a wave well beyond Gloucester, temporarily flooding the water meads along its banks.

As the day wore on, the two trows raced along, butting their blunt bows into the choppy waves that were higher now they were in the estuary proper. Dick Button was hauling closer, it seemed to Laurence, and every now and again he thought he saw someone stand upright in the waist of the vessel as if judging the distance between them, then getting down again as if reluctant to show himself too plainly. Ahead of them he could see the slight haze that was Bristol, the smoke of domestic fires and commerce telling them the location of the town.

"I fear he might overtake us," murmured Quince lugubriously, fearing his bonus disappearing. Laurence's spirits were depressed too. He looked towards Bristol where the buildings were already resolving themselves out of the haze.

"Is there no stratagem you can think of?" he asked hopefully. "Perhaps cut across his bow?" Quince shook his head and looked out over the waters.

"It's a question of load – see how Dick's boat rides higher than we." There was, indeed some small difference, enough, it seemed to give Dick Button the advantage.

"There is one chance," said Quince, frowning after a few moments thought. "It's risky, and it all depends on whether I can get us into position before Dick catches us."

"Why is that," Laurence replied.

"There is a channel between two mud flats in the approach to Bristol. It is completely dry at low tide but this channel is covered as the tide rises. I think the water is high enough now for us to get through. It means a small change of course giving a more direct route to the docks. Dick will know what we are about when he sees us alter course. It is too narrow for two vessels to pass side-by-side but we might get ahead if we use it. If I can hold him off then he will have to go the long way around it, beating into the wind and then come in well behind us."

"Then let us try," he enthused.

"I would never try it normally, and I have a full load," muttered Quince yet clearly tempted with the thought of his bonus, six groats, but only three if the other vessel were to beat him into Bristol. Suddenly the gambler that was the soul mate of every trow owner got the upper hand. He barked his orders to his churl to slacken the jib sails and hauled at the tiller. The trow came upright as the wind moved from ahead to just behind and across the steorbord side. Immediately their speed increased. Laurence watched their companion. At first the trow kept to its former course, the men in the waist looking across at the Joan as the gap between the two began to widen. He thought he could detect some kind of argument, judging my much waving of arms and pointing towards the Joan. Suddenly the companion trow changed course to follow theirs. If ever there had been doubt that they were being deliberately followed, this confirmed it.

Now that both vessels had the wind over the steorbord beam, the advantage was with the trow with the lighter load. Both vessels were scudding through turbulent muddy water where the waves that were breaking over the shoals at once betrayed their position and posed a threat of running aground. The water looked ugly and dangerous. Laurence hoped there were no rocks lurking beneath. Quince stood by the tiller, his eyes darting about looking for the channel, his jaw clamped with steely determination. This was more than a race; it was a competition between two trow owners that would be talked about in the alehouses along the river for weeks to come.

Dick Button's trow was getting too close. If he kept this up he would be in Bristol some minutes ahead of the Joan. Quince permitted himself a quick look back and moved the tiller to take the trow slightly to ladebord. Encouraged, the companion trow eased to steorbord, clearly manoeuvring upwind to steal the wind from their sails and overtake the Joan.

"That was a bad move, master Quince," grunted Laurence.

"Wait and see," replied the trow master with a twinkle in his eye. He constantly switched his glance from the channel to their pursuer. As the other trow came down on them he eased the tiller taking the Joan to steorbord. That meant if Button moved to ladebord, he would be unable to get past the Joan, as the wind would be taken from his sails. On the other hand, if he took the steorbord course, it would be the Joan who would have her wind stolen but that would place Button close to the edge of the channel. After some hesitation the other vessel did the same, keeping the same course ready to get swiftly past them and clear for Bristol. Dick Button, it seemed, hoped to beat them to the narrow channel. Laurence could see the trow clearly now – a figure similar to Quince at the tiller, another in the bow and yet another in the waist of the vessel swathed in a cloak with its hood raised, obscuring the face of the wearer. The two trows looked to be on a collision course where Dick Button's trow would impact upon the side of the Joan.

"He's trying to force me to ladebord," grunted Quince, "but I believe he has left it too late." As the trow began to come up to them, it suddenly slowed, then with a shudder, came to an abrupt stop and heeled dangerously. Dick Button hastily released the main sheet letting the sail free to flap idly in the breeze.

"He's aground," whooped Quince while his churl in the bows jumped up and down, waving his cap at the other trow now falling rapidly astern. "He would never have passed me in this channel anyway, though once clear he would have beaten me easily on this tack. But It's not over yet," growled Quince, turning his attention to his steering. "I am not clear of these flats and the tide is still in flood. Dick will float off shortly, but if we can stay out of the mud ourselves I am sure we will be in Bristol first." As if to warn them they felt the vessel scrape against the mud hidden beneath the river waters on the ladebord side. Quince hauled at the tiller and got them clear. All around the river was patterned with swirls, eddies and whirlpools where the tidal flow stripped the river of its silt and piled it in hidden flats that were constantly changing. Had it not been for the superior river craft of Quince, they too would be grounded.

It was a grateful Laurence who finally bounded across the plank from the trow to the quay at Bristol. He turned to wave farewell at Quince and the churl. The dog followed him onto the quay looking for scraps and perhaps a rat to dispatch. Out in the estuary he could make out Dick Button's trow with its disconsolate crew and passenger. The trow had floated off in the rising tide and now could only follow them in. He picked up his bundle and, having paid a jubilant Quince his deserved six groats, turned and wended his way to disappear between the boxes, bags and trade goods piled along the quay. He soon found the vessel he was looking for, a carrack, among the many that used the port, in which Cornelius had arranged passage for him. He would get aboard and keep out of sight until clear of the English coast.

* * *

Brittany was his homeland, yet St Malo had no fond memories for Laurence de la Halle. The last time he was here his accommodation had been the town goal; three months of his life he had no wish to repeat. The voyage from England had been largely uneventful, though the Breton vessel did alter course once to avoid what were unidentifiable sails on the horizon. Rather than risk a possible encounter with English ships, the master took himself clear. The situation between the English court of King Richard III and that of duke Francis II of Brittany was diplomatically delicate, but the mariners in the narrow seas cared little for diplomacy where there were grudges to be borne and plunder to be gained from each other. As soon as the carrack was safely tied to the quay he gathered his few belongings and, bidding the master farewell, went ashore.

Holding his breath for as long as he could, he stepped swiftly away from the harbour with its smells of rotten fish and general stench and entered the town. This proved to be hardly less noisome, the narrow streets holding jealously on to their odours. He was looking for a particular house, the habitation of a wealthy cloth merchant and friend of Cornelius Quirke. Being somewhat familiar with St. Malo, he soon found the house he was looking for. It was in a street leading from the very cathedral dedicated to St. Vincent, where the Tudors had sought sanctuary from the English, who were with bishop Robert Stillington. The bishop and his entourage failed in their attempt to bring Henry Tudor to England and the court of King Edward in the year 1475. The door was located part way up the side of the building and accessed by a short flight of steps. This elevation placed the door and the windows of the dwelling well above the street, a sensible precaution. A stout oak door provided entrance to the cellarage under the house. This was located at street

41

level but would, no doubt, have no internal means of entering the house above.

It took repeated knocking on the door to get an answer and then only after he had taken out his dagger and hammered away with the pommel. A short, dumpy woman of mature years looked through the small opening, appraising him with hostility as if he had no right to live, let alone disturb the household. She wore a simple black woollen shift with a clean white apron and a scarf over her grey hair. He sheathed the dagger and asked for monsieur Gerard Levoir saying how he had come from England on particular business of great importance. The woman sniffed and grunted something unintelligible and moved to shut the door. Laurence pushed with his hand and leant against it before she could latch it closed. She opened the door again and stood there, five foot of Gallic menace, glowering and cursing him in the dialect of a Breton paysan. He felt himself wavering, but he had to speak to Gerard Levoir so he responded in kind, which made her pause. She had not expected to be addressed in the street language of Brittany. Someone called to her from the depths of the house and she answered, despite him addressing her in Breton, a mad Englishman was trying to get in. A man appeared and asked his name.

"Laurence de la Halle, fresh out of England and wishing to speak with monsieur Levoir."

"Ah yes," he answered. "You are a confrere of my friend . . .?"

"Cornelius Quirke."

"Then welcome to my house," he said standing back and indicating for Laurence to step inside. The paysan woman stood back also, muttering something disapproving under her breath. "I must apologise for Eloise," he chuckled. "She has had some bad experiences in life and trusts nobody. I have taken to meeting my friends in the tavern rather than invite them to try to get past her into my home. You are privileged to get this far."

"I think my response in street-Breton took her aback."

"I heard, and you are correct. If she had believed you really are English you would be wiping spittle from your face by now."

Gerard Levoir was stout, around forty years of age, of average height and with a face that indicated over-familiarity with the wine bottle. He was richly dressed in a linen shirt and woollen hose over which he wore a houpelard of brown velvet trimmed with fox fur. His long brown hair was tied back to hang behind. He led the way along a short passage to a chamber furnished with a table and benches along with comfortable chairs either side of a stone fireplace in which blazed a goodly fire. Papers littered the table and a shelf contained an assortment of bowls and bottles. A tapestry depicting a stag hunt hung by one wall. The floor was tiled and cleanly swept and in a corner was a niche with a statue of the Holy Virgin where a candle glimmered for illumination of the figure, or perhaps to light the way to heaven for a loved one. Eloise could be heard moving along the passage to her place in the *cuisine*, the sabots she wore clattering on the wooden floor. Somewhere deeper in the house she was greeted by a female voice and the chatter of children. Gerard shrugged off the houpelard and threw it over a bench, it being hot in the chamber. He invited Laurence to divest himself of his travelling cloak, which he too threw over the bench. Soon the two men were sitting by the fire each clasping a beaker of wine and deep in conversation.

"Eloise is a servant who came along with *ma femme*," Gerard informed him with a shrug. "She is protective of my family, especially when I am away on business."

"We have a wolfhound that does much the same job," chuckled Laurence, "but is less savage, I think." Gerard laughed and drank from his beaker while Laurence told him of his desire to contact the Tudor exiles.

"You are too late, monsieur Laurence," lamented Gerard. "The Tudors are already out of Brittany and into France. The circumstances were unfortunate, so far as Treasurer Landais is concerned. He let them travel freely to Vitré and from there, using a subterfuge, they escaped into France disguised as servants. Duke Francis, now recovered of his illness, made to stop them but it was too late." Gerard went on to describe the current political situation.

Duke Francis of Brittany now had no bargaining power with King Richard, yet there were some encouraging signs. He had recalled his warships from the narrow seas and King Richard had taken steps to curb those pirates operating from English ports such as Fowey and Plymouth along with ships putting out from Devon and Cornwall. The king had decreed that the port a ship had come out of should compensate damage done by that ship. Nevertheless there were still acts of piracy aplenty in the narrow seas. Brittany was now in a very vulnerable position. France was renewing its ambition to subdue the dukedom and bring it under French authority. The Breton court was a maelstrom of intrigue, made worst due to the incapacity of duke Francis, who had only just recovered from his illness. Treasurer General, Pierre Landais was heading the government but he was highly unpopular with certain Breton nobles, who favoured France. He had overthrown the corrupt Prime Minister, Guillaume Chauvin, whom he had imprisoned.

"Has the entire English contingent of exiles gone into France?" asked Laurence.

"No, many of them are still at Vannes and in fear of their lives, having been abandoned there by Jasper and Henry's rapid departure." Laurence considered this for a moment. Those Englishmen remaining in Brittany were trapped, being unable to return to their homeland and now without the man whose cause they had embraced. He thought that there was some kind of justice in this, yet some advantage might be made out of it.

"I must get to the duke," said Laurence with determination. "Where is he?"

"He is at Nantes, I believe." Laurence felt a wave of elation. He would be able to see his family, who resided there, and his father, duke Francis' personal armourer. Simon, his father, would be able to give him trustworthy advice and information. He would set off as soon as he could.

3 – Paris

The armourers' forge at Nantes was busy, the air ringing with the beat of hammers and the atmosphere thick with sulphurous fumes from the tempering tanks and the acrid smell of hot iron. Simon de la Halle was stroking a highly burnished cuirass that was hanging from a wooden frame, his fingers tracing the intricate design of the embossing on the breastplate.

"There might be more work of this kind if we become part of the kingdom of France," mused Simon.

"Surely you are not contemplating defeat, father?" Laurence said with some surprise, "and our resistance will hardly bring us less business." His father gave a shrug and continued regarding the harness with the respectful eye of a craftsman. He was becoming stout, though his arms were still sinewy and strong. Simon rarely did any rough work these days, preferring to concentrate on what he did best, embossing, tooling and decorating fine armour. He was dressed in the robes of a prosperous merchant, which is what he was, a craftsman at the top of his profession. His son, Laurence de la Halle, was following a similar route in England where he had built a reputation for crafting the finest harness for the king and many of his highest lords. At the same time, their respective forges made the more mundane weapons, halberds, swords, helmets, war axes, arrowheads, mail and plain armoured pieces for the lesser nobility.

When he first went into England, Laurence was surprised there was nowhere that a complete set of harness was made. The finest harness of the nobility was imported and indeed, he habitually imported steel plate and partly formed armour from Italy and altered it to fit his customers. Much of his work was maintenance and alteration due to damage from the tourney, or in war. Then, too, men tended to become more robust as they matured and their harness had to be adjusted to accommodate a stouter frame. Where that harness was of the finest steel and embellished with intricate design, only the artistry of a master armourer could bring it back to its former splendour while ensuring the maximum protection in the field.

"I am becoming weary of the continuing arguments here in Brittany, sighed Simon "Some want to remain independent and others see opportunity in being part of a greater country."

"France is not that great a country," replied Laurence. "For centuries her fields have been trampled over in pointless wars that have resolved nothing. It might bring us plenty of business, but surely we are better off standing to one side, as we are now, and let France take the consequences of her own policies."

"You know that duke Francis is ill and, between you and me, he will not live long. With but a daughter to follow him, it is unlikely she will be able to hang on to the dukedom when he has gone. We must look to the future." Laurence considered the duke's daughter and heir. Anne of Brittany was the only surviving daughter of the duke's second marriage to Margaret de Fois, a princess of Navarre and duchess of Brittany.

"France is all but ruled by a woman at this time," he pointed out. "It does not appear to have dampened the ambition of their government."

"Ach," snorted Simon. "Ann of Beaujeu will have to give way to her brother Charles when he reaches his majority, though it must be admitted at the moment she is stirring the government of France into pursuing their father, Louise XI 's dream of incorporating Brittany into that kingdom. Certain lords here at the court of duke Francis are in league with her. As a counter measure, duke Francis is making overtures to Louis, duc de Orléans who is involved in intrigue against the French regency for his own purposes. You know of the conflict in France between the houses of Orléans and Bourbon – similar, I suppose, to the wars between York and Lancaster in England?"

"Orléans - he is another who has ambitions of monarchy and thus, as the late duke of Buckingham recently demonstrated, cannot be relied on," said Laurence. "I believe that Brittany will someday need to call on England for help against her bigger neighbour. That means we must make peace with King Richard."

Simon de la Halle stroked his short beard, deep in thought. Presently he turned his eyes upon his son. "I am aware of your loyalty to the English King, and I respect that. But you must tread carefully when you meet with duke Francis. He believes that Henry Tudor has a debt to him, not unreasonably, seeing as the Tudors have been entertained in exile here for years. It may be he considers Tudor as a better ally than your King Richard?"

"But Henry Tudor is not king of England and that is what matters. Has this one man's ambition blinded everyone so that they cannot see straight? He has no claim to the English throne and a full blood prince is sitting upon it, the inheritor of a long line of Plantagenet monarchs. This whole business with the Tudors is madness. I have an audience with duke Francis so I will wait and hear what he has to say."

"The duke will not be in a good mood. Pierre Landais has angered him by letting the Tudors get into France. I suppose that has put paid to your mission for King Richard?"

"Not necessarily," replied Laurence. "Though I believe the man I need to talk to, Thomas Grey, is one of those who went into France with Henry and Jasper. If I can get to France too, I may yet be able to fulfil my mission."

"The situation is fraught with danger, my son. How will you get to Paris, which is where Henry Tudor is? You will need a passport from either King Richard or duke Francis, or a safe conduct from the French government. How are you going to explain the nature of your mission?"

"I have an idea to put to duke Francis, but it will need his permission, as you say, and a passport from him."

"I worry for you, my son," said Simon, his forehead creased with a frown, "and I have your mother constantly in my ear telling me of her fears - as if I can do anything to order your life." Simon spread his arms hopelessly.

Laurence placed his hands on his father's shoulders. "Don't worry; I am not engaged in anything more dangerous than any other messenger is - less, seeing as nobody knows the nature of my business."

"Well, get you off to the palace. I have had a word with Sir Gervaise, you know him of course, the duke's champion knight. He will get you straight to the duke."

* * *

Duke Francis the Second of Brittany was showing in his face and general demeanour the signs of his recent illness. Laurence knelt before him looking up at where he sat on the ducal throne. Draped over it, the cloth of state was richly embroidered with ermine designs in black silk upon a white satin ground. His hair was neatly curled under but where it had once been a deep chestnut now it was streaked with dull grey. He was wrapped in a gown of red velvet where the edges were embroidered in a design of entwined ivy using threads of gold. The great hall of the palace at Nantes was crowded with courtiers and diplomats from the various estates and countries that traded with Brittany. Pierre Landais stood obsequiously beside the duke while Sir Gervase Montaine knelt

47

before him beside Laurence. To one side stood a tonsured priest robed in a simple brown habit with a wooden carved crucifix hanging from a gold chain arranged around his neck. A rosary was looped into the white rope belt about his waist.

"I am pleased our sister of England, queen Elizabeth, is well after her spell in sanctuary," intoned the duke superciliously. "We have had our own problems here with our health, as you are aware." He spoke as if he was tired and his voice lacked the regal firmness it once had.

"Indeed your grace," replied Laurence sympathetically. "Though she has not had to endure illness as you have." He noted that the duke referred to Elizabeth Wydville as a queen when, in fact, she was now merely dame Grey - still, best not to notice the error. "She has asked me to convey assurances of her well-being, and that of her daughters to her son, Thomas Grey, who I had thought was with the Tudor exiles at Vannes."

"Yes, you are unfortunate," murmured the duke with a cold glance at Landais. "He is away into France with the earl of Richmond." A flicker of anxiety showed itself briefly on the treasurer's face; then the consummate courtier composed his features and smiled benignly on Laurence who continued to address the duke.

"So I understand, your grace. I hope to follow him into France with your permission." *Richmond? Duke Francis was using Henry Tudor's affected title.* He wriggled uncomfortably, being yet on his knees, hoping duke Francis might deign to raise him. If the duke noticed his discomfort he failed to respond so Laurence and Sir Gervaise remained as they were.

"We have the problem of the English exiles, your grace?" Sir Gervaise inserted. "Close on three hundred of them abandoned by Richmond." At hearing this, Pierre Landais leaned toward the duke and spoke softly into his ear. Francis nodded and setting his lips in a firm line, fixed Laurence with a hard stare.

"You tell a pretty tale, master de la Halle. Perhaps you will enlighten us as to your true purpose at our court?" Laurence took his eyes off the duke for a moment and looked nervously around at the circle of courtiers standing within earshot. Duke Francis was quick to notice and indicated with a wave of his hand for his henchmen to move the crowd further down the hall. Now just the duke, Landais, Laurence, Sir Gervaise and strangely, the priest remained gathered around the dais.

"That is what I fully intend to do, your grace," he said hurriedly, anxious not to let duke Francis think he was dissembling. He was, after all, his agent in England. "As with his brother, King Edward, King Richard of England is keen to get the Tudor, the earl of Richmond into England. Richmond's recent invasion of that realm demonstrates his ambition is towards taking the English crown for himself." Laurence decided that it might be best to use the putative title of Richmond when discussing the Tudor with duke Francis. "There can be no more pretence that there is an offer for Richmond to return there to live peacefully. King Richard has decided to provoke Richmond into invading again before he has time to strike any further alliances with France." Duke Francis raised his hand to pause the narrative.

"Richmond has a debt to us. You seem to be favouring the English king. Why should we fall in with Richard of England's plots?"

"I am not about to suggest we do anything to disturb Brittany, your grace," continued Laurence nervously. "If Richmond were to invade England he would likely be destroyed and therefore no more a pawn of the French. That would let you negotiate a treaty with England to form an alliance that would strengthen Brittany should the French attempt further to encroach upon your realm. While Richmond is in France, he is a nuisance threat that confuses the issue."

"On the other hand," put in Landais suddenly, "If Richmond were to win the English crown, his obligation to your grace would remain to our advantage. It seems to me that we should do what we can to resolve the problem between Henry Tudor and England. Brittany cannot lose either way. It is prevarication that endangers us."

Duke Francis leaned back and pondered while Laurence and Sir Gervaise remained uncomfortably on their knees. "You have a letter, do you not, intended for Thomas Grey who is, I understand, with Richmond in France?"

"I have your grace. Dame Grey, that is the lady Elizabeth Wydville has made her peace with King Richard and wishes her son to return to England, where the king promises to restore him to his estates without penalty. The intention is to encourage others to desert Richmond and thus provoke him to precipitate action where he can be defeated." The priest who had been standing quietly listening to the conversation stepped forward and with an inclination of his head to the duke, addressed Laurence.

"And what about the two princes, the sons of King Edward?" he snapped coldly. "We understand they have been murdered by the English king. What sort of woman would make peace with King Richard, the murderer of her babes?"

"The two princes were not murdered," your grace," said Laurence looking directly at the duke. "That is just a rumour put out by lady Stanley and the deceased duke of Buckingham to disturb King Richard's peace. One of them, Edward died of a malady, a sickness he suffered long before he went into the Tower of London. As for his brother, Richard of York; it was I who got him from the Tower secretly so that he could be taken to safety." The priest had sharp features and dark eyes that suddenly seemed to glitter with curiosity. He leaned forward close to Laurence and rasped in a subdued tone:

"One of the princes lives, you say, and taken to safety. Do you know where he was taken?" Laurence instinctively mistrusted the priest, even though a man of God. Perhaps, the priest being close to duke Francis, he should tell something of what he knew regarding the whereabouts of the boy, but he had resisted confiding in anyone so far, not Anna, nor his father, not even Elizabeth Wydville the boy's mother. Besides, he knew there were many at Francis' court in league with France and against an alliance with England. Richard of York's continued existence relied entirely on his place of concealment being revealed to nobody.

"I am afraid not," he replied as firmly as he could. "I handed him over to one of King Richard's henchmen myself, who took him away. Only King Richard and one or two of his most trusted friends know where the boy is. All I know is that the king is keeping him safe to fret and discomfit Henry Tudor. The fact he is alive and well is the reason Elizabeth Wydville has made her peace with the king." The priest regarded him with a bleak stare that brought to his mind the story of the serpent in the Garden of Eden. There was a tapestry in the family church he used when at Nantes depicting the Temptation of Eve and the expression on the face of the serpent was what he was seeing now.

"I do know that Elizabeth Wydville was not above child murder herself," growled the priest. "Two sons of the earl of Desmond in Ireland were killed at her behest when she was queen of England. It seems the earl had made some remarks about the validity of King Edward's marriage to her. That is a tale which has come back to bite her!"

"Yes, I know the story," replied Laurence. "And I have no liking for the Wydville woman either, but I know nothing more than what I have told your grace." Laurence addressed his remarks to the duke. "She has written to her son asking him to come home and with King Richard's personal assurances of safety."

Sir Gervaise put a hand on Laurence's arm. "If I might make a suggestion, your grace?" The priest glared at him. It seemed he still had further questions for Laurence.

"You may speak, Sir Gervaise," intoned the duke.

"We have around three hundred of Richmond's followers kicking their heels at Vannes and wondering how they are going to leave. I would advise you pack them off to the earl of Richmond, in Paris, and relieve yourself of the burden of their continued presence. They are serving no useful purpose to anyone at the moment. Master de la Halle, here, can accompany them ensuring his safe passage while getting him into the company of the Tudor retinue. If he can persuade the marquis of Dorset to desert Richmond then so be it. We can stand back and observe events without enmeshing ourselves in unnecessary intrigue."

"That would be a neat solution, your grace," inserted Laurence hopefully.

Duke Francis nodded and made up his mind. "Do you have a plausible story to cover your defection to the Tudor English?"

"I have," returned Laurence. "We have already touched upon it. I shall pretend that the alleged murder of the two princes has embittered me towards King Richard and I can no longer stomach my work as his armourer."

Francis indicated he was satisfied with that and raised the two men from their knees. "Master de la Halle, you will go to Sir Edward Wydville and Sir Edward Poynings at Vannes. They head the English contingent there. Inform them of my decision. I shall send funds sufficient to carry them to the earl of Richmond. That should get you into the English company – how you fare afterwards with them is up to you." Duke Francis waved them away. As they backed from his presence, Laurence could not help noticing the curious expression on the face of the priest and the considered way he watched as they disappeared into the mass of courtiers who were now clamouring forward to besiege the ducal throne once again.

* * *

51

The mighty fortress of *Le Louvre* rose stark and white in the sunshine that reflected from its bastions just inside the city wall of Paris, its round towers with their conical roofs pointed towards a blue sky and the upper parts of the *Grosse Tour*, the massive keep at its centre, were just visible inside. Once a fortress on the outskirts of Paris, now it was a royal palace located within the boundary walls of the expanding city. The retinue of former Tudor exiles approached along *le Rue St Honoré*, entering by the gate where, at the beginning of the century Jeanne d'Arc was wounded in her abortive attempt to wrest Paris from the English, who occupied the place at the time. Already the stink of the city assailed their nostrils, though that was only to be expected. Paris had never been the more fragrant of cities.

It was a bedraggled troop that trotted into Paris, though they attempted to make a brave show as they came to meet up with their lord, the earl of Richmond, Henry Tudor. The journey across France from Brittany had taken its toll of horse and rider. Their train had left with scant resources and little money, though duke Francis had given them some to help them on their way. Now they rode with heads high, dressed in the green and white livery of the Tudor. Turning right at the *Rue St Denis*, they headed towards the Seine where the *Pont aux Changeurs* would take them across the river to the *Ille de la Cité* and bring them to *Le Palais du Roi*. Henry Tudor and his uncle Jasper had been allowed chambers within the edifice, though others of their retinue were lodged in the area around the vast palace.

Laurence's interview with Edward Wydville, Elizabeth's brother, had gone better than expected. Wydville accepted the story proclaiming his disgust at the murder on the orders of King Richard of the sons of King Edward. All in his company were unhappy with the new rule in England, especially those who had been involved in Buckingham's failed rebellion, not to mention Lancastrian sympathisers. Men such as these enthusiastically embraced any mutterings of discontent with Richard's reign. Thus, Sir Edward had not probed the plausibility of the tale too deeply as he was preoccupied with the welcome news that he was free to follow the Tudors into France, which favourably disposed him to the armourer. He already knew that Laurence was a master armourer, having seen him at the court of King Edward. Laurence had once maintained the harness of his brother Anthony Wydville, who had been executed by King Richard, a fate that had been his also had he not fled to

Brittany and the Tudor; more pragmatically, he immediately realised an opportunity for having work done on his own harness.

So it was that soon after their arrival in Paris, Laurence spent a few days, gladly so far as he was concerned, working on adjustments to Sir Edward's harness along with other repairs to that of the English nobles, men who were eager to get themselves into battle trim, even though they were here peacefully in France. All entertained the notion that soon they would be fighting in England against the cruel tyrant Richard the Third. His father had supplied him with a few tools necessary for basic work, though his own tools required for delicate, refined ornamentation were back in England in his home forge at Gloucester. One after another man-at-arms came to him at the forge close to the castle where he had been quartered, each needing some repair or alteration to his iron. Impoverished though they were, Laurence still managed to extract some payment for his work, which gave him a frisson of satisfaction. These were traitors to the English crown and though he had no particular allegiance there, yet traitors were universally to be despised.

There had been no sign of Henry Tudor, his uncle Jasper or Thomas Grey and Laurence was anxious to speak to the latter and deliver his letter. Cornelius had briefed him as to the character of Thomas Grey and the others he could expect to find in the Tudor retinue. He knew Sir Edward Wydville was a firm adherent of the Tudor cause, but Thomas, his nephew, was weak and prone to vacillation. Elizabeth, his mother, might be blind to his shortcomings, but King Richard had chosen well in selecting Thomas for a possible deserter. He might well be tempted with the restoration of his property should he return to England. His family greed and self-seeking could always be relied on and here it would be used to advantage.

It was the third morning after the Tudor men's arrival in Paris that Thomas Grey turned up at the forge. Laurence was engrossed in working on the fixing of a visor to a sallet when a shadow fell across the work, causing him to raise his head with a look of annoyance. The fellow had something of familiarity about him and it was a few moments before he realised that here was his quarry. Thomas Grey was a man in his early forties, handsome once, not unlike his uncle Anthony, but shorter and thicker around the middle. He had the same brown hair and eyes, which perhaps was the reason for the likeness but when he spoke the similarity ended.

"My uncle, Sir Edward, tells me you are recently out of England and come to us here at Paris," he piped in a high-pitched tone. "If you have fled the court of the murdering usurper Richard Plantagenet I expect you can give me news of my mother? The rumours of her conduct are disquieting to me."

"I can understand that, my lord," said Laurence as he put the sallet to one side to stand and sweep a bow. Looking around to satisfy there was nobody near enough to overhear their conversation, he lowered his voice to speak conspiratorially. "I cannot, for the moment venture an opinion except to say I have spoken to her and she has entrusted me with the carriage of a letter that is for your eyes only." This statement took the marquis slightly aback, but his experience in years of practiced intrigue prevented him from crying out in astonishment. Instead his eyes darted about the courtyard where Laurence had set up a temporary workshop. This was near to where a team of farriers were tending to the needs of the horses in their care and showing no interest in the master armourer who had intruded into a corner of their space.

"You have it with you, this letter?"

"It is safe in my chamber, my lord," replied Laurence. "Shall I go and get it for you?"

"No, no," replied the marquis hurriedly. Laurence understood that even though they were seemingly innocently discussing the art of the armourer, if he was to be observed passing a document to Thomas Grey, soon others would hear of it and want to know what was written therein. He had no doubt that someone invisible to them would be observing somewhere among those who were apparently bustling about the courtyard pretending to mind their own business. That was the nature of a royal palace. "I shall send a servant to conduct you to my lodgings away from here. If anyone asks what you are about, say it is to discuss my harness. I wish to get it into fighting trim when we go over to England."

"Very good, my lord. You can depend on my discretion." Laurence took up a pair of gauntlets with gatlings embossed and gilded, clearly the property of a wealthy nobleman. They examined and discussed the gauntlets for a while to allay suspicion before Thomas Grey stepped back to take his leave. He gave Laurence a brief nod, turned on his heel and walked swiftly away. His reaction to the existence of his mother's letter was encouraging. The man was a natural dissembler whose desire to have secret information from England not shared by others overcame any superficial loyalty he might have had to Henry Tudor. He picked up the sallet and carried on with his work. At some point he would have to go to his chamber for the letter, but it was unadvisable to go there until the memory of the marquis of Dorset's presence had receded somewhat in the brain of anyone who might have been curious about it.

It was well after the ninth hour, when the bells for Nones had rung in the surrounding churches, that the marquis' servant came for Laurence. Dressed in the green and white Tudor livery topped with a green acorn hat, he was a spidery, supercilious youth who, he considered, could do with a whipping to temper his arrogance. Laurence was sitting quietly by his forge casually rubbing a shine into one of a particularly fine pair of vambraces when he flounced up. The lackey spoke as if he were a noble himself instead of an insipid youth.

"Master armourer, my lord, the marquis of Dorset commands your immediate presence," he intoned nasally. Laurence paused at his task and regarded the youth coldly, but with an indication of amusement at his lips. Then he returned to the job, rubbing away at the armour, which clearly needed no further embellishment. Annoyed at the armourer's insouciance the youth spoke again with a petulant sneer. "My lord the marquis will brook no delay . . ." Laurence fixed him with a glance of menace that provoked a choked pause.

"Is there a dog in the kitchen where your master resides?" asked Laurence as he slowly placed the vambraces in a straw-filled box. The youth's eyebrows lifted in surprise.

"I do not understand your meaning, master armourer."

"Well, a spit may be turned by a wheel, where a dog is set to run inside it. It seems the kitchen can spare its spit boy, so I assume there is a dog wheel there – the marquis will be dining on cold meat else." The youth stepped back, his face flushed with anger.

"You insult my master when you insult his servant," he snapped. "My father is Sir Geoffrey Blyth and I am squire to the marquis of Dorset.

Laurence got to his feet and suddenly shooting forth his right arm, grasped the youth by his tabard front and hauled him onto his toes. The boy found himself inches from a fearsome black-beard under lancing eyes and a deep scar down one side of his face. Even elevated thus he was still a good foot shorter than the armourer.

"I make harness for the highest in the land and kings have spoken to me better than you are doing. Now, wait here while I finish what I am doing and keep silent. If in the unlikely event I ask you to speak at all you will address me as master de la Halle." With that he spun the youth to one side and propped him against the wall of the forge before releasing his grip. The youth slumped down and only just managed to prevent himself sliding to the ground in shock. It would be some minutes before the penetration of the glittering blackness in those eyes faded from his senses. His hat had fallen into the mud and he had trodden on it. Keeping a wary eye on Laurence, he bent down and retrieved it. The hat was a fine one and he was upset at the mess it was in but too shaken to do more than scrape the encrustation off with his fingers.

Dressed as a prosperous merchant, Laurence followed behind the subdued youth, content to let him pick the cleanest way through the filth in the streets between the *Palais du Rois* and the great cathedral of Notre Dame. If there were any hidden depths beneath the foul puddles in the roadway then the boy could be the one to step into them. It appeared that the marquis of Dorset had his lodgings in the environs of the cathedral, which rose in gothic splendour above the lesser buildings of the city. Laurence noted the gaily-painted statues of the saints in the many niches in the stonework and the coloured walls that blazed resplendent in the late evening sunshine. Gargoyles leered down from above while carved demons and devils threatened damnation to the sinners below. By the great west door, and in the square before, beggars and cripples were contending with the carved grotesques for sheer ugliness, demonstrating that if humanity could be so degraded in this world, how much worse would it be in the next. Tomorrow he might enter the cathedral and find a priest to confess to, though not of course regarding his mission for King Richard. He had heard the cathedral reliquary had a part of the True Cross and one of the nails that pinned Jesus to it. He wondered which of them it was. He fingered the phial suspended on a silver chain around his neck. Within it, he knew, were filings from the nail that fixed Christ's feet to the cross, so it could not be that one.

The youth led him to the gatehouse of what looked to be a new stone-built residence. They passed by the guard, who acknowledged the youth but eyed Laurence suspiciously, as is the way with such men. They entered a court and a short flight of curved steps led to a fine oak door studded with nails and, he noted, reinforced with ornamental iron. There were no windows on the ground floor, but arrow slits were set in the walls along its length. It was not exactly a fortified house, but clearly the owner had taken pains to ensure it could be defended if necessary. The Paris mob had a deserved reputation for riot, so this house was well prepared to withstand all but the most determined attack. Even the royal family had to leave Paris at times to avoid the mob. At the moment there was much activity in the courtyard with horses and riders milling around and he recognised the predominance of Tudor livery. At the door the youth spoke through a square grill to someone within. Presently they heard the grinding of heavy bolts being withdrawn and the door swung open just wide enough to let them enter.

Laurence found himself within an enclosed stone chamber where a flight of steps led upwards to the first floor of the house. The porter, an old fellow with a bent back leered at them aggressively. There was but a small fireplace where a fire burned with a table and chair set close to it. He was well versed in the construction of castle defences and though this was supposed to be a residence, yet he recognised that anyone breaking through here would have to get up the narrow steps, where they could be picked off fairly easily. Parisian houses, it seemed, had regard for such contrivances.

Passing through a stout door at the top of the stairs they stepped into a hall hung with arras. A long table set to one side was littered with what looked like maps and untidy heaps of documents. A scribe sat at one end scribbling away. The others in the chamber, Laurence recognised, as members of the Tudor retinue with whom he had come from Brittany. The household was obviously prosperous, even though Henry Tudor himself had scant resources. Then he remembered that Sir Edward Wydville had fled to France with a considerable portion of the treasure of the deceased King Edward the Fourth after it was discovered that the marriage between his sister Elizabeth and King Edward had been bigamous. When they learned the duke of Gloucester had taken the young prince Edward into his protection and was coming to London, he took the fleet to sea while the marquis of Dorset and queen Elizabeth tried to rally England to their defence. Nobody would rise in favour of the Wydvilles and so it was that Elizabeth took herself and her children into sanctuary at Westminster Abbey. Soon, her son Thomas, marquis of Dorset joined her, but not until he had used his residual authority to extract the remainder of the late king's treasure from the Tower of London. Later the marquis escaped from sanctuary and hid, not to emerge until he joined with Buckingham in his rebellion against King Richard. After the uprising was defeated he fled to his uncle, Sir Edward Wydville. No wonder the Wydville faction could afford to live well in Paris.

It was also apparent he was in the household of Sir Edward Wydville because the servants other than the Tudors had his device on their tabards, a shield with field argent with a fess and canton gules having a crescent in the upper dexter quarter. The youth led him through the hall and along a corridor lit from above through small circular windows, then knocked upon a door. Surprisingly it was the marquis himself who opened it. When he saw whom it was he stood back to let Laurence enter while stopping the youth.

"Attend upon me here and let no-one enter," he commanded. The youth glared malevolently at Laurence but otherwise kept his counsel. Thomas Grey shut the door firmly and led Laurence to the opposite side of a small chamber where wooden shelves made up into pigeon holes were ranged around the walls and a single desk and stool stood beneath a lancet window. They were obviously in some sort of scriptorium as the pigeonholes were filled with scrolls. The late afternoon sun streamed in through the narrow slit like a sword of light, in which silver and gold reflected from dust motes floating like disembodied souls.

"You have the letter?" asked Thomas rhetorically. Laurence reached into the wallet suspended from his belt and withdrew the document, which he handed to the marquis. Thomas Grey inspected the seal carefully, then, breaking the wax he opened it and read. There were two pages and the marquis took his time reading them. Presently he looked up and regarded Laurence shrewdly.

"You have my mother's confidence?" he enquired cautiously.

"Yes, and that of King Richard."

The marquis frowned at that, seemingly not quite ready yet to believe where his mother had written indicating her trust in the man who had killed his brother Anthony and his step-brother Richard Grey, not to mention others of their faction.

"I realise this is a difficult decision, leaving the Tudor and returning to England. I would not urge it on you myself, but your mother is better placed to advise you than I am," ventured Laurence. "All depends on how sure you are that Tudor will triumph if he invades. He will be meeting with a general who has never been beaten in battle while Henry Tudor has never fought a battle in his life. Moreover, Tudor is unknown to the English people having spent most of his years in Brittany. Apart from a few malcontents there will not be many in England who would rise to his banner, while King Richard can raise levees from across the whole of his realm. Once Tudor is defeated, where would that leave you - forever an exile?"

The marquis screwed the letter in his fist, his mind in turmoil. He turned and paced the room, clearly undecided as to the best course. In common with all exiles, his resolve was wracked with doubts though the confident character of the others, Sir Edward his uncle, Jasper Tudor and those lords who, having backed the wrong side, had been driven from England gave him pause to think they might succeed. Then there was the Lancastrian faction, implacably opposed to the house of York waiting a chance to remove the King. Lord Stanley, married to Henry Tudor's mother would certainly hold back, he might even be persuaded to come over to the Tudor. Yet King Richard held the throne and he was the inheritor of a long line of kings while the Tudor had hardly any claim at all.

"Another consideration," put in Laurence, intruding into his thoughts: "could Henry Tudor hold on to the throne of England even if he managed to wrest it from King Richard? A king with a dubious bloodline is in a precarious position where there are many others present who can better his claim. It is not just a question of who is most likely to come out on top, but can he remain there? Henry Tudor is a clerk, not a warrior. A final victory for King Richard would at least bring stability and thus security to the realm of England, would it not?"

Thomas smoothed out the letter and looked at it again. "My mother says here that the prince Richard of York lives. Is this true?"

"It is, my lord. That is something I can vouch for personally, being the one who got him safely out of the Tower of London."

"Where is he?"

"Alas, I cannot say. Only the king knows, though he will undoubtedly bring back the boy once the Tudor problem has been dealt with, if only to show the stories spread about him were untrue."

Thomas Grey folded the pages and thrust them into a pocket in his gown. "I must think carefully on this," he said at last.

Laurence nodded and decided it would be best to remain silent and let the idea of a return from exile work in the mind of the marquis. His mission to deliver the letter and sow seeds of discontent in the mind of Thomas Grey was complete and now he had the problem of getting away himself. Being supposedly pledged to the Tudor faction he could hardly ride through France to the coast without suspicion and that would lead to questions about why he had come in the first place. On the other hand, if the marquis suddenly took off for England, he would be left behind and inevitably the Tudors would be looking for whoever had encouraged him. His plan had been to leave France first and let the marquis with his better resources make his own plans for escape afterwards. How to do that and keep a whole skin was now his main concern. He fingered the reliquary that hung around his neck and uttered a silent prayer to St Barbara, patron of armourers, to send him a sign.

* * *

The sign came, as he might have expected, brought by a man in full harness. He rode triumphantly into Paris at the head of a substantial troop of men-at-arms. As always with divine intervention the sign was preceded by despair before the revelation of its true purpose.

John de Vere, the thirteenth earl of Oxford had broken out of Hammes castle, where King Edward had confined him in 1474 after he had surrendered the fortress of St Michael's Mount, Cornwall. He had taken the Mount with the purpose of raising Cornwall against the king and had sent to King Louis of France for aid. Nothing came of the business and Oxford found himself under a siege, which he was unable to sustain. It seemed that though a prisoner at Hammes castle he had befriended and subverted his guard, captain of the castle James Blount, who was here in Paris with the earl. Laurence considered this must be a setback for King Richard while greatly raising the hopes of Henry Tudor, who was struggling to gain the support of the French court for his cause. Oxford was the last serious Lancastrian leader and, unlike Henry, a good general. Laurence decided to have another talk with Thomas Grey to try to figure out what effect the arrival of the earl of Oxford had on him.

The *Palais du Roi* was alive with courtiers, merchants who were vying for business, and servants, all it seemed to Laurence, constantly on the move, a confusion of colour and chatter. He had spotted the Wydville servants amongst the rest, mingled with the green and white livery of the Tudors and the blazing star badge of Oxford. He found Thomas Wydville in an annex to a chamber where Henry Tudor, his uncle Jasper and the earl of Oxford were in close conference. He wondered if it was useful that Thomas was not, at the moment, included. That might help him provoke resentment in the vacillating breast of the marquis. He saw him now, standing in conversation with a dark-skinned man dressed as a soldier, bare headed and wearing a plain brown leather doublet and grey hose. Thomas was clad in a pale green gown over a dark green doublet and yellow hose. His chapeau was black velvet with tassels of plaited gold. He wended his way casually through the throng until he managed to place himself close and in plain sight of the marquis. Thomas caught sight of him and immediately beckoned him over.

"Sir James," he said addressing the man with him. "May I present master Laurence de la Halle, erstwhile armourer to the tyrant England and now another who has joined us here in France." Laurence swept an elegant bow and glanced with curiosity between the two men, inviting a more detailed introduction. The marquis was speaking in English, which meant the other man was a native of that country. "This is Sir James Blount," continued the marquis. "He has come here with the earl of Oxford and he too has joined our cause." Laurence suppressed a grimace of disappointment, as it seemed the marquis had dismissed the idea of abandoning Henry Tudor. He was clearly swept along in the general feeling of euphoria that was the effect on the Tudor contingent of the earl's unexpected presence.

James Blount scrutinised the armourer with the arrogant diffidence of a professional soldier. Fortunately Laurence had come dressed in simple garb similar to the soldier and so was regarded favourably as Blount's face relaxed somewhat.

"Master de la Halle is another who has joined our cause," intoned the marquis with a smile of satisfaction.

"It is well," said Blount. "If we are to succeed our army will need the skills of the armourer. I see you are acquainted with battle yourself, or has that scar another cause?"

Laurence touched the scar on his cheek. "It is the result of a close shave with a war axe, Sir James," he replied humorously.

"That is a most prodigious nick from a barber who shaves his customers with a pole axe. If all our English barbers were to serve us thus there would be no more shaving there, I think."

"I got caught in the fight at the Tower of London last year during the attempt to rescue the two princes Edward and Richard," he explained, hoping the ambiguousness of his statement wouldn't provoke further question. He had been caught up in the fight, that was true, but on the side that drove off the attack, not the rescuers who were in league with Margaret Stanley. It was while Laurence was recovering from his injury that Prince Edward died of the malady that had been troubling him for some time. Later, he helped get away from the Tower the remaining prince, Richard of York, to preserve his life.

" You have seen the two princes?" asked Sir James.

"I had been working on harness for prince Edward, which is why I was at the Tower that day. After the attack failed, the boys were closely mewed up and I never saw them again. It is because of their murders that I have left England. My wife died and there is little to keep me there." He gave the marquis a blank stare. Through his mother, he now knew that one of the princes was alive and that Laurence was lying. *Will the marquis keep the information to himself, or disclose it?* Laurence held his breath. He need not have worried; the courtier in him prevented the marquis revealing a secret of such magnitude unless there was a decided advantage in doing so, and at the moment there were many options to keep open.

"Master de la Halle is a Breton, so he has no particular loyalty to England, while our liege lord, the earl of Richmond owes Brittany a debt of gratitude," he explained by way of diverting the subject of their conversation. Laurence felt some relief. Now that the marquis had failed to disclose his secret, he could hardly denounce Laurence as an agent of his mother, Elizabeth – nor deny the message requesting him to desert the Tudor and come home.

"Quite so," said Laurence. "It was with the connivance of my liege, duke Francis, that Richmond was granted safe passage to France. Indeed, it was from Brittany and with duke Francis' help, that he sailed last year to join the rebellion of the unfortunate Buckingham." Hopefully that explanation would be enough to allay any suspicion regarding his presence here with the Tudor faction. At the same time it reminded Thomas Grey that King Richard had easily seen off the Buckingham threat. Being part of it, and thus in exile, the marquis was only too aware the rebellion collapsed through lack of support by the nobles of England.

Sir James gave a nod of understanding. "Unlike you, I have a wife and she is yet at Hammes, a castle under siege. It was too hazardous to bring her to Paris and I considered her to be safer there. Lord Dynham has sent troops from Calais to retake the castle for King Richard. The men of the garrison are not persuaded to join Tudor, yet they fear retribution due to my leaving there with my lord Oxford. If we can drive off Dynham's men then we shall have a valuable asset in our hands. My lord Oxford is planning such an expedition now."

Laurence at once saw an opportunity to get away from Paris. "I should be pleased to offer my services in the expedition, Sir James. If we can raise the siege then no doubt the castle garrison will be in need of some work on its harness?"

"For myself you would be a welcome asset, but the decision rests with my lord Oxford."

"I shall speak to his lordship," said the marquis.

Laurence stood on a low hill looking towards the English camp outside Hammes castle. Of the two inland castles guarding the approaches to Calais, a rebel garrison held Hammes while the other two miles away at Guisnes was still tentatively loyal to the English crown under the command of lord William Mountjoy, the elder brother of the treacherous Sir James Blount. The troops besieging the fortress were from Calais, where a limitless stream of men could be deployed. The earl of Oxford had been sent by Henry Tudor in an attempt to relieve the besieged garrison. It soon became apparent that they were never going to be able to raise the siege. Laurence had come here with a small troop led by Thomas Brandon, one of Henry Tudor's most loyal captains with the intent of getting inside to reinforce the garrison. He stood there with his sergeant, looking across at the castle. Laurence stood with them, having volunteered to join their expedition.

"We will wait for nightfall and approach along the fields to the east of the castle," said Brandon confidently, as if it were merely a matter of a country stroll.

"We mun use the ditches," intoned the sergeant lugubriously.

"Of course," replied Brandon. He was clad in a simple jupon. It appeared he had already thought on a night operation and left his iron with the baggage. Brandon was a small man, but well muscled and tough. He tended to lead his men from the front and thereby commanded their respect. Laurence was clad in leather doublet and linen hose, not exactly the rig he would have chosen, but it was all that was available to him. Brandon had no problem with that. His plan was to be a clandestine approach, then, hopefully, obtain help from the garrison to get his men inside. If they had to fight in the open then they would be overwhelmed and their ploy was lost.

The men with them were similarly clad, each having a long dagger at his belt and a short sword suspended from a hanger. They were sitting in a group behind the hill, just out of sight of the castle.

"How do you expect to get inside?" asked Laurence tentatively. He hoped that once there he could bide his time until the siege was lifted and thereby reveal himself as an agent of King Richard and obtain passage out of there. It was a plan; not much of one and it would have to be modified by circumstance no doubt, but it was a plan.

"I must let the garrison know who I am and that I intend to reinforce them. There is a possible way across the marsh to the castle. It is impossible to get a large force across without heavy casualties, so it is lightly guarded."

"It sounds somewhat desperate, Sir Thomas," replied Laurence. "For one thing, if we get close why should they not suspect a trap?"

"They will, at first, but I am known to several there and once I can identify myself I am assured of entry."

Laurence was disturbed at this intelligence. It rather suggested that there was a subversive component in the English army that could turn either way, in favour of their rightful king, or the usurper Henry. These were English men but much depended on the tales of murder associated, albeit falsely, with King Richard. Poison, he realised, spread insidiously and contaminated opinion. The garrison, cut off from the mainstream of English politics, were vulnerable to the false dissemination of corrupt fabrication and might be easily swayed by Tudor lies. Clearly the garrison had been upset by the stories coming out of England regarding the fate of the two princes and the way in which the throne had been taken from Prince Edward, who many assumed was the rightful heir of King Edward the fourth. Laurence realised that the best way of resolving the situation was, as King Richard wanted, to bring Henry Tudor to battle. Once Tudor had been defeated then the young prince Richard could be brought back and the true story told. That would resolve the problem and restore stability to the realm of England.

"We will take up our position in that wood," said Brandon pointing to where a strand of trees came close to the marsh. The troop moved off to get in position ready for their attempt to get into the castle.

"How will you communicate with the castle?" asked Laurence, still worried about the response of the garrison. As soon as they see a troop of men outside the walls they are likely to let fly at us?"

"Leave that to me," replied Brandon. "The earl of Oxford has been in regular contact with some of his followers in there. This adventure is not as mad as it seems." With that Laurence had to be content. Already the light was going and flocking birds were twittering in the trees, getting ready to settle for the night. He drew his woollen mantle close about him to keep out the November chill. There was a cold wind coming from the marsh and he didn't relish having to tramp around through swamp.

Presently they moved off, wending their way along channels running with sluggish water, but obscured from the view of the English camp. Clouds scudded indifferently across the sky. The moon was yet to rise but there was just enough light to let them find their way. Every now and then, Brandon led them away from the castle to avoid sentries. He seemed to know his way through the mire, though the going was difficult. Soon the fortress loomed ahead of them. The place was in darkness to preserve the night vision of those on its walls watching for the approach of a force such as they were now. Brandon stopped them within bowshot of the castle walls. They were in a deep rivulet that seemed to emerge from the massive walls of the castle.

"Wait here," he commanded. The men squatted down patiently, clearly used to the ways of their leader. "Master de la Halle, come with me. I might need you to return with a message." Laurence stepped forward, wondering how Brandon was going to communicate with the garrison. A shout would alert the English to what was going on as well as inviting a shower of arrows from above. Brandon beckoned his sergeant forward. "When master Laurence returns, follow swiftly and silently. You know what to do." The sergeant nodded and tipped the brim of his helmet with his fingers.

Bent low to hide themselves from the sentries around the English camp, they waded knee deep through water that was running away from the castle. The channel was circuitous and deeper in some places than others. Finally they came to the castle rock and there they came upon an iron grill. It seemed the castle used the flow of water to discharge waste into the swamp. The smell here was foul and Laurence tried to breath as shallowly as possible to limit the effect on his olfactory senses. The grill was half submerged while slime and tendrils of weed hung from it or streamed in the sluggish flow of water.

Brandon gave a low whistle to which there was a similar response from behind the grill. The shadow of a sentry appeared and there were whispered words exchanged. Laurence heard a rasp of iron and saw the grating move inwards slightly. Apparently this was some sort of gate.

"Give a hand here," whispered Brandon. Laurence waded up to the gate and saw that it was only partly open, the bottom being fouled in filth. Both men pushed while the sentry on the other side stirred the ooze with the bottom of a halberd. Gradually they were able to open the gate until it was wide enough to allow one man to squeeze through. Beyond he could just make out a split in the rock, a passage barely wide enough for one man – it seemed it cut through the foundations of the castle. Brandon turned to him.

"I shall go into the castle and speak with the guard. Once they know who we are they will let us in through here. Get back to the men and pause before coming forward. I will need some time to talk to the guard and prevent them attacking you as you approach." With that, Brandon squeezed through the gate and disappeared into the darkness beyond. Laurence turned and waded back along the channel. When he reached the troop, the sergeant seemed to know what to expect and made no attempt to move off. They waited in the cold and wet, hidden in a shallow depression lined with mud. They could hear noises from the English camp, whose soldiers had no need to keep silence and which served to mask any noise that they might make when they eventually moved off.

Laurence was just wondering how long he should give Brandon when the sergeant looked at him expectantly. He knew his leader's ways and so it seemed prudent to get going. They moved as silently as they could along the channel, mud sucking at their boots. They were just about to turn into the channel that led to the gate when there was a shout. Dark shapes of men appeared behind and above them. The besiegers must have spotted them. In this channel they would be trapped.

"Quick, you men, get going," said the sergeant. He grabbed Laurence by the sleeve. "We mun hold them back while our men get into the castle," he growled. He had half a dozen men with him while the other thirty or so scurried away. Black shapes leapt into the channel behind and were bearing down on them. Soon there would be others and Laurence realised that he would have to fight or die here. He drew his sword and faced the first ones. They retreated close under the castle walls and they could hear shouts above them as the garrison saw what was happening. In the darkness it was impossible to distinguish one from another. He heard the snap of crossbows as the garrison fired into the night. The men above disappeared as they were sitting targets for the defender's archers. He could hear arrows being loosed and it seemed the defenders had spotted more attacking troops coming to the aid of their fellows. Hopefully they would be held off until Brandon's men could get inside. Allowing but single entry, it would be impossible for anyone who was unwelcome to get in at the gate.

The attackers approached cautiously, aware of the danger from the castle ramparts above while realising their advantage over the men caught below. Fortunately for Laurence and the others the attackers had no crossbows otherwise they would have been cut down. They had pikes, though, and in common with the rest of

Brandon's men Laurence was lightly armed with just sword and dagger. The sergeant was a seasoned fighter and as one of the pike men came close enough to lunge in the constricted space within the channel, he managed to sweep the spear head aside and strike under his guard. The man screamed and went down. The sergeant grabbed the pike, sheathed his sword and faced the others coming along the channel. Laurence stood by him, his sword arm extended. Torn with anxiety, he had no wish to attack these men but had little choice. The fate of the leading man, and the continuing threat from above slowed down the attacker's advance. Gradually they retreated along the channel getting so close to the castle rock that what light there was in the sky was blotted out. Behind them, one by one, Brandon's men slipped through the gate and into the castle. With just Laurence and the sergeant left outside, they still had about a hundred yards to go when figures leaped down behind them. The sergeant attempted to get his pike around to respond to the new threat when one of the attackers, seeing his chance, lunged at him, plunging the spearhead into his back. With a strangled cry the sergeant fell back into the cloying mud in the bottom of the channel. Laurence was now cut off and trapped in a circle of pike heads, their points aimed at his throat. He had no choice other than to drop his weapons and stand still, hoping they would spare him.

"Let us get away from here," he heard someone say and bring the traitor. My lord would put him to the question." He was pushed roughly along the channel until they were beyond bowshot when he was forced up and onto firmer ground. Surrounded by angry soldiers, a sudden blow to his stomach put him on his knees. He was shoved face down in the mire while his hands were pinioned behind him then he was kicked until he could manage to struggle to his feet. They jabbed, punched and kicked him all the way to the English camp where he was thrown into a low stone hovel, by appearance once the habitation of some animal, probably a pig. A wooden palisade was placed over the entrance and jammed into place. He lay there in the filth, listening to the raucous noises of soldiery. His captors had declared him traitor, which, he supposed was only to be expected seeing as the earl of Oxford was one. He had been caught with Oxford's men who were clearly intent on reinforcing the garrison of Hammes castle, an English fortress presently by treachery, being denied to the crown. Dressed as a common soldier, he could expect to be summarily hanged. His only hope was that whomever the lord was who would question him might believe his story, but there was small chance of that.

He knelt in the confined space and vomited onto the ground, then fell over on his side and drifted off into a state of semi-consciousness.

4 – A Pack-Horse in Great Affairs

Laurence was hardly aware of his surroundings, knowing only that he was confined within an enclosure that prevented him stretching out to his full length. His hands hurt almost unbearably, his bonds bit deeply into his wrists and he was cold. He drifted in and out of consciousness fitfully until the dawn. The first light merely illuminated the gloom of the sty and the stench was causing even his strong stomach to heave. He could hear the voices of men outside and he detected they were of the rough sort, brutal and unlikely to give any consideration to the suffering of their prisoner. He reckoned the door must face the east because early morning spears of light lanced through gaps in the palisade that sealed him within his enclosure. At this time of year he knew the day was well on its way and he reckoned that his captors would have already eaten, which meant he might be confined here for many hours yet without food or water.

As it turned out, he did not have long to wait. He heard gruff voices and the sound of the palisade being freed and thrown aside. Light streamed in and he was grabbed by the feet and hauled out. Nobody other than a man bound with his hands behind his back can known the difficulty of standing, especially when being kicked around, but somehow he managed to get to his feet. There were half a dozen men around him, shoving him roughly towards a nearby pavilion. Outside was a table where a man, obviously by his dress a noble, sat with his captains standing either side. Behind them his servants stood in attendance, leering evilly at the prisoner. He regarded Laurence with contempt tinged with indifference. The two captains stared at him coldly, clearly anticipating the dreadful inevitability of his fate. Laurence stood in front of the table with two soldiers behind him, bedraggled, coated in mud and filth, stinking of the latrine and the sty where he had been confined.

"You wear no livery, yet I think you have been taken as one of Oxford's men," stated the noble, looking him in the eye.

"If I might know to whom I speak?" began Laurence. Immediately one of the soldiers behind kicked him to his knees then, with the aid of the other, raised him to his feet again. The noble stared at him curiously. He ignored his request for identification but leaned back in his chair as he recognised the cultured but accented French tone of Laurence's voice.

"Are you a Frenchman?" growled the noble. "Be it understood that will do you no good here. We can deal with French spies as easily as English ones. Why were you and those others with you attempting to get into Hammes castle? "

"Answer my lord Dynham," shouted one of his captors.

"Lord Dynham!" said Laurence brightly. "Why, my lord, surely you recognise me from the court of King Edward?" Laurence knew this lord. He was John Dynham, Baron Dynham, a faithful follower of the English crown and now in the service of King Richard. Lord Dynham regarded him with curiosity. He could hardly identify the wretch in front of him, encrusted as he was with mud and filth.

"There were many at King Edward's court who are now attainted traitors. You have been caught in the company of those forces who have joined with the treasonable Henry Tudor. Do not think that any previous attendance upon poor King Edward's court will influence me. I suppose I must ask what you were doing there?" Dynham sighed laconically and indicated to a lackey to fill with wine the goblet at his hand.

"I was at court as the king's armourer," stated Laurence hastily. "My name is Laurence de la Halle. I am in the service of his grace King Richard who is waiting upon my report. I am his personal armourer, too."

"Laurence de la Halle? Yes, I remember the name. If I recall you are Breton, and the Tudor was supplied with ships in his recent bid for the English crown by duke Francis of Brittany. Duke Francis has financed the Tudor again and helped him into France where he is plotting treason. I find you before me having been caught in the company of Oxford's men; moreover, you also made harness for Anthony Wydville did you not, executed for plotting against the life of the king? It seems your loyalties have a certain ambiguity."

"My lord, I am in France on the business of his grace King Richard." Laurence felt his plea slipping away. He could think of no way of convincing Dynham of his loyalty to the English crown.

"That business being?"

"I cannot say, my lord. My report is for the ears of the king alone."

"That, my friend is a stupid statement. If I had a desire to hear your report I have the means to extract it. As it is, I have listened to your pathetic story long enough. Be assured, I know a dissembler when I have one in front of me. It may be that you once had some business with the English court but that goes for several other traitors I can think of. Rest assured, I shall *report* on your behalf the fact of your hanging to the king." With that Lord Dynham waved him away.

"My lord, you mistake me," cried Laurence.

The two guards took hold of him and dragged him off, lord Dynham having turned his attention to some papers in front of him. A group of soldiers, one with a rope, joined them, obviously looking forward to the entertainment. They shoved him before them, directing him through the camp to where a gibbet had been erected. This was a feature of any camp where there were regular executions for misdemeanours such as desertion, stealing supplies and food from the baggage, or any offence against the military code. They waited while a crowd gathered to witness the spectacle with Laurence standing in dejection, his head bowed. One of the guards had snarled into his ear that he had been with those who had captured him. It was one of his men who had been wounded by Brandon's sergeant. The man was likely to die so it was with some relish his fellow in arms had the job of dispatching Laurence.

"What's his offence," someone called.

"A French spy of Oxford's," replied the guard. "One of those who did for Jemmy Woodman." There were angry shouts at this information and a stone whizzed past his ear almost striking the guards. "Less o' that," he shouted with annoyance. "Let us get clear first." The guard stepped away and a whole battery of missiles came out of the crowd striking Laurence until he fell to the ground.

"Enough now," called the guard who stepped forward and with his companion hauled the armourer to his feet. "We aren't heathens to stone a man to death." Laurence swayed, his mind reeling. His body was a mass of pain, from his bonds and from the impact of the objects thrown at him and he could taste blood on his lips. He was trembling in every limb as much due to the result of his treatment as for fear. The guard slipped a noose around his neck and shoved him under the gibbet. He began to panic as he realised he was to die without benefit of clergy.

"A priest," he managed to croak. "Get me a priest."

The guard ignored him and simply spat a curse while throwing the rope over the rail of the gibbet. Half a dozen men ran forward to seize the rope ready to haul him up. The guard faced him and noticing the silver chain around his neck, ripped it off and examined the silver reliquary. He grinned at Laurence and slipped it into his pocket when a commanding shout of authority was heard.

"Stop this at once, in the name of the king!"

Laurence raised his head in surprise. Shoving his way through the soldiers, who parted for him, was Sir James Tyrell. He had with him a trio of men-at-arms, one of whom took the noose from around Laurence's neck and offered him an arm for support.

"This man will answer before King Richard himself," he declared to the crowd. "He is now in my custody." The soldiers had no choice but to comply. Sir James Tyrell was Master of the king's Henchmen. "Get him onto a horse and take him to Guisnes castle," he commanded. "And release his bonds." The guard, who a few moments ago would hang him, took his dagger and with a sullen expression on his face cut the ropes at Laurence's wrists. The pain in his hands became almost unbearable as the blood began to flow back into them, but at least that told him he was alive.

"My reliquary," he rasped. With a guilty eye upon Sir James Tyrell, the guard hastily took the object from his pocket and thrust it into Laurence's hands. He could hardly feel it but he managed somehow to push it into a pocket in his doublet. He nodded his thanks to the man who had given him support and stood upright, determined to walk unaided. His gait was uncertain, and he had to accept help getting on to the horse Tyrell had ordered for him, but once in the saddle his wits began to return as he realised he was free.

"I think you should ride downwind until we arrive at Guisnes," called Tyrell as he sprang into the saddle of his mount. Laurence flapped a weary hand at him and managed a grin that was lost beneath the encrustations on his face.

* * *

A bevy of giggling French serving girls brought water and cloths to the tub where he stood washing the filth from his hair and body. His flesh was stinging virtually from head to foot from a myriad cuts and abrasions. There were livid bruises around his ribs his arms and his legs, though he didn't think any bones were broken. Tyrell had sent in some clean clothes while his were washed and cleaned. The cleansing had a restorative effect upon him and he was able to swap lewd jokes with the wenches. Having regained his normal composure and fully dressed he went to seek out the man who had saved him.

A servant conducted him to a large chamber where Tyrell welcomed him and a friendly log fire blazed in a huge fireplace. He walked stiffly now that his skin had dried and his injuries were smarting. Tyrell signalled for seats to be brought near to the fire. They sat facing each other illuminated by the glow of the flames and a quartet of candles on a table nearby. Four lancet windows normally lit the chamber by day, but these were shuttered, the weather having taken a turn for the worse. He could hear the wind and rain lashing the wood as if some malevolent sprite was frustrated at being shut outside. The arras hanging by the walls swayed gently in the moving air and he felt a cool draught at his feet where the air was charging the fire. There were two others in the chamber, servants of Sir James. One stood by the door while another took up a position behind and to the side of his seat.

"I believe this is the second time I have rescued you from hanging?" grinned Tyrell.

"I know, Sir James," replied Laurence who responded with a wry smile. "And I think your timing is improving. The last time I was actually suspended before you got to me. I would have appreciated it more had you arrived earlier. You might have saved me from a beating."

"So much for gratitude. Here you are, alive and well and smelling somewhat sweeter than when I found you."

"I am forever in your debt."

"That thought pleases me," said Sir James. "I recall I still owe you something for the harness you made for me. Perhaps we can come to some agreement?"

"I shall take off the interest; a most generous discount considering the time it takes you to pay anything at all." Tyrell gave a chuckle and indicated for his servant to fill with wine two pewter goblets that were on the table. The servant handed one to his master and the other to Laurence.

He regarded Tyrell quizzically. His stocky frame was dressed in a linen shirt and hose under a blue velvet mantle lined and trimmed with fur - rich attire; velvet was expensive but more common in France than England. A short beard neatly trimmed to a point framed the round face. A fierce, dark mien was an attribute as it lent him an air of ferocity that was tempered by a naturally jocular disposition. Nevertheless, his appearance was one that generally had men jumping to his command. He was the last person Laurence expected to find at Guisnes castle and, it seemed, he was here with some authority. It had been Tyrell who had taken into hiding the young prince Richard, after Laurence had surreptitiously removed him from the Tower of London. The last time he had seen him was last year. They were together with his men attempting to entice

Henry Tudor to land on an English shore. The Tudor had not been fooled and fled back to Brittany. Laurence cursed that enterprise. If it had succeeded, then he wouldn't have been here now having narrowly escaped a hanging.

"Your mission to get that traitor Thomas Grey to abandon Tudor is, I must say, good strategy, but I cannot stomach the idea of him being restored to his lands. Sometimes I fear for the policies of our king."

"I don't know that I agree," returned Laurence. "So far Grey has made no attempt in that direction, but I have a feeling he will do so for the sake of his mother. If his defection causes Tudor to invade now before he can persuade more to join him, as Oxford has done, a twisted expression of sycophancy on the face of Thomas Grey at court will be a price worth paying. In any case, who is to say he won't overreach himself at some future time and put his head on the block?"

"You give me cause to hope," said Tyrell flippantly. "But you miss my point. Consider the present situation. I am to open negotiations with the treacherous garrison of Hammes with the object of letting them walk free to join the Tudor, if they so wish!"

"The king has ordered that?!"

"He has sent me here to take command of the garrison at Guisnes, seeing as the present lieutenant, William Blount, being the brother of that traitor James cannot be relied on. That is fine and sensible; but letting a whole garrison free from retribution when there is a clear conflict of loyalty to the crown defeats my sense of reason. The Pale of Calais is part of the kingdom of England after all and that includes the castles of Hammes and Guisnes. King Edward would have taken the castle and hanged the lot of them."

"Well, it does make some sense," said Laurence. "Diplomatically, it can do the king's credibility with European monarchs no good where an English army is besieging an English castle located within English crown demesnes."

Tyrell nodded and took a thoughtful pull at his wine. "Perhaps you are right, and in any case the whole of the garrison might not accept the king's amnesty. Those that do we will be well rid of and we can always deal with them after Tudor is gone. Calais has enough men to replace them and bring the garrison back to its proper strength. I shall ensure the rest of them stay loyal, there is no question of that!"

"I am sure that is why the king sent you here. We live in unquiet times and so it will remain while the Tudor lives. The sooner we can get him into England where King Richard can dispose of him, the better."

"If that is any time soon it is likely I shall be stuck here and miss it all."

"Be assured, if I am lucky enough to witness Tudor's destruction I shall render you a full account – which brings me to the question of my return to England. I should like to get there before the Yuletide feast."

"There are plenty of ships at Calais, but while this weather persists they will not put out to cross the narrow seas."

"Some of them are eager to carry trade goods across and will sail should there be a period of sufficient calm."

"I suppose you will be looking to my purse for the means to purchase passage? If you had one when you set off with Brandon's men there was no sign of it when we found you."

"I didn't even feel its loss. It could have been taken anytime after my capture. There is any number of cutpurses in the army. I had a fair amount on me too, payment for the work I did for Tudor's men in Paris." He looked at Tyrell pertinently.

"I shall settle my outstanding account with you. Then I can wear my iron with a clear conscience knowing I helped you on your way to England."

"Your generosity is seconded only by your humanity, Sir James." Laurence raised his goblet and Tyrell did likewise, both men touched their cups and smiling together, drained the contents and held them out for a refill.

* * *

Laurence stayed at Guisnes castle long enough to witness the procession led by Sir Thomas Brandon with his own men, James Blount's wife and those of the garrison who would join the Tudor. Happily there were few of the latter; most had decided to remain once they had the word of Sir James Tyrell that there would be no retribution. It appeared that many had been reluctant to hold the castle against their own countrymen but had been intimidated by Sir James Blount, their commander. As Tyrell had pointed out to Laurence, King Edward would have hanged them without mercy and they were uncertain regarding King Richard, so held out in fear of their lives, their loyalty to the English crown otherwise undisputed.

The next day he bid Sir James Tyrell goodbye and departed Guisnes for Calais, riding a borrowed horse and accompanying a small train of supply wagons. He managed to find lodging at an inn near the harbour and was fortunate that the weather cleared after a couple of days there, which encouraged some vessels to put to sea. His passage across the narrow seas to England was subsequently fast, though the motion of the ship tormented his bruised body and his stomach lurched with each plunge into the troughs of the waves. The sea was not his natural element and although he was rarely sick, even a short voyage made him ill and he would remain in low spirits until his feet were on firm ground once again.

The ship he had taken passage on came in along the Thames River and so he was spared the long and miserable journey through Kent to London. It was with great relief that he entered the apothecary's shop at last, shook the wet from his mantle and, giving Beast his due regard of a pat on the head, presented himself before Cornelius and Anna. She gave a gasp of surprise when he entered, and the thought came to him she might have thrown herself into his arms had they been alone.

"Welcome back," enthused Cornelius. Laurence was pleased to note that the apothecary seemed to be restored to health. "We have been wondering if you could get back to us. The weather has been bad for weeks now and I see few signs of improvement."

"Yes, we thought that the delights of Paris might hold you until spring," intoned Anna with a tinge of cynicism despoiling the gladness she otherwise radiated.

"Paris is a dreary place unless you are of the nobility," he responded, "and then it is wont to be dangerous. The people there are in a permanent state of disquiet and the poverty is even worse than here in London." He looked at them quizzically. "How do you know I have been in Paris? When I left it was to go to Brittany."

"I have my agents in France, as you should have realised," said Cornelius. "I managed to track you as far as Paris, then you disappeared until you turned up at Guisnes in the company of our old friend, Sir James Tyrell."

"Have you any idea how I came to be there?"

"Only that you were captured trying to invade the fortress of Hammes in the company of Oxford's followers."

Laurence wondered how much of the tale he should tell. The part about the hanging would be particularly harrowing for Anna as that had been the fate of her first husband and she knew it had nearly been his, too. He would leave that bit out. He told them the story more-or-less as it happened except Tyrell turned up sooner than he actually did.

"I left the marquis, Thomas Grey in a state of indecision," he told them as he brought the tale to a close. "I had some initial success and thought that the plan would work. However, Oxford's arrival boosted the Tudor fortunes and undid my efforts. To make matters worse, at least part of the garrison at Hammes Castle deserted to the Tudor. I suspect I went to a lot of trouble for nothing."

"Not a bit of it!" exclaimed Cornelius. Anna too was smiling at him triumphantly. "We had word just yesterday that the marquis of Dorset had ridden off to come home to England."

"Had ridden off?"

"Well, yes. Unfortunately Henry Tudor sent his man Humphrey Chaney and some others after him and they caught up with him at Compiègne and *persuaded* him to return with them to Paris."

"So the scheme was a failure after all," said Laurence disconsolately.

"Not a bit," replied Cornelius joyfully. "It will have disturbed the Tudor greatly to have someone who knows of his plans desert him. It must have some affect on the rest of his followers, which was the whole purpose of the scheme. King Richard does not actually require the marquis to come to him, merely attempt to do so. Henry must be plaiting his legs wondering if any others might be thinking to do the same. It can only force him to bring his plans to invade us forward, irrespective of whether he is fully prepared or not."

"Yes, I suppose that is correct," said Laurence brightly. "But I wonder what tipped the marquis over the edge? I know he was encouraged by Oxford's arrival and then there would be the men from Hammes to increase their numbers. That would rather tend to encourage him to stay with Tudor."

"No, that is not correct. It was the arrival of the men from Hammes, along with Brandon and his men, that made him decide to leave the Tudor."

"I don't follow your reasoning."

Cornelius clapped his hands with apparent delight and stood with his back to the fire. Anna went to the table and poured them both a beaker of ale from a jug. Handing it to them, she looked at Laurence with a smug grin. Obviously she knew the answer to his question.

"You must know, seeing as Sir James Tyrell will have told you, that King Richard offered a free pardon to any in the garrison at Hammes who stayed, while letting free any others who wished to leave?"

"That is so. Sir James and I discussed it and he was not happy at all."

"Maybe not, but the mind of a king operates differently to most men. In this case it bore fruit. The free pardon extended to the wife of James Blount, a traitor to the crown who, if things were as they should be, deserves a traitor's death. She was in the castle and the king has now restored her to her husband, in spite of that man's crime against him. It was a decision that made the marquis of Dorset realise King Richard's word could be trusted. Moreover, his lack of spite in restoring the woman to her husband convinced him that the king's merciful promise to him, should he return to England, would he honoured. That is what made him desert the Tudor. He will not be the only one in the Tudor camp to think on it either, in particular the Tudor himself."

"Wonderful!" exclaimed Laurence. "That means any advantage gained by Oxford's escape from Hammes, or the defection of part of its garrison has been negated."

"Quite so. I think you can consider your expedition to have been worthwhile. I have sent a message to the king, who is with the queen at Westminster for Yuletide. I expect he will wish to thank you personally once he knows you are back with us."

Laurence looked about the room. While they had been talking he had been aware that there were people missing, Philip and Mother Malkin. He wasn't too concerned that the old crone was absent, but he did wonder where Philip might be.

"Oh, he is about with doctor Maddison," Anna informed him. He thought he could detect a look of disapproval on her face so he decided to push the matter further.

"No doubt he is preparing him for his studies. He is to go up to Cambridge soon. We should be grateful the doctor is taking an interest in him."

"That depends – the doctor has some strange ways," she sniffed and busied herself rearranging some jars on a shelf.

"You do not approve of Philip's association with doctor Maddison?"

Anna stopped what she was doing and exchanged glances with Cornelius, who deigned not to notice. She sat on a stool and

Laurence settled himself on a bench, regarding her with a puzzled frown that demanded an explanation.

"You know of the man Colyngbourne?" she said rhetorically.

"The traitor, yes. He is to be tried for treason, then executed I suppose." Laurence knew of William Colyngbourne. He had been caught along with another, one John Turburvyle, both having written to Henry Tudor asking him to invade England and take the throne from King Richard. Colyngbourne had been a gentleman usher at the court of King Edward and a servant of the king's mother, Cecily. Knowing he was a traitor, Laurence had taken his name in vain last year, pretending to be one of his men when he and Tyrell were attempting to entice Tudor to land on an English shore. He knew him to be a Tudor agent because of the rhyme he had attached to a door of St. Paul's – all London knew it better than their catechism:

> The Cat, The Rat, and Lovell our dog
> Rule all England under an Hog.

That was a clear reference to William Catesby, Sir Richard Ratcliffe and Viscount Francis Lovell, close followers of the king whose badge was a white boar. He had no idea why Colyngbourne favoured the Tudor cause, it having no legitimate claim in blood to the English crown and he a former servant of a Yorkist king. Perhaps lady Stanley had got to him as she had with others? The man had gone into hiding, but he and Turburvyle were found and imprisoned just before Laurence went off on his trip to Brittany.

"There was a great trial at the Guildhall," Anna informed him. "King Richard was much angered by Colyngbourne's mocking doggerel and he appointed a powerful commission to hear the case. There were about ten sitting in judgement; Viscount Lovell was one, the duke of Norfolk another; and also appointed was lord Stanley."

"Curious that," interrupted Cornelius. "Lady Margaret Stanley had almost certainly encouraged Colyngbourne in his treasonous activities. I think that the king might have been delivering a warning to him, making him part of the process of condemning a traitor."

"I think you are correct, husband," said Anna. "The commission sentenced Colyngbourne to be hanged, drawn and quartered while John Turburvyle was sent off to prison. The execution was carried out just the other day on a new gallows specially built on Tower Hill. That is where Philip comes into it."

"Philip!" cried Laurence in horror. "What can he possibly have to do with such a dreadful spectacle?"

"He was taken there by doctor Maddison. The two of them were spectators in the very front."

"But why? The boy is barely ten years old, though I know there will have been many a churl there much younger than that."

"I am informed," continued Anna with a sigh, "that it is because of Holy Church. Apparently, apart from on the battlefield, there is no other opportunity of examining the internal parts of the human body. Holy Church does not allow such explorations."

"You mean it is part of his learning?" said Laurence, aghast.

"It would seem so," she replied. "While the whole disgusting procedure was being carried out the doctor calmly pointed to certain attributes of Colyngbourne's insides, even paying the butcher who did the job to let them get a close look at the entrails before burning them in the fire." Laurence sat open mouthed, hardly knowing what to make of it.

"It is unfortunate that a physician should have to go to such lengths," stated Cornelius flatly. "But if Philip is to be a physician he will have to become inured to human suffering. He will discover sights just as harrowing as those on the scaffold and inflicted on innocents too. Consider the healing skills of Mother Malkin, much prized hereabouts. She learned those on the battlefield and in the camp of many an army. At least Colyngbourne was the master of his own destiny and paid the price for his own decisions, the rest of us are helpless in the hands of God."

Laurence was shocked by what Anna had told him, but he understood something of what the doctor had been about. Anna understood too, he was sure, but that didn't stop her concern for the developing mindset of her boy, nor his either. He decided the conversation should take a turn for the better and a change of subject was called for.

"Soon it will be the feast of Yuletide," he declared joyfully, "when we can disport ourselves gladly in our celebration of the coming into the world of Our Lord. Let us think on the renewal of life rather than death."

"Well said, Laurence," cried Cornelius. "Wife, spread the board and let us feed, not yet a feast perhaps, but we can enjoy the delights of anticipation."

* * *

Brightness was dominant at court, found in the colours and fabrics of the gentlemen, knights and their ladies, tapestries and arras hangings and in the myriad of torches in the corridors and candles in the halls of the palace at Westminster in the final days of the year fourteen eighty-four. Brightness, too in the chatter of the courtiers, the scholars and churchmen resplendent in their finery as they contemplated the celebration of the coming of the Christ Child, yet with a touch of the primitive, the echoing grandeur of ancient times when the Yule log was burned for the twelve days of Christmas and part of it preserved until the following year when it would light the new Yule log. On the eve before the Christ Mass, known as Adam and Eve Day, apples were placed in bowls on tables along the walls, though correctly they should adorn the nearby trees, which they would have, should this be in the country rather than a royal palace in the city of London. Holly adorned the pillars of the great hall, its red berries once white, turned red by Christ's blood and mistletoe, a recent decoration now the church had declared that it helped mankind to recognise witches and, as a bonus, protected against the plague.

The great hall was hot. Torches blazed in sconces along its walls and the air over tables set in rows down its length shimmered in the light of candles. Already men with their ladies were moving to their places, carefully chosen according to rank. Gentlemen ushers showed them to the tables while lackeys scurried back and forth dispensing wine so that no man or his lady might have to sit unattended. Jewels glittered in a myriad of colours where they were fastened to the fabric of doublet, or suspended at the throat of a lady, or stitched here and there into an already rich fabric. Beyond the great hall, in lesser chambers, the lower orders were similarly accommodated, the language coarser and the jests more ribald, but none the less good-natured. Here jugs of ale and wine were placed for the guests to serve themselves. Anyone approaching the Palace of Westminster could not help but salivate at the smells of cooking coming from the great kitchens and outside, the poor of London thronged, waiting for the bread trenchers of those inside, sodden with the juices of the choicest meats to be distributed amongst them along with any other largesse that the king might see fit to bestow upon them.

And this was, indeed, a generous king. His followers had been well rewarded for their service to him and any man who displayed the quality of loyalty that was enshrined in his own motto – *Loyaulte Me Lie* – Loyalty Binds Me was assured the reciprocal support of his king. King Richard the Third was determined to bring to his people good laws, peace and prosperity, where noble and commoner, each in their allotted station could be assured honest reward for their service and toil.

The table at the far end of the hall was yet unoccupied. The king would not appear before the people were all assembled to greet him and his queen, and the great kitchens had finally prepared the best of viands for the feast. Minstrels played in the gallery above and all was chatter and noise. Then at last, a hush fell over the hall. The minstrels had stopped playing and expectation was in the air.

A curtain obscured the door through which the king and his queen were expected to come. This shook slightly and it was apparent to everyone that the door behind it was now open. The curtain parted and a strange twisted face appeared thrust through the gap. Just three feet from the ground, it leered at the assembled people then disappeared. After a few moments it appeared again looking around the room as if wondering what everyone was waiting for. The face disappeared again and then a leg was thrust through the gap in the curtain, clad in bright yellow hose. The disembodied leg gave a little jig all of its own and the people began to laugh, having realised at last who this was. The leg was withdrawn and after a pregnant pause, a giant phallus of impossible dimensions appeared, which jiggled about for a few moments then withdrew. At this the company was in uproar. Next a veiled herrin was thrust through the curtain, which swelled as if a woman was the hidden possessor of the headwear. The curtain began to jerk rhythmically and cries of falsetto ecstasy rang out whereupon, with a long drawn-out sigh of great satisfaction the herrin slowly disappeared behind the curtain.

There was a pause when the whole hall held its breath, then the curtains sprang apart and a short dwarf of a man leapt through holding his arms out to be recognised. He swept an elegant bow as the assembly cheered and applauded. Here was the king's jester, Jolly John. The little jester was clad in multi coloured doublet and hose, with the traditional cap and bells on his head. To the shock of the people, he bounded on to the dais and sat on the king's seat with his feet upon the table, inviting the servants to serve him. With great show they declined to do so and pointed for him to get out. He jumped up and ran down the hall to a side door, which after turning to the audience ensuring he had their full attention, he flung open. The clarions sounded a fanfare and then, entering through the door came the king, escorting his queen. The hall exploded with delight as Jolly John, genuflecting and bowing escorted the royal couple through the middle of the mass of courtiers to the dais where they sat down. Following came the king's chief retainers and their wives. Viscount Lovell was there along with Robert Percy, Richard Ratcliffe and William Catesby the lawyer. Archbishop Rotherham, as a prince of the church took a place next to the king. Beside him was the duke of Norfolk. To Laurence's delight, his son Robert had come along in his retinue and, though too lowly to be attending upon John Howard at the royal table, he had been brought with a few others to see to his master's more mundane wants.

Finally, almost as if to eclipse the splendour of the king and his friends came Elizabeth Grey with her five daughters. The crowd gasped in unison at the sight. They were robed as splendidly as the queen. Who now could say the king had not been true to his promise of care? Elizabeth of York, the eldest of them attracted most attention and speculation. Everyone knew Henry Tudor had declared his intention to marry her and though the possibility was unlikely, yet she was the most desirable heiress in England. She was wearing her mother's jewellery and it seemed that light radiated and sparkled from her as she walked with her mother up to the dais. Both women sank down in obeisance, and though the mother knelt in front of the queen, the daughter was before the king and looked up softly into his eyes while smiling enigmatically and displaying a good deal of white throat as if offering herself as a sacrifice. Here was another brazen Venus, oblivious to the court, intent only on her own schemes and probably aided by her witch of a mother.

Others at the table were clearly uncomfortable with this performance. Ratcliffe and Catesby in particular whispered together while glaring at the two women. Their wives could have lanced them to shreds with their eyes should the pair ever turn their attention from the royal couple. Lovell was on the far side of the king next to Norfolk and the archbishop and he too scowled down at them making his disapproval plain. Robert Percy looked to the queen, concern for her written in his face. The king, though, seemed captivated by Elizabeth of York, as indeed would any man were such a lady to gaze up at him with those eyes. The queen, though, was unimpressed.

"We are pleased to have you join our revels, Lady Grey," said Queen Anne without a glimmer of expression. "Your daughters, too. You have our permission to take your places." The queen lifted her head and looked out across the assembly to where the jester, Jolly John was standing. With no further prompting he sprang forward and skipped up to Lady Grey and with exaggerated gallantry raised her to her feet and made a dumb show of wonder that somehow depicted her faded beauty. The bizarre antics of the dwarfish jester made it impossible to ignore him as he turned his attention to Elizabeth of York. He swept her a low bow and scampered around giving her no choice but to tear her attention away from the king. The crowd began to applaud and with the laughter of the crowd in their ears, Lady Grey and her girls were escorted by the jester to their places at one of the side tables at the top of the hall, their frozen faces betraying their attempts at containing their fury. Jolly John came and bowed before the queen, who plucked a white rose from one of the table decorations rarely grown out-of-season by the palace gardener and threw it down to him, clearly delighted at his performance. The jester clasped the rose to his chest and sighed with a show of passion, then kissed it and having bowed to the queen, scampered away.

When all were seated, King Richard looked up at the minstrels' gallery and signalled for them to strike up a melody. Thus began the great banquet. The king's armourer was favoured and had a place in the great hall at the end near to the dais. It was with some sadness that he had departed the apothecary's shop dressed in his best finery leaving Anna and Cornelius behind. Cornelius, it seemed, had a place but he would have been situated in a different hall and so declined, citing ill health, even though he was now recovered from whatever had ailed him. Laurence noticed that Queen Anne was looking ill and though trying hard to engage with her ladies and other courtiers, the strain seemed to be telling on her.

Not being married he was seated with Edward Brampton, a Portuguese Jew who had converted to Christianity and was also alone. An elderly courtier and his wife, who was considerably younger than her husband sat opposite. She was wearing a blue silk gown and her brown hair was arranged under a dark blue herrin dressed with diaphanous gauze of white. He had the feeling he had seen her somewhere before, though there were many ladies at court, he could not place this one. By the look in her eyes it appeared she was not displeased with the seating arrangements, favouring with a coquettish smile the handsome man with the interesting scar on his face. Brampton knew Laurence fairly well, having had some repairs to his jousting armour done by him. He was a favourite of King Richard and had engaged in many a clandestine scheme for him as well as other more overt tasks. It had been Brampton that Richard sent last year to attack the ships of Sir Edward Wydville, who had usurped command of the English fleet. King Richard, then the duke of Gloucester had seized control of the kingdom after the Wydville attempt to deprive him of his protectorship. Edward Brampton was authorised to offer a free pardon to those sailors in the fleet who would desert the Wydvilles. That resulted in just three ships being left under Sir Edward Wydville's command and he fled to France with his remaining followers and a part of the king's treasure.

"The king has favoured me with the tale of your expedition to Paris," whispered Brampton, not wanting to share his knowledge with the lady opposite, who was taking a decided interest in them. "You did well there."

"Thank you, Sir Edward," he replied. "Though I was nearly hanged for my trouble." The two men laughed together, both having had similar adventures in the service of King Richard. "I wish they would hurry with the feast. My belly is growling a counterpoint to the lute. I suppose we must wait until the ceremony of the Yule Boar is enacted. It has great significance to his grace the king and although it was never a feature of King Edward's court, King Richard has revived it. It is a northern custom hardly known here in London. I have a part in it and I think you might be included too."

Just then the minstrels paused and the hall fell silent. Through the door that led from the kitchens, two servants in royal livery carried between them a huge platter with a full roasted boar, surrounded by apples and other delicacies. Following was the head cook and six of his minions. Two heralds preceded them then, after bowing to the royal couple, raised clarions to their lips and blew a fanfare as the great roast boar was placed on a trestle table immediately before the dais. The cook, resplendent in green festive hose made his obeisance and stepped back. The king stood and came down to stand behind the boar. His close companions and squires of the body followed him. Viscount Lovell came first and placing his right hand on the boar, swore faithful allegiance to the Crown of England. The others followed in due course and swore the same oath. As they returned to the dais, Brampton gave Laurence a nudge and indicated they should go too. Each of the king's loyal knights and chief retainers came forward and placed their hand on the boar to swear their allegiance.

When all had settled back into their places, and with the king returned to his queen, the head cook stepped forward and began to cut pieces of boar meat and place them on platters, which were taken to the king's table. At once the doors to the kitchen burst open and a troop of servants paraded in with steaming dishes of ham, fowl, fish, flesh of every kind served with a variety of sauces and savouries. Platters of meats were placed onto the tables and everyone took their daggers and set to, cutting their choice of meat and placing it on the bread trenchers in front of them. Serving men went around replenishing the silver goblets of the knights and the pewter ones at the lower end of the hall. Ewers constantly refreshed the water in the finger bowls. The minstrels started up again and all was gaiety and chatter.

"I do think this carol is one of the most beautiful," commented the lady opposite, leaning towards Laurence letting him get a view of her ample bosom. "How think you sir?" Somewhere above a solo voice was singing to the accompaniment of a viol.

"*There is no rose of swych vertu*," Laurence responded with some amusement as virtue was not something he was beginning to associate with the woman. "A carol of Our Lady. It is an old song. We sing it in Brittany, too."

"Ah, you are Breton? I thought you might be French by your accent?"

"My family reside at Nantes."

"Indeed – you are a long way from your home."

"My home is here in England. I have the honour to serve his grace the king as his armourer."

"Now I know who you are," she laughed. "I should have recognised the face."

"It is not now one that attracts the ladies, madam."

"*Au contrere*," she gushed. "We ladies like a man who clearly has something of the adventurer about him."

"Then I am afraid I would be a disappointment."

"I have to agree with monsieur de la Halle, lady Staunton" cut in Brampton with a grin. "If you were to know his history you would appreciate he is the most boring of men."

"Lady Staunton! – Now I know where I have seen you before. You are in the service of lord Stanley, are you not?"

"My husband leases his lands from the Stanley estates in Lancashire." She sat back and gazed at him with soft, dark brown eyes. "I remember – you were here recently to see the king on a private matter and I entertained your lady while you were with him."

Laurence wondered if lady Staunton had somehow arranged it so she could sit near him. Anna had informed him the lady was curious regarding his business and his son, Robert. It was impossible she had no previous idea who he was.

"She is not my own lady, but a close friend who wanted to see the spectacle of the lady Grey and her daughters coming from sanctuary. She has a husband."

"So have I," returned lady Staunton, flicking her eyes sideways. Her aged husband was busily engaged in reaching down the table for a favourite morsel, clearly taking no notice of her. "I shall ask the minstrel to play another noel for him – *Owt of your slepe aryse* – though I think it will do no good. Once abed, Sir Charles sleeps soundly until wakened by his servant." She took up her goblet and drinking, gazed pertinently at him over the rim, then after a moment she carefully placed the goblet down on the table. "It is a carol for two voices, a *fauxbourdon*."

"I believe the *fauxbourdon* has a place for a third vocal harmony to be introduced?"

"Ah, but if the third voice is discordant, it may be omitted."

Edward Brampton, who had been enjoying this exchange, sent them both a knowing look and busied himself cutting a slice of ham. He gave Laurence a nudge.

"I hope you are taking note of what I am doing here," he said. "It is a law applied to all converts from Judaism that they are witnessed eating ham at Yuletide."

"I believe, Sir Edward, that your faith, as your loyalty, is undisputed," said Laurence.

"Nevertheless, witness that the law is now observed," he replied. "Sometimes it is necessary to do that which is required, in spite of one's personal taste." Laurence had the feeling he was not entirely comfortable consuming the ham, but he set to bravely enough.

"You are quite right, Sir Edward," sighed lady Staunton "when you lament some of the conditions we find ourselves in. But as you are no doubt aware, there are ways of compensating what we lack in one part with another. After you have done your duty with the ham, there are other meats and sauces you might like to taste." She spoke to Brampton but turned her head and glanced at Laurence before regarding a baron of beef. "May I trouble you for a slice of that beef, monsieur Laurence. I find it just beyond my reach."

The beef was in easy reach, but he sliced some with his dagger and placed it on her trencher, then cut some for himself.

"I will take some of the sauce," she said softly. "It is pleasantly *piquant*, with a hint of darkness; rather to my taste." He spooned some of the sauce over the meat.

There was no doubt what was on the lady's mind, and her husband, one step from his dotage, was busy feasting and quaffing wine. Either he wasn't the jealous type or lady Staunton was the one who dominated their relationship. He could easily believe the latter to be the most likely. In any case he was taking no notice whatever of his wife.

"Do you reside in London, monsieur Laurence?" she asked.

"My main forge is at Gloucester, but since my wife died I have left the running of it to my steward there. Most of my work for the king and other nobles is carried out at Windsor Castle. This night I am sharing with my son who has lodging nearby among the retainers of the duke of Norfolk. When in London I live near to the cripple gate with my father-in-law."

"And his fair wife?"

"Of course. She is guarded by a huge wolfhound." Lady Staunton sliced a morsel of meat from one of those Laurence had cut for her and popped it in her mouth. She chewed it slowly while gazing at him with a coquettish smile at her lips.

"Does she need such protection?" she busied herself cutting another morsel.

"I was jesting, madam. She sleeps with her husband."

"I do not. Nor do I have a great dog to guard me."

"Does your home, then, have a moat and drawbridge?" he chuckled.

"As a matter of fact it does, which serves both to keep the unwanted out and the favoured in. Here in London we have taken chambers at the White Boar Inn. It has no moat, but the locks on the doors are good. While nobody could get in there, I have noted that a determined felon might reach up to my window and get inside, should I be foolish enough to leave it unshuttered. Mind you, my husband keeps his purse close to him along with my jewels so he believes there is nothing in my chamber worth the having."

"I suppose that depends on your sense of values," responded Laurence. "I recall that Holy Writ tells us a good woman is beyond price."

"Yes, and a bad one is like to be thrown down from a high place. I count myself fortunate to have taken a chamber close to the ground where, should such be my fate, I might survive the experience."

"And are you a bad woman?"

"We are all sinners and Eve was the first to fall."

"I suppose this being Adam and Eve day has put that idea into your head."

"Oh, my head is full of ideas, sir. Tell me, at what time does your son expect you to join with him?"

"Robert is unlikely to be in a condition where he would have any idea of time, being in the nearby hall with his fellows in the duke's service. I think the wine will be flowing just as freely there and he has not a strong head."

"I understand – Sir Charles will be in the same condition." She cast her eyes towards her husband who was draining his cup having seen a server approaching with more wine. Edward Brampton was talking to a courtier sitting on the other side of him. Lady Staunton leaned forward and fixed Laurence with her soft brown eyes. "There is a lane at the side of the White Boar and I believe the third window along on the first floor lights my chamber. The sill is barely above the reach of a tall man. Just call Isabella and the shutter will open to you." She smiled and leaned back, then turned to her husband. "I see you are making the most of the king's largesse," she quipped gaily. Sir Charles laughed drunkenly and held his goblet out for a refill. She took up her own cup and sipped at the wine, her eyes dark above the rim focused intently on Laurence.

* * *

A single candle lighted the chamber, painting the flesh of lady Isabella Staunton with a yellow blush. Laurence was laid beside her, his hirsute body a stark contrast to the smooth skin tones of the woman. Both were breathing heavily after the vigorous exertions of their lovemaking. Lady Isabella Staunton, shackled to a geriatric sot, was making the most of the liaison she had orchestrated and Laurence, long deprived of the warm comfort of a woman had entered the fray with enthusiasm. As their breathing returned to normal Laurence listened for any sign that the maid sleeping on the other side of the door might be astir and listening. All that could be heard was the creaking of the timbers that was the feature of any inn and the usual scampering of rodents somewhere in the woodwork.

"You speak little, my love," whispered Isabella. "Not that I am complaining; I much prefer action rather than words. If you are worried that my maid, Dorcas will run to my husband then fear not. His man also sleeps outside the door to his chamber and unless I am badly mistaken, they will be doing on the hard floor what we are doing in this soft bed."

"I am not used to clandestine trysting, Isabella," he said quietly.

"Well, that tells me your lady, the apothecary's wife, is quite safe from your attentions. I find that interesting. You and I are in the same case, I think. I have a husband who is unable to serve me properly, and you a woman you cannot have because of your conscience."

"She is not my woman."

Isabella turned to face him and stroked his arm. "You have never had her, then?" Laurence tensed, his face betraying his confusion. "You *have* had her – do not try to deceive me *monsieur*, a woman can always tell."

"It is not what you think," he muttered. "It was a long time ago and well before I met my wife." He told her of the great march, when he first entered England in the company of King Edward and how he was there when Edward won back his throne.

"And did you get her with child?" She smiled wickedly and kissed him on the shoulder while gazing into his eyes. "Ah, I see confusion there," she chuckled.

"She has a son who was recognised by her first husband."

"Her first husband! Then she has been married before?" Laurence stiffened as he began to realise he was giving away too much to this woman who, so far as he was concerned, was just someone to sport with. "I see I have said something to upset you," she sighed and pouted. "It is just that I know you have a son already, in the service of the duke of Norfolk."

"That is so. I had thought he would follow my trade, but he seems to prefer the idea of becoming a squire to a knight."

"An adventurer, just as his father." She stroked the scar on his face with the backs of her fingers.

"Let us hope your son, your *sons*, prosper rather better than the sons of the late king. The poor creatures; so cruelly murdered." She leaned towards him and regarded his face keenly, as if inviting a comment.

"Such is the fate of princes," he replied non-committally.

"Their deaths do not affect your loyalty to King Richard? I find that strange, seeing as you are otherwise quite a honourable man. I speak knowing of your behaviour towards the apothecary's wife. Mind you, there are those who believe the princes are not dead, but hidden away?" He could see enough by candlelight to observe a raised eyebrow.

Laurence felt a prickle of apprehension causing the hairs on the back of his neck to rise. He knew lady Isabella Staunton was familiar with lord Stanley and through him, probably the lady Stanley - Margaret Beaufort. If she were a servant of the Stanley's then he would have expected her to prosecute with vigour the lie that their uncle Richard murdered the two princes. Why would she want to make out the possibility that the princes lived?

"I have learned it is wise not to dwell on matters that are of no further consequence."

She nodded and smiled enigmatically. "You have become a courtier, *monsieur*, not just a mere artisan armourer."

"That has always been so, my lady. I was brought up close to the court in Brittany. My family work only for the highest of noble knights."

"It is my experience that you serve their ladies particularly well, too." She lay back in the bed and pulled him to her. "Let us make love one more time before the dawn wakes the world and we must part."

He felt a wave of lust sweep over him as he took hold of her. No doubt this was a dangerous woman, but at the moment she was just a woman, and a most beautiful and lustful one, too. He would deal with that aspect of her character for now and consider what to do about the rest in the full light of day.

5 – The Fruit of Rashness

It had been an easy drop from the window of lady Staunton's chamber, though he had almost landed on a bundle that cursed him to damnation in spite of this being a Holy Day. As the shutters closed softly at the window above, he made his way from the inn and walked towards the massive stone magnificence that was Westminster Palace.

The bells for Matins were ringing in all the churches around Westminster as Laurence made his way through the surrounding streets, where the first rays of the morning sun let him pick his way about the potholes and general ordure thrown down there. It was the morning of Christ's nativity and the joyous peals were particularly prolonged. A thin crust of ice lay over the mud in the streets, which collapsed crepitatiously under foot. Occasional flakes of snow were adrift in the still air floating as if in thought, wondering whether or not to descend to earth in a full-blown snowfall. The area was unusually populated due to the feasting at Westminster Hall. The poor and destitute had gathered around the hall last eve, attracted by the promise of trencher bread and waste scraps that they knew would be distributed after the feast. Some were still lying in alleys and doorways, huddled into their rags against the cold and waiting for the dawn. He could smell wood smoke from the morning fires lit by servants and somewhere the sulphurous tang of a sea coal fire.

Robert had a place along a wall on the floor of the great hall itself with his fellows in the duke of Norfolk's household. Laurence had a pallet there, too, but unused. He would invent some story about having found another place to sleep – not exactly inaccurate and he was reluctant to tell his son an outright untruth on this day. Robert was unlikely to bother where he had slept, especially if he was suffering a thick head.

There was a disconsolate air about the great hall, as might be expected the day after a feast. Already servants were sweeping the floor and moving the tables and benches away. Dogs were sniffing around, licking vomit and rooting for scraps amongst the rubbish. The king had ended the revels some time before the ringing of the Midnight Office. He had wished to take up a vigil with his queen in the hour before the coming into the world of the Christ. He had always been a pious man, but since the death of his son, and with the obvious degeneration in Queen Anne's health, he had become even more devout.

Laurence looked about among the servants in the hall, but could not see Robert anywhere. He supposed the boy would be attending if not upon his grace of Norfolk, then one of the squires in his household. There was nobody there he recognised, except perhaps one fellow hurrying through the hall towards St. Stephen's chapel. It was merely because the man turned his face particularly to regard him that he noticed him at all. Something about the man's demeanour was disturbingly familiar, but he had other things to occupy his mind – not least his encounter with lady Isabella Staunton. Then there was the king's business. He must make his way to Windsor Castle and the armoury there to finish some work he was doing on the king's harness.

He managed to find a mount at the palace stables. There was a kind of equestrian exchange between Westminster and Windsor involving a small fee to the head grooms. It was a scheme that was both convenient to those moving between the two palaces and as a way of exercising the spare horses. The nag provided for him would just about get him there, he hoped. A troop of soldiers was also off to Windsor Castle and he asked their sergeant if he could join with them. There were some parts of the road that were stark and lonely where padders and other brigands, no respecters of a Holy Day, would lie in wait for travellers. The sergeant was only too pleased of the company. He was a loquacious fellow and though Laurence would have preferred to sort through his own thoughts riding in silence, he found himself engaged in idle chatter. The wind came up as they started off across Lambeth Moor yet the snow maintained its casual sporadic drifting making the ride endurable if not actually pleasant. It was not until midday, when the walls and towers of Windsor Castle came into sight that the snow began to fall more heavily and by the time they rode into the lower bailey it was almost obscuring sight of the upper turrets of the castle.

The bell for None was ringing as they pulled up and dismounted by the horseshoe cloister, recently finished and inhabited by some of the clergy of St. George's Chapel. This latter edifice was still under construction, but priests were appointed to serve the royal apartments and other chapels in the castle. Laurence thanked the sergeant for his company and strolled across the lower bailey towards the upper bailey and the entrance to the armoury. On the way he had to pass a small chapel used by the armourers, smiths, farriers and others. He decided to enter the chapel as his soul was in need of solace. He joined the company assembled there and knelt with them when the priest elevated the host while an acolyte swung a fuming censer. Muttering a paternoster he crossed himself and fingered the silver tube of his reliquary. Wreathed in fumes of incense, it was easy in imagination to conjure images of his family who would on this same day be attending the None mass in Brittany, his mother, father and brother; and also those working for him at his forge in Gloucester. Desperate to keep from rising in his brain the vision of lady Isabella Staunton, he prayed for the souls of his dead wife and children, ever conscious of the hope he was thus speeding them through purgatory to heaven. Perhaps they were already there? He had paid a large enough sum to the chantry priest at St. Michael the Archangel in Gloucester where their mortal remains were interred. Finally he prayed for his two living sons which, when thinking on Philip, inevitable tormented him by causing him to picture the face of Anna Quirke. As he rose to his feet, he crossed himself before a statue of the Holy Virgin and realised he was in urgent need of shriving.

With something of a haunted look about him he shuffled with the crowd of worshippers from the chapel into the castle precincts.

"Give you good den, master Laurence." He looked around at the speaker.

"Peter - give you good greeting." Peter Heap was one of the armourers at Windsor Castle. Laurence had first met him on coming into England from Flushing with King Edward back in fourteen seventy-one. He had been apprenticed then to Nicholas Olds, the king's armourer and they had all come over together. A boy then, now he was a man – a Viking, thought Laurence. He had that kind of appearance with cropped blond hair and a neatly trimmed beard. When dressed for the forges, and when wielding a hammer he was a very Thor.

"I have the king's cuirass ready for you to work on, master Laurence. I have been expecting you here for some days."

"Yes, I was held up at Calais for longer than I expected. Shall we get along?" The two men made their way towards the armoury, which was situated under the great round tower located in the upper bailey but looking down on the lower. The guards at the armoury nodded to Peter as they entered through the door and acknowledged Laurence, whom they recognised as the king's armourer, by standing to attention as he passed. They walked by racks of weapons, pikes, halberds, war axes; then there were more sophisticated weapons: crossbows, crannequins to wind them and tubs crammed full of arrows. There were shelves heaped with harness and the better pieces hung to display their embellishments. Laurence noted with satisfaction there were enough arms here to equip a small army.

The armoury was full of noise as the artisans beat metal into the required shape, working both hot and cold. There were three furnaces ranged against an outside wall where the fires could be vented into flues that carried the fumes to exit at the top of the tower. Just inside the door two churls were turning a pair of barrels with mail inside along with fine sand, which cleaned the mail and got rid of any rust. A plume of steam rose from one of the quenching tanks and spread across the ceiling as an armourer plunged hot steel into it. Laurence found his own corner where his tools were kept along with his forge clothes. There, arranged on its frame, was the king's cuirass. It had become necessary to alter the breast and the back plate as the king's bodily dimensions had changed causing a small problem with the flexibility of his harness.

"Leave me for a while, if you would," he said to Peter while contemplating the harness. Peter gave a bow and withdrew, knowing that Laurence would have to consider carefully how he was going to rework the metal. As his personal armourer he had intimate and discreet knowledge of the king's body and had constructed the harness not only for protection, but to account for, and disguise away certain anatomical peculiarities. This was something that afflicted most men, some rather more than others and it was his job to hide them. The king would wear a surcoat over his cuirass in the field, which would prevent anyone noticing his tendency to incline to the left, but at other times he must appear perfectly formed.

The plates, back and front were articulated, each being made in three parts. This was battle armour and the wearer had to be able to move naturally inside it. Laurence had used Milanese plate in its construction, but designed it in the English fashion where the iron was equally thick on both sides, being designed for the English style of combat, which was on foot rather than mounted on a horse. Where he had used fluting as decoration it was rounded and less pronounced than the Italian fashion, giving small purchase should an enemy get close enough to the king to deliver a blow. Not only must the cuirass allow the body to bend, it had to let the king pivot his torso too. He had made it with rather more volume on the right than the left and this caused him some concern. The right shoulder of the king being higher than his left meant there was extra space to be accounted for in the vulnerable spot under the arm. When they had tried the harness, the king reported some small difficulty in turning to his right and this was where Laurence would ease it. He knew King Richard was preparing himself for the hoped-for conflict with Henry Tudor and on that day he was determined to be in full battle trim.

He marked the plates where he would reform the steel and took the cuirass from its frame, ready to work on it. Peter Heap had been keeping an eye on Laurence and when he saw he was ready to start work came over to him.

"I have a furnace ready for you to use, master," he said, "and Maud is here to work the bellows for you." Laurence looked around and there was Maud Mudd, a forge labourer who always managed to be around when Laurence needed her. She was a huge woman who dominated the workshop and the men who worked there. Laurence had saved her from prison and possible execution by coming to her defence after she had beaten a farrier senseless in retribution for similar treatment he had handed out to his wife. He had pointed out that while it was lawful for a man to beat his wife, there was no law that covered the beating of a man by a woman. The castellan at Windsor, confounded by having no law to refer to, had no alternative but to release her and, seeing the fellow she had beaten recovered, less a few teeth, there the matter was closed. Afterwards Maud regarded Laurence with favour, a condition she reserved for just one other man, her paramour Long Tom. He was a scrawny fellow, a farrier of good nature and clearly fond of Maud. Shortly after her release she had been useful to Laurence in finding out certain things from the castle servants, which got him out of a tight spot.

"I shall be pleased to have your help, Maud," he said with a smile. "I'll call when I need you. How is Long Tom?" Maud grinned at him showing her tooth.

"He be well enow, maister," she replied. "He likes t' be workin' I' the stables this weather, but they ha' him shoein' in castle yard. He wur kicked a few weeks since but there wur nothin' brocken, thank the saints." They both crossed themselves.

"I must disassemble this harness first," said Laurence. "After that, I will need to soften the metal then re-temper it after working, so there will be bellows work needed at my furnace."

"I have some blood to bring up from the butcher fer t' quenchin' barrels, but just call when you want me." With that she turned and strode swiftly away, her wooden sabatons, just visible under the hem of her dress, crunching the ash and cinders that lay around on the forge floor.

* * *

A few days later, the king's harness shone brilliantly in the light of the forge fires helped by refracted sunlight sneaking through windows high above in the walls. Laurence had made the adjustments he hoped would solve the problem with flexibility. Maud Mudd had spent some hours restoring the shine, burnishing the metal with oil and powdered chalk rubbed vigorously with a leather pad, then finishing it off with a soft cloth. The embellishments around the edges of the restored plate would have to be re-gilded, but Laurence would fit it to the king's person for his approval first, before getting the gold decoration applied. He was standing with Maud Mudd and Peter Heap admiring the cuirass, each of them enveloped in a glow of satisfaction at the artistry involved in the armourer's craft and in which each played a part, when a coarse fellow turned up at the door asking for master de la Halle. He was wearing a plain leather doublet and brown woollen hose. At his waist was a belt from which hung a short sword and a dagger. A black acorn hat adorned his head and his face was unshaven but covered in stubble. The condition of the forge floor, with curled bits of sharp metal and cinder lying around discouraged him coming inside for fear of cutting into the leather soles of his boots. Laurence went over to speak with him.

"What is it you want of me?" asked Laurence.

"I have been sent by my master who would talk to you of certain matters," he said in a tone that somehow managed to convey both mystery and menace.

"You will have to be more specific," returned Laurence, not liking the fellow's tone or his demeanour. "Who is your master?"

"I am not at liberty to say," he replied slyly. "He is not inclined to advertise his presence in England. He does, however, have something to say to you of great importance concerning recent events in France?" The fellow raised an eyebrow to signify that Laurence might suspect something of what this was about. It could only refer to his attempt at cajoling Thomas Grey to return to England, but he knew that particular matter had been resolved when Henry Tudor brought the marquis back into the Tudor fold. Perhaps it was something to do with Tudor plans for invasion? It appeared the only way to find out was to go with the man, though there was something about the fellow that caused a slight chill of apprehension.

"Wait here while I get into my boots." He was wearing sabots, as were the other forge workers. He went to his closet where his boots and cloak were kept. On the way he took Peter Heap to one side. "I shall go with this fellow to discover what is the business of his master. It may be of interest to the king. When I leave can you get someone to follow and discover where he will lead me, just in case there is foul play afoot?" Peter nodded emphatically.

"There is an apprentice who is just the boy for the job. He will not be much use to you if there is violence, but he will be able to follow you without being observed."

"As to the possibility of violence, I will strap on my sword and dagger."

"A wise precaution, master."

Laurence took his time getting himself ready so that Peter could arrange for the boy to follow. He saw the boy leave the forge and no doubt he would position himself somewhere in the busy upper bailey and wait to see where they went.

"Where are we to go?" he demanded as he left the armoury. The man had managed to get past the castle guard, which was curious if he was engaged in a clandestine activity for someone who could not honestly declare himself.

"Just into the village. It is not far."

"Do *you* have a name – and how did you manage to get by the castle guard?"

"Yes, Jemmy Capper, in the service of lord Thomas Stanley. I carry messages for him and perform other services, as he requires. The guard here know who I am."

Laurence was shocked by this revelation and his thoughts began to race. He knew that Thomas Stanley was at his estates in Lancashire and would probably stay there until spring. Whoever he was to meet it could not be him. Lord Stanley would simply have summoned him to attend him here at the castle. Perhaps this was something to do with lady Stanley. She was with her husband and under house arrest since her involvement in Buckingham's rebellion last year, but she had agents at court and was no doubt in regular communication with her son, Henry Tudor. She would have a good idea regarding his invasion plans. There was treachery here somewhere and it took all his self-control not to reach for his sword and loosen it in its scabbard, or look around to see if the boy was close by.

Windsor was large for a village. The people that lived there generally served the castle so the homes of servants, tradesmen and merchants clustered around its walls and along the river. It was just after midday and the streets were crowded with people going about their business. Jemmy Capper led him to an inn and stood to one side of the door indicating he should enter. The sign above the door was a fetlock, this being a badge of Edward IV. It seemed the landlord had not felt the need to change it when King Richard came to the throne. Laurence stopped and looked up at the building. It was constructed of stout oak timbers having plastered wattle and daub infill except the ground floor, which was brick. The upper story protruded over the street. He had no particular interest in its architecture, but wanted to make sure the boy who was following knew where he had gone. After delaying as long as he could without provoking suspicion, he ducked under the low lintel of the doorway and entered the inn.

Most of the clientele were huddled around a huge fireplace at one end of the main room and took no notice as Capper began mounting a plain oak staircase, indicating that Laurence should follow. He led him along a gallery and knocked at a door. The door was opened from the inside and he stood back while Laurence went through. It was a large, comfortable room - a table with papers and writing implements scattered upon it, chairs, a cupboard with wine goblets and beakers on a silver tray. A window glazed with diamond panes at one end let in the afternoon light, illuminating the presence of those others in the chamber. There were three men, four including Jemmy Capper, who having closed the door leaned with his back to it. Two of the men were clad similarly to Jemmy, but even more brutish in appearance. They glared at Laurence menacingly, as is the normal habit of such men, but made no move. The third man was sitting in a comfortable chair with his legs stretched out in front of him and regarding Laurence with a supercilious smile. Clearly a noble, Laurence recognised him at once – Sir Reginald Bray, agent and confidante of Margaret Stanley and Henry Tudor. He had somehow been pardoned by Richard the Third after the Buckingham fiasco, probably as a favour to lord Stanley but Laurence had seen him recently in France with the Tudor. He looked between the men in the chamber and deliberately loosened the dagger in its scabbard. Sir Reginald gave out an amused grunt.

"That will do you no good, master armourer," he said with a smirk. "But rest easy; you are in no danger. Please, be seated." Bray swept his hand over at a chair beside his own."

"I think I prefer to stand for the moment, thank you Sir Reginald," growled Laurence with a bravado he was not entirely sure he felt. "And I think I would prefer your minion here to move from behind my back to where I can see him. He turned his head and looked at Jemmy Capper. Bray laughed out loud.

"As you wish, master armourer." He waved Capper away from the door and the man moved to the other side of the room where Laurence could see him.

"It seems introductions are not required between us," intoned Bray, "so I shall get straight to the point. "There is a matter of a missing boy I would like to discuss with you. No – do not interrupt, you do not yet understand the significance of what I have just said." Laurence had opened his mouth to protest his ignorance of any lost boy. It had become immediately apparent that he was here because of the disappearance of the lord bastard Richard of York. He well knew the Tudor was desperate to discover his whereabouts. He had noted with alarm the singular expression. Had Bray discovered that there was only one of King Edward's sons unaccounted for?

"Your inference escapes me, sir," replied Laurence.

"I refer to Richard of York, the youngest son of King Edward the Fourth. He is lost and I would discover him. I believe you can help me in this."

"You are mistaken if you think I know anything of the two boys."

Sir Reginald laughed out loud. "Come, come - you and I both know there is only one boy left alive of the two and you will tell me where I can find the living one."

"You deceive yourself if you think I know anything of the two boys. They are gone I know not where and that is all." Bray fixed him with a determined stare and opened his hands in a deprecating gesture.

"Perhaps I should tell you what I know of your involvement in this business, then you will realise where your best interest might lie?"

"If you insist." Laurence's mind was in turmoil. He had no idea what was happening here so it might be as well to let Bray tell him what he knew. It was doubtful he had the whole story otherwise Laurence would not be standing here now, but an idea of the extent of what he did know might help.

"First of all there was your sojourn into Brittany and the court of duke Francis. I must admit that until then I thought the boy might be somewhere in England, and your journey to your homeland rather threw me off the scent. You were followed to Bristol by Capper, here." Bray paused to let the effect of his words sink in. Laurence remembered the shadowy figure that had dogged him down the river Severn. He had thought the man had something of familiarity about him, but he had never been close enough to recognise him, yet, thinking on it – hadn't he been the man in the Bell Inn at Gloucester who had sneaked away having discovered that Laurence was leaving the next day on the king's business? Bray must have been having him watched even earlier than he had thought likely. He looked at Capper who grinned at him triumphantly.

"You managed to evade Capper at Bristol but my sources at duke Francis' court informed me that your mission was to attempt to get the marquis of Dorset to desert our cause. That, I admit was a disappointment because until then I believed you might lead me to where the boy princes are hidden. It was then that I discovered you knew one of the two boys was dead, that being Edward, the elder of the two. I was not surprised to hear this as the boy was already sick when he entered the Tower of London."

Laurence thought back to his interview with duke Francis and recalled the interest of the priest attendant upon him. The court of duke Francis was replete with spies for France and it seemed certain the priest was one of them. He had been particularly interested in the fate of the princes, though Laurence had, fortunately, deprived him of any further information, pleading ignorance. Hopefully that same tactic would sustain him now.

Sir Reginald continued: "It seems you know rather more of this business than is apparent to the casual observer, but I *monsieur*, am not quite so casual.

"You speak treason, though, Sir Reginald - or something very close to it. As he has generously granted you pardon your attitude towards King Richard is beyond contempt." Bray's eyes glared at him in anger; then he took on a smile of indifference.

"It all depends on your idea of treason. I believe lack of constancy and vacillation between one cause and another is treachery. Who do you serve, *monsieur*, King Richard or duke Francis?"

Laurence ignored the gibe. "Then why plead for pardon from your king and when he grants it, work against him. Skulking in France with the other exiles would be the honourable course, yet here you are in England, reluctant to show your face," snorted Laurence in disgust. "Though I suppose it is an indication of shame, which is some sort of admission of guilt."

"There is no point in continuing this argument," said Bray indifferently. "I have my loyalties and they are ever constant. The rest is strategy. What concerns me now is the whereabouts of prince Richard of York."

"For what reason?" snapped Laurence, noticing that Bray referred to him by his defunct title *prince* Richard. "To place him on the throne of England and confound the plotting of your master Henry Tudor? Is that the intent of your mistress, Margaret Stanley? Even though illegitimate, the lord bastard Richard still has a better claim to the throne than your master. I smell murder in this."

Bray waved his hand in casual dismissal of Laurence's words.

"I do not expect you to agree with me, indeed it is not necessary that you do. What I want from you is information. Now you see these men here," he looked around at his henchmen. "I have no doubt that they could extract everything you know on this matter. However, I think it possible you may not know the exact whereabouts of prince Richard, in which case, rendering you *hors d'combat* as it were might be counter productive. It is better you should work *for* me and obtain the information I need. Though you might not know where the boy is right now, you are the best one to find out, being in on the secret from the start. Alas I have no other close enough to King Richard so you have the task."

Laurence laughed in his face. "If you think I would ever contemplate such a course, then you are sadly mistaken; what is more I am not so helpless as you might think. I am not without my own friends in England and the king would hear of it. If anything should happen to me you would find yourself a hunted man and Henry Tudor would have one less traitor to rely on."

"I am sure your threat is no idle one, *monsieur*, which is why I expect you to come to my aid entirely on your own volition."

A thrill of apprehension fluttered down Laurence's spine. Bray was far too sure of himself. There was something he had not yet been told, nevertheless he would defy him until whatever threat he was holding back materialised.

"I will leave, now, Sir Reginald. You and I have nothing to say to each other." He slipped the slim blade of his murderer from its scabbard and crouching in defence, directed the point at each of them in turn while backing to the door.

Neither Bray, nor his henchmen made any movement to stop him. "You are free to go, *monsieur* Laurence. As I said earlier, you are not in any danger from me. Capper here will always be somewhere close to you from now on and you may contact me through him when you are ready. I bid you good day."

With considerable disquietude, Laurence felt behind him for the door latch, opened it and stepped outside. The principal thing he noted as he closed the door on them was the amused expressions on the faces of Sir Reginald Bray and his henchmen.

The snow was falling fast and had already covered the streets and roofs of the houses when he stepped out of the inn. As he walked back towards the castle the boy whom Peter had sent to watch his back joined him. The lad had not been necessary after all but Laurence had been unable to spot him as he followed him, so he might be useful in the future.

"What is your name, boy?" he asked him.

"Sam Fosset, master," came the reply.

"Well Sam, when we get back to the castle there will be a small reward for you."

"Thank you, master," the boy replied, touching his cap.

* * *

King Richard pronounced the alterations to his armour satisfactory when he tried it on. The successful fitting put him in a better mood. He had spoken his thoughts to Laurence as his harness was fitted. The privy chamber had been cleared of all others, as it always was when the king's armourer or his tailor was in attendance. Perhaps he had detected something of disquiet in his armourer's manner thus provoking the desire to express what was on his mind. Laurence was already privy to the secrets of his body and so could be trusted with something of his thoughts. True, he had priests to confess to, but his troubles concerned his relationship with God of a kind he was reluctant to share with clergy.

He was afflicted by bouts of melancholy as he contemplated the future. His heir was dead and his physicians were unable to halt the deterioration in the health of his queen. He would never be able to produce another heir of his own blood. It was futile to combat God's will, and he could not understand why, in spite of the numerous chantry and chapels he had dedicated throughout the land, God was working against him. The business with Henry Tudor was, in some respects, the least of his worries and the possibility of the Tudor

103

attempting to invade his realm gave him someone mortal he could actually fight. He could not rail against God, but he could hate Henry Tudor with a vengeance and heap upon him all the frustrations of his life.

"My agents inform me the Tudor is desperate to invade and is assembling an army of sorts. Your mission to get the marquis of Dorset to desert has stirred him." Laurence bowed in obeisance. "Once we have the Tudor, perhaps whatever evil spell has been cast upon us will be broken? For sure our whole life, and that of our dead brothers, has been affected by witchcraft." The king and Laurence crossed themselves.

"I think you are correct, my lord king," replied Laurence. "It began with Elizabeth Wydville and her mother Jacquetta of Luxembourg, then there came Elizabeth Shore to distract the late king, your brother. Those have been dealt with so far but there is still Margaret Beaufort, the lady Stanley. She affects great piety, but it is simply a subterfuge to cover her black iniquity." Laurence held his breath, realising he had spoken too particularly regarding lady Stanley. She was of a noble family after all and his opinion, though shared by the king, might be considered impertinence. The king, though, accepted his statement without thought for protocol; rather it brought to his mind his concern regarding the woman.

"Has she a better channel to God than us through which to provoke our distress?"

"How could that be? Your grace is an anointed monarch, God's representative on earth, excepting his holiness at Rome."

"Perhaps this is a test of our faith," he murmured, "and she a tormentor sent by God to try us as the Holy Book tells us Abraham was tried, though *his* son was saved at the last moment. Perhaps that was where we have failed God? Abraham had been willing to sacrifice Isaac, but we had prayed fervently that our son be saved. I fear my dear Anne will soon join him."

"I have pondered much on this too, especially after I lost my wife and children, though my son was saved, at least for a time. If prayers pleading for the preservation of our loved ones were to be accepted by God every time we utter them, then the world would be overpopulated I suppose, and heaven peopled only by old men and women. Hell, we are told has no shortage of human souls either. Evil is not easily defeated – when it is we will be hearing the last trump!"

"True, there is much evil in the world and the Tudor is its present embodiment," snarled King Richard. "He is governed by avarice, having not a vestige of royal blood to give him even a semblance of righteousness in his cause. The same infection is upon his followers too and no good will come of it, whatever our fate may be."

"It is certain, your grace, the matter will have to be tried in blood. When that happens I will make sure your earthly armour is the best in the world. Let us hope the church can make your spiritual armour so fine."

The king stretched out a steel-clad arm and regarded it in contemplation. He moved it, trying it for ease of movement.

"With Tudor gone, our troubles are likely to diminish. Should, by some chance, the Tudor vanquish us it could only be by treachery and its cousins, greed and ambition; then God's will be done and England must take the consequences. We would not want to live in a realm won and ruled by such as Henry Tudor."

"Nor I, my lord king."

It was with a heavy heart Laurence took his leave of King Richard. The threat made by Sir Reginald Bray hung over him and the knowledge he was being dogged by his minion did little to help him. His discourse with King Richard had unsettled him further, with its underlying theme of treachery and discord of which Sir Reginald Bray was a decided practitioner. He would arrange for the gilding to the king's armour, where he had reformed it, then get himself to London and Cornelius Quirke who might be able to throw some light on the situation.

* * *

He was about to go down to the river to take a passage across and down to London when a servant in the livery of the duke of Norfolk, red with a white crosslet, called to him.

"His grace the duke is rather annoyed with your son, in fact, I believe he is considering letting him remain with you, never to return to his grace's favour."

Laurence stopped dead in his tracks. "What do you mean? I have no idea what you are talking about." The lackey took him aside. He was not quite so haughty as most of his kind.

"I know Robert, and I am the first to admit what he has done is out of character. I would have thought better of him. His grace the duke is a firm taskmaster I know and he spares his pages rarely, but he is fair with them and Robert showed much promise."

"You must tell me what you mean," said Laurence, increasingly worried for the well-being of his son.

"Then you are unaware that he has absented himself from the duke's household without permission nor had the courtesy to make a request to do so?"

"I do assure you I know nothing of this. When did it happen?"

"Shortly after the Yoolis feast. Robert was there with the other pages at Westminster; then he was not. You were there yourself with him, master de la Halle – you must have known what was in his mind?"

"No, I am as much in the dark as you. The last time I spoke to him was, as you say, just before the Yoolis feast. He was fine then and looking forward to the celebration. I believe he is content in the service of the duke of Norfolk."

"Well he has not been seen since then and it is supposed he has returned to his family."

Laurence was almost overcome by a feeling of dread as realisation swept over him. This was why Sir Reginald Bray was so sure of himself: he had his son Robert captive somewhere. It was, in a way, a clever ploy – to use the secret captivity of one boy to force him to reveal the whereabouts of the other. The whole idea suddenly descended upon him like a leaden cloud. He had last spoken to Robert just before they parted; he had entered the great hall at Westminster and Robert had gone to a side hall where the pages and lesser squires were placed. He had warned him against drinking too much wine, he being but a boy and not having the head for it. If only he had returned to the hall where they had their pallets for the night. Then it came to him – lady Isabella Staunton, whose husband leased his lands from lord Stanley! Her distraction had prevented him detecting that his son was missing. His failure to take up his sleeping pallet meant he did not miss his son and the next morning he simply assumed Robert had returned to his duties with the duke of Norfolk. Guilt at his adulterous tryst with the lady had provoked in him some relief that he had no need to explain his absence to his son, not realising it was Robert's disappearance that required an explanation.

It must be Bray who was responsible for his absence. He is the chief confederate of Lady Stanley and it is she who needs to find Richard of York. Discovery would mean the boy Richard's death, of course, and if he failed to get the information Bray wanted, then Robert's life was in danger too. Panic showed in his face and the duke's servant became alarmed as he realised Laurence knew no more than the duke himself.

"If I might suggest, master de la Halle, the duke should be told of this," said the servant. "If Robert has come to harm while in his household, it becomes his business to find out what has happened to him."

"Yes, but just let me think for a moment." The two men stood quietly while Laurence, his thoughts racing, tried to fathom out the best course to take. If he went to the duke, and that was something for the sake of Robert's reputation he could hardly refuse to do, then how much of the story would he tell him? If he informed him as to the plot hatched by Sir Reginald Bray, to find Richard of York's hiding place, then Robert might never be found as the duke's men would hunt Bray down and the king would hear of it. On the other hand, not to speak out could be seen as an act of treason, seeing as he had discovered a plot to disturb the crown and kept silent.

Perhaps a story might be concocted that didn't involve disclosing Bray's plot, but he would need to speak to Cornelius first. In fact he would have to speak to the apothecary before he took any further steps. Perhaps he could use Cornelius' contacts to discover where Robert was being held? He put the thought out of his mind that his son might have been murdered already, telling himself that Bray would keep him alive at least until Laurence had disclosed where the boy the lord bastard was living. Of course, he could tell him what he wanted to know right now, but his conscience would not permit it, at least until he had made some attempt to confound Bray and his mistress, Lady Margaret Stanley who, he knew, was behind the whole thing. He was torn between a steely determination to overcome Bray's plotting and the desperate need to get his son to safety.

"We must not presume harm has come to him," said Laurence at last. "I will go to our home in London. There may be a simple explanation and I am loath to approach the duke without having first looked into the matter of Robert's absence myself."

This being quite reasonable, the servant nodded in understanding. "I will inform his grace I have spoken to you and what you have said. I presume you will present yourself to his grace in due course? He will be here at Westminster with the king for the next few days. He is anxious to get to Framlingham Castle though, as he is having some building work done there and he is keen to see what progress has been made." Framlingham Castle was in Suffolk and the duke's main residence.

"I will return here as soon as I have made some effort to find my son. I would prefer to furnish his grace with an explanation, which I am sure will be a simple one."

Satisfied for the moment, the duke of Norfolk's man made a short bow and walked off back to the palace of Westminster. Laurence stood on the quay and hailed a convenient boatman. He clambered into the boat and as they moved off into the river, something made him look back. There, leaning casually on a post by the quay from which they had just left, he saw the cloaked figure of Jemmy Capper.

* * *

It was a worried group that assembled in the apothecary's shop. Cornelius, Laurence and Anna were seated together while Mother Malkin stood listening by the table along with Philip. Laurence told them of his meeting with Sir Reginald Bray and how he wanted discovered the whereabouts of Richard of York.

"There is no doubt we are in the same case as Margaret Stanley and her minions," said Cornelius bitterly. "The only difference between us is that we have the lord bastard Richard hidden to preserve his life while Robert's is under a dire threat. There is no guarantee he will be returned to us unharmed even if we were to disclose the whereabouts of the York boy."

"I think Bray will assume that, having betrayed York, his consequent murder will prevent us disclosing our part in the business," said Laurence.

"That is unlikely," put in Cornelius. "Bray and his kind do not allow those who know their business to live long lives. In the aftermath of a suspicious death there is ever the possibility that any one of us could be arrested and tortured by the king's men, thus revealing the details and purpose of the plot. Consider also that after the destruction of the Tudor hope, a distinct possibility if he dares to invade King Richard's realm, Bray, should he survive the conflict, might wish to ingratiate himself with King Richard. That would not be possible if his plot to destroy the lord bastard is revealed."

Anna gasped and looked to Philip, who was listening intently with the curiosity of youth. They had decided to let him remain while they discussed the problem so that he would be alerted to any future danger that might be directed at him.

"All of us are in peril, it would seem," she whispered almost to herself. "What surprises me is it is two weeks since the Yoolis feast and we had no idea Robert was missing. Did you not miss him when he failed to come into the hall where he had his sleeping pallet?"

Laurence had been dreading this question. He might just have disclosed his tryst with the lady Isabella Staunton to Cornelius, but he was reluctant to do so in front of Anna and Philip.

"I assumed he was with his fellows in the duke of Norfolk's household," he replied lamely. "It is very well being wise after the event, but at the time I had no need for concern."

Cornelius tugged at his beard, his brows lined in thought. "You say you are being followed by one of Bray's minions?" Laurence nodded. "Then he is now aware you know your son is missing. A clever ploy that - to let you discover it for yourself. It has put if not actual distance, then some time between Robert's abduction and your awareness of it, making it harder to discover where he might be while increasing our anxiety. Did anything occur at Westminster that might give us a possible line to investigate?"

Laurence realised he must, at some point, introduce the involvement of Isabella Staunton, but he would do so carefully to obscure his rash liaison with her. "I was approached by someone, a lady we have met before who took an interest in Anna."

"A lady at court who knows me?" gasped Anna.

"Yes, Lady Staunton; you remember her. She looked after you that time when I was attending upon his grace the king."

"Ah, yes. That was the day when Lady Grey and her daughters came out of sanctuary," she said, recalling the woman. "She had something to do with lord Stanley." Her eyes opened wide with understanding. "She approached you at the Yoolis feast, you say?"

"She did, that is she was sitting with her husband at the same table as I was. Her conversation was with regard to Robert. It was just a casual reference to his being in the household of the duke of Norfolk and what a fine squire he would make."

"She asked me about you and your family while you were with the king," said Anna with an angry frown. "Her connection with the Stanley family must make her suspect in the affair. She is from the north of England I think from her accent."

"Yes, her husband leases his lands from lord Stanley." He mentioned again the fact that her husband was there to deflect suspicion he might have had something other than a casual conversation with the lady.

"And did she have anything more to say to you other than a strange interest in your son?"

"Very little of consequence, as I recall," he replied carefully. This much was true. It seemed the intent of the lady was simply to distract him while Robert was removed from the palace. She would have taken great care not to say anything that might arouse his suspicion, therefore the rest, he told himself, was irrelevant to the issue of finding Robert. What did bother him was the recollection that Lady Staunton had wheedled out of him knowledge of Anna and his illegitimate son, Philip.

"It will not take me long to discover where the lady Staunton lives, nor where she is now. Do you know where she was lodged?" asked Cornelius.

"At the White Boar Inn, Westminster village," responded Laurence without thought.

"How do you know that?" snapped Anna immediately. "I seems a strange thing for a lady to disclose in a casual conversation with someone she hardly knows. It is not as if she would invite you to visit her there?" Laurence fought hard to keep any semblance of confusion from his face.

"I think it was a casual mention. She and her husband could not be accommodated within the Palace of Westminster and it was contentious with her." Anna frowned at him but made no further comment. He realised how easy it was to give away a secret. "How long she remained at the inn I have no idea. The weather could prevent her going into Lancashire so she might still be somewhere in or close to London." He turned to Cornelius. "Let us forget about Lady Staunton for the moment and think what we can do to find my son and your grandson. I could let Bray have the information he wants," he muttered in despair. "After all, the lord bastard is of no significance either to us or to King Richard." Cornelius put his back to them and tugged fretfully at his beard as he contemplated this course. Anna looked between the two men, her face a mass of bewilderment. This was a situation none of them had ever imagined and it was replete with danger whatever course it took.

"Let us get clear what is at stake here," she said at length. "For us Robert is a priority, but the Tudor must have the lord bastard Richard out of the world seeing as the boy has a better claim to the crown and his declared plan is to marry the boy's sister. If he were ever to gain the crown then he would force parliament to overturn the *Titulus Regius*, the document that proclaims their bastardy and thereby legitimise King Edward's children. That would make Richard of York the rightful king of England. Thus we must presume that Bray, working for the Tudors, is contemplating the lad's murder."

"Yes, we know all that. What is strange to me is that the present plot is premature," said Cornelius throwing himself into a chair and staring at the fire. "It is certain that the Tudor will lose should he invade."

"That might make the lord bastard a future threat to King Richard," ventured Laurence. "The king might not be so concerned if the boy is done away with, especially if it is Tudor who is to blame?"

"That depends upon many things," continued Cornelius. "The lord bastard has no legitimate claim and remember it is also suspected his father, the late king, was but a half-blood prince himself. King Richard need not fear him."

"I agree," responded Anna. "The lord bastard is still one of the house of York though. While he lives there is no way clear for any Lancastrian claimant, no matter how obscure. Moreover, if the boy is murdered now, the blame will be placed upon King Richard because there are already rumours abroad to that effect. If that happens and you, Laurence, have given away the location of the lord bastard to those who would murder him, you will be guilty of high treason."

Laurence, his face ashen, clutched at the reliquary about his neck and leaned weakly against the table. "Yet he is my son, the only part of Joan I have left – you too sir," he directed at Cornelius. The apothecary seemed to shrink within his gown at the statement. He was less robust after his illness and not able physically to sustain great distress. They all fell silent for a time, each desperately reflecting on the problem when Mother Malkin stepped forward.

"I con find whear t'lod is taken," she declared firmly as if such a proposition was beyond dispute. Each of them had a different reaction to this statement. Laurence discounted it immediately as the delusion of a frail old crone, Anna was saddened by what she thought of as senility in her old friend and Cornelius looked at her with amusement. It was Philip who responded enthusiastically.

"Yes," he piped up. "We can ask Peter Otteler to help us. The two of you could do it."

"What are you raving about, boy?" snorted Laurence disdainfully rejecting the contribution of the youth. The lad was only here so he could be apprised of the family problem and thus on his guard.

"Wait a moment," interjected Cornelius, "let the lad speak. Otteler you say? " The name of Peter Otteler had provoked his sudden interest. Philip came and stood beside Mother Malkin. The two had developed some sort of bond and the old crone delighted in revealing her healing secrets to the boy who was a keen listener and learner.

"Peter Otteler is a skilled scryer and diviner," gushed Philip hurriedly. "We visit him most times when we pass his shop on the way to gather herbs and simples. He lives in the lane just outside the Cripplegate. Doctor Maddison consults him regularly and he has been able to find many things hopelessly lost. He has located missing people too."

Laurence thought on this while his fingers crept automatically to his reliquary. Perhaps it was time to get a similar device for Philip if he was associating with cunning men and women. Everyone knew there were those whose art let them uncover secrets despite them being hidden from everyone else. It was quite normal for physicians such as Doctor Maddison to consult astrological tables, in fact it was an essential part of his art, and it came as no surprise that for the more difficult cases a scryer might also be consulted. Of course, they could do harm too and Holy Church did not approve of their activities, though there were such even amongst the clergy.

"How could he possibly help us?" he asked.

"Mother Malkin has abilities of her own and the two of them have worked together before now," replied Philip. "Their combined power is quite potent."

"How do you know this?" inserted Anna, herself surprised by the arcane knowledge of her son. She looked anxiously at Laurence, and both of them recalled their recent conversation regarding Philip's attending a public execution.

"Doctor Maddison has told me of his skill," he replied enthusiastically, seemingly undisturbed by his association with necromancy.

"Master Otteler will find t'lod," repeated Mother Malkin, "and time's a wastin'."

"I know of this man, Otteler," said Cornelius. "It is certain he has the ability to find things. He discovered the whereabouts of Widow Lambert's sow, which it was supposed had broken free from its sty and wandered off. It turned out Calen Bright had it safe tethered behind his house. I remember - Calen got himself shrived soon after to rid himself of any guilt at *finding* the beast then keeping it to himself."

"Let us consult this Peter Otteler and see what he can do," said Laurence with some uncertainty. "It is sure *we* have no idea where to look for the boy." He was unhappy at the thought of using a necromancer in this way, but he had to admit it was better than meekly giving in to Sir Reginald Bray.

"I'll go to him now," said Mother Malkin, "while tha' stops here. We mun wait while nightfall. He willno' want to scry till then and there will be a good moon tonight. Get sommat o't lods, so tha' Peter con feel for 'im."

* * *

They had left the city by the Cripplegate and Philip with Mother Malkin on his arm led the way by orchards and vegetable plots to the house of Peter Otteler. Laurence walked behind with Cornelius. The city gates closed at curfew and they would spend the night at Otteler's abode while Anna remained in the city. Here and there the few houses erected outside the protection of the city walls were closing their gates and shutters against any night prowlers. Presently they came to a walled compound with a gate that remained open. It seemed they were expected because a small boy closed and barred it after they had passed through. A two story thatched building of wood with wattle and daub infill confronted them. Apart from a small glimmer at a single doorway caused by a fire burning somewhere within, the house was completely shuttered with not a chink of light showing.

The boy ushered them into a chamber, lit by a small fire and where deep shadows obscured the corners and form of the place. Laurence fingered his reliquary and muttered a paternoster under his breath.

"Bring a glim for our visitors," boomed a disembodied voice somewhere in the darkness. A shadowy figure, that apparently had been seated in a dark recess stood and moved casually to stand in front of the fire. All that could be seen was the silhouette of a man in a voluminous gown and wearing a cap on his head. He was of medium height and he stretched out his arms to shuffle his sleeves away from his hands, though for a moment, Laurence feared he was about to hurl some enchantment upon them. This, Laurence assumed, was Peter Otteler, the necromancer. The boy scuttled to the fire and, finding a pair of rush lights, lit them and brought them around to give some illumination.

"We shall have candles, too," said Otteler. They could see him now and it came as a sudden shock to Laurence as it was obvious by the whiteness of his globes, the man was stone blind. Of course, the others knew this and had not thought to tell him, taking it for granted everyone knew Peter Otteler. He was quite old and he wore a white wispy beard, poorly trimmed. The boy delved into a wooden box and took out two candles, which he lit from a rush light. The walls of the chamber were fitted with shelves that held a variety of pottery from fine drinking cups to the more mundane – plentiful clay bowls and vessels of every kind. Under the shuttered window was a table fitted with a wheel under which was a treadle that rotated it. Peter Otteler was a potter. Laurence should have known as soon as he entered the house as now it came to him, the smell of wet clay. No wonder the place was in darkness – the blind potter had no need of light, but would no doubt be grateful in his working hours for the cooling air that wafted through his window as, according to his trade, he pedalled the treadle of his wheel.

"Come, be seated everyone," he intoned fraternally. "Boy, fetch drink for our guests. I take it ale will be acceptable?"

They all muttered their thanks as they looked around for something to sit on. There were several chairs in the chamber and they drew together close to the fire where Otteler waited until they were all seated before settling himself into what was clearly his own chair. The boy brought a pitcher of ale and some cups and placed it on a table by his master before withdrawing into the shadows, no doubt having a place for himself within call. Otteler reached for the jug without difficulty, as if he had been sighted and taking up each cup in turn, poured ale for them. Every cup had the same level of liquid and not a drop spilled. The only dispensation was that he offered the cups in the general direction of each person, relying on them to take it from him.

"Your work is most fine, master Otteler," began Laurence by way of opening a dialogue after looking around the shelves. "The more so when your infirmity is taken into consideration."

"I do not concern myself with what you think of as an infirmity," replied the potter. "My trade suits me well. Man is made of clay so I am content to use the same material as God himself. I see with my hands and my other senses." Laurence found himself confounded by this statement. It was completely the opposite of what he had expected.

"It is not just through your hands that you see, master Otteler," inserted Cornelius. "You have the sight; not as common men have,

114

but that which can penetrate into the darkness where things we cannot see are hidden."

"I have some small ability," agreed Otteler modestly. "Marjory tells me you have lost a youth. You want my help in finding him is that not so?" He turned towards Mother Malkin.

Marjory! Who was Marjory, thought Laurence with surprise? The potter must mean Mother Malkin. This was the first time he had heard her called by another name. Everyone that knew her and in the family addressed her as Mother and never bothered to enquire as to her Christian name, if indeed it was a Christian name?

"He be somewhere near," uttered the old woman. Otteler nodded in agreement, though there was no way in which either of them could possibly know that. "I have a shirt of his for you." She pulled a linen shirt from beneath her mantle.

"We will take it with us," was the reply. Mother Malkin stuffed the shirt back beneath her mantle.

"Take it with us?" asked Laurence. "Are we going somewhere else?"

"Aye, to t'mantic mirror," she replied as if he would know what and where that was.

"Tell me about the youth you are looking for," said Otteler. Laurence described Robert to him and explained that he had been abducted to get him to reveal a secret. "Where the boy Richard of York is," stated Otteler flatly. "He be far from here."

"You know of whom we speak?" gasped Laurence. How the potter could know that was disturbing. Otteler laughed.

"It is not due to the black arts, never fear. There are certain advantages to being blind – one of them is people imagine I am deaf too. I hear things when I am walking abroad that would not be uttered within hearing of the sighted."

"Yes, I have seen you myself at the kilns arranging for the firing of your pots," said Cornelius, smiling at the idea of a man being thought deficient in all his senses simply because he had lost but one. Perhaps this had something to do with his ability to find folk?

"We should set off now." Otteler got to his feet. "It is nearly dark and though I know the way, you might need some light to prevent you stumbling. There is a good moon tonight otherwise I would have had to delay scrying."

Laurence had been wondering about scrying. Usually it would involve the use of a ball of crystal, or a polished mirror of black stone. Mother Malkin had mentioned a mantic mirror, one that can divine the future, but why go out doors and how could a blind man make use of these? Perhaps the crone would look into a scrying object for him and let him see through her eyes?

Everyone got to their feet and went to the door. The boy appeared and went out into the courtyard to open the gate for them. Mother Malkin took the arm of Peter Otteler and led the way outside while Cornelius followed, apparently fully apprised of what was to take place. Laurence had heard much about the scrying art but had never witnessed it, preferring to keep himself well clear of those practices not approved by Holy Church. Following the others, he signed himself and took hold of his reliquary. At least he had a proper talisman against the evil eye. For some reason the fact that the necromancer was blind exacerbated his fears rather than soothed them. If Cornelius had not been with him he doubted he would follow so readily.

They walked for a way between the houses outside the city until they reached a small wood. Wending their way between the trees along a path just visible in the light of the rising moon they had to stop every now and again to wait while a casual cloud obscured the moonlight. Because of this it took some time before they halted before a small lake at the very edge of the wood. Beyond were cultivated fields with just an occasional skeletal tree punctuating the landscape. The day had been clear and it was too early yet for frost to coat the scene. Above, dark clouds drifted across the sky and when they covered the moon, a silver border traced an abstract pattern over the darkness where a few stars were appearing.

"Not here," whispered Otteler to Mother Malkin. The old crone bobbed her head in understanding. She turned and beckoned to the others to follow and set off with Otteler along the fringe of the lake, tramping through wet mud and moss while casting her eyes at the moon. Soon she stopped.

"This be the spot," she said to Otteler. The potter turned to face the lake, the hood of his mantle drawn over his head. The surface of the water was perfectly still, reflecting black from a sky where the moon was, for the moment, hidden behind a cloud. Was this the mantic mirror Mother Malkin had spoken of? Otteler reached into the folds of his mantle and withdrew a white wand and a white moonstone suspended from a leather thong. He stood still; head bowed with his arms hanging loose, the wand in his left hand and the moonstone in the right. Mother Malkin draped Robert's shirt around his shoulders.

Presently the moon illuminated the fringes of the obscuring cloud turning the edge to a band of silver. Soon the full moon shone down on the lake tracing a shimmering band of whiteness across to where Otteler stood. As though he could sense the moonlight, he lifted his face. The globes of his blind eyes glowed with surreal light, the dominant feature in a face framed within the shadow of a hood. He lifted his arms and the wand also took on the moonlight reflected from the shining blackness of the water. In his other hand was the stone held palm upwards and offered to the moon, the leather thong dangling between his fingers. Slowly, he turned sideways with his arms still outstretched, moving his head so that his face was always washed in a full flood of moonlight. He stopped when the wand was before the moon and the stone at the other extremity so that the light passed into the wand and transferred through his body to the stone. He raised the stone above his head and presented it to the moon where it glowed with unnatural energy.

Laurence and the others were frozen to the spot. None of them, except perhaps Mother Malkin, had ever witnessed a ritual such as this. Otteler stood thus until another cloud drifted by the moon and Laurence swore afterwards and to the end of his days that the silver outline of the cloud as it slid by traced the facial profile of his son Robert.

Otteler dropped his arms and slumped into a position of exhaustion. Mother Malkin reached for his hand, took the boy's shirt from his shoulders and drew him away from the lake. He went with her, moving as a man who was asleep. In silence, with Laurence and Cornelius, stunned and deeply immersed inside their own thoughts, the small band made its way back to the potter's house where the boy, looking for their coming, opened the gate for them to enter. The night was not yet over. Mother Malkin opened a cupboard and withdrew a scroll. She unrolled it across a table and placed stones at each corner to keep it open. Candles were brought. It was a crude map of London and the surrounding districts along the river. Peter Otteler approached the table and took the white stone from within his mantle. Letting it hang from the thong, he passed it slowly above the surface of the map, right to left, he was less than a third of the way down the map when the stone began to describe a circle. It was in the general area of Westminster. He moved it around the spot until satisfied he had found its focus. He turned his sightless eyes upon the spot beneath the stone.

"There!"

* * *

117

"We think we know the general area where Robert might be held," said Cornelius. "There are but a few houses, yet how do we discover exactly which house?" They had entered the city as soon as the gates opened and made their way back to the apothecary's shop where an anxious Anna awaited them.

"I have an idea about that," replied Laurence grimly. "We will need some help in getting him free once we find him. I have some friends at Windsor who might help. There is a lad there who has shown himself capable at following people discreetly. After that, everything depends on how many we are to deal with."

"If you are thinking of having Jemmy Capper followed then I don't give much for your chances," responded Cornelius. "He is a servant of lord Stanley and will be more than capable of ensuring he is not followed."

"I am aware of that and I do not intend to have him actually followed. I shall instruct the lad to take himself off to the part of Westminster indicated to us by Peter Otteler. He already knows Capper, having followed the two of us when he first took me to Sir Reginald Bray. I shall give Capper a message for Bray asking to meet with him. All the lad has to do is hang about in the general vicinity of where we believe Robert is being held. He will not follow Capper; hopefully Capper will come to him. It should be a simple matter when he arrives there to observe which house he goes to. The man will be looking out for someone who would follow him. He will hardly suspect a lad already waiting at his destination before him."

"Well there are several things I can think of that is wrong with your scheme, Laurence," said Anna ruefully. "For one thing you are placing a great deal of confidence in this necromancer, a blind one at that; secondly Capper will go with your message to Sir Reginald. If he is not staying at the same place where Robert is being held, what then?" She had also thought Robert might not be alive, though she refused to voice that idea, it being too terrible to contemplate.

"You were not there when Otteler cast his spell," said Laurence, remembering the strange, silvered outline in the sky. "I am convinced we have the right location." Anna gave a shrug of her shoulders and kept her counsel. "Bray is in London as an agent of Henry Tudor and thus may not readily show his face. This limits the number of places he might be securely hidden. If Robert is not with him, then he would need two of them and I am counting on his not wanting to have too many people in London knowing he is here. He can no more rely on his fellow conspirators than the king can trust his courtiers. When you are surrounded by traitors you suspect everyone."

"Your reasoning is sound in that respect," said Cornelius. "Let us hope the necromancer has guided us to the right spot."

"It might be a good idea to have Capper followed, though," suggested Anna. "He would shake off a shadow of course, but afterwards that would make him less cautious at his destination. Why have someone followed when you already know where he is going? In any case he would be looking out for a different person than the boy?"

"That is simple to arrange," said Laurence. "Meanwhile I shall send word to Peter Heap at Windsor Castle, telling him something of our trouble and asking him to come to us here along with the lad Sam Fosset."

The following morning, Philip came into the shop to inform them that Peter Heap was on his way from the quay at the river. He had been sent there to act as a harbinger so that Laurence could draw away Capper, who he knew would be somewhere close, while his friends entered the shop. The purpose was to render the spy unaware there was anything untoward afoot. He threw on his mantle and went out, making his way from the Cripplegate along the city wall to Gayspur Lane. It was as he turned the corner that Jemmy Capper showed himself.

"Sir Reginald is fast losing patience with you, master armourer," he growled. "He has other business and needs to be away."

"I can't help that," responded Laurence impatiently. "Does he think I can just go up to the king and ask him where is the lord bastard?"

"You seem very casual about the whole thing, sir," said Capper. "I would expect alacrity; you want your son returned to you I take it?" Laurence glared at him.

"As it happens I am expecting to hear something of interest soon. Where can I find Bray?"

"I will get word to him when you have something sensible to tell him, then I will let you know where he would meet with you."

Laurence nodded in acknowledgement and shoving past him, walked off along the lane. He strolled about for a while then made his way back to the apothecary shop.

When he arrived there he was greeted not only by Peter Heap and the boy Sam Fosset, but to his surprise, Maud Mudd was there too.

"She twisted my arm when she heard you were in trouble," said Peter with a grin. "If you have ever had your arm twisted by Maud you will know why I had to bring her." The huge woman folded her arms and frowned at Laurence, daring him to deny her. Anna, who had never met her was overawed and simply spread her hands hopelessly. Mother Malkin had taken Beast out into the garden after the animal had bared its teeth at the strange woman as her shadow fell across his lair when she entered the shop.

"Greetings to you all," said Laurence. "I am pleased to have you here. Shall we gather around and I shall inform you of our plan?"

* * *

"Sam easily found the house where Bray is," gushed Peter Heap excitedly. Everything had gone quite as planned. Laurence found Jemmy Capper and asked for a meeting with Sir Reginald Bray. Peter had been given the job of following Capper. As predicted, Capper lost him at the river when he took a single boat across and upriver towards Westminster. Sam Fosset was already at the spot where the necromancer had indicated and sure enough Capper appeared. He went down a small lane between two houses and disappeared. After a few moments, Sam followed and discovered a wall at the end, which was too high to climb. The houses either side had no openings at ground level, but one of them had a door at the top of a flight of steps. That could only have been where Capper had gone. Sam went back into the street and noted which house it was, then waited. Presently Capper came out of the lane and stalked off towards the Thames where he took a boat downriver to the city. They knew where he was going because soon after he was lurking in Wood Street where Laurence found him.

"What did Capper tell you?" asked Cornelius as Laurence came into the shop.

"I am to go alone this evening to the inn at the Sign of the Fetlock again at Westminster. I suppose Capper will be there and so will the two thugs who were his previous attendants. I think he spotted Peter following him, which is all to the good as he will be encouraged to bring muscle as insurance in case I have friends behind me."

"Did he promise to bring Robert there?" said Anna hopefully.

"No, he said I would have to satisfy myself as to Robert's well-being with Sir Reginald."

"I have some intelligence from my informants in the city," said Cornelius. "I know who the house belongs to where Bray is holding Robert."

"Whose is it?" Laurence breathed expectantly.

"Sir John Fitzwarren is the owner, but at the moment it is leased to Sir Charles Staunton," gushed Cornelius.

"Lady Staunton's husband!" snapped Laurence. "They must be using it while the weather improves. Their home is in Lancashire and to get there is hard travelling at this time of year. Sir Charles is not robust."

"It also means," continued Cornelius, "there will be few servants and those he does have will be domestic servants. Sir Charles is not a martial knight and lives quietly."

"Then we can break Robert out of there?" suggested Peter Heap.

"The house is well built and difficult to get into," said Cornelius. "If we could find a way of forcing an entry, I think it would not be too difficult to find Robert and bring him out."

"One problem is the two men Bray keeps with him, not to mention Jemmy Capper. There will be at least four robust fighting men against us," said Laurence, and Bray is a trained knight. It could easily end in Robert's death and perhaps our own too, unless . . .?"

Peter Heap looked at him. "You have a stratagem?"

"When I go to meet with Bray at the Sign of the Fetlock his two henchmen will undoubtedly be with him, and Capper, too. They were there at our last meeting. If so, it means they will be out of the house."

"Yes, but that means there would be just me and Cornelius to get inside," said Peter turning to the apothecary, "and with respect sir, I do not think you would fare very well even against servants?"

"My husband will certainly stay well out of it," snapped Anna.

"I can get inside," put in Maud Mudd, who had been listening with interest at what was being said. "At least I can get the door open. It will be a strong man who would prevent me forcing my way in once the bolts are back!" They all regarded Maud with astonished interest. She was known for her prodigious strength and the idea of her forcing her way into the house was not impossible.

"But how to get it open first?" queried Laurence.

"By the office of a cheese," she replied with a grin that exposed her tooth.

"A cheese?" they chorused.

"Aye. It will have to be a large one, mind." Clearly enjoying herself she beamed at them. "I will turn up at the door with a large cheese sent as a gift for the table of Sir Charles. Usually, fortified doors have a small flap covered with bars for the interrogation of visitors. It will be impossible to squeeze a cheese through, so the door must be opened. I shall need a new dress, though," she sighed, looking down at the coarse and patched woollen one she had on. "I must appear a pretty maid." They all looked at each other, not daring to speak and wondering if she was serious, though her face remained passive. The idea of Maud disguising herself as a pretty maid was hilarious, but she was a woman and the right clothes might soften her appearance.

"There are still just two of us," said Peter. "We have no real idea what resistance there will be once inside."

"There is only one thing for it," said Laurence. "I will have to ask for help elsewhere. I believe I know whom to approach. It is risky and if we fail there will be difficult questions to answer afterwards."

Anna stepped forward and pushed Cornelius protectively back to one side. "Mistress Bold is a seamstress living in Silver Street. I am off there now to buy a dress for mistress Mudd. You should come with me," she spoke directly at Maud. "We want one that fits properly if you are to become a maid once again." With that she reached for her mantle and taking Maud by the arm, bustled her out of the shop. It seemed there was more than one determined woman in their party.

6 – His Castle of Care

Laurence knelt before the king, his face raised as he made his report. Kneeling beside him was the recently knighted Sir Edward Brampton. Here in an ante-chamber to the great hall of Westminster the king sat in a chair on a low dais accompanied as always by his secretary, John Kendall and nowadays the ubiquitous William Catesby. Richard Ratcliffe was there too along with the duke of Norfolk. The king's face was tired and drawn, yet his eyes were bright and his brain keen. Everyone knew the queen was dying and the strain of it so soon after the loss of his son and heir was taking its toll.

"What we would like to know is why you failed to come to us when you discovered the reason for your son's abduction," said King Richard sternly.

"I would try to recover him myself first, my lord king, rather than add to your present anxieties." Laurence knew this was a lame excuse but it was the best he could come up with. "I did enlist the help of your loyal knight Sir Edward Brampton who, along with my own people and a small troop of his trusted men got the boy out."

"Happily for you everything turned out well. Norfolk here, has told us something of the business and we are most intrigued. We shall come to the matter of the lord bastard Richard later. For now we would have the tale from your own lips. Perhaps you, Sir Edward could tell us your part in this?"

Brampton settled himself on his knees, not the most comfortable of positions but the king had declined to raise him. "Master de la Halle came to me asking my help in getting his son from a certain house not far away from where we are now, in Westminster. He had good reason to believe his son was being held hostage there until he revealed the location of the lord bastard Richard. Of course, as soon as I heard the details I advised him to post straight to your grace, but it seemed things had got to a point where precipitate action was required. Seeing as the threat was to the peace of your grace's realm, naturally I complied with his request."

"Yet the traitors managed to get away?" growled the king.

"Well, they were not actually there, your grace, though we have Sir Charles and Lady Staunton under house arrest. Master Laurence had drawn Sir Reginald Bray and his minions away to the Sign of the Fetlock Inn so as to reduce the defences of the house. When word was brought to them by one of the household servants as to what had occurred they fled. Master Laurence was lucky to escape with a whole skin. He was the only one with any real fighting to do."

"And this woman we have heard of, a veritable Boudicca it would seem. She was the one who entered the house first and did most of your work too, did she not?"

"Indeed, your grace," Brampton chuckled. "She beat on the main entrance door and when a servant responded by opening the viewing flap, she presented him with the sight of a great cheese which she declared was a gift for Sir Charles' table. The servant went off to inform his master and when he returned slid back the bolts that secured the door. As soon as the door began to open, Mistress Mudd, that is her name, your grace, flung it back sending the man skidding by the seat of his hose across the entrance hall. The rest of us, who were waiting by the wall out of sight rushed into the house. By this time Maud had the servant in a headlock and unable to move."

"We shall consider her for a captaincy in our host," laughed the king. "And soon you found the boy?"

"Yes, your grace. There were just a few household servants there, mainly women. The lady of the house, a very virago, once she realised what was happening came at us with a dagger, but she was soon subdued. Sir Charles was in his cups and hardly knew what was happening. A maidservant showed us a trapdoor leading down to the underdrawing of the house and there was the boy. He was cold and in a filthy condition, there being no latrine down there. The ladder had been withdrawn to effectively imprison him. As we replaced it he shot out of the hole like a rabbit running from a ferret."

"The lad is well after his experience?" asked the king turning to the duke of Norfolk.

"He is, your grace. He is returned to us in as good a condition as when he disappeared. It seems he was taken at the Yoolis feast after being plied with rather more drink than he could take. He has been chastised for allowing himself to be so easily defeated and is now returned to his duties."

"And you, master de la Halle, tell us of the traitor Bray and your part in this. You may stand, both of you." Laurence, who along with Brampton was feeling the stress in his knees rose gratefully to his feet.

"I had arranged with Bray's minion, Jemmy Capper who, I understand is in the service of my lord Stanley, to go to the Sign of the Fetlock in the expectation I would reveal the location of the lord bastard Richard in exchange for my son. Sir Reginald was unaware we had discovered where Robert was being held and my purpose was to keep him and his henchmen there while Sir Edward, along with mistress Mudd and one of your armourers at Windsor, Peter Heap tricked their way into the house."

"It must have been difficult for you, master de la Halle, not being there personally at the rescue of your son," said the king reflectively. No doubt he was thinking of his relationship with his own lost son, the little prince Edward.

"That was the hardest part for sure, your grace, but I was the only one Bray would talk with. I had to get him and his men out of the house in case our attack caused Robert's death. When I met Bray I argued with him saying I wanted sight of Robert before divulging my knowledge. He responded that Robert would be freed only when he had the lord bastard. In this way I was able to stall them to gain time for the others to act, but it wasn't long before Bray's patience ran out. I think he was anxious to be away on some other business and he was in danger of arrest while in England. Believing I now knew where the lord bastard is living, he threatened me with torture, having two henchmen and Jemmy Capper there who were only too willing to perform that office. I drew my dagger, a rondel with a useful pommel, as they came towards me. It was at that moment a servant, who had escaped from the house, came running in and told them of the attack. Realising there were armed men abroad who would soon be looking for them, and now having nothing to threaten me with, the traitors fled. One of them came at me but I managed to draw my short sword to fend him off. You will find him at the foot of the stairs in the Fetlock Inn, dead from a throat wound."

"You have escaped harm?" asked the king.

"I have Bray's curse upon me, your grace, he flung that at me as he rushed out of the chamber, but no other hurt."

"Sir Edward," intoned the king turning to Brampton, "how is the pursuit of the traitors progressing. Do we have them yet?"

"Bray has very good escape routes, your grace, and having got away by the river will be hard to find. I have sent word to the ports as I expect he will run to his master, Henry Tudor. We do have Sir Charles Staunton and his lady."

The king stood and paced the floor for a few minutes while everyone else remained silent. After a while he came to a decision.

"We shall send Sir Charles and lady Staunton under arrest to their estate in Lancashire where they will remain confined in their house at our pleasure. I would not wish to draw attention to this business, which is what will happen if there were to be a trial. Sir Richard, you will attend to that."

"I shall, your grace," said Ratcliffe who had been listening to the dialogue with interest.

"As for the lord bastard Richard, I think we should move him to a safer place. It would appear the Tudor is looking for him and I am not sure Flanders is the best place for him. We were once exiled there ourselves and have an association with that country through our sister Margaret, duchess of Burgundy. You placed him at Tournai, master de la Halle. Is he secure still?"

"He is, your grace. My uncle, as you know, is a citizen of Tournai and he found him a place with the Osbeck family. Jehan Osbeck is a boatman and plies the river with trade goods. The young lord spends a good deal of time afloat on the river, disguised as a boatman's son."

"Let him remain there for the moment," said the king. "We are presently engaged in certain matters with the court of Portugal, your homeland I know, Sir Edward." Brampton bowed in acknowledgement. Ratcliffe and Catesby exchanged looks though their faces remained carefully expressionless. "I would have the boy educated in a gentler household. My sister Margaret would be fittest for the task, but that would inevitably expose the boy. We will think on this further."

"And as for the traitors, your grace?" said Brampton. "They are still at large and have many hiding places, yet if they remain in England we shall have them."

"We are not overly concerned," replied the king. "Obviously we have the Tudor much disturbed and it only remains for us to turn the screw a little tighter. You have all heard the rumours regarding us and the lady Elizabeth?" Everyone looked to the other, each suddenly white with apprehension. "I see you have," he continued. "We would have it run a little longer. If the Tudor believes I have designs upon the woman he wants for his own queen, that can only disturb him further. Desperation provokes desperate measures and the sooner the Tudor comes the sooner he can be disposed of."

Laurence felt the scar on his face tightening. There had been rumours abroad that the lady Elizabeth of York and the king were closer than uncle and niece should be. He had thought these rumours to be malicious, put about by the king's enemies. That might have been so at the beginning, but listening to him now it was apparent that King Richard himself was complicit, or at least compliant. Was his reticence in denying rumour a ruse to get the Tudor to invade? He remembered how the lady had flattered the king boldly in front of his queen at the Yoolis feast. Everyone knew the queen was dying and the king must look to the future. He needed an heir and the queen was not going to provide one, yet, at just thirty-two years of age, the king could expect to remarry, beget an heir and rule until his majority. Laurence was not sure he wanted to remain in this company and become privy to such secrets, but until he was dismissed he must stay, caught in a web of intrigue and therefore deprived of any room for manouvre. Recent events had brought him close to treason and the more he was taken into the king's confidence, the harder it would be to extricate himself should things take a turn for the worst. He shook this thought from him even as it entered his mind. King Richard was clearly in full control of his realm and, excepting the intervention of malign influence, must triumph. The Tudor was the final obstacle to peace and once the king had removed him, everything would come right.

"Sir Edward," said the king decisively. "You shall wait upon us here at Westminster for the present. You will shortly depart on a particular mission." Edward Brampton swept the king a low bow of obeisance. "As for you, master armourer, hold yourself ready. You have our order for arms and harness for the men-at-arms of our Lance and household. Our own harness is in good trim and it is our intention to go into Nottingham to be ready for the Tudor. Our information is that he will invade this year. You will attend upon us when we go there." King Richard turned to some papers on a table by his side and John Kendall bent over it with him. The duke of Norfolk rolled a map out across the table. It seemed the audience was over. Laurence bowed in obeisance to the king and backed towards the door, which a servant opened for him. Edward Brampton and Richard Ratcliffe soon joined him in the passage outside.

"You have been very lucky, master de la Halle," intoned Ratcliffe flippantly. "Had you been in the presence of the late king Edward, while you might have escaped with your life, you would probably have spent time chained to the wall in a dungeon somewhere, just as a warning."

"Yes," agreed Brampton." Coming to me for assistance was the right thing to do."

"I am grateful for your support, gentlemen. I realise how dangerous are these times and like to remain so while the Tudor problem remains unresolved."

"And you being the king's personal armourer did you no harm," put in Ratcliffe, "yet that fact might just have easily been your undoing. Those of us close to the king, and privy to his secrets have the greater potential for treachery. If any one of us were suspected of anything less than absolute loyalty, we might expect summary execution."

"There is the example of lord Hastings to confirm you in that opinion, Sir Richard," said Brampton. "I think the fact you, *monsieur*, were acting to secure the safety of your son had much influence with the king," he said turning to Laurence. "If there had been a sniff of personal ambition on your part, you would not be in the world right now, I believe."

Laurence realised just how close he had come to a charge of treason even though any idea that he lacked loyalty to the Crown had never entered his mind. His danger had been the consequence of his close association with the king. As his personal armourer Laurence was privy to knowledge other courtiers could never have; the particular dimensions of his body, for one thing. In that respect, his tailor was in a similar position, of course, but in the case of his armourer, the king would tend to discuss matters military, something he would not think to speak of to his tailor. Then there was the clandestine work that in the past he had carried out for the king; now he had learned something of the problem with the queen's declining health and the need of a monarch to secure the succession.

Laurence knew the king's marriage was a love match. He had been there when the king, then the duke of Gloucester, had rescued the lady Anne Neville from where his brother, the duke of Clarence had hidden her. Laurence was the one who had discovered where she was being held. The two brothers were in dispute over the Neville estate but that did not diminish the duke of Gloucester's love for the lady. Now she was keeping to her chamber, critically ill and nearing the end of her life. She was suffering from the same affliction as her sister, Isabelle Neville, the duke of Clarence's duchess who had died shortly after giving birth to a fourth child that had died even before the mother. The king was clearly teasing the Tudor with the rumour of a possible match with Elizabeth of York;

the woman Henry Tudor had declared his intention of marrying. In reality that could never be. She had been shown to be illegitimate along with her brothers and sisters and thus any issue from such a match would be diluted by bastardy. That went against everything King Richard stood for and the basis on which he had taken the throne from his nephew Edward."

"For a man who has just escaped a possible charge of treason, your face is writ large with concern," said Ratcliffe, breaking into his reverie.

"I am struggling with the matter of the lady Elizabeth of York," he replied. "I can see why the king might use the idea of marriage to her to discomfit the Tudor, but the rumours I have heard going abroad do him no good with his people."

"Well said, master armourer," responded Ratcliffe. "Both Catesby and I have made the very same point to his grace. She is too close to him in blood and it is unlikely the Pope would grant a dispensation for them to marry. Have no fear. It is the king's intention to make a public statement to properly refute the rumour, but I agree, it is a fine line he treads."

"If it is any comfort, I can add something to set your minds at rest," said Brampton. "His grace has opened negotiations with the court of Portugal with regard to the hand of the princess Joanna, sister to King John the Second. Believe me, the matter is being considered seriously. It is upon the negotiations for a future match that is my mission to Portugal for the king."

"And there is still the Infanta Isabella of Spain, who might yet be considered," added Ratcliffe. "She is just fourteen and more than capable of bearing him an heir, though her mother, Queen Isabella, is still bristling at her rejection by King Edward as his bride in favour of the commoner Elizabeth Wydville back in fourteen sixty-four."

"Both are regal princesses and any issue would be of full blood royal with no potential for mischief as there is with those of dubious lineage," said Brampton. "An alliance with King Richard and either of them would provide England with a stability regarding her monarchy the realm has not had for many years. In particular, Joanna of Portugal is directly and legitimately descended from John of Gaunt, son of King Edward III and thus of Lancastrian blood. Marriage to her would unite the houses of York and Lancaster."

"The best hope for England's peaceful future, then," gasped Laurence.

"Yes," said Brampton emphatically. "It disposes of all those doubts of illegitimacy that have benighted the realm. No monarch can sit comfortably on a throne where there are those in the world with a better claim in blood to threaten him. If the monarch fears his security then the whole realm suffers."

"I shall get myself away to Gloucester," said Laurence enthusiastically. He was thinking he would be unlikely to get himself into any more trouble while at his forge. His work was a comfort to him and he would immerse himself in his craft while greater events in the world worked their course. Before he left he would go to Windsor Castle where he would reward Peter Heap, Maud Mudd and the boy Sam Fosset in appreciation of the help they had given in freeing his son. In particular he looked forward to seeing Maud's face when he told her the king himself had commended her bravery. The two others would be similarly delighted. Briefly, a thought of lady Staunton drifted into his mind and he wondered at her commitment to the Tudor cause? He had believed her merely caught up in the affairs of her husband, who had his estate on Stanley lands, but the description he had heard of her flying at the intruders with a dagger rather belied the idea of passive support. He shrugged off the lady's image as he took his leave of Brampton and Ratcliffe.

* * *

"The fluting of this piece is in danger of being spoiled by the condition of the hammer," said Laurence the armourer while holding the tool so the light reflected from its polished striking head letting him find any blemishes that might transfer to the work.

"I had already put that to one side for reforming," replied John Fisher. "Here is another. The head is hardly used." He handed Laurence another hammer from several arranged in a rack along one wall of the forge, each one with a different shaped head. He regarded its polished surface with a practiced eye and nodded in appreciation. The two men were working side by side companionably at the Gloucester forge. Laurence was sitting at a stake plate working on one of a pair of greaves he was finishing off with its decoration, both enhancing its appearance while reducing its deliberately oversize dimensions to fit the proposed wearer. He placed the greave on a creasing stake and, holding the piece with one hand, proceeded to hammer along the edge, following a pattern he had traced with a lead scriber. It was intricate work and each blow had to be placed precisely so as to flute the metal to the correct depth without blemish, vitally important when armour was formed from the outside. He glanced over to where John Fisher was working.

"I look forward to seeing that on Sir John," said Laurence, referring to what appeared to be a whole armoured leg of steel John was tapping away at.

"Yes, I am hoping he will be able to sit his horse naturally and nobody who doesn't know him any the wiser." The armoured leg was, in fact, a false one, the knight to whom it would be fitted having lost his leg above the knee. "It locks in two positions, one for riding and the other for standing. There are one or two features visible on the outside that I have managed to disguise as decoration, but most of the mechanism is within."

"At least nobody will be able to wear it but Sir John Wetherby," chuckled Laurence. Sir John was a local Gloucestershire knight who was eager to get back into fighting trim, having fully recovered from an amputation necessary due to infection after being kicked by his horse. John Fisher had made his original harness and it was with professional interest the armourer had taken on the project to make him a false limb.

"Not unless they have a hole through their knee joint where the pivot pin goes," laughed John. The two men worked away steadily for a while, each concentrating on his own piece of armour. Around them, the forge resounded with the sound of hammer blows as the other smiths worked at the more mundane tasks of forging halberd heads, lance points, rondel daggers, caltrops and a variety of weapons according to the order of the king. The days were lengthening and around the forge the first buds of spring were swelling ready to burst in the branches of trees and bushes where they had lain dormant through the winter. The air was alive with birdsong. Two weeks earlier, the thaw of winter snow had flooded the stream at the forge, stopping their work. Laurence had moved himself into the town with John Fisher and took a chamber at the Sign of the Bell to be well looked after by Gurden. Having moved their tools into the upper chamber of the adjacent house, they simply had to wait for the waters to recede. Afterwards the compacted earth floors of the forge and the house were stamped down hard again and the fires relit letting them continue as if nothing untoward had happened.

Suddenly, the air became unnaturally chill and the light began to fade. It was well before evening and a sense of dread pervaded those at the forge, as if the hand of God had somehow fallen across them. Everyone stopped work and silence was absolute; no birds sang, the chuckle of the nearby stream being all that disturbed the air. The men stood upright and turned their faces to the sky. The sun was visible above the sallows along the road to the forge and they could see that its disc, though faint through thin cloud, was half obscured by a giant shadow. Though they had been told there would be an eclipse this day, most had forgotten the predictions of the town's astrologers, the movements of the heavens being an unfathomable mystery to most folk. Laurence, along with everyone else, crossed himself and fingered his talisman while muttering a paternoster, the prayer seeming most apt at this moment: "Our Father, which art in heaven . . ." Soon darkness fell upon them and they stood in awe, gazing with fear at the black disk that had been the sun. Had not the sky darkened such as this when the Lord Jesus Christ gave up his ghost on the cross? Then, as if God had decided he had shown enough of his power, a diamond spark of brilliance burst from the edge of the blackness and spread across the earth, bringing light and sunshine once more. They watched in silence, open-mouthed as the sun was restored to its full glory, then, muttering softly to their companions, and crossing themselves mightily the men returned to their work, though the chatter that had flowed between them previously now ceased and each worked enveloped within the secret depths of his own mind.

"It is hard to subdue treasonable thoughts," reflected John Fisher as he worked away at the knee joint of the armoured limb. Laurence supposed the remark had been uttered as a natural consequence of what they had just witnessed. "The tales we have heard of the king, the murder of his nephews, his queen being ill by poison and his courting of the woman Elizabeth of York, all this cannot be just rumour?" Laurence put aside his work and turned to face his friend.

"I am aware that here in Gloucester you are far from events at Court, but I am the king's own armourer and, believe me, if any of what you say were true, I should quit England and never look back. There is much you don't know and what you think you do know is based on lies and deceits put about by the king's enemies."

"I hoped you would say something of that sort, master Laurence," said John with a tinge of relief in his voice. "There are matters that do not tally with the stories we have heard. For sure, the king's justice is much appreciated by the commonality and he has never overburdened us with taxes and other charges; rather, here in Gloucester, with our new charter granted by King Richard, trade has improved in the town. As for the present, though he must raise revenue for the protection of the realm, he issues us with proper security for repayment."

Laurence sighed, wondering how much he should reveal to John. "All I can tell you is the rumours of a liaison between the king and Elizabeth of York are untrue. The king will make an announcement to deny it soon, you will see. As for the murder of the two princes, I can personally vouch for one of them being alive and well at this very moment. The queen is gravely ill and the king has been advised by his doctors not to share her bed for fear of the malady transferring to him. This has led to certain malicious rumours that he has spurned her while in fact he is in agony of mind. He recently lost his son to illness and now he is about to lose his queen, imagine how that must feel; he is but a man? Having said that, as a king he must be about the business of begetting an heir and thus he is the slave of his dynasty. Here is much material for mischief." Laurence stopped there. He would have delighted in informing John of the mission to Portugal of Sir Edward Brampton with a proposal for the hand of Princess Joanna, the coming together of the houses of York and Lancaster and the peaceful future that an alliance between princes of true royal blood would secure for the realm, but he was sworn to secrecy.

John hung his head, somewhat abashed at revealing his doubts about the king. Laurence could hardly blame him. Few people were privy to the intrigues of the Court and were therefore, prey to rumour, having nothing else to go on.

"You too were willing to forswear your king, master Laurence, for the sake of your son," came the comment of a woman behind them.

The two men lifted their faces in surprise at this new voice. Gurden Fisher stood just inside the forge with a basket under her arm. She smiled somewhat uncertainly at them, wondering if she had overstepped the bounds of modesty. Women were not supposed to discuss such matters, unless, of course, they were of high degree. She was an innkeeper's wife and ex vagabond. John Fisher showed no surprise at his wife's intervention and if Laurence had wondered at her indiscretion, then he soon dismissed it.

"Good den mistress Fisher," he said, greeting her and eyeing up the basket. "Where is Molly this afternoon."

"Up to her elbows in laundry," came the reply. "I thought I would bring your vittles myself this day." She placed the basket onto a bench and took off the white cloth that covered the contents.

"What have you brought us, wife," said John rummaging about in the basket.

"I think you will find a flask of ale and one of Rhenish for master Laurence," she replied. There is eatables too, if you be interested?" John found a stool for his wife and set her down upon it. They brought out some bread, cheese and two birds of some kind, woodpigeon perhaps? Breaking off chunks of bread, with Gurden, all three sat together quietly indulging their appetites and thinking about the woman's statement. It was not the first time the adventure with Robert had been mentioned. The friends had spent some time before the fire in the Bell discussing the exploit. Laurence, of course, had been careful to edit out certain details regarding lady Staunton, though he thought he detected a knowing smile on Gurden's face when the lady's name was mentioned.

"The king's government is blighted by treason," said Laurence.

"I suppose treason is akin to blasphemy," muttered John Fisher half to himself.

"Your meaning?" asked Laurence.

"Well, blasphemy is often spoken accidentally, say as when you step on a nail in the forge and give forth of an oath."

"Or curse a curmudgeonly customer at the inn," put in Gurden.

"We have no idea how these might be taken when we stand before God at the end," said John. "Your attempt to free your son without informing the king of the threat to his government is such as this."

"Let us hope that God is as charitable as King Richard, then," said Gurden. "It is our expectation that our true feelings are laid bare at that time and if honest, detected as such."

"I would not have the conscience of lady Margaret Stanley when she stands before God, no matter how many prayers she sends to pave her way," said Laurence, "nor her husband neither."

Gurden smoothed out her apron and wriggled on her stool to compose herself. She had turned out to be a sensible woman with strong opinions garnered from the vicissitudes of her life, but which had not deflected her from a natural charity. "Yet she must believe that her plotting is on behalf of her son, not herself. In that she might seek redemption."

"It is lust for power that motivates her, and her spouse," snorted Laurence. "Her son is but a tool to be used, her husband, too, I should think. Her vision is dynastic and her son merely the first stepping stone."

"You are correct in that, master Laurence," said Gurden. "But can you not see how her vision might justify her treason? You acted for the love of your son alone, which you think of as laudable, but her love of family is just as intense. Working against King Richard is not treason so far as she is concerned; rather not to do so would betray what she believes to be her destiny. In the same way, if it had come to it, you would have given in to the demands of Sir Reginald Bray to secure your son – treason."

"Well that could be said of us all," inserted John, "but how many of us make a bid for the crown to secure our own?"

"It is a question of degree and in that is the core of all ambition," replied Gurden. "Noble families conduct their intrigues at one level, the rest of us at a variety of others, but all are the same – self elevation. If there were no kings it would still be so."

"But the Tudor has no claim in blood to the throne of England. All is ambition with no other substance," snapped Laurence irritably.

"I remember some years ago, when in Spain with some English mercenaries, two of them were playing a game of nine men's morris in a tavern there," mused John.

"There is a morris board carved into a cloister seat at the abbey here in Gloucester," Laurence interrupted. "The nine men are represented by holes and I think it is called nine-holes as a consequence."

"I haven't seen that, and it describes three-men's morris. I am speaking of the greater game where each player has nine men each with twenty-four points on the board. I was about to observe that this is a game of strategy, as you know. If a player can place three of his pieces, or men, in a straight line horizontally or diagonally across the board he may remove one of his opponent's men from the game. This continues until one player is reduced to just three men. Then, at the third level, that is the endgame, the rules are changed such that a player might fly o'er to land at any vacant point on the board. The game is won when one player has reduced his opponent to just two men, or rendered him unable to make a legal move. One of the mercenaries I am speaking of cheated and made an illegal move at this stage whereupon a fight broke out and the one who should have won was beaten insensible and robbed of his purse. It seems to me this is the sort of play we are now engaged in with the Tudor."

"Yes, the king has managed things so that if Tudor does not act soon, he will be so reduced as to be forced to either abandon the game, or lose," replied Laurence.

"Or cheat to win, which is the point I was making," said John. "I often think of the board as being played by nobles of high degree, such as lord Stanley or the earl of Northumberland. They have their own objectives and make their own rules seeing treachery as an option, a reluctant one perhaps, but permissible should circumstance allow"

"Something not allowed in an honest game," inserted Gurden sagely. "Little wonder that kings turn out to be tyrants more often than not, surrounded always by the threat of treason. This present one is somewhat like a moth struggling to free itself from its cocoon. Once free it must spread its wings in the sun before it can fly, which is just the moment when by chance a passing bird might consume it."

"Yes, a hostage to fortune and that too is part of God's scheme," intoned Laurence, fingering his reliquary.

"It seems the passing darkness has depressed our spirits," said Gurden sitting upright and tugging at her dress. "This eve there will be game pie on offer, though you will have to guess what meat is in it." She laughed and clapped her hands. "The season of spring is upon us and soon the roads will be passable. You will be away then, master Laurence, and I hope, when you return to us it will be with good tidings."

"Well said, wife," agreed John. "Tonight we will dine on your game pie in our Bell Inn and drink to a better and prosperous future." All three raised their beakers and drained them. Gurden got to her feet and retrieved her basket then bid them a jocular *adieu*, as Laurence had taught her, before taking herself off to the town. The two men returned to their work in better spirits for her visit.

* * *

Laurence was on his knees before an effigy of the Holy Virgin, the patron of an old Norman church in the small market town of Ilkeston, just a few miles from his destination at Nottingham Castle. The church of St. Mary the Virgin was located on top of the southernmost of the Pennine hills, popularly known as the Backbone of England. This range stretched in a line up north through Derbyshire and Yorkshire as far as the Cheviot Hills on the Scottish border. Beside him was the tomb of one Nicholas de Cantelupe, an earlier lord of the manor. A chantry chapel had been erected by the side of the chancel at the expense of the knight's wife, Joan, which caused Laurence to reflect upon his own wife also named Joan. *O vos omnes qui transitis, per viam attendite et videte, si est dolor, sicut dolor meus.* O all ye that pass by the way, stay and see if there be any sorrow as my sorrow. After his devotions to his wife and children, his prayers were for the health of the king, who had lost his queen back in the early spring. Anne, daughter of the Kingmaker Richard Neville, died on the day of the eclipse, sixteenth of March, though it was some days before the news reached Gloucester.

He had discovered that Ilkeston had a charter granted by King Henry III to hold a weekly market and two annual fairs. They had arrived yesterday, on the eve of the Thursday market. Outside the church, in the market place, mercers, cutlers, and medicine men along with a motley gathering of traders could be heard, as if from another world, busy shouting their wares. He had travelled here with a train of them who would make Nottingham their final destination. The presence of the market today meant most of them would remain at Ilkeston until tomorrow but he would journey on with the few who would not tarry when the city of Nottingham was but twelve miles away.

His thoughts returned to the king and his dead queen. She had been one of the king's last links with his childhood and the castle of Middleham. He knew that Richard was in the habit of confiding his hopes and plans in his queen and the two of them were united in grief when their little prince, Edward of Middleham, Prince of Wales had died last year. No doubt that had exacerbated the queen's own frail health leading to her premature death. Now he was alone with but a few friends he could rely on, yet the business with Buckingham must have shaken his confidence, even in them. That duke had pretended the closest of friendship yet within just a few weeks, Buckingham had betrayed him by declaring for the Tudor. Buckingham's rebellion had been easily put down, and no doubt the Tudor would fare no better when he finally arrived on England's shores, but afterwards, the residual stench of treachery would likely infect the realm for some years.

He got to his feet and made a final prayer to the Virgin before turning and walking towards the door in the west portal. A robed friar was standing there, regarding him in expectation of oblation. He dropped a few coins into the grimy hand that appeared from under his cassock, which just as rapidly disappeared accompanied by a muttered *pax vobiscum.* There was no sign of the incumbent parish priest who he had learned was one Robert Edmund. That was a pity because he had not been shriven for some days and he was reluctant to confess to the friar, who looked to be a shifty fellow.

Stepping out into the morning light he looked around at the bustling fair where farmers, peasants, servants of the local nobility and goodwives milled around arguing and haggling with the vendors. Three or four beggars, squatting by the base of the church tower, cried for alms alert to the fact he was a stranger to the town and therefore not immured to their distress as the town folk were. He ignored them and strode over to where the wagons of the merchants were parked, guarded by some boys who had been slipped a few coins for the purpose. Already those merchants who were to travel on to Nottingham were getting their oxen into the traces. Laurence took the sacking from the back of his horse, where it was tethered in a nearby field and led it to his cart. Soon the small train of six wagons and Laurence's cart set off down the hill from the town and into the Erewash valley. They splashed across a ford in the stream, a tributary of the River Trent, which fortunately was deceptively low and quiet. He looked at the deeply cut banks, evidence that this stream could arise suddenly to a great height. The broad water meadows on each bank testified to its tendency for flood, which, no doubt, was why the good folk of Ilkeston kept safely to their hill.

They plodded on along the well-worn road, though not without having to negotiate around a series of prodigious potholes, until the houses of Nottingham came into view with the great castle rising on its sandstone mound above the town overlooking the River Trent. Bells for nones were ringing in the holy houses as they entered the city by the west gate. Laurence could not help wondering if Anna's stepfather still had the alehouse at the sign of The Pilgrim cut into the base of the castle rock, or if he did, would he remember the tall dark armourer who had deprived him of the servile services of his stepdaughter.

He wasn't looking forward to meeting with the king, though that was his purpose here. Cornelius had kept him informed of events and it was more or less definite that the Tudor was about to invade. Where he would actually land was anybody's guess and so the king had taken up residence at Nottingham Castle, this edifice being at a central position in England and he could get his forces into action quickly once it was known where the Tudor had landed. Laurence was somewhat surprised at the king's choice, though he supposed it made sense militarily. Word of his son's death had been brought to the king while on a previous visit to Nottingham and since then he had called the fortress here his Castle of Care. He would not have come here by personal choice, particularly so soon after the death of his queen. The fortress had been improved by his brother, King Edward and had lavish royal apartments, but these could not compensate a bereaved heart.

Looking around, King Richard was certainly ready for the Tudor invasion. Nottingham was replete with soldiery, to the uncertain satisfaction its citizens. The alehouses, whorehouses and taverns were happily doing brisk business along with many mundane trades, such as that of farrier, smith and mercer. Armourers too, were tending to the needs of the men-at-arms and those few mercenaries already gathering around the king. Of course, the greater part of his army would be brought into being once it was confirmed the Tudor had landed, and where. Already the king had sent out Commissioners of Array calling upon the men of Northumberland, York, and Norfolk, the king's allies. Included were others of uncertain loyalty. Principals among these were the levees of lord Stanley and his brother William who, as English lords, had sworn allegiance to King Richard. Laurence too, had been called to the king's side.

Approaching from the east, he turned south towards the gate, the only way to get into the castle, which rose stark, one hundred and thirty feet upon the southwest corner of castle rock. He was stopped at the south gate while the guard took a cursory look at the contents of his cart. This comprised his personal chest and the tools of his trade. Passing through the gate he came into the vast lower bailey. Here were the dwellings of the castle trades, the farriers, grooms, blacksmiths, butchers and the stables. Some soldiers had erected tents, there being limited room for them within the castle itself. Horses outnumbered the soldiers at Nottingham Castle, it seemed, as he looked around the outer bailey. One stable block in particular took his notice. The horses here were all greys and he knew these must be the king's own mounts. He wondered which one of them was "White Surrey," the king's favourite.

He beckoned over a groom from the stables and, dropping a few coins into his readily open hand, ordered care for his horse. It had performed well hauling his cart from Gloucester, which though fairly light, was work the animal was unaccustomed to. From now on it must serve him when he rode out with the king. Firstly, though, the man accompanied him as he drew the cart containing his tools and belongings towards the main gate of the middle bailey where he knew from his previous visit the armoury was located. They passed over a stone bridge, which traversed a deep ditch between the lower and middle baileys at the end of which was the main gate. The gate here was fortified by a portcullis with another in the castle wall beyond. Anyone trying to invade through here would be caught in the tiny court between the two and cut down. The castle guard knew him as the king's armourer and so, with little hindrance he was waved through. He found the armoury amongst the buildings of the middle bailey and let the groom take his horse out of the traces to be led off to the stables.

The castle armoury was located in a tower that stored armour for the nobles of the king's household knights. To his delight he found Peter Heap there along with some others he recognised from London and Windsor. They all gathered around to greet the king's armourer and to share any news they had. Laurence could tell them little other than the Tudor was expected this summer.

"The king is away hunting over Tideswell, which he calls his larder," Peter informed him. "He will be back tomorrow so you have until then to settle yourself here."

"Are any of his closer henchmen here?" asked Laurence. It was probable that King Richard's favourite esquires would ride to the hunt with him, but there must be someone at the castle who could deal with any urgent business.

"Kendall is here, and Sir Richard Ratcliffe. Sir William Catesby is with the king along with viscount Lovell, Sir Robert Percy and lord Strange."

"Strange!" Laurence spluttered in surprise. "Lord Stanley's son and heir. What is he doing in that company?"

"Ah, yes," said Peter taking him by the arm and drawing him away from the other armourers. "He is hostage for the conduct of his father. Lord Stanley has retired to his lands in Lancashire and, when the king sent for him, he made his excuses, claiming he has the sweating sickness."

"If he has then good riddance to him. I cannot believe he will survive that affliction," snorted Laurence, thinking of the death of his own wife and children from the malady. "I refuse to believe a word of it," he said dismissively. "Stanley is planning mischief along with his wife, the countess of Richmond."

"Henry Tudor's mother, Margaret Beaufort," said Peter with a nod of agreement. "Everyone thinks the same, which is why the king is keeping lord Strange close as surety for his father's conduct. He hopes that lord Stanley will capitulate and bring his forces into the field for his king, or at least stay away from battle rather than risk the life of his son."

"He calculates well. When the Tudor falls lord Stanley is in danger of losing all. As chancellor in the king's household, and having fought with him against the Scots when his grace was duke of Gloucester, he knows the king's mind better than most men. Perhaps he believes his son is not in any great danger? The king is sensitive in this regard, being grief-stricken still for his own son and heir. He is perhaps crediting lord Stanley with a tenderness of heart the man does not possess." Laurence recalled lord Thomas Stanley's avuncular features, always smiling and pleasant when at court yet the lord was always ready to turn with events to serve his own interest. That was not unusual, everyone else inclined to the same and even the king, when duke of Gloucester, had conspired to obtain lands and incomes for himself. That had been a cause of dissent between him and his brother George, duke of Clarence. Shifting loyalties was a constant worry for any monarch, but some lords were more false-hearted than others and in this regard lord Stanley was in the vanguard.

"Still, it is peculiar that he displays such reluctance in the king's cause," mused Peter. "I would have thought he might at least pretend to be an ally. He is cutting down his options else."

"Which smacks of treachery to me," considered Laurence. "There may be something afoot we are not aware of as yet. So far as I can see, when Tudor comes the king will be able to field a host far greater than he, a clerk who has never fought a battle and who fences merely with a barbed pen. His battles are fought from behind arras, which tapestried ground is counterfeit being that of the spy and dissembler, a contest at which he excels. Stanley is a warrior lord of great experience. He must know what the Tudor is and thus calculate at nought his chance of attaining the crown of England, unless there is some plot that the king is unaware of. His grace must look to his back, I fear."

Their conversation came to a halt with this thought and both men stood mute for a few moments, shuffling their feet idly in the sandy ground of the middle bailey and thinking when and how treachery would show its twisted face. Presently, amid much shouting and cracking of whips a train of oxen trundled into the middle bailey hauling a wagon creaking and groaning, piled with what looked to be handguns. Another followed it bringing a pair of cannon on wooden mounts. A third was covered over with oiled cloth and all three took up much space, halting outside the armoury tower. From the third wagon, the off-ox clambered down from his seat beside the driver and approached the two men.

"A load for the St. Barb," he called out as he approached, identifying the armourer as someone of authority by the richness of his attire. Laurence looked to Peter for help. Hopefully he would know the location of the St. Barb, a building where gunpowder and shot was stored. It was so named after Laurence's own patron, Saint Barbara, patron saint of armourers and artillerymen. Peter pointed out a squat stone building by the west wall. The off-ox nodded and climbed back up beside his driver who lashed the team into motion, steering the oxen towards the St. Barb.

"The king had that built earlier this year, well away from important buildings," stated Peter. "If there were to be an explosion there, it would carry away the wall above the town but hopefully leave the rest of the castle intact."

"Yes, the king has always had an interest in guns and artillery," said Laurence. "I remember some years ago he had a gunner at Middleham Castle. He was influenced by his upbringing with the earl of Warwick, who used guns at the battle of Barnet, not that it did him much good; Warwick missed everything he shot at."

"Perhaps the king plans to use gunpowder against Henry Tudor?" ventured Peter.

"And frighten him away from battle," laughed Laurence. "A whiff of powder will no doubt provide a taster of the hell fires he will inevitably end up roasting in!" The two grinned at each other. "Is the king's harness here at the armoury, or in his privy chambers?" enquired Laurence, suddenly remembering he was here by royal command and had better attend to his duty.

"Aye, in his privy chamber under the care of one of his esquires. Sir Richard Ratcliffe will know the king's mind regarding it."

* * *

The great hall of Nottingham Castle was a hive of activity as courtiers, knights, their squires and castle servants hurried about their business. None, it seemed was still. In the minstrels' gallery above, the court musicians were playing, providing a delightful musical background that complimented the brightness and colours of the arras hanging around the walls of the hall. Most of these depicted hunting scenes while along one wall they displayed interpretations of the Garden of Eden. Laurence entered to the sound of a single melody played on a lute. He recognised it as

Unicorns in the Mist, one of his favourites. He knew the king had taken to having music played in the hall as a desperate distraction; an attempt to thrust away the demons of his melancholy occasioned by the death of his queen. Sir Richard Ratcliffe saw him as he entered and, taking him by the arm, conducted him to the king who was standing amid a group of his courtiers. He waved them aside when he saw Laurence approach. The armourer went down on his knees and lifted his head to show his face only to be immediately raised by the king. Close by was the harness Laurence had sent up to the great hall that morning.

"The gilding is tastefully under-stated," said King Richard as he looked at his harness on its frame. "It declares this is battle armour, not frippery meant merely for the tilt yard."

"It will withstand the heaviest of blows, your grace," declared Laurence. "Gilding of the spaulders, couters and poleyns declares your majesty as does the pattern of entwined roses down the sides of the cuisses and greaves. Your grace's cuirass, I have left in the white and though of the finest polished steel and worthy of display, will be covered by your surcoat. Nothing will get through this armour."

"And my helm, master armourer?"

"It is here my lord king." Laurence swept a gold cloth cover from the helm, which he had placed on a table next to the king's harness. It was a masterpiece of the armourer's art. An armet with gorget, it was made of the finest Milanese steel and further tempered to harden it so that no single blow could penetrate, then highly polished to sparkle in the sun. A gold circlet was fixed around the brow. This too was of steel and gilded. The king had first asked for a solid gold circlet but Laurence advised against this as gold, being a soft metal could be cut through in the heat of battle and the king would not want to lose it. The pivots of the visor were formed into gold roses. At his neck the gorget, which would fit below his helm to protect his throat, was embossed with entwined and gilded Yorkist roses.

Next, King Richard drew the jewelled rings from his fingers and handing these to his squire, reached for his gauntlets. He slipped his hands into the leather gloves to which steel had been fixed over the individual fingers. Finger parts were polished steel while the gatlings that covered the finger joints, each having an embossed rose, were gilded to compliment the style of the full harness.

"I have left the rerebraces and vambraces again in the white as plain polished steel," your grace," explained Laurence, pointing to

143

the armour of the upper and lower arms. "This, I believe, will draw
the eye to the wings at the couters, which, as you can see are
embossed and gilded. I have replicated these at the wings for the
poleyns, except the leg harness, being larger than that for the arms,
allows for the decoration there. I have left the lames of the sabatons
plain, my lord king, to ensure perfect flexibility at the feet,
important if you intend to fight on foot. Should you be mounted,
then your spurs are gilded and the roundels have a single rose at the
centre." King Richard clenched his fingers, trying out the flexibility
of his gauntlets then drew them off. He took the rings proffered by
his squire and slipped them back onto his fingers while regarding
the harness critically. After a few moments he nodded in satisfaction
and faced his armourer.

"You have done well, master de la Halle," he enthused. "Our
harness is a masterpiece that combines the latest style with fighting
practicality." Laurence swept the king a low bow of obeisance.
"Master secretary Kendall, here, informs us he wishes to ride into
battle by our side." John Kendall who, as always, stood close to the
king ready to take down any orders he might issue took a step
forward and with a grim face bowed to the king. "He has no battle
armour and we would have you attend on him immediately. Pay
particular attention to his gauntlets," chuckled the king. "We would
not have his writing hand *hors de combat*." Everyone laughed at the
king's jest. Laurence smiled at Kendall. The secretary was rather too
old for the cut and thrust of battle, being around sixty years, but then
so was the duke of Norfolk and he would ride at the head of his
men. In any case, Laurence mused, if Kendall remained close to the
king and his household knights he would be as well defended as
King Richard himself.

Laurence backed away as the king turned to his courtiers, who
were eagerly clamouring for his attention. Messengers were coming
in at regular intervals from France and from various ports along the
south coast of England, all reporting on the current state of the
Tudor's invasion fleet.

* * *

The word came one afternoon in August when the court was at
its brightest. Minstrels were playing in the gallery above the great
hall and Jolly John was capering around sometimes amusing the
gathered nobles, sometimes annoying them with his antics, but
always distracting them until the word came. Then all was

determined. His household knights gathered around the king, his principal advisors were voluble in their advice and in all this the king stood as if in isolation. Though many proffered their opinion, yet he alone was the one who would command and direct them into their respective places. The Tudor had landed in Wales, at Milford Haven with a few Frenchmen, about five hundred English and a small force mainly of Breton mercenaries, not nearly enough to cause the king concern.

Laurence had spent his time waiting for the word making battle harness for John Kendall and others in the king's service. He had also found armour for himself seeing as he would be going along with King Richard's household knights. He didn't expect to take part in a battle but armour was a necessary protection against probing missiles such as arrows or crossbow bolts. It was plain but serviceable white armour, which he had reserved for such an eventuality from his own stock. His surcoat would be murrey and blue, the colours of the house of York and embroidered on it a white boar, the *blanc sanglier*, King Richard's personal sign. On his right shoulder would be pinned a silver boar badge. The king had given these to all his followers, silver for his immediate retinue and pewter for the rest.

He was watching one of the forge boys putting a final polish to the king's armour, when Sir Robert Percy entered and espying the king's harness nodded in approval.

"His grace has commanded that his harness be sent up to him," he said authoritively. Robert Percy was a well-built man of medium height and a long-time friend of the king, having known him since childhood. He was clad in his court dress of red silk doublet and hose and a short blue mantle richly trimmed with sable. He wore a jewelled dagger at his belt. "His squires will be here presently. I see all is ready?"

"It is, Sir Robert. I shall attend upon his grace when he is fully harnessed. Will he ride out of Nottingham steel clad?"

"He will, to put on a brave show for the people. That is if the Tudor has not been brought to battle before the king can get to him. He has landed at Milford Haven and must march through Wales then cross the River Severn and into England."

"Has Tudor a large force?"

"We cannot tell at present, but if the reports of our spies in France are reliable, then he has but five-hundred English traitors with him, his fellow exiles; the rest are a rabble of mercenaries. He has probably less than two thousand in all."

"Might he be stopped while still in Wales?" wondered Laurence. "Such a small army could easily be defeated."

"Rhys ap Thomas has an army that could bring him to battle, but the king has some doubt regarding his loyalty. He sent for his son as hostage but ap Thomas refused the king, which is suspicious. The boy would be in no danger should his father remain loyal. The Tudor has been making all sorts of promises for advancement to several nobles should he unseat our king and it is possible the Welshman might succumb and turn traitor. The best we can hope for is that he is merely keeping his options open."

"I suppose the Stanley's are included in your assessment?" said Laurence.

"They are. Our spies report an exchange of letters between lord Thomas and his brother William and Gilbert Talbot presumably pledging support. We have also discovered that Sir Reginald Bray has collected a large sum of money with which to pay for more men."

"So that is what Bray was doing in England recently," gasped Laurence. "I wondered what he was about; it was not just to discover the whereabouts of the lord bastard Richard of York."

"That is correct and I suppose he will have been subverting Rhys ap Thomas and Sir John Savage, both Welsh landowners. No doubt that is why the Tudor has landed in Wales. He expects to pick up more men there. However, our spies say the men of Wales have not bothered flocking to his banner and Rhys ap Thomas, though on the march, has yet to join with him, so that part of his plan is stillborn."

"It would be well if the Tudor could be defeated before he meets up with the king," mused Laurence, whose mind could not shake off a sense of dread when there was so much suspicion of treachery amongst the nobility, though not the English people who were more than happy with the king's just government.

"I cannot share your opinion on that, master armourer," snapped Percy with a tinge of annoyance in his voice. "I should think you would want the harness you have made testing in a real conflict. There will be little profit to you if we return to London with our harness unscratched?"

"That is true, Sir Robert," replied Laurence anxious to clear up the misunderstanding. "It is the constant talk of treason that has unsettled me."

"Rest calm," replied the knight. "Court politics was ever thus and if we were to give dissemblers and rumour mongers much credence we would be incapable of government. Remember that spreading falsehood is part of the game. When you give it too much thought you risk becoming a casualty without ever striking a blow."

Laurence understood this. He immediately thought on the young man with a hidden identity at Tournai and how it was rumoured King Richard had murdered him and his brother, or the scandal of a supposed alliance with his niece, Elizabeth of York. This was a war being fought on two platforms. King Richard had encouraged the latter rumour regarding marriage to Elizabeth of York to provoke the Tudor into invading, a strategy that had certainly worked. He had publicly refuted that rumour; it only remained for Tudor to be brought to battle to end the conflict once and for all. At this very moment Sir Edward Brampton was in Portugal negotiating a genuine marriage contract between King Richard and the princess Johanna. The lady had already declared her interest in the match. Afterwards, with the king wedded to his Portuguese bride the two houses of York and Lancaster would become one. The king was but thirty-two years of age and quite capable of siring an heir to secure the throne of England for the future.

Suddenly everything was set abustle as two of the king's squires of the body entered the armoury to have the armour conveyed to his grace. Sir Robert and Laurence bowed to them as they gave instructions to the forge servants then made their way together out of the armoury to head for the royal apartments where a king was waiting to be attired in his battle harness.

7 – Treason!

Laurence reflected on his position here in the line of soldiers marching out from under the battlements of Nottingham Castle then through the town taking the road to Leicester. As the king's armourer he rode along with the royal procession. Ahead was the splendid cavalcade of the king, his henchmen and household knights. They stretched four abreast for half a mile and he could just make out the banner of the white boar and the royal standard of England that marked the king's position at the front of his men. With a thrill of pride, he imagined he caught a glint of sunlight from King Richard's helm, shining and declaring the splendour of his house as he passed by the people of Nottingham who cheered him on is way. Behind Laurence was the rest of the king's army. The bulk of his men-at-arms were horsed now but would dismount for battle when they met with Tudor's pitiful army. Further back were the yeomen archers, foot soldiers and supply baggage, including the king's artillery – cannon and handguns. All were in jubilant mood as they marched in their places under the bright banners of their captains and liege lords.

His thoughts went back to the first time he had been part of such a march. He had been at the end of the line then, with the baggage. Edward Plantagenet, erstwhile king of England, along with his brother Richard duke of Gloucester, after being chased out of England the previous year, returned at the decaying port of Ravenser in the north with just a few men, far less that the Tudor had today. To keep away from the fighting had been Laurence's main concern at that time. Duke Francis of Brittany, his liege lord, had sent him to join Edward's army, charged with getting into the English court to keep him informed of events there. It mattered little who it was actually sitting on the English throne. If Edward had lost at that time, he would have attempted to join the court of the Lancastrian king, Henry the Sixth. In fact, he had actually met the defunct king and sat by his side as they observed the battle of Barnet together. As it was, and against impossible odds, Edward had won through to wrest back the crown he had lost and now, with many adventures under his belt, Laurence de la Halle found himself riding in full harness towards battle, a loyal follower of the house of York and Edward's brother, King Richard the Third.

Fighting in the cause of a king in a country not his own would have seemed to him folly back in fourteen seventy-one. He would have stayed in relative safety at the rear with the baggage and the armourers' camp, ready to flee should the battle go against Edward. In the years afterwards, he had fallen in love and married an Englishwoman, gained a family then lost to disease his wife and two daughters leaving him but one legitimate son. The other woman in his life had also bore a son, Philip, who was now at Cambridge studying towards becoming a physician. His legitimate son, Robert, was somewhere ahead with the household knights of the duke of Norfolk, serving as a squire. That meant his duty was to take care of the spare horses and, with any luck, stay out of the fighting. Because of this there was nowhere in the world he would rather be than here, sharing the perils of his son along with the man whom he was pleased to regard as his king despite his Breton heritage and his obligation to his liege lord, duke Francis the Second of Brittany.

He was broken out of his reverie by a shout from behind. Turning his head he saw a familiar figure riding along the outside of the line. He was armoured but with his visor up. Nevertheless with his face partially obscured, it took Laurence a moment for recognition.

"David Morgan," he shouted in delight as the soldier came up to him. The Welshman was a follower of Sir James Tyrell, who at this time was acting as captain of Guisnes Castle near Calais. Laurence and David had become firm friends, the Welshman speaking a dialect not unlike Breton and they delighted in conversing thus to the confusion of those about them. The two men immediately fell into their mutual language.

"What are you doing here at Nottingham?" asked Laurence. "You are usually skulking around the Welsh Marches in the service of Sir James Tyrell."

"That I have been, my friend," he replied. "Sir James has instructed me to send him word of the Tudor invasion. His spies have been providing King Richard with regular reports from France and he sent word when Henry of Richmond sailed from the Seine. He guessed the landing would be in Wales so that is where I have been."

Is Sir James well?" asked Laurence. "I wonder if he is discomfited with the recent appointment of the king's bastard, John of Pomfret to the captaincy of Calais?"

"Sir James bears it well. The lord bastard John is but seventeen and in need of serious counselling. That is one reason the king sent him to Calais. It gives him real responsibility while under the guiding wings of Sir James, who is thus content though I believe he had sights on the promotion of his own son who is there with him." Laurence was pleased for John who had been but a child when he first met him at Middleham Castle. A vision of the mysterious woman who was his mother came to mind. She had been briefly at Middleham, too, before the king's marriage to the lady Anne Neville. He knew she had married and wondered how she was faring in the world.

"Tudor expects the Welsh to rally to his banner, I believe," said Laurence, forcing his mind back to the present. "Is there any movement there?"

"Very little. Of course, my agents have been busy spreading the story that the rebels are few in number and unlikely to succeed in their objective, true of course, which keeps men at home. There will be no great rising in Wales, you may depend upon it."

"What about Rhys ap Thomas and John Savage. It is said they are contemplating joining with the Tudor? Both are considerable landowners in Wales and might raise some men."

"Ah, yes. It seems that Rhys ap Thomas had, as his tutor in his youth one Lewis Caerleon who, as you may know is physician to Margaret Beaufort, lady Stanley and also Elizabeth Wydville.

"Yes, I know of him. He has been slinking between lady Margaret and her minions for some years."

"It is through that connection where lady Stanley might have subverted Rhys ap Thomas to her cause with who knows what promise of future advancement. The king suspects this and has extracted an oath of loyalty from him, but has not gained the custody of his son."

"The same applies, of course, to her husband and his brother, William Stanley. All sorts of promises have been made, but everything depends on the Tudor unseating King Richard. When that fails those who sided with the Tudor will find themselves in dire straights, which is why they appear uncommitted to either cause," growled Laurence.

"Well there is good reason why they should consider the outcome of the approaching fight rather less than certain."

"Really; it seems to me that Tudor, a clerk who has never seen a battle could ever hope to defeat England's most experienced general."

"True, so why is he here?"

Laurence sank his chin onto his chest in contemplation of this remark. It had been something that had lurked at the back of his mind and he had no answer. For some time he had suspected something lay behind the otherwise rash actions of the Tudor faction, but had put it down to the manic ambition of Henry's dam, Margaret Beaufort and the hatred of the defeated and exiled Lancastrians for the house of York, which clouded their judgement.

"I have discovered, through my contacts among the Welsh marches that Henry of Richmond has been in communication with lord Stanley and his brother, William. I have no idea what was discussed, but it would hardly be anything regarding the welfare of King Richard."

"I can add something," said Laurence, pleased that he could bring his own information to the conversation. "You might be aware that the king has lord Stanley's son, lord Strange as hostage for his loyalty?" David Morgan gave a nod of understanding. "When the king sent to lord Stanley reminding him of it, the lord replied stating: *I have other sons!* Upon questioning, in fear for his life lord Strange revealed that Sir William Stanley has declared secretly for the Tudor."

"But the Stanley's have yet to publicly reveal themselves, which tells us they are waiting to determine the outcome of the battle when King Richard meets with Tudor," said David.

"A dangerous game - overt treason and I would not be on the receiving end of the king's wrath in the aftermath of battle," stated Laurence with conviction.

The two men fell silent for the moment, each pondering upon events. Around them the scents of high summer wafted in the slight breeze, while the thudding of thousands of hoof beats, the creaking of saddle leather and casual chatter of the soldiery drowned out the birdsong that otherwise would accompany them on their way. Somewhere in front they could hear floating in the air the song of minstrels, commanded by the king to play and sing their way to Leicester. There the king would wait upon the man, a bastard claimant, who had the temerity to challenge his throne. Warrior Plantagenets had ruled England for over two hundred years and it was unthinkable that a mere clerk might unseat this one. Presently, David Morgan, who from the expression on his face had been struggling with a further thought, decided he would speak of something more. Confident that, by using their Breton dialect the two could not be understood, even if overheard, he nevertheless leaned towards his friend the better to speak softly.

"I know of someone who, though close to the king and enriched by him is yet working with lord Stanley to secure his own position. He too is manoeuvring to gain an advantage should the king lose."

Laurence's face registered shock at this statement. Who could it possibly be? King Richard had by his side only those he trusted implicitly. Chief among these were the men set down in the seditious doggerel that had been the downfall of its author, William Colyngbourne: The Cat, the Rat and Lovell my dog, rule all England under an Hog. These were William Catesby, the lawyer, Sir Richard Ratcliffe and Viscount Lovell, the latter two his friends since childhood along with Robert Percy. There was Brackenbury, loyal to the house of York and above reproach. John Howard, duke of Norfolk had command of the king's archers and would lead the attack against the Tudor. Henry Percy, The duke of Northumberland was doubtful, that was true, but not a close confidant of the king. Other than these Laurence could not think who David Morgan could be speaking of and therefore the threat to King Richard was likely to be small.

"You must say who you mean, my friend," said Laurence querulously. "I cannot think who it could be."

"Catesby," David whispered.

"Catesby!" barked Laurence. David Morgan drew back and signed to him to keep his voice down. Speaking Breton, it was impossible anyone who might overhear them would know what they were speaking of, and the name of the king's chief advisor was hardly a secret, but Laurence's reaction might cause a perspicacious listener to wonder at what was being said. "Catesby has become one of the richest landowners in England, a circumstance entirely due to his closeness to his grace the king," he growled. "He was the one who steered through Parliament *Titulus Regius*, the document describing the king's legitimate title to the throne. He is Speaker of the Commons."

"Think back to the cause as to why King Richard deposed his nephews."

"As I have just said, it is set down in *Titulus Regius*. They were shown to be illegitimate and therefore debarred from the throne."

"That is so and the reason was King Edward's pre-contract with lady Eleanor Butler a daughter of one of the Talbot's whose family were the earls of Shrewsbury. What you may not know is that William Catesby is related by family to Margaret Beaufort – she is the half-sister of his stepmother."

Laurence was, indeed, astonished by this information. "That makes William Catesby and Henry Tudor cousins by marriage," he surmised. "I hear that Gilbert Talbot will join the Tudor with a few men, but Catesby has no levees here that might be used against the king," muttered Laurence looking around fearfully.

"I am not saying he is plotting any personal involvement. He is but a lawyer and will in no case put himself in harms way, which is the reason for his vacillation. You remember the fate of lord Hastings?"

"Yes, he was executed by the king for treason – he kept to himself the Butler pre-contract and the illegitimacy of prince Edward, thus depriving King Richard of his rightful claim to the throne."

"It was Catesby who disclosed the pre-contract to Richard who called in a reluctant bishop Stillington, seeing it was he who had been its legal witness, and thus Stillington became the public face of the business. Catesby, though, had privately informed Richard of the contract beforehand and absolved lord Thomas Stanley from any knowledge of it."

"Did he?" gasped Laurence. "I wondered at the time why lord Stanley had escaped Richard's retribution and too, why Stillington has lost the confidence of the king. Being clergy, though, he is not subject to a secular court. You seem to be saying lord Stanley knew of it too, through Catesby's affiliation with lady Stanley. She, of course, needs the children of King Edward to be legitimate if her son Henry is to marry Elizabeth of York. Any progeny from that union would be bastards else."

"Quite so. Catesby, in protecting the life of lord Stanley, has insured himself should the Tudor triumph over King Richard leading to the subsequent rise of the Stanley's, lady Margaret being then the new king's mother. He will be able to call in the favour and ingratiate himself in what would be a new reign. Should, as we expect, King Richard destroy the Tudor, then no harm done and lord Stanley will be on his own."

Laurence drew back and leaned against the cantle of his saddle, his mind whirling with the ramifications of what he had just heard. The extent of the Tudor subversion was now becoming clear. For months he had wondered at the temerity of Tudor ambition and he, along with Cornelius had often conjectured upon it. While there were those even so close to the king ready to manipulate and betray him it was little wonder that Henry of Richmond might be encouraged to try and topple him to usurp his throne. Lancastrian subversives had long been working to such an end and even if Henry Tudor was nothing more than their dupe, yet he could provide a figurehead for their ambition.

"We must post to the king with this," snarled Laurence in fury. "Catesby rides beside him at this very moment!"

"We must not," replied David. "For one thing, Catesby is a lawyer and will tear any present accusation we might make to shreds. I think he cannot have much influence on the battlefield, so we might not fear him in that. He is looking to his own advantage afterwards should the Tudor triumph. When the king triumphs he will expect to carry on as he is now. King Richard is simply not ready yet for such knowledge. Let us wait until the Tudor is defeated. Then we can question the Stanley's more closely and extract the truth. It will not be forthcoming until then."

Laurence was forced to conclude this made perfect sense. Another accusation of treason by a close companion would merely upset the king and might even distort his reason, and God alone knew he needed to be clear in his mind if he were to successfully prosecute the coming conflict. Afterward come the truth and there would be many who might fear the outcome. Laurence determined in his own mind that William Catesby would be one of the first to fall.

The two men rode companionably together, chatting of their mutual friends and enjoying the warm weather, which fortunately for men in harness, was pleasant and not too hot. David Morgan teased Laurence over his helm, which was his habitual barbute, completely different to the sallet and visors of the English knights. He rode bare-headed and his helm bounced along, tied to the front of his saddle.

"I do believe this is the first time I have seen you in full harness," chuckled David. "A plain rig, to be sure, but no doubt of the finest temper?" Laurence was clad in a mail coif and haubergeon with steel cuirass over, spaulders protected his shoulders while his arms had plain rerebraces and vambraces with latten at the wrist the only decoration – this remnant testifying to the grandeur of a former owner. He wore half gauntlets; that is steel over but with the palms bare for grip. Plain tassets rode over his cuisses where he sat his horse and his poleyns over his knees were good quality but unembellished with the usual wings at the joint. His legs were clad in mail with the backs having no plate, the better to grip the sides of his horse. A discerning observer would conclude from this he had no intention of fighting other than on horseback. Greaves and steel sabatons completed his leg and foot armour. Over he wore a surcoat fastened around the waist with a leather belt from which depended a sword and rondel dagger. At his saddle, opposite his barbute hung a war axe with a severe crescent blade and a solid hammerhead opposite.

"Indeed, my friend," replied the armourer. "I intend to be as inconspicuous as possible if an enemy manages to get close. Let the nobles display themselves boldly and divert attention from me."

"What, covered by a surcoat of murrey and blue with a great white sanglier emblazoned upon it?"

"Identification – danger comes from our own side just as well as from an enemy." He omitted the obvious codicil to this statement that a surcoat could easily be disposed of in a rout leaving just an anonymous and un-liveried man at arms that might with luck, make his best way from the field. Laurence was not a professional soldier, but it was his business to understand their craft and though he had never been in a full battle before, yet he had heard enough tales to know that, when steel armour is no longer of any use the best defence is intelligent flight.

* * *

Two days later the forces of King Richard were encamped a few miles west of Leicester on a hill overlooking Redemore plain, an area of moor with a suspicion of boggy ground here and there. It was evening and already the prickers had brought news that the Tudor's army was approaching from Lichfield by the direction of Merevale Abbey. Clearly the long awaited battle would come with the morning. Laurence was with the king in his pavilion making last-minute checks on his harness and waiting for further orders. From this vantage point he could see over the plain, the only movement at present being the positioning of the king's artillery. There was a windmill to the south, somewhere before the Redemore marsh, though Laurence supposed the miller would have sensibly abandoned it. To the north west he could see the tower of the church at the village of Shenton while to the east another church, that of the village of Sutton Cheney where the king would rest for the night. Due south could just be seen the village of Dadlington and somewhere past that, though hidden from sight, the village of Stoke.

Beyond Redemore marsh was common pasture and it was expected that the Tudor would come along the line of the old Roman road that cut through to pass below the windmill, its direction almost due east. The prickers, the king's advance scouts, brought word that the banner of Rhys ap Thomas was flying with those of the Tudor. So it seemed he had turned traitor by breaking his sworn oath to his rightful king and one who had awarded him lands, a Welsh Stanley who had at least the courage to turn his coat before battle was engaged. Tudor must be making some very tempting promises, thought Laurence. Below the hill, King Richard's army was getting into position, ready, come first light to move into battle formation under the banners of their lords.

His commanders surrounded the king and they stood gazing out over Redemore, chattering together and planning their strategy. Laurence took careful note of Catesby and he was not difficult to see, being dressed in the finest of robes and having his servants in attendance. Clearly he did not expect to take part in the fighting. Close by him stood a pale-faced youth. This was George Stanley and it seemed the king had placed him with Catesby for safekeeping. Everyone knew the king had given orders for Stanley's son and heir to be killed should the forces of his father move to join the Tudor host. Robert Percy and Richard Ratcliffe were jesting together, keeping the mood of the king and his immediate retainers as light as possible, being fully aware of the responsibility that rested on the royal shoulders. Viscount Lovell, his face cheerful was regaling the king with one of his stories. Brackenbury was there and John Kendall, his face drawn and looking uncomfortable in his harness, sitting by a table with his writing implements ready to despatch written orders. The duke of Norfolk stood by them, mature in years and serious of mien but his expression martially confident. It was towards this lord that Laurence moved to position himself where it might be convenient to speak to him.

"Give you good e'en, your grace," he said sweeping the duke a low obeisance.

"Master de la Halle," acknowledged the duke, glancing at the westering sun. "I suppose you wish to enquire of your boy?"

"Just so, your grace," responded Laurence with some pleasure seeing as how the duke had immediately understood his parental concern.

"He will ride in the lance of my son Thomas, but to the rear with the spare horses. He is well accoutred, especially as you have sent him some good armour, and he will not be in the thickest press of the fighting. Nevertheless, he will still have to acquit himself well should my rearguard be attacked. We march in support of the king's archers." Laurence was partly gratified by the duke's remarks.

Robert would be a squire with the lance of Thomas earl of Surrey and after the conflict could expect some advancement, though he had to survive it first. At just thirteen years he would not be expected to join the fight, but anything could happen in a battle. The one thought that Laurence had to calm his fears was that being with the horses, Robert would be able to ride clear of danger should the worse happen.

"My lord of Northumberland is late arriving here with the king," Laurence ventured, hoping his statement would not be considered impertinent. Norfolk's brow creased in annoyance, but not, it seemed with Laurence's temerity.

"He is close and will be here in time to join battle, but he is tardy, master armourer, he is tardy. Of more concern is lord Thomas Stanley. His forces are to the west of us and he has declined the king's order to join the main army. His brother, William has been declared traitor though he would be rash indeed to join the Tudor at this time. Yet he has a considerable number under his banner and the best hope for us is that he stays out of things as the king believes his brother will." The duke turned his head and glanced pertinently at George Stanley, lord Strange.

"Is Sir William Stanley discovered a traitor? I have always doubted him, but proof of treachery is another matter." Laurence thought it best not to reveal he already knew of William Stanley's treason, not wanting to betray the confidence of his friend, David Morgan.

Norfolk curled his lip is distaste. "He has been reported as having had conference with the Tudor over Stafford way. I have no idea what was discussed, but it could only have been to the detriment of the king. We have enough men in our army to take on the Tudor's puny force and deal with the Stanley's too, though that would turn a relatively minor battle into a major one, perhaps another Towton but without the snow. With lord Strange in our hands it is probable his father will stand aside only to join the king once we have the upper hand. William Stanley must then flee for his life."

"To be sure, your grace, neither would I be Henry Tudor on the morrow. The day is like to be his last and he must know it too. I expect he will try to run."

"Yes, I agree and so does the king. We shall have a pursuit on our hands but the Tudor will hardly escape. His grace the king will have him out of this world and his realm of England at peace once and for all." Laurence thought he detected a tone of weariness in

Norfolk's voice. He was a man getting on in years and whatever the outcome, this would likely be one final battle before his dotage.

"I would speak with my son Robert, your grace, if that is permissible?"

"Of course, you may give my greetings to the earl of Surrey and tell him I have sent you to him with your request. I must stay with the king, but tell the earl he too has his father's blessing for tomorrow."

Laurence stepped back and gave a low bow. "My grateful thanks, your grace." He manoeuvred himself close to the king. He could hardly depart the king's pavilion without leave to go. He approached Kendall who was scribbling away at a paper.

"If I may have a word, master Kendall," he muttered. Kendall looked up and gave him a friendly smile.

"Master Laurence," he said pleasantly. "What can I do for you?" It was always a pleasure to speak with Kendall who, in spite of being essentially close to the king had little of the hauteur that was associated with such as the sycophantic Catesby.

"I have spoken to his grace of Norfolk who has given his permission for me to go to the camp of his son the earl of Suffolk where I might speak with my own son Robert. I would ask you to approach the king for me? I need his leave to go."

"I will right gladly," replied Kendall seriously while getting to his feet. "It will be his first battle. Of course you must go to him."

The king had been reluctant, at first, to let his armourer leave his side, but as he would spend the night at his camp at Sutton Cheney with Norfolk's host nearby, he agreed providing Laurence came to him before the midnight office was rung in the church there.

Norfolk's host was encamped to the north-west of the hill from where the king had his pavilions. Laurence found his way there in the twilight. He looked for the lance of the earl of Surrey. Thomas Howard had joined his father, the duke of Norfolk and the king at Sutton Cheney but he discovered his squires sitting outside their plain round tent, playing dice. The squires stood respectfully when they recognised the king's armourer. He had something of a reputation amongst them, his exploits for the king having been somewhat embroidered in the tales of his son Robert, which his swarthy appearance and the deep scar on his cheek running into his beard did nothing to diminish. They had a bright fire going which, though not needed for its warmth, yet provided illumination for their gaming.

"I hope you are not losing your coin," chuckled Laurence. He was not adverse to a wager himself though cautious in limiting his losses. He would instruct Robert in this after the battle. There was no point in doing so now. No doubt there would be rich pickings for the victors from a grateful king, particularly when there were so many traitors to be dealt with afterwards. Those who had remained loyal would be in the ascendant then.

Robert scrambled to his feet, his face split in a huge grin. He was in his doublet and hose, his armour heaped among that of his fellows. Laurence had provided him with a plain steel cuirass, a sallet with visor and a mail aventail and hauberk so his arms and legs were protected with mail. He wore leather boots. As a squire he would be required to move swiftly to refresh his lord with a spare horse, or a new weapon as required. Usually the lord would retire to the rear of his lance for this, meaning Robert should remain out of the main press of a fight. This was the only comfort Laurence could find. He well knew that once the men-at-arms were engaged, blood lust would cause a rampage among them and their enemy, striking down anyone in their path. At least being in the lance of a high noble, Robert would be accompanied by the best fighting knights under the king's command.

"Keep you visor down when your lance is engaged, and at all other times when in range of the enemy archers and crossbows," warned Laurence. "You will be tempted to lift it for a clearer view, but resist it. Your lord has a bright banner and as you know, Norfolk's is red quartered with the gold leopards of England and a rampant lion with a white bend in the other two quarters dividing six silver crosslets. He fights with a lion rampant on his shield. Your lance is with the earl of Surrey and he has the same arms as his father except the lower quarter of crosslets has the ancient Warenne check of blue and gold. Keep your eyes on their banners and listen for the sergeants. They will shout the lord's requirements in battle. Should the day go badly, or your lance be overwhelmed, get out of the way. You have the spare horses in your charge so you can get clear. Remember you can always rally and return to the fight if you live. There is no reward for the victorious dead."

Robert looked at his father curiously. His descriptions of the heraldry of Norfolk were unnecessary, he being a squire of that house. Laurence realised the advice he was giving was that of a father to a son, not a knight to his squire where the very idea of defeat was anathema. In Norfolk's household, the lad would have had the chivalric code drummed into him, where gallant knights

159

disdain to run and go down fighting if they must. The king himself, an ardent reader of knightly tales, held to this doctrine. Others, he knew, were rather more pragmatic when it came to their own demise, the Stanley brothers being two in particular. Such as these tended to survive while the more noble knights perished.

"I hear you, father, and understand. I shall do my duty and trust to God as the rest of us must."

Laurence could do no more than clap Robert on the shoulder, resisting the impulse to clasp him to his chest in the presence of his fellows. "Then we shall find a priest and pray together," he said and removed the reliquary he habitually wore. "Take this and wear it under your armour. If contains filings from the nail that fastened Christ's feet to the Holy Cross."

"I know, father. You have told me that since I was born, I think."

"Well then, you know its power. I am still alive am I not and there have been times when my continued existence has been in serious doubt."

Robert took the reliquary and hung it around his neck.

"Thank you, father. I shall wear it tomorrow, never fear."

"Then let us find a priest and make our devotions to God and pray we both might come through the morrow's battle. You have a priest here, I take it?"

"Yes, there are several with us."

"Ah, I see one moving over there." Laurence pointed to a group of tents where a friar was threading his way dangling from his fingers a crucifix among his beads. "Let us go and make our peace. Remember especially to ask your mother's blessing through the Holy Virgin."

Robert gave a passing nod to his companions, who had returned to their game. Laurence wondered if he was rather keener to rejoin them than secure his living soul, but that was the way of youth. He called to the friar who, seeing here two that were in need of a shriving, raised his hands in orant display while they approached.

* * *

Dawn found the first of the Tudor army seeking their positions opposite the Royal army of King Richard. Laurence could make out the banners of the earl of Oxford, remembering well the blazing star that had been his undoing when he faced King Edward at the Battle of Barnet. Mistaking it for the Sunne in Splendour banner of Edward, Oxford's men turned on each other in confusion leading to their rout. That would not happen today; they were getting into line opposite Norfolk and unlike Barnet, there was no fog to obscure the ground. Edward de Vere, thirteenth earl of Oxford was a serious and experienced commander and therefore probably the most dangerous general in the field, second only to the king himself. He looked in vain for the Tudor banner and supposed the pretender, useless as a general or even as a fighting knight, would keep safely to the rear. Others would do his fighting for him this day, God help them. Laurence crossed himself in sympathy for those who must fight and die for a traitor and bastard claimant.

King Richard's squires had strapped him into his battle harness and Laurence made a final inspection, pronouncing it ready for war. He stood among the king's commanders, the same who had been there the night before. The king seemed unconcerned at the approach of the Tudor host; rather he was looking to the south-east beyond Sutton Cheney where the first sighting of the earl of Northumberland's army was just visible, their harness and banners dark against the early light. He listened as the king's commanders conversed together.

"Can't see lord Stanley from here," he heard Ratcliffe say to lord Brackenbury, "but Sir William is forming up over there." He pointed to the south.

"Yes, replied Brackenbury, "right beside us and the Tudor, useless but well positioned to join either side should he decide to do so. His brother, Thomas Lord Stanley is over by Market Bosworth according to my prickers."

"That is just to the north and unless he moves soon, away from the battle. His son is here with us, so let him remain skulking where he is," growled Ratcliffe. "If he attacks, his son is a dead man and if not, after the battle, having failed the king his head will be forfeit."

"I would gladly do the execution myself," snapped Brackenbury. "Sir William is already pronounced traitor so the two can go together – one block will serve both."

Suddenly the air was rent with the sharp reports of gunfire. The king's guns had opened up on the Tudor line, discomfiting them before they could get into position. As well as the heavy guns, lesser and crisper bangs came for a few dozen handguns. These might not do a great execution among the opposing host, but they made plenty of noise and belched out huge clouds of smoke to drift across the enemy ranks, giving them a taste of battle even before they had attacked. Everyone around the king looked across to see what damage had been done, but it was impossible to tell at the distance and through the smoke.

Laurence reached for his reliquary before realising he had given it to Robert. Still, the gunfire prompted him to mutter a prayer to St Barbara, the patron of gunners and armourers. He could see that Oxford was getting into formation quickly, no doubt anxious to attack before the guns could do much damage. Once engaged with the king's army, the guns would be unable to fire for fear of hitting their own side. The king nodded to Norfolk who, after sweeping a hurried bow, stomped off to his own command on the right flank where the archers were stringing their bows.

With agonising slowness, Northumberland was getting his men into battle array on the left flank. It seemed to Laurence Northumberland was failing to match the alacrity of Oxford, but as it was Norfolk who would engage the Lancastrian earl that was merely a cause for angry frustration at the moment. He could tell by the king's face he was not pleased and no doubt Henry Percy, earl of Northumberland would have some explaining to do after the battle, unless he acquitted himself with rather more vigour.

Looking around at the scene, the king's army was huge, greatly outnumbering the Tudor by more than two-to-one. Laurence thought he could tell something of the king's plan. Norfolk would attack Oxford's centre and if successful, push him back. If he was unable to achieve this, then Northumberland would strike the Oxford flank, thus destroying the main part of Tudor's army. William Stanley might cause a problem should he be foolish enough to join with Oxford, but the king's army at Norfolk's back should easily overcome both. The worrying thing was the army of Lord Stanley. He was six thousand strong and if he attacked in support of Tudor the battle would become bitter and protracted, though the king still outnumbered his enemies, even should both Stanley brothers engage to support the Tudor.

Laurence wondered about the feelings of the common soldiers in both Stanley camps. They were here ostensibly to fight for their anointed king. Would they willingly commit treason and engage fellow Englishmen for the sake of a usurper who had brought a foreign invading army to their shores? He pushed the thought away and considered that, on balance, Thomas lord Stanley would prefer not to test them and remain over by Bosworth and join in on the winning side, which, if everything went as it aught, would be King Richard.

Clarions sounded as horses were brought for the king and his household knights. King Richard climbed into the saddle of his favourite destrier. Laurence knew this was White Surrey, one of several greys the king had, no doubt to complement his badge of the *blanc sanglier*, the white boar. The horses of the king and his knights were barded, each having a glittering criniere at the neck with steel peytral and croupier to protect the chest and hindquarters under a bright, embroidered caparison. Horses were powerfully shod with protruding nails at their shoes and calcans to stop them slipping on soft ground. A polished chamfron with spiked rondel covered the face of each mount. A mounted squire rode to the king's side and handed him his battle helm, the one Laurence had made for him. With his helm strapped down, but with his visor up to show his face, he beckoned at his fellow knights to gather around him, then off they cantered to parade in front of the army, splendid in their fine armour, the royal standard of England to the fore with King Richard's banner streaming behind. Those pennants of the banneret knights, their ends cut off square to denote that their title had been awarded on the field of battle, streamed behind that of the king. They made a fine sight and Laurence felt a tug of emotion in his throat as he thrilled with pride at the sight, the resplendent excellence of his craft.

Laurence was left behind for a time with the serving men and those not riding to show themselves to the army. The young and pale-faced George Stanley, lord Strange, was standing outside a pavilion craning his neck to observe the battlefield. Behind him, his face grim and cold stood William Catesby. A few moments ago he had been all smiles and encouragement while in the presence of the king, but now as a non-combatant he stood in his fine riding clothes, a sword and dagger at his belt and two brutish henchmen close by.

"It should be soon now," came a voice at his side. Looking around he found John Kendall in his battle harness, holding his sallet ready with its visor.

"You really are riding into battle?" gasped Laurence with astonishment. He had provided Kendall with good plain white harness, but had not really expected him, a penman, to actually ride by King Richard's side today.

"Don't be too surprised, master de la Halle," he chuckled. "I did some soldiering in my youth before I took up the feather. I never did like too much exercise." He patted his stomach, which though generously proportioned was yet less than corpulent. "I shall stay close to the king. I do not expect many will get past his household knights, you know who *they* are. I consider myself courageous, but not stupid."

"You echo my own philosophy, master secretary."

"The king is sanguine though," he intoned lugubriously. "You have heard that he has appointed as his heir the earl of Lincoln, John de la Pole?"

"His sister Elizabeth's son, yes, I know that but I cannot believe the king imagines he will perish this day?"

"No, but illness or accident may carry him off as anyone else and he has been much shaken by the loss of his queen and his son, the prince Edward."

"But he might yet produce an heir – I think on the present negotiations with Portugal. I believe the princess Joanna is amenable to a royal match?"

"If all works out well, then we shall see but until then the king must have an appointed heir and at the moment that is the earl of Lincoln."

The camp burst into a flurry of activity as the king returned and dismounted. Looking over to where the earl of Oxford was moving forward he gave the command for Norfolk to advance banners. A pursuivant galloped off to the duke with the order and immediately it was delivered, John Howard, who had arranged his archers on each flank of his men-at-arms, ordered them to shoot. At the same time the king's gunners set off a final carronade. Norfolk's army advanced on foot towards the enemy. The duke had wisely sent the horses to the rear, as they would be of limited use on the Redemore plain; furthermore there was a bog over by his right flank that had to be avoided. Laurence could see them, relieved that Robert would be out of the front line of battle.

Perversely, the smoke from the guns drifted across the plain and obscured the first clash as the armies came together. When it cleared sufficiently they could see a mêlée of men-at-arms struggling in a mass around Oxford's centre. King Richard looked to Northumberland with his army on his left and sent an order for him to advance on Oxford's flank. Laurence looked beyond the fight below, trying to see where the Tudor was. He could make out the standards of Rhys ap Thomas advancing and approaching behind Oxford but no sign of the Tudor, who had diplomatically adopted the red dragon banner of Wales in an attempt to garner support in that country. Few Welshmen wanted to fight for the English throne. It hadn't worked as he planned with only Rhys ap Thomas and a few others joining him. Soon the pursuivant returned from

Northumberland, who had, as yet, made no move. King Richard ranted at the poor fellow who knelt in terror before him. Word soon filtered through that Northumberland was observing Sir William Stanley in case he joined in and would not move in support of Norfolk. *Had Northumberland been made certain promises too?* His army was larger than Oxford's and could easily defeat him if only he would engage.

Laurence returned his gaze to the battle. Oxford's centre was turning Norfolk's right flank and his left southwards towards the previously viewed windmill. It looked as though his centre was collapsing. Oxford's men were mainly mercenaries who were fighting hard for their lives. They knew full well they would be cut down mercilessly in a rout. English soldiers would not take kindly to foreign invaders. The English archers were pouring arrows into the enemy where they could without hitting their own while the enemy were replying with crossbows. Soon many of them had thrown down their bows and were fighting hand-to-hand with sword and dagger. No quarter was being given on either side but slowly and inexorably Oxford was punching through Norfolk's line. Dismayed, Laurence looked to where the earl of Surrey's banner fluttered in the right flank above the dust and residual smoke. He was being separated from the centre to be pushed north. The king issued orders for his own army to ready itself to support Norfolk. He sent the pursuivant again off to Northumberland with a direct order for Henry Percy to advance upon the enemy or be arraigned for treason.

Suddenly Norfolk's herald burst into the camp and flung himself before the king.

"My lord of Norfolk is down, feared killed," he cried in anguish.

The king raised himself and took a deep breath, his face deliberately expressionless. This, Laurence and everyone who knew him was a danger sign.

"To horse," cried the king. Catesby hurried up and knelt in front of his sovereign.

"Northumberland is not moving, my lord king. Unless he does so all might well be up with us. There is still time to retreat and reform to fight another day."

The king looked at Catesby with high disdain.

"I have waited and worked long for this day. I am not going to run from a caitiff traitor," he declared angrily. He beckoned for his horse and his squire trotted White Surrey to him. King Richard flung himself into his saddle and held his arm out for a lance while a squire fastened his war axe to his saddle. His household knights immediately mounted their steeds and Laurence spotted John Kendall mounted and ready to ride with the king. Without a second thought Laurence called for a mount. A squire brought him a courser barded with a plain chamfron of cuirboille and a peytral of the same to protect its chest. Robert was down there somewhere and if they were riding to support what remained of Norfolk's army, then he would go too. Behind them the tension of the king's army was almost palpable. King Richard, it seemed, would mount a cavalry charge around the struggling mass to strike at Rhys ap Thomas, who was hurrying in support of his new ally, while the mass of his army would attack on foot Oxford's flank to relieve pressure on the centre. Without the aid of Northumberland it would be difficult and messy with much death and injury, but Henry Percy's recalcitrance left the king little choice.

Laurence placed his barbute over his head and got a squire to strap it down at the back while he secured it at the front. No other had such a helm, it being Italian and based on the old Greek model rather than English sallet. Visorless, the helm was an open slit down the front with two holes for vision. It was a compromise between riding with an unprotected face and the ability to see clearly as well as to breath easily. He looped the thong of his war axe around his right wrist and checked the sword in his scabbard, ensuring it would come clear without catching. He tried to see from his new vantage point on horseback, within the struggling mass of the fight, the banners of the earl of Surrey, but it was too confused a sight.

Suddenly there was a cry from the men around the king. They were pointing to the mid distance, beyond Rhys ap Thomas and well clear of the main enemy army - a group of horsemen with a few men-at-arms and what looked to be pikes. Above swirled the distinctive banner of Cadwallader, the red dragon of Wales. It was the Tudor – it had to be! *What was he doing away from his main force?* He might be behind his army, but separated thus he was in striking distance and a tempting target. The king made up his mind in an instant. If he could catch the Tudor and bring him down the battle was won and much slaughter prevented. To get there they must ride across the Redemore plain directly in front of Sir William Stanley's army, which duplicitous commander still waited and watched for the likely outcome of the battle. There was no sign of lord Thomas Stanley and if the Tudor could be brought down, he would be too late in any case.

Before Laurence knew what was happening they were off, King Richard in the lead with his standard bearers closely followed by his household knights. Beside him rode viscount Lovell, Sir Robert Percy and Sir Richard Ratcliffe. Sir Robert Brackenbury was behind them and close by rode Kendall and Laurence, the latter having but little choice than to be swept along with them, cantering with the accompanying knights of the king's household. Looking around they were pitifully few, no more than two hundred but if they could cut through to Henry Tudor, the battle was finished and these were amongst the best knights in England. He had no wish to be here; rather he expected to be riding to the aid of the earl of Surrey and Robert. The God of battles had dictated otherwise.

They cantered across the front of Sir William Stanley's red liveried ranks and there in the centre Laurence spotted Stanley's banner of the White Hart. He could sense every eye upon the king's band as they cantered past, and still there was no movement. It was as if they were carved chessmen on a board waiting for a game to start. Rhys ap Thomas, observing the direction of the king began to swing his men to the aid of the Tudor. The king, seeing the danger couched his lance and ordered a full charge. They broke into a gallop, the thundering hooves of the horses sending the soft pasture of the Redemore plain flying in clods. Ahead a small force of what looked to be mercenary pikes moved to form a barrier in front of the Tudor. The king was almost on them now, but their defence, with twenty-foot long pikes grounded forward and those behind held by the pike men at the level of the riders was a formidable, probably suicidal barrier. *Surely they were not going to charge into that?* Behind the pikes Laurence caught a glimpse of the Tudor sitting his horse, apparently immobile. Beside him was his standard bearer and Laurence recognised with some surprise the pennant of William Brandon, whose brother he had last seen in Paris. Breaking out from the defence of pikes came another familiar knight, Sir John Cheney, a huge man famous in the joust and he was aiming straight for the king. Whether it was over-confidence in attacking a smaller man or perhaps his horse losing its footing, but the fury of the king's lance strike threw Cheney out of his saddle. Cheney's squire ran to his lord's aid whereupon viscount Lovell following the king let his destrier trample him into the ground, breaking his body under its hoofs while Chaney scrambled out of his way.

Throwing down their lances, the king and his knights stopped and formed up in close rank. Walking their barded horses into the mass of pikes, with sword, axe or mace, they struck the points aside as they went. The defenders could do little to stop them. Grounded as they were, the forward pike men could only steer their points within a small space and relied on a rider impaling himself due to the weight of his charge. With the attackers moving slowly thus, the pikes could only scratch away at impenetrable armour while the king and his knights could easily sweep the points aside. Once beyond the point, a pike man, both hands full, could only look up at the horseman above in the instant before being chopped down to his death. The pikes between the grounded weapons could jab at the armoured knights but these too, unable to effectively pierce good armour, were easily swept aside.

Once having broken through the wall of pikes, the king and his knights spurred their horses and charged at where Henry Tudor was sitting frozen to the saddle of his mount and looking frantically around for somewhere to run. Halberdiers moved in front to protect him. The usurper, who now saw his death carving an approach through his spears, dismounted and cowered behind his men. Sir William Brandon, still mounted and carrying the Tudor standard attacked the king with a mace, aiming at his helm. He managed a strike before King Richard, with a backhand slice carved into his armpit. Laurence was laying about him with his war axe and he recorded somewhere in his mind a certain satisfaction when another glancing blow from Brandon failed to damage the king's armour. The king struck again and down went Brandon, blood streaming from a neck wound and the Tudor standard fell to the ground. There were now just a few halberdiers protecting the Tudor.

Laurence's attention was taken up by the charge of a man-at-arms in full harness. He was wielding a mace the better to crush his helmet. Laurence, though not a trained knight was an armourer and knew exactly where and how to strike and penetrate steel armour. The man swung at his head, and he ducked under the blow. This let Laurence swing at the cuisse covering his thigh. The curved blade of his axe cut through the metal and into the muscle beneath. The knight howled with pain and rage. He was not disabled but the injury caused him to momentarily lose full control of his horse. Laurence spurred his mount around to drive behind the knight and managed to cleave the back of his helmet. The axe had not penetrated far but the knight, shaking his head was slowed letting the next blow chop upwards between the lames of his right pauldron to bite deep into his shoulder joint. Crippled thus, his arm dropped limp, his mace fell into the mire and he was forced to turn away or face his nemesis. Laurence let him go and looked around for the king.

He hardly knew what happened next but the small band was turning to defend itself from the massed charge of red liveried cavalry. Stanley! The traitor, seeing his chance to defeat the king by overwhelming his small force, had come in on the side of the Tudor. Meanwhile they were being thrust towards a deadly wall of halberds. These weapons were a combination of spear, axe and curved blade. A trained halberdier could hook his curved blade into the harness of a knight and drag him from his mount and that is what they were trying now. He saw the king swinging his war axe and hacking at his enemies. Richard had hurled down his lance early in the fight, it being too unwieldy in a thick press of men and horses. The Tudor was frustratingly close, but try as he might, the king could not get to him. Then a halberdier managed to get the hook of his blade under the king's helmet strap and sever it. Richard tore his loose helm free and shook his head in anger, his long hair flying out from his head as he lay about him with greater vigour.

Laurence saw Brackenbury attack only to be brought down by a Stanley lance and then Ratcliffe was pulled from his mount, the press of men being too thick for him to manouvre it. The pressure of the fighting men swept the king further away from Henry Tudor who remained invisible behind his protective wall of halberds and pikes. He could hear the king's voice screaming Treason! Treason! Suddenly there was a cry, animal in sound, then becoming a kind of braying. The king, deprived of his battle helm had gone down somewhere close. Laurence tried to spur his horse to where they had him on the ground, but it was impossible. For a moment he thought he might save the king, but the sheer numbers around the kill was impenetrable. The king had failed in his brave attempt to bring the battle to a close, but his objective was still on the field.

For the moment everyone was focused on the killing ground where the king had been hacked down. The halberds were still guarding the Tudor but their attention too was drawn to the killing spot. If the usurper was killed, then the only man left was the earl of Lincoln, Richard's heir and he would become the next king. Laurence turned his horse and set it at a gap in the halberds. Swinging his axe he crashed through to confront the few men still guarding Tudor. Laurence saw him then, clad in full harness, his surcoat of green and white with the red dragon of Wales at its centre, his visor down and he imagined at that moment the abject fear the coward must be feeling. If only he could have the satisfaction of seeing it in his eyes. Henry Tudor stood rooted to the spot, vainly brandishing a sword and if all were silent, Laurence imagined, he might expect to hear the clatter of his armour as the wretch trembled within it.

With the Plantagenet war cry in his throat, and disgust for Tudor in his heart, Laurence spurred his mount at the usurper, trampling over the fallen standard and stomping the red dragon into the Redemore marsh. Immediately a press of men ran forward to obscure his progress. Laying about him with his war axe, and clad in his Greek style barbute his enemies saw a very Achilles, his armour and axe smoking in the blood of his foes, the very embodiment of martial valour slicing and smashing into their flesh and bones as if invulnerable.

Someone in the enemy halberdiers saw the danger to the Tudor and a dozen or so charged, crashing into their own men in a bid to get at the warrior who, it seemed had somehow risen from Hades to wreak vengeance on their lord. Something struck his head and he felt the steel buckle and tear at his scalp. Their very charge, and the number of men in the field caused Laurence to be swept clear and suddenly he was in the open behind the Tudor line. Realising the hopelessness of his position, he spurred his mount away. Unfortunately, there was a marsh in his way and his mount stumbled and threw him.

Landing breathless but otherwise unhurt, he looked around. He had lost his war axe in the fall but still had his sword and dagger, which he drew from their scabbards. Many were running and riding about him and one had seen where he had fallen. A horseman in the Stanley livery reined his mount to a halt and watched him as he struggled to his feet. The man had his lance at the ready and Laurence's heart sank as he realised the hopelessness of his position. He readied himself for one last desperate fight, though he knew he must be run through before he could hope reach the man armed with just sword and dagger. Then, strangely the horseman turned away and cantered off. He could hardly have failed to recognise a king's man as his surcoat clearly showed the badge of the *blanc sanglier*.

Having no time to ponder on the mystery, and mightily thankful, Laurence quickly looked around the battlefield. All movement was towards the king's lines, which now he was dead, were breaking and running. His heart lurched at the thought of a rout. A man might survive a battle only to be killed trying to get away from the field. Hopefully Robert, if he lived, might heed his advice and ride off to safety. He looked down at his surcoat, which was ripped to shreds where blades, probably of halberds had sliced at him. This made it easy to tear it away. He unbuckled his damaged helm and stuffing the surcoat into it, hurled it into a nearby pond.

Having fallen behind the Tudor line everyone was going away from him. Nearby was a band of soldiers in a Tudor livery. They looked like mercenaries and their captain had just seen him. He stood, dejected, blood from a head wound seeping into his hair. There was nowhere to run. If he were lucky he would be taken prisoner, but seeing as he was not accoutred as a rich knight, and taken for someone worth a ransom, he would likely have his throat cut for economy.

"Stand, fellow and declare yourself," shouted the captain sword in hand. Laurence's ears pricked up at the voice – someone having a Breton accent had addressed him in French.

"A poor soldier who has lost his mount," he tried in Breton.

"Ah, one of use are you," came the reply. "Who is your commander?" Laurence's heart skipped a beat. He had no idea who any of the Breton mercenary captains were. He put his hand to his head and pulled it away covered in his blood.

"Captain – captain – no captain," he stuttered. "Servant of . . ." he let the statement tail off and assumed a vacant expression. The captain looked to his sergeant who had come up but who was anxious to be away to plunder the field.

"This fellow is out of his wits. Take him with you and we shall find out who he is later." The sergeant, his face crestfallen knuckled his forehead and pulled Laurence to him.

"Keep up or get left behind."

That suited Laurence perfectly. He sheathed his sword and dagger clumsily and stumbled after them. It wasn't long before the men were intent on plundering the injured and dead while their shuffling companion was a hindrance in their labours. They came to a small brook that traversed the marshy ground and halted while they looked for the easiest way across.

"Leave me here for a while," suggested Laurence. "I thirst and also can wash my wounds in the water. A cool moss compress might help." The men were only too glad to go along with this suggestion. They could see others of their kind bending over the fallen, slitting throats and looking for booty.

"We form up by the windmill over there," said the sergeant pointing it out. Laurence knew it from his earlier reconnaissance with the king. "Find your way there before nightfall. There are those who can tend your injury in our company." Laurence pretended a sudden weakness and slumped down. He bid the Breton adieu and sat by the brook while they moved out of sight. He would strike west away from the field of Redemore and once clear of immediate danger, perhaps he could use his new Breton mercenary identity to aim for London and Cornelius Quirk where he might earn some respite and get his thoughts into order. For the moment his soul was heavy. He had no idea if Robert lived or no, and a dissembling coward now had the throne of England while a brave and noble king lay dead.

He reflected on how King Richard had disdained the Church before the battle and had no priests with him. The king had said that if God was with him he needed no priests and if not then they were of little use. He had been thinking this way since the deaths of his wife and son, though few thought it more than a passing bout of melancholy. Laurence crossed himself, missing his reliquary but praying to the holy Virgin that it might keep Robert safe. Could it be that God had promoted a bastard claimant over a true and anointed king, handing the crown to a man too feared to fight for it, while destroying the better man? A priest had once told him that God does not see death as a punishment. Well King Richard was certainly beyond punishment here on earth, but his subjects remained and they would have to bear whatever regime Henry Tudor might impose upon them. Perhaps the time had come for him to consider returning to his homeland and leave England to its just desserts.

8 – Leave Taking

Laurence entered London by the Newgate and followed the crowd until he reached the little conduit opposite Fauster Lane. Just a short walk further would bring him to Wood Street, but he considered it prudent to approach the apothecary's shop with caution. His journey had been perilous, though his counterfeit identity as a Breton mercenary had sustained him, even when some he had met on the road regarded him suspiciously. He had been questioned at one point, but the sergeant and his men were unable to understand Breton, so they let him go, it being too much trouble to probe his identity any further. Besides, they had stopped plenty of others such as he on the road.

At this time, men were keeping their opinions to themselves until they could work out what the future would bring under a new and completely unknown monarch. He had sensed the furtive mood of Londoners even before entering the city. He was aware that, as King Richard's armourer, as well as for other nobles, there was the possibility that someone would recognise him and for the moment at least, he wanted to remain anonymous. For all anyone knew he had died at the battle some were now calling the Field of Bosworth, named after the market town near the Redemore plain. The scar on his face gave him away, and so he had wrapped a bandage around his face and jaw to obscure it. A smear of blood at his cheek gave pretended testimony to the presence of a wound received in the battle. The gash to his scalp, though sore, seemed to be healing, but he would be glad of the ministrations of Anna, or even Mother Malkin.

He was swathed in a cheap woollen cloak picked up from the battlefield, as were the good leather boots he was wearing. The former owners would have no further need for clothing. His armour had to be left behind a hedge for some lucky peasant to find and sell. One thing he did not want to be mistaken for on the road was a man-at-arms, who would be taken up and closely questioned thus destroying his persona as a Breton mercenary.

He hung around the conduit watching as servants and goodwives hurried to and fro, drawing water for their households. It was some time before he saw someone he knew. It was one of Able and Goody Wood's children, about ten years of age. The family had a carpenter's shop next to the apothecary and were friends of

Cornelius. Able and Goody Wood had been the witnesses to his marriage contract with Joan. He waited by the corner of Fauster Lane, knowing she would have to pass the spot on her way to Wood Street after she had drawn water in the pail she carried.

"Why maister Laurence," she gasped with shock as he tugged at her sleeve. It was a few seconds before she recognised him, fearing at first he was attempting to accost her. "Master Cornelius feared you be dead."

"Not yet, mademoiselle," he whispered cheerily, keeping his voice down to encourage her to do the same. "How are things with your mother and father?"

"They are well, but much distressed that the king is slain." Laurence knew that the Woods had been loyal to the House of York.

"And master Cornelius; is all well there?

"Drear, maister," she said shaking her head. "There is much dole in the house. They fear for you maister and young Robert, too."

"Is it safe for me to approach?"

The girl looked about her furtively. Laurence might wish she could show more guile. Anyone watching could tell she was being secretive, thus drawing attention to them. "Maister reckons as how we be watched," she whispered, "us being faithful to King Richard." Laurence thought about this for a moment.

"Can I trust you to deliver a message to master Cornelius for me, and stay silent should anyone question you?"

"That you may, sir."

"Then tell him you have spoken with me and ask him to throw a rope over the wall of the herb garden just after the curfew has rung. I shall climb over then and enter the house hopefully unobserved."

"I will," she answered.

"Then get you gone. Don't look back and walk slowly. Remember to keep our secret."

The maid went off and Laurence hoped she would manage to get back safely without looking as if she were on a subversive mission. He glanced casually around at the crowd. Everyone seemed bent on their own business and few, he had noted, concerned themselves with the kind of bonhomie that was usual between the city tradesmen and vendors and their customers. Though he had heard the people of London dutifully turned out to cheer their new king as he entered the capital, the mood had instantly turned dark the moment he disappeared into the palace at Westminster. Tudor agents, formerly no doubt Lancastrian spies who had, until now maintained clandestine identities, were free to prosecute the interests of their king. The city goals were beginning to fill and already there had been an increase in hangings at Tyburn.

Laurence spent the time to sunset strolling in the thickest press of the crowd, where he was lost in the thronging mass. As the time for curfew approached the streets began to thin and this became a problem. He didn't want to be taken as a vagabond so he made his way to the lane at the rear of the apothecary's shop and huddled into a nich between a wall and a hawthorn bush, which gave him cover from anyone passing the end of the lane. At the appointed time, just near to his hiding place, a rope was flung over the wall. He stepped from the hawthorn and glancing up and down the lane to ensure all was clear, he grabbed the rope and pulled himself up and over the wall.

The sight that met him would stay with him for many a year after. His brain took in and recorded a tableau - Cornelius in his black gown and leaning on a stick, Anna by his side and the diminutive form of Mother Malkin holding the spiked collar of Beast. The great wolfhound was the first to move. Pulling free of Mother Malkin's grasp, the hound bounded over to him before jumping up, its great paws on his shoulders and slapping at his face with its tongue. Anna stood, her hand over her mouth gazing with a mixture of distress and relief, a multitude of emotions chasing over her face. Laurence opened his arms in greeting and Anna, overcoming her temporary immobility pulled the dog away and threw her arms about him, bursting into tears and sobbing uncontrollably.

He crushed her to him for a moment, then, holding her away turned and drew the rope back over the wall and threw it over the bole of the tree to which it had been tied. Anna tore herself away and they all walked silently through the garden, thick in the twilight with the heady scent of the herbs that were cultivated there, and entered the house where Able Wood stood grinning a greeting, the little maid Jocelyn by his side.

"I see the fair demoiselle delivered my message," chortled Laurence, smiling down on the girl.

"That she did," said her father. "I thought it best to come here with her. We suspect the houses in this street are being watched. Having the girl with me might allay any suspicion that something is happening." He nodded at Cornelius as he spoke.

"Yes," agreed the apothecary. "We have not been approached yet, but others have. It cannot be long before we are questioned."

"I suppose I am to blame for that," mused Laurence with concern in his voice. I am well known as the king's armourer and connected to you." He sat down on a chair by the fire while Anna unwrapped the bandage from his face. Mother Malkin came over and probed at the wound in his scalp. It said something for his gratitude to be safely with them that he neglected to sign himself or mutter a prayer against the evil eye. In fact, after seeing her standing with the apothecary and Anna as he scrambled over the garden wall, almost as part of the family, he was beginning to warm to the old crone. He let her snip away some of his matted hair and then wash the wound.

"We thought you might have been killed in the battle," inserted Anna, "there being no news of you, and those enquiries we made among the Tudor mercenaries here in London were of no help." Mother Malkin, muttering some incantation to herself, went to a shelf, took down a pot and proceeded to smear a piece of linen with some of the contents. She returned to Laurence and placed it on his wound then bound it around his head with a linen strip to hold it in place.

Cornelius waved a hand towards a table upon which were beakers and a flask of wine. Anna poured and handed the beakers around. "Reports of the battle are confused and I suspect embroidered by the soldiery, as is their wont," he said matter-of-factly. "It worries us that we have not had a visit from the Tudor agents. I cannot bring myself to say the king's men, though that is the case now. Had they known you lived and escaped, I would expect them to come searching for you here. On the other hand, if they are uncertain that might account for them not coming, rather they will wait and watch to see who turns up. It was sensible of you not to come here directly."

"You have taught me well," replied Laurence. "For all they know I am either dead or escaped. If alive I could be anywhere: Gloucester where is my business, or Brittany my homeland. Perhaps we should let them wonder for a while yet?"

"If I may leave now," inserted Able Wood. "The less I know of this business the better. I cannot be made to disclose that of which I am ignorant and I have my family to think on." He looked down at his daughter. Able had a wife and sons as well as this maid and what he said was quite reasonable. Laurence thought on how it was just two weeks after the battle and men already feared the agents of the new Tudor king.

After Able and Jocelyn had gone, Cornelius got them together in a huddle by the fire. Anna sat by his side while Mother Malkin found a stool to one side. Laurence sat and swirled the wine in his cup.

"Able has made a serious point," said Cornelius bleakly. "If questioned he will hardly let his family suffer even for our sakes and who could blame him. However, I think we might not need to worry too much for the present. It is *this* house the Tudor agents will be interested in and not just because of you, Laurence. I am known to run couriers on the continent and here in England. Not all of them will remain silent. Some are bound to make their peace with the new regime and information is a saleable commodity."

"And Henry Tudor's world hitherto has been that of the plotter and spy," said Laurence. "He has little or no acquaintance with the chivalric code that was the attributes of King Edward and King Richard, indeed, having spoken on the road to some of those who fought for him, it appears he ran from the battle not once, but twice! Even his own men despise him."

"How is that?" gasped Cornelius. "All we know is that he was part of a heroic victory!"

"I was there at the end, and I saw Tudor cowering behind a wall of French halberdiers," stated Laurence firmly. He decided not to mention his own attack on the Tudor lest it upset Anna to know how close he had come to being brought down. Luckily she had not made note of it. "Henry Tudor never struck a blow, his fighting was all done for him, including the command of his army – that was left to the earl of Oxford. King Richard managed to get within a few feet of him and would have finished him had not William Stanley come in on the Tudor side."

"I have heard something similar to what you are telling us," remarked Cornelius. "French halberdiers are boasting in the taverns of London that it was they who won the battle for the Tudor."

"There is something in that," continued Laurence. "I joined a band of Breton mercenaries on the way here, pretending to have lost my reason. As I am clearly Breton they assumed I had been one of them and so I listened intently to their stories. It seems Henry Tudor disappeared the day before the battle, leaving his army, which later we were told was for a meeting with William Stanley, though it seems that was not encouraging and nothing seems to have come of it. That may be true but the rumour going around his men at the time was that he had to be *persuaded* by those captains with him to return to his army. Then, when the battle commenced he remained at the rear ready to run should his army be defeated and at one point that is what he did do!"

"He actually ran away!" snorted Anna, her eyes wide with surprise.

"Yes; again he was pursued and brought back so as not to demoralise his army any further. Having thought on this since, it is my belief that is why he had become separated from his army when King Richard spied him with a small retinue. It is a cruel twist of fate that had he not run and remained invisible to the rear, King Richard would have eventually won the battle, though with much slaughter. As it was, the king imagined the exposed Tudor represented a chance to finish the business quickly. We charged the Tudor with King Richard and but a few knights and you know the rest."

"There is something about the involvement of Sir William Stanley you seem unaware of," said Cornelius. I suppose from your position in the battle that is to be expected." Laurence looked curiously at the apothecary. "Consider the position of Sir William and his relationship with his men. We know that King Richard had previously upset certain nobles with his lawmaking, which tended to favour the people of England rather than the nobility."

"Yes, Northumberland in particular was irritated by the local population in the north. People there preferred to approach the king when he was duke of Gloucester, trusting to his ideas of justice rather than those of the earl."

"Just so, and although Sir William and his brother lord Thomas might wish to take up arms against their king, to what extent could they trust their soldiers to follow? Remember, they would be asking them to attack their anointed king, the last in a long line of Plantagenet monarchs, for the sake of a bastard claimant, a man most of them knew nothing off. Moreover, Tudor's army was mostly mercenary, or rebel Welsh. The Stanley men are all English. I believe lord Stanley held back not because of a reluctance to aid the Tudor, but because he could not trust his men to follow him. The same goes for Sir William."

That was something Laurence had already thought on. It was true that King Richard was generally popular with common Englishmen and many of them in the armies of the Stanley brothers would have been extremely disturbed by any order to move against him.

"But Sir William Stanley's men did enter on the Tudor side?" said Laurence flatly.

Cornelius smiled knowingly. "I have had reports from certain of Sir William's men. Apparently they charged into the fray in the belief they were going to King Richard's aid!"

"What," gasped Laurence. "I was there and Stanley's men were certainly fighting with the king's men."

"Think back on the battle of Barnet? You observed that particular conflict I believe?"

"Yes, you know I did, with old King Henry the Sixth. We watched from a nearby hill."

"Then you will recall how the battle was won, or rather, how the Lancastrians lost it. Remember the charge that morning of the earl of Oxford."

"I recall it well. Oxford's men had chased on horseback after lord Hastings' men who were running from the field. Oxford caught up with and rallied his men then returned to charge into the morning mist that obscured the field. The battle line had rotated and he ran into the back of Montague's men, also fighting on the Lancastrian side who, mistaking Oxford's banner of a blazing star for the Sunne in Splendour of King Edward immediately turned on them. Oxford's men cried treason and the Lancastrians began fighting amongst themselves, giving King Edward the victory, leading to the death of the earl of Warwick."

"Yes, a misunderstanding that altered everything. The same happened on the Redemore Plain. Sir William Stanley, a serial prevaricator certainly, was waiting to see how the battle would work out. Observing King Richard's gallant charge he immediately saw how once Henry Tudor was down, the battle would be over. Stanley too had seen how vulnerable the Tudor was and how he might be finished off. He charged to Richard's aid in the expectation of redeeming himself for his vacillations of loyalty should the king kill Henry Tudor. His men would have no trouble in following then. King Richard's knights, knowing of the Stanley penchant for treachery, assumed he was coming in on the side of the Tudor. They thought they were being attacked and thus fought with Stanley's men who in their turn had to defend themselves. The confusion deprived King Richard of his close support at the critical moment, which led to his death and once that had occurred, Stanley immediately changed sides again in an attempt to win the accolade of the Tudor and avoid another charge of treason."

Laurence considered this. It was true that in the tumult of battle, and with the threat of uncertain loyalties in King Richard's nobles, it would indeed be only too easy to make such an error. Everything was happening so quickly and there had been no time for communication between captains. Had the king brought down the Tudor, Sir William Stanley, already attainted by the king, would probably have lost his head in the aftermath. Joining in with Richard's last gallant charge would have absolved him. What Cornelius said made perfect sense. Suddenly he recalled the lone horseman who, though having him at his mercy, turned away.

"I wondered at the time why Sir William simply watched as we cantered along the front of his host. Just as the king, he too must have seen the vulnerability of Tudor and the time to intervene to save him would have been at that moment. Rather, he let the king charge past and waited until the Tudor's banner fell before intervening. He cannot have known whether the Tudor lived or no."

Cornelius continued his tale. "The story has further credence. Afterwards it was lord Thomas Stanley who actually presented Henry Tudor with the crown. His brother William was shouldered aside and even now has not been promised much in the way of reward, which you would expect had he really saved the Tudor. Henry Tudor simply muttered something about how Sir William came to his aid rather late, yet he favours brother Thomas who made no move with his army whatsoever. I suspect he could not trust his men to follow him either. So far as they knew, they were there to support their king and an order to attack him would have been to command them to commit treason against their lawful monarch."

"The Tudor suspects Sir William but confused circumstances do not allow him to prove it," mused Laurence.

"And a successful outcome for King Richard was closer than we thought," growled Cornelius. "Henry Tudor has the Devil on his side."

Laurence could only nod his head in agreement, hardly trusting himself to speak. This was not the time to inform them that he almost avenged the king by striking down the Tudor. Had he done so they would find themselves in a much different case today.

Suddenly, Anna jerked her head up and glared at Laurence as she realised what part he had played in the battle. "You were actually there!" she snapped. "You mean to say you joined in that mad gamble?" He explained how he had mounted up with the intention of going to the aid of the earl of Surrey, where Robert was, and how the last minute change-of-plan was unavoidable. She regarded him with horror. "All those with King Richard were killed!"

"Not so," declared Laurence, "though the slaughter among his knights was great; those who died sold themselves dearly. Some managed to get away, myself for one."

"We have scant news of Robert and what we do have is not good," said Cornelius grimly. "Surrey is taken and was wounded. He is attainted as the others."

"Attainted!" exclaimed Laurence. "On what grounds. He was fighting for his anointed king?"

Cornelius sent Anna a knowing glance and she looked sadly into the fire, avoiding Laurence's gaze. "Henry Tudor has decreed the date of the commencement of his reign as being the twenty-first of August, the day before the Battle of Bosworth."

"What, with the true king still living?"

"He has declared King Richard a traitor and all those who fought with him, seeing as he claims to have been king before the battle."

Laurence stared at them, lost for words.

"Yes, said Cornelius. Now we know the kind of man we are dealing with, though even I cannot believe such calumny. No man will ever again be able to fight for his true anointed king without the threat of treason hanging over him should he find himself on the losing side." Laurence almost choked on his anger.

"On my way here after the battle, I tried to console myself with the thought that, as a native Breton, the throne of England is not my concern. I came to England at first prepared to serve whoever was king and my own liege is duke Francis the second of Brittany. Now, having married and lived amongst you English I cannot in conscience contemplate serving the Tudor. He is a caitiff that feared to fight for his crown, letting others win it for him. His previous plotting was mostly done for him by his accursed mother and his uncle Jasper. The three of them had been attainted by King Richard for high treason and treason is the method they have used to steal his crown." He jumped to his feet and clenched his fists. "Well let him try and keep it. I predict he will not live long!"

"Henry Tudor is in accord with you there," smiled Cornelius, "when you say he will not live long. He has appointed a yeoman guard two-hundred strong to protect his body so if you are thinking of attacking him you will have a fight on your hands."

Laurence stamped about the room, twisting his face in a rage, his emotions churning with a mixture of disgust and frustration. It was, strangely, Mother Malkin who calmed him. She had been sitting quietly listening to them when she got to her feet and took Laurence by the hand. He drew it back, startled at her move, fearing she might be casting a spell over him. Perhaps she was, for after a moment he took her hand and patted it comfortingly, reassuring her he had come back to himself.

"Having learned of this some days ago, we have come to terms with it, but I can assure you we feel the same as you," said Cornelius placatingly. "The man is a coward and devoid of honour. Such as he are hard to dislodge because he surrounds himself with those who do his dirty-work for him, as we have seen. We must not expect anything more of him."

"When I think of the courts of King Edward and King Richard," Laurence reflected. "In both cases the monarch was approachable by his nobles, indeed both kings walked comfortably among them. It is the same in Brittany."

"It has always been so, except when a monarch loses the trust of his people."

"But this is the first in England who doesn't have it to begin with," snorted Anna.

"A country having a frightened monarch with a dubious claim at its head will not be a happy land, that is certain," lamented Cornelius.

"There is nothing for it but to look to our own safety," said Laurence coldly, "but first we must find Robert. This is the second time he has been lost and both the fault of the Tudor, damn him to hell."

"Philip too," whispered Anna. "He is probably safe at Cambridge for now, but if anything should be said against any of us, how long might that remain so?"

"I am reluctant to say it but at some point we must make some kind of peace with the Tudor," growled Cornelius. "He is king now, at least for the moment, and if we display less than complete acceptance of his rule we will be destroyed."

"When such as the earl of Northumberland capitulate without even making a single move to help his king, then where does that leave the rest of us?" stated Anna. "In a way he is worse than the Stanley's who have always been vacillators when it comes to positive commitment, though it must be admitted petty jealousy and self-seeking are his ruling passions too."

"I do not have to accept Tudor," snapped Laurence furiously. "What you say is true and there were many at King Richard's court who fit your description, but none dealt with him as treacherously as Northumberland. As for me, I owe my allegiance to duke Francis and no other."

182

Cornelius gave an impatient grunt. "Tudor is unlikely to give that much consideration seeing as you actually fought with King Richard rather than remain with the other armourers."

"That would have been no guarantee of safety," said Anna ruefully. "Sir William Catesby remained with King Richard's camp, having spared the life of lord Strange then throwing himself at the Tudor's feet, and look what happened to him!"

"Catesby! What did happen to him?" Laurence could hardly contain his surprise.

"Hanged," said Anna matter-of-factly. "Two days after the battle."

"Henry Tudor's mercy extended sufficiently to allow time for him to make his will, and that was all," muttered Cornelius.

Of all those left alive after the battle, Laurence would have thought Catesby the favourite to be first to ingratiate himself with the new monarch; indeed, from what Anna said that is what he tried to do. Briefly he told them what David Morgan had said regarding Catesby. Cornelius nodded sagely at the tale, having little cause to doubt it.

"Catesby miscalculated badly there," he intoned grimly. "The idea of King Edward's children being bastards is not something that would agree with Tudor plans, it would seem."

"Or his mother's. Catesby's revelation confirmed King Richard as rightful monarch," agreed Anna. "What is more, if Tudor has parliament overturn the charge of bastardy, to let him marry Elizabeth of York and produce legitimate offspring, having a lawyer around who knows the truth is a risk not worth taking. He has already demanded that all copies of *Titulus Regius,* which Catesby put through parliament be collected and destroyed, so it is certain that is what is in his mind."

"I wonder what this means regarding the bastard Richard of York?" mused Laurence. "Tudor knows he is out there somewhere and if his sister is legitimised, then that will make him King Richard the Fourth!" His face lit up at the thought. He smashed his right fist into his left palm. "That is surely where the future lies."

"Before you get too carried away," intoned Cornelius worriedly, "remember the Tudor knows of your involvement in that particular scheme. If he finds out you live, then you are a marked man."

Anna gasped as she too realised the danger. "The very first thing Tudor did even before arriving at Westminster was to send for the earl of Warwick from Sandal Castle where he was living comfortably under the protection of King Richard. The lad now languishes in the Tower of London," she said sorrowfully. "It is not hard to work out he will be looking for prince Richard, too."

"Young Warwick stands before Richard of York. All that is required is for his attaint to be reversed, easier than overturning the material fact of bastardy, and he too may be king – another Edward!" Laurence reflected on the situation, somewhat brightened with the prospect of removing Henry Tudor from the throne. The earl of Warwick, being a full blood prince and son of the attainted duke of Clarence, though but nine years of age and simple minded, so it was said, might still revive the fortunes of the house of York.

"We must not forget John de la Pole, earl of Lincoln," put in Cornelius. "He is legally King Richard's heir though I hear he has pledged himself to the Tudor."

"For today," enthused Laurence, "just for today. I believe Lincoln has brothers, too. There is much material here. I don't fancy the Tudor's chances once the present debacle is behind us and men come to their wits."

Cornelius sat down sadly and gazed into the fire. "We must all realise that what we are saying here is now classed as high treason, speaking of the death and destruction of a sitting monarch, much as we despise the man." Laurence snorted disdainfully.

"I remember Sir Reginald Bray saying something about it. He was convinced he was loyal because he was true to his cause in spite of an opponent of his house being king. The difference is that King Richard was a full blood prince while Henry Tudor has a most dubious bloodline and no legitimate claim."

"As indeed, we might say of the late King Edward. Remember Blaybourne the archer? Edward's right was by conquest and Henry can make that his claim too." Laurence thought about this for a minute.

"It seems to me treason is a betrayal of yourself and in that I must agree with Bray's point. The problem of swearing allegiance to Henry Tudor is that he requires a denial of former loyalty as if it meant nothing, and thus distorts the moral definition of the term. His idea of loyalty becomes a mere compulsion to conform with no personal integrity involved. He does not require honourable loyalty, just the forced compliance due a bandit who happens, for the moment, to have the upper hand."

"What you are saying, and with some justification in this case, is that the Tudor idea of treason is a legal concept with no moral obligation attached to it. Thus while formerly we might have discussed Tudor's bastard line freely, today to do so is high treason."

"That is exactly what I mean. For me the Tudor is not my king so I can hardly speak treason when I pour scorn upon his house, but to accept him would betray my former loyalty and that would indeed be treason."

"While you live and earn a living in England you are honour bound not to speak against the country's monarch. You might not think to do so is treason, but it is sedition and that is just as bad. I would not like to argue the point at your trial," said Cornelius. "Such fine distinctions count for little on the gallows."

"Let us not speak of gallows," cried Anna in distress. She slumped into her chair, her face covered by her hands. Mother Malkin came to her and stroked her hair while glowering at the two men.

"Anna is right," said Cornelius sympathetically. "There are more important things to consider at this time, such as what has happened to Robert and also we must look to Philip's future welfare."

Laurence nodded in agreement and with some shame that he had let his righteous ire confound his proper duty to his own people. He recalled what his wife Joan had once said when he was kicking off at the duplicity of lord Thomas Stanley for always seeking to be on the winning side. She pointed out that lord Stanley was looking after his own interest despite who was sitting on the throne and she hoped that, given the choice that is what he, Laurence, would do if his family were at risk. It was a subdued and pensive group that sat by the fire, each pondering on what to do next and fearing the spiteful retribution of Henry Tudor.

* * *

As it turned out the problem with the whereabouts of Robert solved itself. He turned up the following day, tired, very hungry and dishevelled, but otherwise alive and unharmed. He had been brought to London with Thomas Howard, who had been stripped of his title earl of Surrey and placed under guard in the Tower of London. Robert had been with him when he was taken and thus allowed to accompany his lord as a servant with a few others.

"Were you observed coming here?" Cornelius asked Robert anxiously after the clamouring generated by the relief of his safety had died down. The youth was given a cup of ale, which he downed in one.

"I informed the Tower guard where I live in London. If I had not done so they would not have let me out."

"Quite so." Cornelius turned to Laurence who was overjoyed to have his son with him. "Perhaps they think he might lead them to you? Not many escape confinement in the Tower so easily."

The assembly fell quiet at this statement.

Might you have been followed here?" asked Laurence. Robert opened his mouth to speak.

"It matters little if he was," inserted Cornelius before the youth could say a word. "However, anyone watching can hardly know *you* are actually here seeing as Robert arrived alone. There can be little doubt that he was released purposefully. It is not difficult to work out that the Tudor, knowing of your involvement with the removal of prince Richard of York, would wish to have you under lock and key. He may not be certain you know the actual location of the prince, but he suspects you do and there are those in the Tower who could soon discover your secrets for him."

Laurence shrugged this statement off, but Cornelius shook his head in despair, knowing only too well that bravado was a quality soon disposed of when a prisoner was alone in a cell with the Tower torturers.

"You are a man with too many encumbrances to proclaim such disdain," he said morosely. "You have a son here, and there is Philip, then Anna; and am I too conceited to believe myself also? Should any of us be threatened with such horrors as the Tower can produce, would that cause you to tell all you know, and without the executioner so much as waving a glowing bar of iron in your face?"

"You are so fond of telling us you are Breton and therefore not tied in loyalty to the English throne," cried Anna. "So would you tell Tudor where the bastard prince is hidden to save any of us, seeing as his uncle, the true king is slain? What does a bastard prince matter anyway? Where does your loyalty lie? Which of these two treasons would you choose?"

Laurence gave a long and anguished cry and slumped in his chair, his face in his hands. Preoccupied with getting free of the battlefield, he had not given time to ponder on the need to adapt to the new reign; he was still attached firmly to the former. Cornelius and Anna had clearly thought on this. Their previous attachment to the house of York was problematic; much depended on whether the Tudor could hang on to what he had gained, and seeing as the crown he had won was not due to his own efforts, it was far from certain. This being so it was likely Henry's apprehension and desperation would lead to severe measures against any that threatened him. Laurence, and Cornelius, with their intimate knowledge of King Richard's clandestine business were in great peril along with those associated with them.

I cannot come to terms with Tudor as easily as you think," mumbled Laurence, staring into the fire. "It would be a simple matter to approach him directly and volunteer the information he wants, but there is a very good reason why that would be fatal."

"Which is?" queried Cornelius, a worried frown creasing his face.

"Because I tried to kill him!"

He looked up at them as each gasped aloud and stood stricken with apprehension. He explained his attack on Henry Tudor at the point where King Richard had been slain. He was the only one there wearing a barbute helm – it had almost become his trademark and someone was bound to have identified the Achilles who had raised his war axe against Tudor and come so close to striking him down. Also he was a witness to Tudor's cowardice, something else that would mark him down for death.

Silence descended on the room. The only sound was the crackling of logs alight with flames flickering in the fireplace, and the draught in the chimney.

"I think we must get clear of London," said Cornelius quietly after a moment's reflection. "In fact, it would be better if we evacuated England altogether, at least for a time."

"If we can get to Brittany, we would be safe," said Laurence encouragingly. "I have money there, in the care of my father. There is more at Gloucester, in the vault of the abbey church."

"You can forget that at Gloucester for the moment," murmured Cornelius. "You can be sure Tudor's agents will know of it and be waiting should you be foolish, or greedy enough to try to remove it. As it happens, I too have money in Brittany, at the house of my friend, you have already met him, Gerard Levoir." Laurence remembered well the man and in particular his housekeeper, Eloise. "He is a banker, among other things, and entirely to be trusted."

"Then all that remains is to get out of England," said Laurence. "It means leaving all we have here behind and starting afresh, but that is better than the alternative. Tudor's agents will probably confiscate our property in any case and with our lives forfeit too."

"Were it that simple," whispered Anna, looking under lowered eyelids at Mother Malkin. "We have one here dependent on us."

The old crone picked up on her meaning almost as if she had been expecting it.

"I will go to Peter Otteler," she stated emphatically. "He has a place for me and the dog too." Anna fixed her eyes upon the old woman, tears forming in her eyes. Mother Malkin stood determined and upright, her chin thrust out resolutely. Laurence, for the first time, saw the inherent kindness in the old woman and all his former fears of her necromantic powers faded to be replaced by a certain shamefacedness.

"At least you would be safe there," Anna said pensively. "Beast will be an asset too, because Peter Otteler is blind and that boy he has with him is often beaten by the local youth. How useful to have a guard with a keen pair of eyes. Peter regularly has some of his pots stolen by vagabond boys."

Cornelius grunted in agreement. "We can get Mother clear without a problem. The hound follows her everywhere as it is and nobody will dare molest her when she goes on her way. She will be followed, though, we can be sure of that and perhaps we should coordinate our own departure with hers in the hope that she will draw off at least one of our watchers."

"You can be sure you will not get far, even if you manage to get out unobserved, and that is most unlikely," said Laurence coldly. "There is just a small chance of a way out. Tudor is after me and if I appear suddenly somewhere away from here that is sure to draw all attention to me and away from you. If you can arrange passage out of England for yourself Cornelius, with Anna and Robert I can find my own way."

"Providing you can escape the Tudor," cried Anna, "and that might prove difficult, if not impossible once it is discovered you live."

"It is certain none of us can get away if I am included in your company," returned Laurence with disarming practicality. "On the other hand, if I am assured you three are safe, then I can move without encumbrance. It is our only option."

"The only loose end is Philip," mused Cornelius. Anna jerked her head around and looked at him fondly, concern for her son registering in her face. "I can leave money with doctor Maddison for his continuing education and once out of England I can always send more. He is not connected with Laurence and should be safe at Cambridge as long as he immerses himself in his studies and keeps his head down." Laurence and Anna exchanged covert glances at this remark.

"It is a good plan," stated Laurence. Anna hung her head morosely, accepting that this was the best way out of their predicament, probably the only way.

"So we have a plan," growled Laurence. "What we need now is a way of executing it. Luckily nobody knows I am here, but once I show myself outside all hell is likely to break loose and this house will be infiltrated and guarded. There will be no escape for you then. I need to appear suddenly and well away from here so the watchers will instinctively chase off after me, thus giving you the chance to escape."

"Then we need to think of a way to get you out unobserved," said Cornelius.

"You need not concern yourself with me," put in Robert suddenly. "I shall return to the earl of Surrey's service, though he is just plain Sir Thomas Howard now."

"What, in the Tower of London?" snapped Laurence in shock.

"He is lodged there as comfortably as anywhere," replied Robert. "There are several of us with him and the expectation is we shall be released once King Henry has confidently established himself."

"In spite of the earl being attainted? He is like to lose his head I should think." Laurence looked at his son with concern.

"Everyone who fought for King Richard was attainted," said Robert. "It was a device merely. The king cannot execute them all; he needs the nobles if he is to secure his throne and lord Thomas has already made a declaration of loyalty to him."

"In spite of his father John Howard having died fighting the Tudor?"

"Others have done the same, the earl of Northumberland chief amongst them. My lord Thomas is a realist. There is no other way at the moment. In any case, what is there for me in Brittany other than exile."

"You are my son," growled Laurence. "You will have a place at the forge when I set one up."

Robert shook his head. "I am an English soldier, father. That is where my future lies and I was well placed to become a squire before the battle. The lord Thomas will have need of loyal retainers when he is freed and one day he might even get his lands back."

"Well I hear the earl of Oxford is installed at Framlingham Castle," interrupted Cornelius who had been listening with equal concern. "Thomas Howard must not expect to return there." He turned to Laurence and spoke softly. "There is some sense in what the boy says. If we are taken together then it will be the death of us all. He has a much better chance with the followers of Thomas Howard than with us. Once things calm down and we can see more clearly, then he might return to us."

Laurence nodded, the apothecary was correct. Each of them had a better chance acting as individuals than together. He looked grimly at Robert. The boy had grown strong in the service of the defunct duke of Norfolk. Approaching his fourteenth year he was already as tall as his father, though somewhat leaner. He had his mother's eyes - black just as the apothecary, her father; also something of her independence of thought. A faint hint of hair was appearing on his chin and soon he might even cultivate a short beard. His declaration of intent was brave of him and Laurence felt a thrill of pride that ran as a silver vein through his blood and stirred his heart.

Robert smiled at his father and took a slim chain from around his neck. "Here, father, it is best you take this back. It has done its job for me, now you need its protection more than I." Laurence took it and fingered the silver reliquary suspended from the chain. He made the sign before slipping it over his head and tucking it into his doublet.

Laurence addressed Cornelius. "How will you and Anna get away?"

"Don't worry about us. I have my route already set out. In my business it is always prudent to have an escape plan. We shall leave by the river and take ship for France. From there we will take another for Brittany. When *you* get there, make your way to the house of Gerard Levoir at St. Malo; he will inform you as to where we are. As for you, try for Pembroke. I shall write down for you the names of three Breton vessels that regularly call there and whose captains are known to me. Give my name and discretion will be assured, though there will be a price to pay, of course."

Laurence smiled as he thought on the choice of departure. Tenby, just a few miles from Pembroke was where Henry Tudor and his uncle Jasper had fled England and into exile back in fourteen seventy-one. It had been one of Cornelius' captains that had taken them to Brittany rather than their preferred destination of France, citing contrary winds as his excuse.

"Talking of money, I shall need a full purse and I would like to escape with as much of my own as I can."

"That is sensible," agreed Cornelius. "You have enough lodged here with me to serve your needs. I would advise that you have two purses – one you show when making a purchase, and another hidden with the bulk of your coin. Most men have a good eye for judging the contents of a purse and tend to adjust their price accordingly. Make sure your visible one is not too heavy."

"All that remains is to work out how I am to leave here undetected," said Laurence tugging at his beard.

It might not be too difficult," replied Cornelius with a knowing chuckle. "You must climb into the rafters and work your way along. Several of the houses in this street join together at the roof, separated merely by thin wattle panels. One of these in this house can be pulled away letting you get next door. It is some time since I climbed up there myself," he smiled, "but you will see how to get through. You will have to quietly cut out some of the panels in the houses further along and hopefully any slight noise you make will be put down to rats. When you get to the end gable you will find the wattle is daubed and more substantial, being the outer wall. However, this can be removed because there is a great beam there extending into the lane, which is used as support for winching grain into the upper floor of the corn merchant below. They remove this panel when securing the winch and it is held in place by wedges. That is your way out."

"It is still near this house and the lane is likely a lurking place for any watchers," mused Laurence.

"I agree. You will have to judge the best time to get out. All that entails is slipping a rope around the hoist beam and climbing down it. Try and get it free, if you can so nobody will know you got out there. We shall try and time things to coincide with Robert's return to the Tower and Mother Malkin's departure for Peter Otteler's house. They will take difference directions, which should draw off any close observers sufficiently for you to get away unobserved. There is unlikely to be more than two seeing as Tudor's spies are unaware of where you are as yet."

"What time shall we set?"

"I suggest the bells for prime should be our signal," said Cornelius. "Anyone watching will be weary at that time in the morning and glad of the chance to move off after Robert and Mother Malkin. We shall bestir ourselves at matins so there is some activity here to waken their suspicions, then go when prime is rung."

Laurence still tugged at his beard in thought. "I will need a horse to get clear of London," he mused. "I wonder how that might be arranged?"

"There be stablin' at Peter Otteler's," put in Mother Malkin, "tho' he has but an ass."

"Then leave that to me. I shall see there is a horse and tackle there by the morrow. I think we must revise our plan. Mother – you must leave this afternoon. Anyone following you will have returned once they see you are staying with the blind potter."

"I mun gather mi two-thri things before I go." The old woman trotted off to her closet.

Laurence felt a strange sadness wash over him as he contemplated the departure of the old woman. He was still unsure of her powers with regard to the teachings of Holy Church, and her healing skills were a mystery to him. He watched her now as she bustled about in the closet where she slept, muttering to herself as she searched for the few things she had in the world and stuffing them into a sack. Anna was watching her too, her face a picture of concern and love for the woman who had been her companion on the great march with King Edward all those years ago. It seemed everyone had much regard for Mother Malkin other than he. Robert was fond of her but not overly, as his father. Philip was closest to her, learning from her the healing properties of the plants in the garden and how to make them into potent medicines. Cornelius had her make up his recipes for his clients and even the great dog Beast followed her everywhere. Peter Otteler, too, appreciated her and would be pleased to have her with him. A fleeting thought that she might have bewitched them all, the residue of a doctrine taught to him from birth, faded to shame that he hadn't treated her more kindly. Anna hurried over to help her and finally, when she was ready placed a good woollen cloak around her shoulders.

Mother Malkin said her goodbyes to each of them in turn. Anna, of course, was crying, but that was her way and expected. The moisture in the eyes of Cornelius Quirke was harder to explain, as was the lump that he, Laurence, was feeling in his throat. The old woman came to him last of all and turning her face up, looked boldly into his eyes. What was written in her wizened face he could not fathom except he thought he could see a deep wisdom in her eyes as if he was gazing into mystic crystals. He resisted the impulse to sign himself and instead took her hands in his and gave them a gentle squeeze.

"All will be well," she whispered, or at least he thought she had. The words somehow came into his head and he was not sure if the old woman's lips had actually moved. She withdrew her hands and beckoned to the great hound, which lay in the rushes attentively watching them as if it knew something was afoot. Beast jumped to his feet and padded over to her. She took the collar Laurence had made, leather with iron spikes and fastened it around his neck. Laurence smiled to himself. It would be a brave man that attempted to accost Mother Malkin accompanied thus. Picking up her bundle she went with Anna and the hound into the outer shop. There was a clinking of a door latch, a few whispered endearments and then the closing of the street door.

When Anna returned they stood in silence for a while. The house seemed to have lost a presence and Laurence found, rather than asking protection against the evil eye, his lips formed instead a prayer to the Holy Virgin for Mother Malkin.

"Did you see anyone follow?" asked Cornelius.

"There was a fellow leaning by a post who slouched off after her," Anna replied. "I watched him through a chink before I closed the door."

"The hardest part of our plan comes after Robert has left us," growled Cornelius. "When you, Laurence, reveal yourself there will be a pursuit for sure, but much depends on what the Tudor agents expect to do with us. Once it is realised you are no longer on your way to us here, it is likely we shall be taken, being no longer useful as bait. How you are to reveal yourself then get clean away is going to be difficult enough as it is. For a short time attention will be all on you. That is when we must leave, but how to time it so we act together when we will have no idea where you are?"

"I have thought on this," replied Laurence. "You may leave the details to me but disclosure will be around the time vespers is rung tomorrow. News will reach London probably around the bell for matins. You should leave then."

"I fear for you," cried Anna. "What if you are taken? That will surely follow when you reveal yourself."

Laurence held up his hand to silence her. "I shall ride south from London, then after I am sure to have been detected, I will strike north then west and make for Wales. Hopefully I can lose myself in the country.

"But how will you reveal yourself without being immediately taken up?"

"With the help of God," came the enigmatic reply.

Clearly trusting that Laurence had a workable scheme, Cornelius nodded his head and looked to Robert. "Ready yourself for the morning, lad," he intoned. "I am away now to see a client. We must appear to be working as normal." With that the apothecary put on his cloak and picked up a wallet he used to convey his simples and other cures. "Also I have a horse to procure."

* * *

It was with a heavy heart that Laurence rode well clear of Windsor. He thought of his friends there now, Peter Heap and Maud Mudd working for Henry Tudor. He had thought he might go to the chapel of the Virgin at Eton, but considered that too populated. His escape from the apothecary's shop had gone as planned. He took leave of Robert, giving him a father's blessing. Anna wept, of course, and leaving her behind with Cornelius was almost as much as he could bear. He would have held and kissed her but had to be content with the touch of a soft hand and a winsome smile. When he arrived at the potter's house he found his horse saddled up and ready. The beast was companionably tethered in the stable with Otteler's ass but the house was quiet except, he heard, for the whimper of a great hound behind the bolted door. He led the horse out and after leading it for a short distance; he mounted up and was soon mingling with those others who were on the road going away from the city.

So it was, as the sound of the vespers bell rang across the fields he found, to his surprise, a church not far from Eton, at Upton cum Chalvey that was dedicated to his own named patron, Saint Laurence. It was very old, obviously Norman with a square tower and built of flint and pudding stone. Part of the tower was mantled in ivy and the wind soughed in the branches of surrounding elms. He tethered his horse to a yew tree in the churchyard and hearing the chant for vespers pushed open the door and entered.

Incense hung in the air and the building was lit dimly by the few candles around the altar where half a dozen brothers stood together celebrating the sunset office. Careful not to disturb them, he settled himself into a niche by the door and, letting his eyes become accustomed to the gloom, looked around. The walls were painted with biblical themes and he noted a particular image depicting the Holy Trinity. In a niche opposite was a brightly painted statue of the patron, Saint Laurence holding firmly on to a gridiron, the symbol of his martyrdom and Laurence's own armoury mark. There were several hamlets nearby and he supposed this place served them all, it being too substantial for a single country village church. It was a good omen, almost as if God had caused him to come here.

Presently the office came to an end and the brothers trooped out through a side door to wherever their quarters were, while one stood back regarding the visitor expectantly. Laurence pushed his back off the wall and approached the priest.

"Good e'en, Father," he said bowing before the priest. "I am a traveller in need of shriving."

"Indeed, my son, you look as if you have been on the road all day." The scar on Laurence's face was more pronounced in the flickering half-light provided by candles and lent him an aspect of mystery, which was all to the good.

"I have, Father, and must rest before I press on tomorrow." He regarded the priest carefully. A lean fellow in a clean white habit, he probably had some personal status in the community. Most country priests were rather less particular both in dress and personal cleanliness. This one was rather delicate in his appearance. Hopefully this might be the kind of man he needed for his plan to work.

"We have no accommodation here for you," he said cautiously, "though I might send to find you shelter in a hayloft nearby."

"That would suit me fine," replied Laurence. "Before then I would seek to be shriven. My sins lie heavy upon me. "

"Then come and kneel with me by the Virgin and unburden yourself." The priest took him to where a statue of the Virgin stood in a niche beside the altar. There Laurence made his confession, careful to state he had been King Richard's armourer and a fugitive after the battle at Redemore, which men now called Bosworth Field. He felt tension in the man as he listened with great concentration to his tale. He told of those he had struck down in the battle and wished for expiation for the blood on his hands. He could have stayed with the armourers' tents, but elected instead to ride with the king and much guilt was upon him. He was on his way to Southampton to take ship for his home in Brittany and wished to be clear of England and the blood of battle. Passage across the narrow seas was always perilous and he would be free of his sins before he travelled onwards.

After benediction, Laurence felt better in himself and clear in his mind. The man was a priest after all and his confession would erase much guilt from his soul. He had been careful not to lie, saying he would take the road to Southampton. His omission, that he would leave the road after a while and strike west, was a small sin that would have to remain with him until another shriving, whenever that would be. If he had guessed aright, a greater burden would lie with the priest should he send to Windsor for the Tudor's men. He knew a priest could not betray the confessional but there was nothing stopping him reporting the sighting of a certain man on the road to Southampton. Priests were adept at such subtleties of conscience and he was gambling that this one, being so close to Windsor, prospered by keeping well in with whoever sat on the throne.

They stood and walked out of the church to the yew in the churchyard where Laurence had tethered his mount, a sturdy brown rouncey of the sort he had ridden when he first entered England with Edward Plantagenet and his nineteen year old brother Richard. The priest called to a man plodding his way wearily homeward from the fields. The churl came up, knuckling his forehead.

"Can you find a place for the night in your barn for this gentleman?"

"Aye, if he con pay," grunted the churl. "There be no other shelter near and the curfew be ringing." The curfew bell had indeed begun to toll the end of the day and all the good folk would be covering their fires and bedding down for the night. Laurence reached into his purse and flipped him a silver penny. Even in the dying light, they saw the churl's eyes brighten as he caught it. A half penny would have been enough to set his heart askip. Making his farewell to the priest, whom he hoped was already scheming to send to Windsor, the churl, a farmer, led him from the churchyard towards a distant glimmer where his wife had lit a rush light to welcome him home to his farm. He would be safe until morning.

The farmer had managed to extract a further half penny by offering him food and drink which caused him to recall Cornelius' dictum regarding demonstrating an over-generous purse, and so, crammed with coarse bread with surprisingly good cheese and a passable ale, left alone in the darkness Laurence slept fitfully in the upper loft of a hay barn.

He woke as the bell for matins rang in the church and, looking between the loose planks of the hayloft he noted a lay brother hurrying away on an ass in the direction of Windsor. The priest had not disappointed him after all. Soon he was down and seeing his mount well fed with corn after the disposal of another half penny, he climbed upon the beast and informing the farmer of his intended route, he set off trotting his horse slowly along the road until well out of sight, when continuing just a little further he struck across the wild country. Having ridden with kings he knew that even whole armies could pass within a few miles of each other and not be detected. With luck and depending on his long sword and dagger for defence from casual felons, he would make the Welsh marches and then on to Pembroke. Tudor's men might chase him to Southampton if they would. By the time they realised his trick he would be well gone and so, he fervently prayed, would Anna and Cornelius.

9 – Vannes 1495

The lime washed walls of the Château de l'Hermine shone splendidly in the spring sunshine, while the conical roofs over the towers glowed dark as a raven's wing. The guard at the main gate watched the horseman disinterestedly as he passed by to ride along the city walls. Clearly a nobleman of some sort, he was heading for the Porte St. Vincent, the main entry gate into Vannes, the capital of Brittany. After a brief conversation with the guard there, he passed through into the city and continued through the narrow streets until he came to the Place de Lices – a great open space, which this day displayed the stalls of local paysans busily selling their wares but when required was a tournament field. The rider looked around at the houses and shops that fringed the field until his attention was drawn to the northern quarter by the noise of hammering on metal. He dismounted and led his horse through the press of people towards the source of the noise. The acrid smell of hot metal, the occasional whiff of steam and the glow of heated charcoal furnaces told him he had found what he was seeking.

Laurence the armourer was sitting in his place by the unshuttered window where the light was good. Behind and around him were several armourers and smiths working away at hot iron. There were two furnaces, one open and the other enclosed by an iron door. Someone opened it as the traveller approached and a sulphurous cloud belched forth, lit by the blasted coals, red and yellow like a hell fire. The other open furnace glowed white as a paysan woman pumped away at a bellows while a metalworker used a pair of tongs to turn his ironwork in the fire. Somewhere at the back of the shop, a loud boiling hiss preceded a great cloud of steam as a smith plunged hot iron into a quenching tank. In baskets all around were quantities of arrowheads and other metal components of battle, while ranged against a wall were halberds, finished and fixed to their shafts.

On a bench in front of the armourer was a breastplate upon which his concentrated attention was fixed. The metal was dull, seemingly coated with some substance and the armourer was scratching at it with what looked to be an iron stylus. Beside the breastplate on the bench was a paper with a design to which he constantly referred. It had been ten years since the rider had last seen him and the grey strands in the armourer's long hair and short pointed beard were certainly more pronounced than of yore. As the shadow of the newcomer fell over him, Laurence grimaced with annoyance and sitting back, he looked up at the man. It was a few moments before he recognised him, then, with a cry he jumped to his feet.

"Eduardo Brampton! he exclaimed. "Sir Edward; *Quelle surprise* - what are you doing here at Gwened. Laurence immediately addressed him in French knowing that Breton was not one of Sir Edward's languages. Nevertheless, Brampton smiled at his use of the Breton name for the city of Vannes.

"I am here on the business of the duchess of Burgundy," came the reply. "Let us not bother with that right now. How goes it with you, my friend? I see you prosper."

The sight of the armourer prompted Brampton's remark. He was dressed in the latest Italian fashion, as fitting for a master armourer at the top of his craft. He wore an open-fronted doublet over a low-necked chemise of fine linen, gathered and trimmed with an embroidered silk band. His hose was plain brown in fine wool with a pair of incongruous sabots on his feet. His long hair came down to his shoulders and his head was adorned with a draped pointed hat having a tassel embroidered similar to the silk trimming of his chemise. Around his neck was a silvered cord, which disappeared under the front of his chemise. "I see you still have your sacred reliquary," said Brampton pointing to the cord.

Laurence laughed and withdrew a small silver reliquary. "Yes, it has served me well and I would be loath to leave it off." The armourer regarded Brampton quizzically. "You look as if a good meal and a bumper or two might serve you at this moment?"

"Indeed, master de la Halle. If you hadn't suggested it I would have taken you by the arm and led you off, except I expect you might be the one better placed to recommend a suitable tavern." Brampton grinned while loosening his cloak to drape it over his right arm. He was wearing a brown velvet doublet with sleeves buttoned to the wrist and dark green hose. A pair of black leather boots protected his feet. He was ten years older than Laurence, though subterfuge and adventure had lined his face making him look every one of his fifty-five years.

"Let me attend to your mount," said Laurence with an air of practicality. "First I must put on some different footwear. These sabots are sensible here in the forge, but tend to clatter on the boards of a tavern." He gave a little skipping dance by way of illustration before sitting down at his stool and reaching for his shoes. Presently he stood and called to a youth who was turning a barrel full of sand and mail to clean the metal links of the chain. The lad had been keeping an eye on his master, as had the others employed in the forge and hurried over.

"Garçon, take this horse to my stables and have the groom see it is rubbed down and fed. Afterwards take master Brampton's baggage to my house." He patted the bags tied either side of Brampton's saddle.

"At once, master," said the boy.

"You have your own stables?" Brampton wondered.

"I have a place with stabling for twenty horses."

"Twenty! Business must be very good?"

"Sufficient at the moment. I had the best of it during *La Guerre Folle*," Laurence snorted derisively.

"Ah, yes," said Brampton with a nod of understanding. That had been a period of conflict with France that lasted until after the old duke Francis II died. Francis was contending with France, whose policy was to annex Brittany. Duke Francis allied himself with the duc d'Orleans, King Charles' brother who also had designs on the French throne. There was a protracted war, the end of which found Francis capitulating and conceding vassalage to King Charles. Then duke Francis accidentally fell from his horse and died from his injuries. His daughter and only heir Anne succeeded him but was forced by treaty to marry Charles VIII of France. Thus Brittany was now a province of France.

The garçon led Brampton's horse away and after Laurence had given some orders to his forge master, led him off through the streets of the city.

"You will lodge with me, of course," said Laurence as they walked along.

"I should be most glad to do so," replied Brampton.

"Here we are," said Laurence, stopping outside the door of a tavern. "Le Rose Brave. This is my house."

"A tavern!" ejaculated Brampton.

"And why not?" replied Laurence with a smile at his lips. "Can you think of a better abode for a man who lives alone?"

Brampton and Laurence entered a large room where a series of tables and benches were crammed with patrons noisily drinking wine and eating from steaming platters while conducting business or just conversing with each other. In the centre a grand staircase indicated the way to the upper floors where patrons could take a bed for the night and conduct themselves as they would. At the far end a great stone fireplace stood ready piled with wood, which as the weather was warm, remained unlit. A *servir fille* hurried over as soon as she spotted Laurence.

"Good day master," she said, dipping him a curtsey. "And you good sir." Brampton swept her a gallant bow. "I will let missus know you are here."

"Merci, Giselle. I shall take my usual table." The girl skipped away while Laurence showed Brampton to a table in a quiet corner behind a screen and protected by a woven cord across to discourage casual entry by the denizens of the place. They had barely seated themselves when a woman bustled over to them.

"Good den, master Laurence," she said in accents that betrayed French was not her native language. She carried a flask of wine and two silver goblets that she placed on the table. "A flask of Rhenish as usual. Is that agreeable to the other lord?"

"It is," laughed Brampton. "Do I detect an English accent somewhere?" The woman flushed. She was dark and stout with a pleasant mien that proclaimed good cheer, a decided attribute to her trade.

"Sir Edward Brampton, may I present madam Gurden Fisher," put in Laurence before the woman could answer. "Her husband is patron here and both are long time friends of mine."

"That we are, sir," gushed Gurden, reverting to English. "John is out buying vittles in the market, but he will be along soon."

"I am pleased to make your acquaintance, madam Fisher," said Brampton, studying her with some interest.

"Sir Edward is hungry, having had a trying journey. What have you to tempt him, though I think he will not take much persuading?"

"Game pie. It is just out of the oven and already in demand. I shall cut you the first portions."

"I can recommend mistress Fisher's game pie," grinned Laurence.

"Then that is good enough for me," enthused Brampton.

When Gurden had hurried away Brampton sat back in his seat and regarded Laurence inscrutably. "I see your contacts with England are not entirely broken?"

"Gurden Fisher, you mean. It is a long tale. John Fisher, a fellow armourer and her husband, was my steward at Gloucester where I had my forge when Richard the Third was king. They also had a tavern, which they ran together. When Henry Tudor came to the throne of England he began by persecuting the general population with taxes. He has no particular empathy with the English people

201

and sees them as a source of income merely. John and Gurden were targeted, particularly because of their connection to me. As you know, Henry Tudor was keen to get hold of me and when it was discovered I had got out of England, his spite filtered down to his minions. The result was John and Gurden gathered together what wealth they could and fled here to Brittany. John and I bought a half share in this place and here we are." Laurence spread his arms as if that was all the explanation that was required.

"Your family reside at Nantes, I thought. What brought you here to Vannes?"

"Expediency, that is all, and the wars we were engaged in at the time. We in Brittany have our troubles too. My brother Robert operates the business at Nantes with my father who is now in his dotage. It was considered best for the family to have business interests in two locations and in truth, I did not want to tempt rivalry between myself and Robert."

"A sensible solution. The Italians work that way, setting up individual businesses in separate places but within the same family."

"I know something of what you have been doing since we last met." Laurence informed him. "All of Europe has taken interest and as for myself, a certain delight in some of it."

"Oh, I married again – my wife is Doña Caterina de Bahamonde," said Brampton as if he hadn't heard. "You know, I think, that King Henry, who also took from me my governorship of Guernsey, confiscated the property left to me by my first wife in England. I have had better fortune since."

"I am pleased to say I know of the Doña Caterina," said Laurence bringing the conversation back to Brampton's wife. "She had in her charge a certain prince who has been tormenting the King of England for some years." Laurence's eyes twinkled mischievously.

Brampton grinned at him, his eyes flickering over his face as if looking for something. "Ah, yes. I was in l'*Entre Deux* when I picked up the Prince and brought him to Portugal where my wife Caterina took him as a page. Henry Tudor was getting too close to him at Tournai and his cover identity was becoming fragile. He calls him Perkin Warbeck in accord with the false identity he was given. You know I am now a citizen of Portugal once more?" Brampton's habit of jumping topics was disconcerting and Laurence began wondering about his sudden presence in Brittany. He knew that in King Edward's early days Brampton had left his native Portugal under something of a cloud and it was rumoured murder had something to do with it.

"So I have heard and haven't you made your peace with the English king?"

"You speak, no doubt, of the accommodation I provided at Lisbon for Henry Tudor's ambassadors to the court of Don João II. I am on the Royal Council of Portugal, you know. That was six years ago now. The ambassadors were so pleased with my hospitality that their report encouraged King Henry to issue me with a pardon."

"Given the involvement of you and your wife with the prince, is it not strange that King Henry favoured you in that way?" Laurence lowered his eyebrows with suspicion. He knew Edward Brampton to be an adventurer and somewhat economical with his fidelity. He had grown wealthy with trading interests in Portugal, Burgundy and the surrounding regions. He was all things to all men and would not scruple to seek an understanding with the English crown if it furthered his business there.

"*The Merchant of the Ruby* has moved away since then," he replied laconically. "He is now abroad in the world and identified as Richard of York, so I could no longer be of use to the king; and old loyalties die hard." Brampton sighed as if deeply concerned.

Laurence noted Brampton's mention of the code name that the prince's supporters used when referring to Richard of York. Most of the monarchies in Europe recognised the young man as such and once having met him had no doubt as to whom he really was. Laurence, of course, being complicit in getting him out of the Tower of London and to safety at Tournai, needed no such convincing. Two platters of game pie arrived at that moment, brought by Gurden herself. The *servir fille* appeared also and placed two finger bowls on their table.

"This pie would be served with ale in England," observed Laurence, "and I must admit they have the right idea, though once I would not have believed I could admit to that."

"Variety provokes an appetite that is nurtured on adventure," remarked Brampton.

"John has just returned from market," said Gurden, beckoning to the *servir fille* to place a bowl of manchet bread before them. "He will drink only ale so I must brew some here, though there is not much call for it."

"We shall continue with this fine Rhenish," said Laurence raising his goblet while Gurden filled it for him. She did the same for Brampton. The two men took out their daggers and speared the morsels in the pie.

"When you have eaten John is keen to join you for any news you might have." Gurden looked at Brampton then, having shooed the serving girl away, left them to their meal. Brampton regarded Laurence with a little concern.

"Don't worry about John. He is not one for idle gossip but misses his homeland and still remains faithful to the house of York." This seemed to satisfy Brampton who shrugged and set to his platter with enthusiasm. "You mentioned you are here in Brittany in the service of her grace the duchess of Burgundy?"

"That's right, among other things," mumbled Brampton as he chewed on a morsel. "Duchess Margaret has sent me to you with a particular request." Laurence put down his dagger and scrutinised Brampton with some caution.

"Let me guess," he said jocularly after a moment. "She wishes to become another Jeanne d'Arc and needs a suit of harness." Brampton smiled to himself and continued probing the game pie with his dagger, taking particular interest in its contents.

"Your assumption she has need of armour is correct, though not, of course for herself." Brampton leaned back in his chair and looked casually up at the ceiling. Laurence too sat back, staring directly at Brampton and waited for him to elaborate. Already a thrill of apprehension had caused the hairs to rise at the back of his neck. Presently Brampton put his dagger aside and wiped his mouth with the back of his hand before turning to face Laurence. "It will be for the Merchant of the Ruby."

"Prince Richard of York!" he exclaimed.

Brampton raised his head and looked beyond the armourer into the tavern, intimating that he should lower his voice. "That is correct," he said, returning his gaze to Laurence. "The prince is at Malines with the duchess at this time, but soon will move on England. She has provided him with ships and men, though he must raise more after he lands."

"King Edward did something similar when I was with his army in 1471," stated Laurence emphatically, "but he was battle hardened. The prince is no general, I understand and those nobles who might have aided him in England are discovered and dead. Much has changed since the affair with Lambert Simnel." Laurence was referring to the events leading up to the disastrous battle of Stoke in 1489, where John de la Pole, earl of Lincoln, King Richard's heir lost his life and viscount Lovell disappeared never to be heard of again. It had been a brave attempt to restore the house of York to its rightful place. Margaret of Burgundy had been behind the planning of it too.

"Yes, an invasion of England from Ireland should have served to remove the Tudor except it was poorly armed and badly led. The nobles of Ireland have always favoured York over Lancaster. The intention then was to replace the impostor, Lambert Simnel with Edward of Warwick, who was to be rescued from the Tower of London. He is the rightful king of England, being the son and heir of King Richard's brother, George duke of Clarence."

"Strange, though, that the impostor Simnel now resides comfortably in the kitchens at Westminster by Tudor's order rather than having been dangled from a gibbet."

"I can tell you why that is," replied Brampton. "The Lambert Simnel, as you say, abiding at Westminster is not the same as he at the battle of Stoke. The impostor was killed there."

"An impostor posing as an impostor?" Laurence burst out laughing. Brampton could not help a chuckle too, while casting his eyes around for the presence of anyone who might be taking an interest in their conversation. Laurence had the feeling this was more from habit that immediate need.

"Henry Tudor saw an opportunity for confounding future conspiracies against his crown. The king lives in constant fear of overthrow. The man at Westminster is a creature of the Tudor. Having someone close by who can be shown to be a definite impostor is useful to parade around should a genuine claimant appear. There are several of those, but the one most likely to succeed is the nephew of duchess Margaret, Richard of York."

"Presently at Malines, you say, but presumably bound for Brittany if he wants me to make harness for him?"

"Ah, no," replied Brampton. He lifted his goblet and took a drink while regarding Laurence mysteriously over the rim. With careful deliberation he placed the goblet down. "The duchess wants you to go to Burgundy, to her palace at Malines."

"Malines! - and the duchess has specifically asked for me to go there?"

"She has," affirmed Brampton. "It is only fair to warn you she will expect you to accompany the prince in his mission to win the crown of England."

Laurence sat back in his chair, his mind frantically searching for ways to decline without causing the duchess offence. Brampton watched him, waiting for him to conclude there was no way out - he would have to go.

"I must admit, a chance to be part of a scheme to remove the Tudor from England's throne would give me a certain satisfaction," he said with a bravado he didn't feel. "However, I have little enthusiasm for a mission to England. That country has had me near hanged twice and embroidered my face with a war axe." He fingered the scar on his face, showing pale against his tanned skin. Besides, so far as I have seen all plots against Henry Tudor fail due to the reluctance of the English population to engage in further warfare which brings them no advantage in the aftermath. I think there was a deal of resistance to the Tudor in the years preceding the Battle of Stoke, especially in the northwest and also the city of York. Since then they have been ground down. Tudor is overly fond of declaring any dissidents traitor and thus depriving them of their property and often their life."

"There is truth in what you say," replied Brampton, "but there is much dissatisfaction with the Tudor, his punitive laws and excessive taxes. Why, you have one such here as your partner, so you tell me. Remember, too, the example of the earl of Northumberland."

Laurence smiled at the recollection. The earl had made instant peace with Henry Tudor after Bosworth. The new king needed him to exercise authority in the north, so an accommodation was reached. However, Henry's tax demands provoked the anger of the people there and they demanded the earl negotiate a reduction. This, the earl tried to do, but Henry refused their plea and ordered him to collect in full the taxes as instructed. There was an uprising where his own people lynched the earl. Laurence had heard it was also an opportunity to revenge Northumberland's failure to take King Richard's part at the Battle of Bosworth. Tudor's retribution had been swift and brutal. Upwards of three hundred rebels were hanged, some drawn and quartered, after the earl of Surrey put down the rebellion on Tudor's behalf.

"All this is very well," said Laurence impatiently. "What I want to know is why choose me in particular to make harness for the prince? There are others who could serve just as well. Malines, where the duchess Margaret resides, is a centre of arms manufacture in Flanders. There must be many suitable armourers there."

"It is not just a question of making harness," said Brampton quietly, looking around once more. "There are those about the prince who, while professing loyalty, we suspect cannot be entirely relied on." The thought passed through Laurence's mind that

Brampton could very well be one such, but let it lie there for the moment. "The duchess of Burgundy believes you can be trusted not to betray him and therefore, being beside him, prevent another less worthy getting close. There is also the added advantage that you and he are already acquainted."

"There is the small problem of his illegitimacy. I know the Tudor has caused the English parliament to overturn that, so he could marry his queen, Richard of York's sister and produce legitimate offspring. However, the material fact of his bastardy remains which it does not in the case of Edward of Warwick who remains a prisoner in the Tower of London, so why the sudden change of claimant?" Brampton nodded and set his lips in a hard line while he pondered upon the answer.

"It is largely a matter of who the people might be expected to follow. The reappearance of the true prince provides a potent rallying point for the English. Henry Tudor, in overturning the prince's bastardy, has made Richard of York the next in line to the throne, being the only surviving son of King Edward the Fourth. This, of course, is why Tudor is denying the prince his true identity, or that he even lives. Having discovered the false persona we invented for him while at Tournai, Tudor is simply presenting it as being the true one. He is still claiming the prince's uncle King Richard the Third murdered him. Of course, since it was Tudor's mother, along with bishop John Moreton who fabricated that tale to destroy King Richard's character, he knows too well that Prince Richard yet lives."

Laurence could see the extent of Tudor duplicity, reluctantly admiring the potency of its simplicity. "Peterkin Osbeck, or Perkin Warbeck as Henry terms him; that identity had to withstand close scrutiny to preserve the prince from his Tudor enemies and reciprocally, it seems, serves Henry Tudor just as well to obscure it now."

"Quite so," agreed Brampton, "but nothing can disguise his manner, speech, appearance and intimate knowledge of that time before he went into the Tower for protection. Everyone who has met him agrees he is the true prince Richard of York, though some might waver in accordance with their diplomatic relationship towards King Henry. It was I that took him from Tournai and placed him with my own wife where he spent some time in our household before going off with the merchant Pregent Meno, a fellow Breton of yours. Meno not only removed him further from danger, but got him away altogether when Meno took him on his several trading voyages. It was Pregent Meno who took him to Cork where he was recognised and, after some persuasion, revealed himself as the prince Richard of York come back to claim his right to the English throne. He has also presented himself at the court of France where he was treated according to his proper rank. Not only that, but the Emperor Maximilian of the Holy Roman Empire recognises him and fully supports his claim to the English throne."

"And Henry Tudor has been chasing around ever since, trying to catch him."

"Four years now and no nearer taking him," grinned Brampton. Tudor is beside himself with anxiety, desperate to bring him to heel."

"Despair and sceptred care are his and it is what he deserves. He wanted the crown of England, now he has it but lives in constant fear of losing it again."

At that moment John Fisher found them, concern written in his face. Laurence saw that something was bothering him.

"It's master Cornelius," he said, addressing Laurence after a brief nod to Brampton. "He is asking for you." Laurence jumped to his feet, his face distressed.

"I must leave you for now," he said distractedly. "Master Quirke is sick and not long for this world. I must go to him." Brampton stood and bowed his head in acknowledgement. "John, see to it that Sir Edward has all he needs and give him one of our best rooms."

"I shall," replied John, stepping back to let Laurence by. Wiping his dagger on a chunk of bread, he slipped it into the scabbard at his belt and hurried away without further ado.

* * *

Laurence, his head down, hurried through the busy, narrow streets of Vannes until he reached a modest house in a street close by the Cathedral of St. Peter. Half a dozen steps led to a stout oak door studded with iron nails. It was set into a recess with a small narrow opening to the right, covered by a grill and closed inside, but when open let those within see who was at the door. He beat upon the door with the pommel of his dagger. The side flap opened and a face peered out but instantly disappeared after seeing who was there. Internal bolts slid back and the door opened letting Laurence step inside. He was greeted by a younger version of himself, his bastard son Philip.

At twenty-four years of age he stood a couple of inches taller than his father, rather leaner than Laurence had been at that age, and now sporting a short black beard. He was dressed in a long gown of dark blue wool. Hatless, his black hair was cropped to shoulder length. Laurence wondered, looking upon him now, if he ever suspected his true paternity. Neither he, nor Anna had spoken to him of it, yet even to a casual observer, the resemblance between the two was obvious.

"How is he?" asked Laurence uneasily.

"Failing fast," came the sombre reply. "Philip, recently qualified as a physician, already had much experience in predicting when someone's final hours were nigh. Laurence, his lips set tightly and his expression carefully stoical strode through into the house and up the stairs where he knew on the floor above was the sick room. Philip followed softly behind.

He had been truthful when he had told Edward Brampton he was living in Vannes rather than provoke possible sibling rivalry with his brother at the forge in Nantes, their family home. In fact, he could have located himself anywhere in Brittany, or even in France. There was a particular reason why he had chosen Vannes; it was where Cornelius had come after his escape from England and, more significantly, because Anna was with him. She was the reason Laurence had decided to live as he did, at a tavern rather than take a house of his own. What would he do in a house, with perhaps a couple of servants and no other company? It would have served to exacerbate his loneliness and worse, his longing for Anna, the wife of his erstwhile father-in-law, Cornelius Quirke. *Le Rose Brave* was always full of chatter with friendly company on hand to drive away what might otherwise turn to melancholia.

He was wealthy now, and his reputation for forming the finest armour had brought him plenty of business. Brittany had been in conflict for years, both internally and with its neighbour France. That had quietened down for the time being and recently his forge had concentrated on more mundane harness and weaponry, leaving Laurence with little to satisfy his penchant for high craftsmanship. It was not any better at Nantes. When duke Francis died his father lost his most influential patron and those nobles of France who thronged the Breton court of his daughter, Anne of Brittany, had their own favoured armourers. There too, Simon and Robert de la Halle concentrated more on common weaponry than fine harness. There was not enough work for another artisan armourer at Nantes so the choice of Vannes had been both sensible and compulsive.

As he approached the door to the sick room, it opened and Anna, who had heard their familiar footsteps, stood there her face showing her distress. She was thicker around the waist than when she and Cornelius fled England ten years ago, yet she had retained her intrinsic attractiveness. Her fair hair was long, smoothed over her ears and pulled back into a braid. She wore a pale blue woollen gown with tied-on sleeves where the white chemise beneath was pulled out in puffs between the ribbon ties. He fancied she stood as a summer sky where puff clouds of white drifted across the blue of heaven. Pushing this idea away, he stood in front of her and gazed down into her eyes with real concern.

"He wishes to talk with you, Laurence," she whispered. "I shall leave you together. I fear it will not be long now and the priest is sent for." Clearly fighting to maintain her dignity, her voice trembled as she spoke. She turned aside to let him enter the room, then left and quietly closed the door.

Cornelius Quirke was lying in bed, his head turned towards Laurence having heard Anna speak his name. His beard was completely white, as was his hair, which had been carefully combed giving him a neat appearance that belied the truth of his condition. His arms lay over the covers, his hands and fingers wasted thin with the veins showing blue through paper-thin skin. A small window had the shutters open letting air and light into the room. Anna had placed a bowl of primroses by the bed to bring spring cheer to the chamber. There was a flask of water and a drinking bowl too. Cornelius feebly flapped a hand, acknowledging Laurence's presence while a beatific smile came to his lips.

He sat on a stool that had been placed beside the bed. Laurence patted the withered hand nearest to him, finding it difficult to think what to say to the dying apothecary. Cornelius helped him out by speaking first in a faint but yet clear voice.

"I wanted to say something to you before I go," he whispered. Laurence opened his mouth pretending politely to confound this statement but Cornelius fluttered his hand indicating he should remain silent. "First, I want you to take care of Anna. She is well provided for but in need of protection, especially as she is not a native of this place and cannot easily return to England." Laurence nodded and smiled his agreement. He had already determined on this course anyway but was loath to say so. "Philip has his own trade now and set to be a physician in England. Neither of us need worry unduly about him and I am grateful he has come here to tend me in my last days. I have left some money for him to establish himself wherever he wishes." The old apothecary suddenly became short of breath and began gasping causing Laurence some alarm. Laurence was just about to get to his feet and summon Anna when he calmed and after taking a couple of deep breaths began breathing normally again. "I fear for Robert. His chosen life as a soldier is not one I would have him take, but the world being as it is may not be any more hazardous than another occupation. I know you will provide for him should he need help. He is all we have now of Joan and it is my fervent wish he should marry and bring us children to continue our line."

"That is my wish, too," said Laurence quietly.

"I know Robert is with Thomas Howard who has made his peace with the Tudor. You may be tempted to dispute with him, past circumstances being what they are, but do not let anything separate you. Our family blood is just as precious as that of the nobility and comes before all else."

"If I have learned nothing else in these latter years, that is one lesson I have taken to heart, sir."

Cornelius paused for a moment and turned his head to look upwards. Presently he turned his face to Laurence, his eyes deep and black.

"One thing more then I am done," he gasped. "I know of your feelings for Anna. I always have done. It is the reason I asked her to marry me – to remove temptation from your path."

"Sir, I, I . . ." Laurence stammered his mind a mass of confusion.

"I know you would not have intended to betray Joan and I am aware how you loved her, but men are men and women are women. I simply reinforced your natural loyalty to her by marrying Anna and removing any need for her care that might have confused you. When I am gone you are both free and whatever you decide together, be assured you have my most profound blessing." Cornelius, exhausted by this outpouring sighed and seemed to shrink further into his pillows. Laurence, unable to speak and fighting back tears got to his feet and leaning towards the old man, kissed him on his forehead. Worried that Cornelius might expire at any moment he went and opened the door. Anna and Philip bustled into the room and went over to the bed. A priest was with them bringing the sacraments for extreme unction. They left the room again while the priest performed the last rites, then re-entered after he had heard the apothecary's deathbed confession.

When they returned to the bed, Cornelius was lying on his back, face upwards, his eyes closed. Slowly he opened them and turned his head to let his gaze fall on Laurence and Anna with Philip behind. He smiled gently while the light in his eyes faded slowly from shining black to dullness and his breathing stopped. Anna gave a cry and threw herself over his body while Laurence sat by the bed, he and Anna united in their grief. Philip took his place next to his mother, tenderly stroking her face and dabbing at her tears with a kerchief. A gentle breeze wafted through the open window and somewhere outside the sound of birdsong lilted as if sensing something joyous had just occurred.

* * *

"You should not go!" cried Anna, who then put her hand to her mouth aghast at her presumption. Laurence smiled at her as if her declaration was her right rather than a peremptory outburst. John Fisher, who was sitting with them both in the reserved portion of the *Le Rose Brave*, put his hands up in an orant display that urged calm.

"I cannot see that you have much in the way of an alternative," he intoned to Laurence but with a sideways glance at Anna. "You are a king's armourer, not a mere artisan, and the duchess Margaret of Burgundy is allied in this circumstance with the Holy Roman Emperor, Maximilian who is an enthusiastic promoter of prince Richard of York. If you fail to respond to her request then you are finished and likely to lose much, if not all of your reputation. A king's armourer must always accompany his king otherwise what is he?"

John grimaced and, flapping his hands expansively fell silent as Laurence considered his words. He was right, of course. When a king, or in this case a claimant to kingship, goes into battle he must have his personal armourer close to tend to his harness. Not only in battle but, more particularly, at the courtly tourney where he must display himself in magnificent array and only the services of a master armourer would do then.

"I had thought to remain here in my homeland, that is all," sighed Laurence, "but you are right, I must go into Flanders and from there to England. It seems my fate is bound to that land. Perhaps the tie that binds me is my mother's who was of that race."

"There have been others," said John. "Your wife Joan, Cornelius her father, your sons and one other." He inclined his head to one side to where Anna sat, her hands clasped together in desolate confusion.

At the sight of her, his heart softened and he at once feared for her. His promise of care to Cornelius came upon him and though, should he have remained at his forge here in Vannes he would have fulfilled his vow, the command from the duchess to repair to Flanders, *l'entre deux*, complicated matters in that respect.

"There is a simple solution to at least one of your problems," said Gurden who had come over and heard the last few words. "It is one that gives me some personal satisfaction to suggest and the chance to return to you a great favour - take Anna to wife!" She grinned at him cheekily, one eyebrow lifted archly, knowing that it was Laurence who had inveigled John into marrying *her* back at their inn at Gloucester. Anna and Laurence snapped their heads around to look at each other, both showing surprise and each wondering if the other had really not thought on it also. It seemed they had for a smile of quiet understanding passed between them. "Apparently my suggestion has found some favour with you both," gushed Gurden with a chuckle.

John Fisher jumped to his feet, laughing uproariously and slapped Laurence on the back. "Ha, the engineer hoist with his own petard," he cried joyously, "though not, I think much dismayed?" Laurence was amused by John's metaphor seeing as a petard was an explosive device used to blast down barricades. "Furthermore, as your wife she could travel along with you, at least as far as the court of Burgundy."

"Yes, and she would need clothing fit for the purpose," added Gurden, who looked delightedly at Anna.

"This is going too fast," inserted Laurence. "I have yet to discover whether Anna might consent to be my wife?"

Gurden snorted in derisive amusement while John simply wrung his hands in mock frustration.

"The idea has some merit," said Anna, a quiet smile at her lips. She had been worried on discovering the purpose of Edward Brampton's mission to recruit the services of Laurence. Though she had good friends in Gurden and John Fisher, yet she was a foreigner to the people of Brittany and the widow of an English apothecary had little rapport with the citizens of Vannes. The thought of his going away, possibly for years had been more than she could bear. Her heart was leaping for joy now that Gurden had precipitated matters between her and Laurence. She knew of his feeling towards her and his reaction had confirmed that he needed her too. She pondered on her present position. Circumstances were so different than when they first met. Then she had been the stepdaughter of a crude alehouse owner with no property of her own and no prospects other than a life of servitude, prostitution and a descent into premature ageing followed by a squalid death. Now she possessed money and a small property with a maid of her own and decent clothes to wear.

Laurence approached her and took her hands in his. "It is true I have need of a wife," he said with a twinkle in his eye, and fate has conspired to continually thrust us together, so who am I to argue with that?" He leaned forward and whispered in her ear. "Once we complete the formalities we shall be wed. Consummation has already taken place so we are part way there as it is, yet I think it well to be sure at the first opportunity."

She laughed coquettishly and gave him a playful slap. "Yes, we must observe the rules and make sure we miss nothing out. I would not have you try to get out of it once you have tired of me."

"It is decided," shouted John. "This calls for a celebration." Gurden kissed Laurence on the cheek then embraced Anna while John capered about, lost in delight and deceiving himself that all had been his idea rather than Gurden's.

Anna tugged at Laurence's sleeve, indicating she wished to take him privately to one side. "We have some details to work out," she told him firmly, her face set in determination. "What are we to do about Philip?" This was a delicate question and Laurence took her by the arm to steer her away from the company who, sensing the newly pledged couple had something to say to each other, diplomatically went their separate ways, conveniently serving the needs of the customers at the inn.

"I wonder," Anna began, "how this affects our son? Philip is your eldest and until now a bastard with no claim upon you." She was clearly worried about this question, being a woman with but one child to think of. Women were ever thus and the image of Margaret Beaufort came to Laurence's mind.

"Indeed, seeing as Philip was born while you were the wife of Barrat Thorne, and he acknowledged him as his son, not knowing his true parentage, of course, he is legally no bastard but neither is he in law none of mine. I think that in Common Law if someone is born in wedlock then that person is no bastard. We could try the issue according to Canon Law but in that case the ruling of the presiding bishop would be binding and I would advise it is not sensible to go that way. As it stands, Philip has a claim on your property and, upon our marriage your property devolves to me. That being so, while Robert is my first heir, it is my desire Philip would have an equal claim upon our residual estate. In any case, providing I make that clear in my will and our marriage contract, Philip and Robert will be equally provided for so there should be no problem with inheritance. As for my personal thoughts on the matter, they are both my sons and each conceived in love; I would have neither disadvantaged."

Anna smiled up at him. She had felt some guilt at pressing him so and worried he might react contrary to her wishes. She was no girl to be foolish enough to enter into a marriage contract without assurances in spite of the dictates of her heart while a portion of that belonged to Philip. "The next question, then is: what are we to tell Philip? It is time that he knows who his real father is."

"It is and we must put it off no longer."

They had to wait while Philip returned to the tavern. He had taken to meeting with other physicians in the town to exchange views. These regarded each other with varying degrees of malice born of rivalry and perceived competence. Those trained at the better universities considered themselves superior even when for some, the survival rates of their patients were less than another with lower academic status. Philip, having come out of Cambridge in England was accepted in this company particularly as he was their junior and it was understood he was to return to England soon and, therefore, no rival.

Philip sat before Laurence and Anna and listened patiently, his face betraying nothing while they explained the circumstances of his birth; how he had been a love child conceived while on the road with King Edward's army. After Edward won back his crown and Laurence was caught up in the maelstrom of those times, tending the armouring needs of certain nobles, the two had gone their different ways; then Anna discovered she was pregnant. Being alone, she took a husband to protect her. This was the man he had called father, Barrat Thorne, later hanged for treason as a scapegoat in the cause of the duke of Clarence. By that time, Laurence had met and married Joan, the daughter of Cornelius Quirke. Robert was his son by that marriage. Joan and their two daughters later died of the sweating sickness but by that time, the apothecary had taken Anna to wife. Philip, of course, knew all about this last part, being with his mother throughout her experiences.

Presently they fell silent and looked at him expectantly, wondering how he would take the news that he had both parents in the world where before he had but one.

"I am somewhat relieved that you have spoken to me," said the young man at length, his expression remaining passive. Falling silent for a moment his face took on a wry smile. "You will have noted my beard?" They stared at him wonderingly, trying to work out his meaning. "It is finely trimmed, don't you think?" Both his parents nodded, still unable to fathom what was coming. "It's fine trim requires the use of a mirror in which I might detect the image of my face. You showed me how to burnish brass to provide such an object, if you remember?" He addressed his remarks to Laurence who nodded, recalling he had lectured him on how to obtain a high polish on metal. "I can still remember the face of the man who I called father, but it is nothing like the one I see in my mirror. There is another who is familiar to me with the same features as I, though I think my mother has bequeathed my face a certain softness not present in the original."

Laurence and Anna looked to each other then to Philip, still apprehensive as to his final reaction. Suddenly, Philip smiled broadly at them and they rushed to him, Laurence embracing him with firmness he had not permitted himself before.

"Your education as a physician has not been wasted," declared Laurence, releasing him to be taken into his mother's embrace. "Its first principles, I believe, teach diagnosis from accurate observation."

"Quite so . . .father. We consult the stars also – much of our fate is written there."

"Yes," agreed Laurence. "I have seen that for myself."

The three of them stood clasped together, Anna in tears as usual and Laurence fighting to keep his back. Presently they broke free of each other and seated themselves in their private corner of the tavern.

Having observed from a discreet distance that the three were united as a family, John and Gurden returned to resume their former discourse.

"I can easily manage the forge here for you," said John. "Gurden can run this place without my help and I shall be near her in any case. It will be just as when we lived and worked in Gloucester," he said laconically. Laurence had anticipated he would do that but it was still a relief to have him say so without being asked.

"As for me," inserted Philip, "might I come along with you to Malines? It will be a fine opportunity for me to get close to the court of the duchess Margaret."

"It would be better if you returned to England," advised Laurence. "It is bound to be reported of you if you go to Burgundy and then you will attract the attention of Tudor spies." Philip bowed his acquiescence.

Margaret of Burgundy held a colourful court where nobles from several countries, and also the Holy Roman Empire attended. There were ambassadors from those monarchs who might want her support, or seek to know what schemes she was currently working on. The project to place her nephew Richard of York on the English throne currently was that most pertinent to the times. In particular, there would be spies there reporting back to Henry Tudor and they would have to be circumspect in selecting allies, but that was mostly the problem of prince Richard.

"Fortunately Cornelius trained us well when it comes to subterfuge," Anna pointed out. "There will be much to discover amongst the ladies of the court," she mused. "I am unlikely to find favour with *les grande dames* but their female servants will be a rich source of information for sure."

"If I can make just one suggestion?" remarked John Fisher. Laurence nodded his assent. "Take care how you deal with this Brampton fellow. He has the character of an adventurer and though he was loyal and useful to King Edward the Fourth and also to King Richard, yet both monarchs are no more and Brampton makes his way in a world of living kings, not dead ones. Back then, the Plantagenet monarchs could hardly have been thought of as vulnerable and so loyalty to them would compliment self interest. That is no longer the case."

"Well, Brampton has said old loyalties die hard," said Laurence, "and that is at least superficially true, but you are right, John, we must make our way as things are now. None of us, Brampton included, live in England and thus are not afflicted by the Tudor Law."

"It is not the same for me," sighed John. "I would return to England if I could, and so would Gurden in spite of the suffering of her past. There are many like us presently in exile. We are the lucky ones, being friends with a native artisan armourer here in Brittany. I would not have relished making my way here, or anywhere out of England without the help you have given us."

"The help has been, and is mutual, my friend. I have you to thank for extracting at least a portion of my wealth from England. Just think on this present project and the difficulty I would have been presented with had I not had you to look after my affairs here."

Laurence placed a hand on his friend's shoulder. John did the same and both men stood for a moment in confirmation of their trust in each other.

"I sometimes think that treachery in men has its antithesis, yet it is often disregarded, I suppose being so rare?" Edward Brampton stood there having just come over. He had caught but the last few words of their conversation and supposed they were engaged in a discourse regarding the merits of loyalty over treachery, which they were, though he was seemingly unaware of his part in it.

"Not so rare," declared Anna vehemently. She had taken a dislike to Brampton and the challenge to his opinion had come unbidden to her lips; yet she was not one to retire in confusion even when she had not meant to speak out quite so boldly. "There is much loyalty in the world, in fact, it is a dominant emotion. Circumstances and human greed often grind it down, but, like a flower on a dung heap, it still manages to bloom if only for a single day of its life."

"Most erudite," replied Brampton with a grin. "The ladies of the court at Burgundy will need to treat you with particular care, not to mention the gentlemen."

"I hope I am beyond that season where I might attract the attention of courtly gentlemen."

"You do yourself a great disservice," came the gallant reply. Anna blushed, lost, at last for words.

Turning to the company, Edward Brampton addressed them. "We must ready ourselves for the journey. There is little time to prepare and even now the duchess Margaret is arranging for the victualing of her ships and the preparation of the army she is sending with prince Richard into England."

This statement should have confirmed to Laurence the fact he would be accompanying the prince in his venture, but taken up with the immediate arrangements it hardly occurred to him. Anna, however, took herself to one side and, regarding her new husband under lowered eyelids, feared that their future might not be as definite as she had long dreamed of.

10 - The Merchant of the Ruby

It was without any sense of incongruity that the arms of England were displayed in the great chamber of Malines, only just subservient to those of Burgundy itself. The duchess Margaret sat in stern command over the court before her. Still beautiful, the sister of England's last two Plantagenet kings glowered at the courtier kneeling at her feet. He had been there for some time and annoyance at the disrespect the duchess was showing for the French ambassador in not raising him to his feet was clearly written in his face. The temerity of the duchess having the leopards and *fleur de lis* of the English royal arms flaunting the assertion that England claimed kingship over his land, rankled rather less with the ambassador than the presence of the youth beside her on the ducal throne.

Richard of York, whom the ambassador was now commanded by King Charles VIII of France to refer to as Perkin Warbeck, *le garçon* as King Henry of England called him, was robed over deliberately as Margaret herself in red velvet trimmed with ermine, the exclusive fur reserved only for royalty. Attendants had draped the robes over the steps to the dais, carefully arranged to demonstrate opulence and royal state. Margaret wore jewels woven into her hair while the young man beside her was clad in white damask doublet and hose embroidered with coloured silks and studded here and there with jewels of various hues. Above them, the canopy had two shields, of Burgundy and of England. There could be no clearer definition of the duchess of Burgundy's personal commitment to the cause of her nephew. The French king, though originally only too pleased to accept Richard of York for who he was, had now agreed a treaty with England that changed the course of his diplomacy. He still personally believed in the Prince but asked him to leave the French court according to the terms of his new arrangement with Henry Tudor. Duchess Margaret knew that King Charles had his eye on her duchy and she was determined to keep it safe for her step grandson, Philip called The Fair. Second to her heart was her English nephew and there could be no doubt that should he wrest the throne of England from Henry Tudor, a man she despised mightily, Richard's debt to Burgundy would assure her of military aid against the French while she had the satisfaction of discharging her family duty to her brother's son.

There must be over a hundred courtiers in the hall, thought Laurence the armourer as he contemplated the scene with some amusement. He was standing with Edward Brampton, waiting for a private audience with the duchess and her protégé. Gazing around, he noted the different expressions evident on the less experienced, or more partisan courtiers. Those of the French contingent were showing disapproval while the native courtiers of Burgundy feigned amused indifference. The Germans, being vassals of Maximilian, king of the Romans remained diplomatically stoical, though they too probably approved of duchess Margaret's tactic. Some of them were fighting and jousting knights, and thus appreciated the conduct of the diplomatic battle being fought out now for their delight despite the direction commanded of them by their respective sovereigns. He strained forward, the better to hear Margaret's words as she addressed the French ambassador.

"We thank your king for his past support of our nephew while in France, though his timidity in facing down the Tudor thief we think detracts from his integrity as a monarch." The duchess suppressed a smile as she noted how the ambassador struggled to keep annoyance from his features.

"Your grace is mistaken in our king," he replied coldly. "You know full well that affairs in England have taken a turn for the worse so far as the cause of your nephew is concerned. The support he once had has been largely removed and it was one from your grace's own court that brought that about. My king would have continued in his support else. As it is now, King Henry is firmly in charge and therefore unlikely to be removed by an inexperienced youth." The ambassador curled his lip disdainfully and glanced at the Prince, who affected disinterest.

Margaret's eyes flashed in anger and she sat back to consider her answer. Laurence, observing from the side had much sympathy for the duchess. It had been a close confederate, Sir Robert Clifford, a man she had trusted with all her plans for the invasion of England who had gone over and disclosed everything to the Tudor. There had been dozens of nobles there ready to come to the aid of the Prince but now most were dead, executed along with over two-hundred minor figures. His satisfaction in learning that Sir William Stanley had been one of those whose head had been removed hardly mitigated the fact that his support would have been vital to the success of the plan. It was the extent of treachery on both sides that concerned Laurence more than anything. It was impossible to know who to trust. In England a coterie of nobles had been ready to turn on King Henry while Tudor spies in Flanders, here at the court of the duchess Margaret, had been successful in discovering names and providing information that had brought them to their deaths. Who could divine the true mind of those remaining? Margaret made up her mind and leaned towards the French ambassador.

"You forget that Richard of York is the rightful king of England. The commonality will respond to his banner. If there is treason here at my court then be assured there is yet treason too at the Tudor's court. His mass executions have not endeared him to either the English nobility or the people there, rather it shows he is losing his grip on affairs. Once Prince Richard manages to land and increase his army in England, there will be many defections from Tudor."

"Perhaps your grace is correct in her assessment," drawled the ambassador wearily. "I am sure my king would wish to deal with whoever triumphs, but at the moment he is committed elsewhere and cannot render any further aid." The duchess knew that King Charles VIII of France was currently invading the kingdom of Naples and thus his new treaty with England meant he could concentrate his resources there. This was the reason he had asked, albeit with regret, the duke of York to leave France.

"Then you have our leave to return to your king with a message that his recalcitrance has incurred our most profound displeasure."

The French ambassador got stiffly to his feet and bowing to the duchess, backed away into the mass of courtiers, who made a ready way for him to let his entourage stalk grimly out of the hall. When they had departed, the duchess seemed to sink into something akin to despair, though she fought valiantly to suppress the outward signs to her court, yet those familiar with her could tell her mind.

Laurence shifted his attention to the young man beside the duchess. He was seated where her step grandson, Philip the Fair would usually sit, but had been placed there by Margaret to demonstrate the determination of her position regarding Richard duke of York to the Frenchman. Having previously revealed himself at Cork, the people of Ireland flocked to support him. The Irish favoured Plantagenet rule and despised the Tudor usurper. It was from Ireland that Henry Tudor first heard his worst nightmare had come to life and his determination to capture the lad he called Perkin Warbeck began. Duke Richard of York went also to the court of Maximilian, king of the Romans who to his credit remained a staunch but largely impotent ally. Maximilian had married Mary of

Burgundy, the daughter by a previous marriage of Charles the Bold, duchess Margaret's deceased husband – killed a few years ago at the siege of Nancy. Mary had died tragically after a fall from her horse and Maximilian had remained a widower until now, when he was about to marry Bianca Maria Sforza, daughter of the duke of Milan. As for Mary's stepmother, the duchess afterwards devoted herself to her stepdaughter's son Philip.

Richard of York had at first been welcome at the French court, whose king was ever at enmity with England. Charles VIII had recognised the true identity of the duke of York and found him useful as an instrument with which to taunt King Henry. Now at twenty-one it could hardly be said the youth had acquired much in the way of martial skills in the interim and relied absolutely on the conviction his true identity provided as his right to challenge Henry for the throne of England. He was sitting now, robed in state and completely at ease, as if the delicate condition of his cause was but a trifle. This kind of insouciance was, of course, habitual with kings and was one reason why he was accepted as such. His was not role-play, in spite of what his opponents said of his behaviour.

"The duchess is right to be concerned, even if the Prince appears not to be," murmured Edward Brampton close to Laurence's ear. "There remain few of high degree in England ready to rally to his cause and the recent executions will discourage those that even now might have done so."

Laurence nodded in agreement. He was thinking of King Edward the Fourth and this was his youngest son, clearly delineated not just obviously as in his features, which visibly proclaimed him Edward's progeny, but in his royal manner.

"It is unfortunate that he has not inherited his sire's martial disposition," replied Laurence, "yet neither has Henry Tudor fought in battle. He had to rely on others to win his crown for him and then to defend it afterwards. King Richard the Third was England's best general, yet he lost to the Tudor, albeit due to the blunderings of Sir William Stanley. Think you Richard of York might usurp the luck of the Tudor?"

"King Edward, his father had a similar force at his disposal raised in Flanders after he had been driven from England. We both remember that time, my friend."

"Yes, and I found myself in a predicament then. He had with him a coterie of loyal followers along with his brother Richard, then duke of Gloucester . . ."

"And ourselves, don't forget!"

"Quite so, but are those who will go with the Prince to be relied on? The duchess has called me to the service of the Prince because her trust has been badly shaken."

Brampton nudged Laurence to attention as the duchess rose, looking to the duke of York who also stood and stepped down from the dais, both of them leaving their scarlet robes draped over the ducal thrones. Laurence smiled inwardly at this display as the duchess' ladies tended her dress while she readied herself to walk among the courtiers. This was the Plantagenet way, and the young Prince too was at his ease amongst the crowd. Laurence had never been to the Tudor court, but he knew, as did everyone, that King Henry feared such close familiarity. There had been several plots already against his life and he had earned the dubious distinction of being the first king of England to require protection from his own subjects. Continental monarchs saw nothing ignominious in this, because it was quite normal in most European courts. It was Henry's dubious lineage that they despised; yet politically they would accept his kingship while he could hold on to it.

"I must say I was shocked when Sir William Stanley was beheaded," said Laurence as he watched the duchess move among the throng. "I had no love of the man, though I was not too surprised on discovering he was one of those conspiring to come to the Prince's cause upon landing in England. He had always been favourable to the House of York, saving his own best interest."

"Henry has not forgotten that final charge at the battle of Bosworth," replied Brampton. "His spies must have discovered afterwards that Sir William intended to come to King Richard's aid, but could not prove it. Who amongst his men would admit to doing so after the king was killed and Henry Tudor the victor?"

"Yes, I too thought he had come in on the Tudor's side at the battle, for that was how it seemed to us then. It was afterwards that I learned from Cornelius the extent of Stanley's blunder. The acrimony existing between the separate armies led to a misunderstanding of his intention. Once the Tudor banner went down under King Richard's war axe, it must have seemed to Sir William that the Tudor was finished and therefore his intervention on the side of King Richard was, militarily the right, indeed the only safe thing to do. Had we understood what Sir William was about, then the battle would have gone otherwise."

Brampton agreed. "King Henry would have no problem working that out afterwards, and I believe he was merely waiting for a chance to strike off Sir William's head. He could hardly do so after the battle when he needed the support of the two Stanley brothers to consolidate his victory."

"Yes, and Sir William was the one man in England most able to provide sufficient military support for our present enterprise to succeed. His loss is like to provoke failure." Laurence looked for confirmation of this opinion in his face, but Brampton turned quickly aside as at that moment the Prince approached along with a few of his followers, Yorkist exiles like himself.

Duke Richard of York was the image of his father at the same age. The only difference was his hair, fair as his mothers and he had her brown eyes. Laurence and Brampton swept him a bow of obeisance as he stopped by them.

"You are alone gentlemen?" His voice was that of his father, King Edward the Fourth of England. "Where are your ladies? I had hoped to speak with lady Brampton at least, and, of course, your charming wife master de la Halle."

Laurence bent his head in acknowledgement while Brampton merely smiled."

"They are somewhere close, my lord," said Brampton. "In fact they are here now." He indicated with his arm the progress of the two ladies who were finding a passage between the courtiers towards their respective husbands. Lady Brampton sank to her knees before the duke, closely followed by Anna who mimicked her example. The duke lifted a hand indicating they should rise.

"Lady Brampton, dame de la Halle, most charmed." The Prince smiled at them both though his eyes rested principally upon Lady Brampton, the woman who had taken him as a page in her household. "I would speak with you later. For the moment I have some business with your husbands." He looked over the heads of the courtiers and found the eye of one of his followers. The man came over and bowed before them. "Master de la Halle, may I present Sir Anthony de la Forsse," said the Prince pleasantly. Sir Anthony was a firm, well-proportioned young man of medium height, perhaps just a little older than the Prince. A Spaniard, his father was Bernard de la Forsse who had served King Edward and King Richard, he wore a cherry-coloured doublet cut in the Italian fashion, with a short black cloak of velvet over his shoulders. A short arming sword was at his belt – *something else that would not be permitted at the Tudor court*," Laurence reflected as he and Brampton bowed politely in greeting.

"You are my lord's new armourer, master de la Halle? Sir Edward," he said casually acknowledging Brampton before returning his attention to Laurence." Sir Anthony spoke politely in French, his tone conveying approval of Laurence's position. They hadn't met, Laurence only having arrived at Malines a week previously and Sir Anthony had been away somewhere on the Prince's business. He was duke Richard's closest companion and had been with him in Ireland and France. He was also a famous jouster with a professional interest in fine harness.

"At your service," returned Laurence. He looked to the Prince. "By your leave, your grace, may I present my wife to Sir Anthony?"

"Of course," replied the Prince.

Anna came forward and dipped a curtsey to Sir Anthony who gallantly made her a sweeping bow. Laurence thrilled at this display by a young man to an older, but still beautiful woman. Anna blushed and smiled in confusion. She was unused to the ways of the court, though Lady Brampton had been kindly instructing her and keeping the barbed tongues of the other ladies at bay. They had immediately detected her common stock and largely ignored her, especially when male courtiers were on hand. A few were watching her now, their eyes glowering with jealousy.

"Sir Anthony, how good it is to have you back." Edward Brampton pushed his way forward, anxious to make his presence felt. Laurence might have been annoyed, but he had learned this was Brampton's way. He was something of a braggart, but pleasant in character which ameliorated matters somewhat. Besides, his wife was showing Anna great and generous kindness so Brampton's abrupt, obsequious manner could be tolerated.

"There is much to discuss," replied the knight, eyeing Brampton warily before diverting his attention once more to the armourer. "Master Laurence, I have heard something of you from his grace. If it had not been for you, my lord would not have escaped England as easily as he did."

"It was a simple subterfuge, Sir Anthony."

"Yes," interrupted duke Richard. "It was one of the few incidents from that time upon which I can look back and smile. I regret that your son, Robert is not with us. I understand he is now a man-at-arms in the service of the earl of Surrey, Thomas Howard, restored to that title by the Tudor thief."

Laurence sighed lugubriously. Robert had been the main component in extracting Richard of York from the Tower of London and Laurence was unhappy by his attachment to the earl of Surrey.

"There are many in England who must serve the demands of the Tudor. Surrey has become his creature, that is true, but once your

225

grace wins back his throne, there will be no shortage of men who will be only too glad to rid themselves of their enforced and unnatural allegiance."

"Then let us retire, where we can finalise our plans to that end," said the duke. He moved casually through the gathering of courtiers, his own followers surrounding him to make way. Laurence tagged along behind Brampton, who as usual had shoved himself into a place close to duke Richard and Sir Anthony. He had delayed just enough to arrange for Anna to remain with Lady Brampton while he went into the chamber where the duke would hold council with his followers.

Laurence could not free himself from a feeling of unease at the number of persons within the chamber where the duke had led them. Counting heads he found there were twenty persons present, not including the duchess and duke Richard. It seemed there was little regard for security in this gathering. He stood well back from the duke's main council, while Brampton was seated at the long table beside Sir Anthony and the duchess of Burgundy, who was clearly in control. Most of those in the chamber had been with the duke since his initial appearance in Ireland in fourteen ninety-one. That was no surety of confidence as some previous attendants had already defected to the Tudor and there was nothing to say there were no Tudor spies among them as yet undiscovered. The treachery of Sir Robert Clifford was still fresh in everyone's mind, though Richard of York appeared unconcerned. Laurence's doubts were not placated by the knowledge that Clifford would have been at the right hand of the duchess had he remained with the court of Burgundy instead of defecting to the Tudor. He suspected the youthful prince gained some sort of comfort in being surrounded by such numbers as gathered here.

"Recently an embassy from England had the temerity to approach the council of our Archduke Philip," cried Margaret angrily. "They have accused me of trying to subvert and destroy the Tudor throne - which I must say is true enough." She paused while the gathering laughed. "The Tudor thief says I am plotting to instate a *feigned lad* and has instructed that details of what he claims to be a false identity be published to discredit my nephew's right. Needless to say, the archduke's council, while promising to preserve the peace between our respective lands, informed the Tudor they have no power to order *my* affairs."

"I was present when the English delegation met with my aunt," said duke Richard. "She reminded them that as a child I had been conveyed away from England, which their king knows perfectly well."

"Yes, I shall not be deterred from assisting my nephew who is in every way a most distressed Prince."

"This false identity that Henry Tudor is shouting abroad, Perkin Warbeck, is the very one that was created to protect our Prince from his murderous agents," stated Sir Anthony de la Forsse. "Although it served then to obscure the truth of his birth, nobody seriously believes our Prince is anyone other than the son of his father, King Edward the Fourth of England and the inheritor of a long line of Plantagenet kings. Once established in England there will be no shortage of those who knew him as a child and who can recognise him now."

"It is unfortunate that his mother died two years back. Lady Grey knew he lived," said Sir Edward Brampton. "Henry Tudor had her placed in a nunnery to silence her after the business with Lambert Simnal because she refused to state in public her son was dead."

Sitting next to Sir Anthony was a man in priestly garb. He raised a hand and the assembly fell silent while Margaret gave him the nod to speak. Laurence knew him to be James Kething, an Irishman and associated with the order of St. John of Jerusalem in that country. He too had been a constant companion of duke Richard ever since the declaration of his true identity at Cork.

"We need not concern ourselves further with debating Tudor lies," he snarled derisively. "They will all turn to dust upon our victory. At this moment ships are being assembled ready to transport the true king of England across the narrow seas to his rightful homeland. We have the support of Maximilian, King of the Romans who has sent us German mercenaries and along with our own duchess Margaret has provided fifteen ships in all. We cannot have them waiting forever. It is pointless, moreover damaging, to delay any longer. Tomorrow is the first of July and we have the best of the summer ahead. We must go now."

This statement met with the approval of the whole council, which began to discuss with the duchess the logistics of the enterprise.

Laurence was unimpressed with the arrangements for invasion. He had not seen any particular military general of note stepping forward to lead the expedition other than Sir Anthony de la Forsse and another, Roderigo de LaLaing, one of duchess Margaret's trusted soldiers whom she had appointed to command her Flemish mercenaries. The duke of York himself was untried in battle and untrained in the military arts. This had been brought particularly to Laurence's mind as he fitted him into his harness the day after his arrival at Malines. He had asked the Prince to strike a variety of poses to determine the flexibility and fit of the armour so he could find what alterations might be required, yet his stance was not that habitually found in a trained man-at-arms.

Listening to the naïve optimism of his council's debate, it seemed to Laurence, the duke of York was little more than a pawn in a game of international chess, though he did have a more powerful piece, a queen in the person of Margaret of Burgundy to direct him. So far he had not risen above his current state of being passed from one monarch to another, each sovereign certain of his lineage, but also ready to deny it should political circumstances render him an embarrassment. It was the uncertain government of England and the general contempt in which other monarchs held the Tudor king, along with a considerable number of his own people, which had provoked a nervous Henry Tudor into tyranny. His solution was to destroy all opposition while grinding those under his rule beneath his heel. Could this young man accomplish destruction of the tyrant?

As the assembly broke up Laurence went into the great chamber and found Anna with Lady Brampton. He made a few polite exchanges and managed to extract his wife from her company. The duke of York, Prince Richard was surrounded by his followers, all chattering enthusiastically and Laurence, seeing as he had not been called for, took the opportunity to lead Anna unnoticed to a quiet corner.

"What is it, my love?" she said noting the concern written in his face.

"I think that you should return to Vannes until this venture resolves itself."

Anna snorted disdainfully. "I shall do no such thing. We have only just become man and wife. I cannot do without you now, not after being apart so long!"

"I know that and I feel the same. It pains me to suggest such a course, but I fear this business will not prosper and I would have you safe."

"Then I am the more determined to go with you. Don't forget, I am no stranger to the life of a camp follower, besides I shall make myself useful. I have tended the sick and wounded of an army as you know." She set her mouth in a determined line. "There is another thing. You cannot be trusted to remain out of trouble, even though you should stay with the baggage, yet you always manage to find your way towards the vanguard in a battle." She raised her eyebrows as was her familiar way, defying him to contradict her.

"We shall speak of this some more later," he tried, unable to think of a suitable response.

"We shall not! If you go into England you might be tempted to attack Henry Tudor again unless I am there to prevent you," she said petulantly.

"Well, if you will not return to Vannes, will you remain here, or perhaps go into Portugal with Lady Brampton? Sir Edward tells me they are to return to their home there soon. I am sure they will be agreeable to having you with them."

"You see!" she declared triumphantly. "Sir Edward has no intention of going with duke Richard and he is an adventurer. You have already admitted the venture will not prosper. I think we should both return to Vannes."

"I am loath to leave the Prince. I will lose all credit with the duchess Margaret and probably the king of the Romans too, who is the Holy Roman Emperor. It would be foolish to risk that. Besides, if the Prince wins his crown back it will mean much profit for us. You might even end a lady?"

"A widow more like."

"Just think on it. How many examples have we had in our lives of hopeless causes turning to triumph? King Edward had no more of an army than duke Richard now has when he invaded England to fight for his crown. He was outnumbered at each of his battles, but still won. Even the Tudor, against all predictions managed to become king and he was in a similar case to our Prince, so far as fighting ability is concerned. Tudor had no battle experience and no support among the English. The difference is, duke Richard is the rightful king of England, his father's heir and a true Plantagenet which he can demonstrate to his people."

"If you are determined to go into England with duke Richard, then I shall go too." Anna's eyes blazed defiance and he knew he had failed to persuade her to stay behind. He could force her, of course. He was her husband and she was bound to obey him, yet theirs was not that kind of relationship and it was unlikely she would comply in any case.

* * *

Laurence the armourer stood upon the gently moving deck of the carrack that had brought him to England with the duke of York. At least, he reflected, the choice of Deal on the coast of Kent was an ideal place to launch an invasion. He looked across beyond the sandy beach to the downs, lush and green in the summer sunshine. Seabirds wheeled above them, looking to what they might get from the scraps of the ships, their cries vociferously commenting indifferently on the doings of the men below; or was it seabird laughter? The water here was shallow and the anchorage good, ideal for shipping men and horses onto the beach. There was hardly any wind and the other ships in the invasion force vainly showed their pennants, flags and banners from masthead and yards, fluttering fitfully in the light airs. He looked around to find the craft where Anna was. There was no cabin accommodation in any of the vessels, other than the captain's cabin, and that was reserved for the nobles and a few in their entourage. Anna was with the boys, serving women and baggage in the supply vessel. He found it anchored a little further from the coast and though he strained to see, he could not make out any individual among the figures at the rail. Just as on this ship, everyone was crowding the decks and rigging to view the place where they would land and begin to recapture the crown for their Prince.

Soldiers were readying themselves, and the archers were placing their bowstrings into oiled canvas bags to keep the water out until they got onto dry land. They were mostly a motley collection of mercenaries and adventurers from a variety of countries, here for reward and perhaps some plunder. Laurence wondered how they were to be coordinated for command in battle? Each company might have an English captain, but he would have to issue orders through an intermediary, with all the attendant problems of misinterpretation. Having said that, French was more or less a common language except for a few of the lower orders so perhaps all would be well. Boats had been lowered and hoists rigged ready to swing the horses out of the hold to swim them ashore. Several boats were already heading for the shore, each having but a few soldiers.

He heard someone call his name. Sir Anthony de la Forsse beckoned him over to the stern castle under which Prince Richard was closeted with his immediate captains. Following where Sir Anthony led, he ducked his head under the low doorframe and entered the great cabin. Richard of York was there with James Kething and a man whom he had come to recognise as a close companion of the Prince, John Watre and Roderigo de LaLaing in overall command of the venture. Also in the crowded cabin were two Spanish captains, Diego, known as *The Lame*, due to his having a clubfoot and one Fulano de Guevera. The Prince was standing apart letting an esquire fit him into his armour. He was just strapping the cuirass to his arming jacket as Laurence arrived. The harness was aglitter, being white, that is natural polished steel, made originally in Germany and in the style of that country. It suited perfectly the personality of the Prince, being ostentatious in design with its fluting and embossed designs, the high points being picked out in gold. Laurence had made some alterations to the cuisses over his thighs, and the pauldrons at the shoulders, spending some time in matching the fluting and design with the new work. Afterwards the polishing and finishing of the harness took more hours than the actual metalwork. At Malines there were craftsmen to do the gilding, and Laurence wondered how he would bring the harness back to its magnificent condition if the Prince got it marked in battle. This was tourney armour, and though it was easily strong enough to withstand battle, its intended function was in display. In the tournament field there were armourers and gilders aplenty to quickly restore the outward splendour of rich harness. Of course, it was intended as such and the Prince would need to impress at court, yet a plainer Milanese rig would have been of more practical use here and now.

He bowed before the Prince, who waved his squire away clearly intending his armourer to finish arming him. Laurence tugged at the fastenings but other than getting ready to fit the Prince with his arming cap and helm, there was nothing more for him to do.

"Is your grace intending to go ashore with his first men?" he asked, worriedly.

"No," came the reply. "I shall show myself at the forecastle until they have raised my banners and attracted some of my people, then I shall go ashore with my full force to receive them."

Fulano de Guevera pushed forward. "There is already a gathering ashore. His grace's presence has been noticed."

"Yes, we shall raise our banners then go to them," said Prince Richard enthusiastically. The sooner we begin to recruit more followers the easier it will be to gain more during our march inland."

"Is there anyone close on land who is ready to raise men for York?" Laurence had heard of no specific personage who would be ready to welcome the Prince into England now that Sir William

Stanley had been disposed of along with many others. Across the water was Kent and the men there were known to have a grudge against York, many remembering the executions under King Edward the Fourth. After he invaded in fourteen seventy-one and won back his crown, the men of Kent had joined in a rebellion to overturn his victory and Edward's retribution had been swift and awful.

"When the people see that their rightful king is here, they will come to him, never fear," said Anthony de la Forsse. Laurence wondered at his conviction and the thought came to him that Sir Anthony was speaking to bolster the Prince's resolve rather than offer military advice.

"Let us see what happens when a goodly number of our men land on the beach," offered John Watre. "They will discover who will aid us and how many. For now, your grace should show himself to his men."

Prince Richard nodded his agreement and went out to take a prominent place on the forecastle of the ship where he could be plainly seen, resplendent in his shining armour.

It was not long before a boat returned with a message for the Prince. Richard returned to the deck to receive the messenger.

The men of Kent welcome the duke of York and invite him to come ashore where he might be assured of their best attention.

"Your grace," said Laurence having listened to the message the soldier had brought from the land. "I plead caution. I remember a similar situation when we were tempting Henry Tudor to come ashore in fourteen eighty-three. He too was offshore and had he come to land we would have had him and terminated his venture."

"That was different," objected John Watre. "The Tudor was a usurper and could not have won the throne at that time, rather he was to join with the duke of Buckingham in a rebellion that had already collapsed."

"Tudor had no royal blood to call on either," interjected Sir Anthony. "He was right to be cautious in those circumstances. Our Prince is the rightful king with a claim on the support of his people. The situation is entirely different."

Richard of York paced the deck, clearly with no idea how to proceed. Laurence looked about him in dismay. Was there nobody here who could properly advise the Prince? He decided it best that he speak out.

"May I suggest we land half of our soldiers to establish a safe landing place from where we can explore inland and discover what support we might achieve?"

The Prince brightened at that suggestion. "Of course," he declared clapping his hands in delight. "Let us do that now!" His captains bowed their agreement, though some glared at Laurence, jealous that he had been the one to suggest a coherent plan of action. Roderigo de LaLaing frowned at him but seemed to agree, seeing as he turned and nodded to the duke.

Soon they were standing at the rail of their ship watching as a small flotilla of ship's boats took men to the shore. After a while they could see the banners of the Prince raised on the land beyond the beach to be greeted by men appearing over the downs. At first all seemed well until a troop of horsemen bearing spears cantered along the beach towards the exposed men while another swarmed like a storm cloud over the downs beyond. The dismounted men were soon identified as archers and they unleashed a storm of iron-tipped death at the Prince's men on the beach. Soon could be heard the clash of arms as the horsemen attacked those on the beach. Laurence could see hurried preparation of halberds serried to stem the advance, but the surprise of the attack burst through them and overwhelmed the men behind. Then another troop of men appeared on foot and attacked the small force, which was completely overwhelmed. Some men had made it to the boats and even fewer managed to get into them and pull away from the shore. Others ran into the sea, vainly trying to scramble into the boats whose crews were more intent in getting away than waiting to haul their companions on board.

Of the three hundred who went ashore, less than eighty returned and it was obvious there would be no landing for the Prince here at Deal. The misery was intensified when it was learned the Prince's men had been repulsed without the aid of King Henry, his troops being nowhere near. Fellow Englishmen who had scant regard for Plantagenet blood had driven them off.

It was a disconsolate and disillusioned group that assembled in the great cabin. The same persons were gathered there and each was looking to apportion blame for the catastrophe. Laurence was an easy target, having been the one to suggest landing while entirely ignoring the fact it had been he who had advocated that the Prince remain safely aboard ship.

"We should have landed with our full force," growled John Watre. "There were too few on the beach. We have lost Diego and Fulano de Guevera, two of our best captains."

"I should have been there too," lamented the Prince. He was sitting at the table with his head in his hands. "If they had seen me they would not have attacked."

"If you had landed, your grace," said Laurence, suppressing his anger at the attitude of the captains, "your enterprise would have finished there and you taken for Tudor's reward."

"We cannot go on now having lost so many men," said Anthony de la Forsse. He was thinking on how those remaining would be demoralised by the debacle of Deal beach. Most of them were mercenaries, devoid of any passion for their particular cause. "Already two of our ships have departed empty, taking news of our supposed landing and invasion back to duchess Margaret and the emperor Maximilian." He grimaced and passed a hand over his brow. "Now we must trail after and admit we have failed."

"That is not necessarily so," intoned James Kething. "Our prince has always been well received in Ireland. We should go there and recruit some more men to our cause. The earl of Desmond is ever our friend."

Laurence looked askance at the Prior. The plan was not without hazard. After the debacle that was the battle of Stoke and the capture of Lambert Simnal, Henry Tudor had sent a large army to Ireland and razed to the ground those towns that had lent support to the rebels. Then he had demanded the loyalty of the Irish nobility and those who refused him had their lands burned and pillaged. He had done the same again after the Irish gathered to Richard of York when he first revealed himself at Cork, leading afterwards to his flight to the French court. The Plantagenet cause had not evaporated there, but military support might not be as enthusiastic as hitherto. Still, there was plenty of unrest against Tudor among the Irish population.

"It is our best hope now," said de LaLaing. He regularly travelled between his homeland and Ireland, so it was a natural choice for him. Laurence wondered if he wasn't also a spy for the Spanish court. King Ferdinand and Queen Isabella were presently negotiating marriage between their daughter the princess Catherine of Aragon and Arthur, the son and heir of Henry Tudor and Elizabeth of York, Prince Richard's sister. The whole of the present enterprise was a severe obstacle in those negotiations and regardless of what the Spanish king and queen thought of the identity question, they naturally needed it resolved. The fact de LaLaing was close to the duchess of Burgundy was no guarantee of felicity. Robert Clifford had been close to her too.

"I agree," said the Prince firmly. "The earl of Kildare has been captured by the Tudor and is a prisoner in England, but Maurice Fitzgerald, earl of Desmond is free and resisting the depredations of the Tudor's attempted subjection of Ireland."

"That is correct, your grace," said Sir Anthony. "The arrest of Kildare has caused many of his kinsmen to rally to the Desmond banner. I know that Philip the Fair at the Flanders court has offered support and so has the king of Scotland. There is still much scope for our cause there."

Laurence turned aside while this discussion was going on. He was thinking of Anna. She hated the sea. A short voyage across from Flanders in fine weather was tolerable, but the idea of her having to sail through the narrow sea between France and England then along the south coast and around Cornwall to Ireland would distress her, and the wind was rising. Worse than that, the voyage was not without danger. Tudor ships might attack the fleet, though there were still twelve of them, which might be enough to deter anything other than a comparable fleet of warships. Upon reaching Ireland everything depended on where they made landfall. Castles protected all the major ports and Tudor had placed his own English born constables in those.

The day was advancing towards evening before the fleet raised anchor and finally set sail, turning their backs on England for the moment and retracing their course before turning west into the narrow seas. Laurence was on deck gazing across the grey waters, knowing Anna would be at the rail of her transport looking towards the Prince's vessel. Roderigo was captain and it turned out he was a good sailor. The Prince was ostensibly their admiral, but he sensibly deferred to Roderigo in matters of ordering the disposition of the vessels in the fleet. Fortunately the weather was fair and a brisk breeze was coming from the south bringing warm air but forcing them to tack constantly. Once beyond the narrow seas, the sailing conditions should improve, unless the wind changed, and they would make a reasonably fast passage. He was pleased to note the transport was keeping up with them, if anything sailing a little faster. All things being well they would not lose sight of each other before reaching Ireland.

11 – A Change of Plan

Tongues of flame and sudden ejaculations of smoke shot from The Maria, one of the Prince's ships, which was attacking a merchant carrack attempting to escape the harbour of Youghall. Laurence stood swathed in smoke as the wind whipped the foul sulphurous cloud back across the deck. Looking across at the diminishing space between the ships as the smoke blew clear, he saw splinters of wood falling into the sea, the result of a strike at the poop deck rail of the target ship. Gunners were already sponging out the three cannon ready to apply another charge before the boarding of the other vessel. To his mind, the smell of brimstone always conjured up a vision of hell as depicted in the wall paintings of many a church and he fingered nervously the reliquary suspended from his neck. Flemish soldiers with war axes and heavy falchions were ranked in anticipation of the coming fight. Some were waiting by the rails with grappling irons and rope ready to lash the two vessels together. He sneaked a glance to windward where the rest of the small fleet was following and breathed a sigh of relief when he observed Anna's ship well back from the rest. Hopefully, this fight would be over before she would be placed in danger.

There was no time for a second carronade. The two ships crashed together and the sailors swung their grapples aboard while the soldiers swarmed across onto the opposite deck, though meeting scant resistance. The captain of the merchantman stood on the deck, his sword across his arm in a gesture of surrender. It had been a foregone conclusion. He was a trader and though he had a crew capable of driving off a few pirates, they were no match for the force of professional mercenaries confronting them in the Prince's ship. He was not easily intimidated and a thunderous expression in his face was a graphic reproduction of the fierce carronade that had damaged his ship and forced his capitulation.

Duke Richard stood on the poop deck of his ship and waited for the report of Sir Anthony de la Forsse, who had been sent across to look at the manifest of the merchant vessel. He came back and reported it was carrying bales of wool and a quantity of iron and that he had arranged for it all to be removed and donated to his grace's cause. They would sell it in the town of Youghall once they had rid the harbour of hostile ships.

"The captain, by the name of William Bourget, declares he is a merchant of Harfleur and promises retribution for what he terms our piracy," said Sir Anthony. "His cargo is bound for Southampton and Exeter."

Duke Richard took this statement seriously. "It is with much regret that I have had to attack a vessel of the French," he lamented with something of genuine concern. "However, I have done so without spilling too much blood. Let captain Bourget keep his ship and live to complain to the usurper Henry Tudor that the true King of England has graciously shown him mercy and thanks him for the donation of his cargo to his cause. Moreover, tell him he may retrieve the cost of his cargo should he present himself at my English court in due course." Sir Anthony smirked and bowed his head in agreement. "You might add that had he landed in England the Tudor would have extracted a punitive import duty, so his loss in not too great."

Laurence smiled to himself at the Prince's remarks. He would pay good money to be present should Captain Bourget ever kneel before Henry Tudor and repeat what he had just been told.

As the goods were being lifted from the captured vessel, their attention was attracted by more sounds of gunfire as another of the Prince's ships engaged a second vessel flying English colours trying to escape the harbour. They watched as a similar scene presented itself to that which they had been practitioners themselves. So it was that, as the afternoon wore on they made their way cautiously towards the harbour, which was at the mouth of the Blackwater River, the town of Youghall being a little further upriver. They would not enter just yet, until they were sure of what resistance there might be. The earl of Desmond had many supporters in Ireland and faced with the Prince's force, those people of Youghall who might be in thrall to the Tudor could well be overwhelmed by those loyal to Desmond.

A pinnace scudded across the sea towards the vessels anchored just outside the harbour at Youghall, its triangular sails full and its fluttering pennant forward of the main mast. It was showing the earl of Desmond's colours, but that meant nothing and after the debacle that had been Deal, nobody was going to chance a trip ashore without absolute certainty of a good reception. As with all the harbours on this coast, Tudor had them in a tentative grasp but with Desmond nearby the citizens of Youghall might allow the duke of York to land his army.

The pinnace turned smartly head to wind and hove to just beyond the Prince's carrack. Soon a small boat was pulling across the water between the two vessels. A man in the garb of a merchant was standing forward of the four oarsmen and looking towards the Prince's ship. They pulled alongside where a rope ladder had been hung to allow the occupant to clamber aboard. One of the oarsmen flung a bow painter and a sailor made the end secure. The four, ragged oarsmen came aboard first to form a small, almost comical guard for the other occupant of their boat.

The duke of York stood dressed in full harness cap-a-pied, though with the visor of his armet raised to show his face. Every inch a Prince, his harness reflected in the brightness of the day while the gold trim glinted in the sunshine flooding the deck. A white plume of feathers adorned his helmet and these wafted gently in the breeze coming off the land. His retinue stood around, also clad in harness to display a certain martial determination to whoever was coming across from the town, while their lord in his full armour demonstrated the majesty of his Plantagenet blood. Laurence had ascended to the poop deck and was leaning on a rail looking down on the main deck in company with Don Carlos, a Spaniard and the ship's owner, with whom he had struck up a casual friendship. The Spaniard came from Cadiz and traded regularly with the Breton ports as well as Ireland and England. The voyage to Deal had been familiar to him as he had sailed those waters going into the Thames estuary as far as London; neither was he a stranger to the ports of Calais and Flanders. He knew Sir Edward Brampton, though Laurence felt there was some disquiet in his manner when he had mentioned that name so felt it prudent not to probe too deeply the reason.

The townsman doffed his chapeau and made low obeisance to the Prince, his green velvet gown spread around him on the deck as he fell to his knees. The Prince raised him without delay and the man struggled somewhat unsteadily to his feet. He was about middle age and though he had demonstrated some agility in getting himself aboard, yet Laurence guessed he was getting close to that age where he would be better off stopping on shore. Standing on the poop deck, Laurence and Don Carlos could hardly hear what was being said. Scraps of dialogue came to them but most of it drifted away in the breeze. The exchange seemed friendly enough and soon those about the Prince were sharing what seemed to be gladsome bonhomie while the men about them relaxed and began discoursing individually. They watched as the Prince and his visitor turned and entered the main cabin beneath their feet while the oarsmen returned to their boat and rowed back to the pinnace, leaving their passenger with the duke of York and his immediate entourage who had followed their lord into the cabin.

"It is time we joined his grace the duke," said Don Carlos. "From what we have just seen there will be orders to land in the offing and I must be ready to dispose the ship ready to disembark. Not a moment too soon either."

Laurence understood his meaning. They were running low on supplies, especially for the horses needing fodder and fresh water in far greater quantity than the men.

As they entered the cabin they were met by a cacophony of what might almost be described as celebration, though whatever news the townsman had brought could hardly be so welcome as all that. Laurence and Don Carlos approached the duke of York and made obeisance.

"Captain Don Carlos," cried the Prince lustily, "Prepare to land. We are to establish ourselves here at Youghall. The town is under the control of the earl of Desmond who has men holding the town."

"Excellent news, your grace," replied Don Carlos. "I shall set to immediately while the light holds. With God's grace you shall be ashore before dusk."

"That is what I want you to do," said the Prince. "As soon as we are disembarked we have the town at our disposal."

"Are we to remain here?" enquired the Spaniard.

"For the time, yes," came the reply. "We have further need of your ship, but I will give you your orders after I have heard from the earl of Desmond. The earl is with his main army at Waterford, which city is resisting him in the name of the Tudor."

Don Carlos bowed himself from the Prince's presence and, slapping Laurence on the shoulder, left to give orders to his men. The Prince turned to Laurence.

"Master de la Halle, if you would, get me out of this damned harness."

Damned harness, thought Laurence as he began to unbuckle the leather straps. All other kings and nobles delighted in wearing armour and he had never known them consider it damned. This simple statement told him he was dealing with a courtier rather than a fighting man-at-arms. Even Henry Tudor appeared in armour, though he never actually took part in battle. Did he consider it damned too? Perhaps the world of kings was changing? If the finest armour could not preserve the life of a militant king, such as King

Richard the Third had been, then what use was it to any monarch other than decoration?

He mused upon that thought for a while. On one hand a monarch's harness would be merely for display, as the duke of York was using it here, and in that case it meant much profitable business for armourers of Laurence's class. He would be able to command a fee to match the extravagance of the armour he was making. On the other hand, he had the feeling there was something lost, a past glory. He thought on the tales the troubadours sang: of gallantry, romance and chivalry where everything could be decided upon in one mad brave charge, such as King Richard's at Bosworth; but that, prophetically had fallen to the ground along with Richard's body. He thought on how a knight might pledge his arms to the defence of a lady and fight for her honour. How might a new world order affect that particular aspect of courtly love? Would women be plunged into a nightmare comparable to that which existed before chivalry gentled, albeit artificially, the grosser conditions of men?

It was upon this last question that he remembered Anna was near, waiting in her transport vessel for disembarkation. As soon as his feet touched the quay he was determined to find her and he knew she would be looking for him, too. He had no idea what the Prince would do now, or where he might go. Exile was a possibility and if the saints had a sense of humour, maybe he would find himself in Brittany and become, as Henry Tudor once was, a pawn in a long game of international diplomacy while languishing at a foreign court and ever dreaming of a lost crown.

* * *

"I have heard the duchess Margaret has written to the Holy Father at Rome requesting he overturn the Bull of Excommunication he has imposed upon anyone in England declaring for our duke of York." Laurence was replying to a statement of Anna's that those in England sympathetic to the cause of the Prince could be slow in coming to his banner due to the Pope's edict made at the request of Henry Tudor. "Tudor's argument placed before the Pope was spurious to say the least. It would never have been accepted had there been a counter argument at the time."

Sitting close against the wall of a tavern in the town of Youghall, each was nursing a cup of rough wine. They had spent the night together in a nearby barn, after paying the owner an exorbitant

240

fee and had come here for a coarse meal of bread and cheese. There was no room to be had anywhere in the town. Laurence was greatly disturbed that he could not accommodate himself and his wife in a better abode, but the town was crammed full of soldiery and the truth of it was their strawy bed was very much superior to the sleeping arrangements of many others. Anna, it seemed, was quite satisfied with her lot, stating that she had determined to come with him and therefore must not complain. They had a few possessions with them in a canvas bag, the rest still remaining in their chests aboard the supply ship that lay alongside the quay in the harbour, but which were due to be brought ashore today.

"Tudor has his throne by conquest, not particularly recognised in English law, but pragmatically accepted, as with the late King Edward. Richard of York is a true blood prince," Laurence paused and grinned at her, "that is if you ignore the material fact of his bastardy, overturned by Henry Tudor himself. The Pope is bound to support the blood right of a king over that of a bastard claimant, so Margaret may yet upset the delicate legal situation to our advantage." Anna swilled the wine in her cup, gazing into it as if trying to discern the future.

"There are two dukes of York now," she sighed. "I wonder how this whole affair will be resolved?" She was referring to the news that Henry Tudor had invested his second son, also called Henry, as duke of York - a direct counter to the threat posed by their own Prince.

"It does show the extent of his fear of the real one," returned Laurence with a chuckle. "It means one of them must go sooner or later. I wonder if the Tudor has thought of that? It might be his own son is in danger."

Anna looked about the crowded tavern to ensure nobody was in earshot and leaned close to her husband. "The turncoat, Robert Clifford has been putting it around that he originally went to Flanders in the belief our Prince was Richard of York, but now he knows him to be an impostor."

"Yes and if that had been true he would no longer be walking the world, having returned to the Tudor court. Luckily for him, Clifford, in refuting the Prince's real identity is useful to the Tudor who needs to discredit the Prince."

"Think you his real reason is that he has perceived our Prince has not the aggressive capacity to win and keep a crown? Perhaps thinking so, he returned to the Tudor in an attempt at preserving his own life and interests?"

Laurence sat back in consternation. Anna had voiced his own doubts as to the Prince's martial spirit. When he had been with King Edward back in fourteen seventy-one, nobody doubted the military capacity of their leader - but his one . . .?

"I have no doubt that is Clifford's motive, but his defection and lies helps the Tudor to muddy the waters further. It would hardly matter had we merely the nobility of Europe to deal with; they can tell a true prince from a counterfeit well enough. It is the common people whom we need to convince if we are to win a crown for duke Richard. Unfortunately they are the very ones most susceptible to twisted Tudor lies. I remember well it was the commonality that were stirred against King Richard by rumours he had murdered his nephews and provoked to rebellion. None of that was true either."

Anna took a thoughtful pull at her wine cup. "Yes, the common crowd is fickle to be sure. Some of those who once thought the two princes murdered are now ready to believe one still lives. They can swing the other way at a moment. Dissembling works two ways, think you?" Laurence shrugged in agreement. "This is a war on two fronts," she continued, "one using arms and the other words. Tudor has found that out - he has been troubled by dissent ever since he usurped the crown at Bosworth Field and stories that the two princes live still circulate in spite of his desperate measures to suppress them. Serves him right; he gained his crown by treason and now must continue along the road he laid out for himself, dogged by the ever-present threat to his life and throne."

"You are correct, wife; but for the time we are engaged in the military aspect, where we must fight to win."

Anna placed her cup firmly on the bench before them. "Which brings us to the small matter of yesterday's sea fight. " She regarded him sternly, her eyes smouldering with suppressed anger.

Laurence shifted around uncomfortably. He wondered why she had not raised the matter before now, and supposed her distance from the engagement served to damp down her concern.

"It was hardly a sea fight," he countered. "We were the only ones to open fire and then but once. The ship's captain surrendered when faced with our overwhelming force."

"That may be so, husband, but out of twelve ships in our fleet, you managed to get yourself aboard one that actually went into action! My worst fears are being realised. What if the captain of the other vessel had fired back?"

"Well that didn't happen and in any case, should it come to a real fight, our Prince will remain well to the rear - we cannot risk his life otherwise our cause fails. I must remain with his grace, so I should be among the safest in our expedition."

Anna leaned her back against the wall, smiling smugly. "Well said, *monsieur*, then you will, as a natural consequence of that statement, desire your wife to be equally safe. Our chest will be unshipped soon. I shall have it transferred to your ship and you will just have to find me a place beside you there - in safety."

Laurence drew a sharp breath. He had not seen that one coming though he had been living constantly with the expectation that Anna would try some subterfuge to keep close by him. He spluttered unintelligibly for a moment before giving up. There was in fact, no counter to her argument and he could at least look after her. The transport she was on might well be a target for pirates or Tudor warships should it become separated from the main fleet.

Anna reached forward and broke off a hunk of bread, handing it to her husband along with a piece of cheese, her eyebrows raised in challenge, daring him to contradict her. He stuffed some in his mouth rendering himself speechless rather than admit he could find no fault with her argument.

* * *

The hall in the mayor's house at Youghall was not intended to accommodate so many as to be found in the entourage of the duke of York, as well as the few townsfolk that favoured the Yorkist claimant through their liege lord, Maurice earl of Desmond. Everyone was packed close and a dull background of noisy chatter confused the individual conversations of those gathered there. Many in the town had kept away having been intimidated by the threat of the English king to destroy their houses and businesses should they give aid or succour to those he termed rebels. That had not stopped them buying, at favourable prices, the goods plundered from the captured merchant ships. Those townsmen here with the Prince had previously been victims of the Tudor and thus had nothing more to lose but might yet gain something if they could help Desmond defeat the English forces sent against them.

Richard of York was standing in a bow window from where he had been gazing out down the Blackwater River towards the harbour, which was just out of sight around a bend in the river. He was clad in a fine doublet of yellow silk over plain brown hose, which somehow served to enrich the splendour of the silk. The weather had turned around and a miserable drizzle blurred the view and had turned the streets of the town to mud. Roderigo de LaLaing was with him while close by stood Sir Anthony de la Forsse and James Kething. John Watre, too, hovered close, fingering his chin in deep thought.

"This request is from the earl of Desmond who requires our help with his investment of Waterford," said the Prince, brandishing a parchment he had been holding by his side. "We must make all dispatch. The Tudor has sent Sir Edward Poynings with a small army to contest with Desmond and wrest back control of Ireland. The earl espouses our cause and we are bound to go to his aid."

Laurence was standing amid the other courtiers in the duke of York's entourage listening with interest to what was being decided. Most of his grace's followers seemed to agree that they must take ship for Waterford where Desmond had laid siege to the town these past few weeks. The citizens there were resisting, being adherents of the Tudor King of England while Desmond was encamped just outside the fortified town, unable to get inside. Waterford was set on the Suir, upriver from the large anchorage at the river mouth. The only way there by land was protected by a series of flooded moats and water-filled ditches making a concerted attack difficult to say the least.

"I wonder why Desmond's army has not broken into Waterford ere now?" growled Don Carlos in Laurence's ear. "He has enough men for the job. He has been there a month with no progress so far as I can see."

"Perhaps he is waiting for our ships. We can approach from the sea and distract the defenders while he attacks from the landward side?"

"A futile strategy," bemoaned Don Carlos. "My ship is at hazard being used thus. I would keep the profit I have made here rather than lose it along with my ship by attacking a fortified town." He was referring to his share of the goods plundered from the ships taken in the approaches to Youghall harbour.

Laurence had some sympathy with Don Carlos. His ship was his living and a seafaring life was risky enough without engaging in warfare. He had reckoned on transporting an army to England and then either profiting from the duke of York's victory or sailing away with his fee from Margaret of Burgundy, his vessel intact to resume his peaceful trade.

"It looks as if you have no choice, my friend," said Laurence considerately. "If you sail away and later enter an English port, you will find your ship impounded and yourself imprisoned for a rebel.

As the rest of us, you must carry on with the Prince's quest. Once he obtains the Crown of England we shall all be at an advantage."

"And somewhere between these two hazards, victory or defeat, there might be an opportunity to negotiate ourselves free of the whole business." The Spaniard tapped the side of his nose in the manner of a merchant moneylender.

"Your meaning?" responded Laurence cautiously.

"The English king is affrighted by our Prince, and a fearful man is always ready to negotiate a deal to weaken his opponent."

Laurence looked around, hoping that nobody near was listening to the Spaniard at this moment. Fortunately everyone was focused on the Prince and his immediate advisers.

"Take great care, *senor*," he whispered with something of panic in his voice. "You speak of treason."

"You would inform the Prince?" asked Don Carlos with a grim smile. "I speak as a friend, that is all. It is sensible to have an escape plan for such a sea as we are afloat upon. A roaring tide may have us on the rocks in an instant."

"I understand what you say well enough," Laurence responded. "But for the time, our enterprise depends upon the willingness of many different loyalties, most of them whose interest is only to themselves, and who fight for a cause not their own."

"Such as we?"

"Yes. Our army comprises mostly mercenaries and there are few Englishmen amongst us. We are Flemish, German, you have a Spanish crew and I am Breton. But understand this, our Prince has the support of the duchess Margaret, Philip the Fair of Burgundy, Maximilian who is *de facto* Holy Roman Emperor and also, so I hear, the King of Scotland is on our side. We might add the King of France and the monarchs of Spain, your own country, though I must admit the last two are pragmatic supporters merely despite their private convictions and are not to be counted upon. The point is our Prince has powerful friends who would rather a *bone fide* monarch be seated on the throne of England than a bastard upstart which is the Tudor. You risk much in abandoning the duke of York now before the frail Tudor regime has even been properly contested."

"I suppose you are correct, my friend," agreed Don Carlos with a nod of his head. "I am premature. Let us play at the hazard a little while longer, but bear in mind what I say. We may yet need a way out of our present commitments."

Speaking later to Anna, he recounted his conversation with Don Carlos. They were huddled down in the forecastle of the Maria, Don

245

Carlos' ship, batting against the waves as they ploughed their way to Waterford. The sea was rough making Anna distinctly uncomfortable, but, Laurence noted with some relief, not so bad that she must stand on deck and vomit. It seemed she was gaining her sea legs. As for himself, he felt some slight nausea but nothing very much and even in the roughest weather he never seemed to get worse than he was feeling now.

"The plan is to get ashore and join with Desmond's army," he informed her, "It will be a relief to get our feet on dry land rather than a heaving deck."

"But no nearer England, which was supposed to be our landing," grumbled Anna. "I fail to see how tramping Irish soil is going to get the Prince his crown. I mean, suppose the earl of Desmond takes Waterford - what then? He will have to hold on to it. Even if he lends us some men, the last invasion of England from Ireland came to disaster at Stoke. We know the Tudor is sending reinforcements to his garrisons in all the major towns here so Desmond is likely to have his hands full. I cannot see a way forward."

"Let us think on the situation when we get to Desmond's camp. The Prince must have some plan to get himself into England with an army and he still has many friends."

"We have no other option. By now the duke of York should have been King of England. That was our mission and it looks as if we shall be dragging around after him for some time yet. I advise we stay close to captain Don Carlos. If he decides to get out, then we should go with him and never mind your reputation. That will do you no good if you are dead."

Laurence was forced to agree with her. He reflected again how he was in exactly the same position as when he had joined with Edward Plantagenet, the Prince's father. At that time he had been ready to switch allegiance to whoever won the English throne, but then Edward actually landed on the shores of England. If he had been forced to flee to Ireland, would Laurence have remained with him then? The answer came back to him - probably not. Having Anna with him too made that a virtual certainty.

12 – Bellicosus

The pavilion of Maurice FitzGerald, 9th earl of Desmond, was easily picked out from those others in the encampment. It was colourfully hung with the Desmond banners and his standard: a red saltire cross on a white ground. The whole might be set in the fancy as a jewel in a dung heap. All around was a scene of confused desolation where camp fires smoked fitfully, their kindling being damp, and the ground churned to mud by the feet of the earl's army along with the deeper indentations made by horse and mule. Beyond were the walls of the town, deceptively bare of heads though there was no doubt the camp was being carefully watched for signs of imminent attack upon the town. Waterford's dominant feature was a round fortified tower that commanded the approaches along the river. The Suir was wide enough at this point for the Prince's ships to stay just out of range of the guns that had been placed atop the tower.

The day had dawned warm and clear after a few days of dreary drizzle. Tents and pavilions were steaming in the July sunshine. As usual, Laurence had smelled the army before actually bringing it to sight as he tramped along behind the duke of York from their landing place on the bank of the river Suir above the town. The Prince was mounted along with Sir Anthony de la Forsse, Roderigo de LaLaing, James Kething and John Watre while everyone else in his company must march along a well-trodden trail. They passed a company of Gallowglass, well armed native mercenaries who gave their military service in return for grants of land.

Other Irish soldiers were a poor lot, dressed in long woollen jackets and scant leg wear. Some had shoes, some sandals and a considerable number were barefoot. They were naked – that is without armour though a few wore helmets of several types, no doubt plundered, or picked up from a battlefield somewhere. All had daggers but few seemed to be armed with either sword or halberd. Laurence knew them to be brave and determined fighters, but their general lack of body armour and proper weapons made them easy pickings for a well-supplied army. Men as these had fought for the earl of Lincoln and Lambert Simnal at Stoke Field and had been slaughtered there by the trained army of King Henry under the earl of Oxford. *This answers Don Carlos who wondered why the town had not been taken after a siege of four weeks*, thought Laurence as he dragged his boots out of the sucking mud. No doubt the earl of Desmond awaited the arrival of the duke of York for the use of his ships and fresh mercenaries. Nothing Laurence could see around here encouraged him to believe the Prince's enterprise could thrive by association.

The procession halted in front of the Desmond pavilion where a dozen of the earl's followers and captains waited to greet them. Fresh rushes had been put down to obscure the mud beneath. The Prince seemed somewhat confused by the absence of the earl himself. As duke Richard reined in his horse, the Irish captains stood away from the entrance while a litter was brought outside, borne by four Gallowglass. The litter had a chair mounted on it draped in green velvet and here seated was Maurice FitzGerald, earl of Desmond. He was a heavy, thick-set man of around forty years with a neatly trimmed, twin pointed beard. His eyes were dark brown under heavy eyebrows and his face was ruddy in complexion. Bare headed, his long hair was drawn back and tied neatly behind. His robe was yellow and richly lined with sable while his lower limbs were covered over with a golden cloth of state; this to hide the deformity in his legs which had rendered him lame. He waved a generously beringed hand in greeting to the duke of York.

"Welcome back, my lord Richard of England," he called, raising himself slightly in his chair. "Please forgive me for greeting you thus, but I am stricken as you can see." The earl signed to a servant who brought a wooden stool to the Prince to help him dismount. The duke of York climbed down from his horse, strode confidently up to the earl and clasped him firmly by the hand.

"My lord Desmond, it is good to see you again. Please do not worry about courtly protocols. We are here to join hands in battle, not to dance a carole. The only pipes we have brought with us use gunpowder and sound a sterner note."

"Bravely said, your grace," Desmond replied. "The city has good ordnance too, otherwise it would have been taken by now."

Laurence kept his face straight at this last boastful statement of Desmond's. While waiting for the duke of York to arrive, he heard the earl had been busy attacking and plundering the lands to the north held by the English and their Gaelic allies, particularly the Butlers. Thomas Butler was a friend of Henry Tudor, who had restored to him his title 7th earl of Ormond in return for his fidelity. He was also 8th earl of Carrick. At one time his daughter Anne had been contracted in marriage to this same earl of Desmond but which event had never happened. The present countess and second wife of

Maurice FitzGerald is a daughter of Lord Barry, the White Knight of Kerry, who Laurence hardly expected to be here with the earl. He pondered upon Desmond's strategy – was he warning off the Butlers or merely stirring up a nest of vipers that might come to sting them?

The Prince signed at those others in his retinue to dismount and they did so, lining up in front of Desmond and the duke, kneeling in obeisance before being told by Desmond to rise. Those with the Prince stood and went inside with the earl. A man-at-arms came out of the crowd of soldiers clustered curiously around the earl of Desmond's pavilion and the remainder of the Prince's followers, including Laurence, were conducted towards several smaller pavilions nearby that were apparently reserved for their use. The rest of the Prince's army would disembark later from the ships and find their own places in the encampment.

Laurence began to think about how Anna might be accommodated. It looked as though he would be sharing the ground within his allotted pavilion with several other men. The Prince's personal armourer he might be, but in a siege camp such as this, there were no places for women other than the usual camp followers. An idea came to him and he began to look about the camp for the armourers who must be set up somewhere. Perhaps a bed within a forge, temporary though it might be, could be a possibility?

As expected, the camp of the armourers and smiths was easy to find, not too far away from the bulk of the soldiery and near to where the horses were herded. Martin Boylan was the forge master and he was pleased to discover an artisan armourer with the duke of York's men. Fortunately, he spoke French so the two could converse naturally. He was a proficient armourer himself, but was overwhelmed by the demands of the nobles in the earl of Desmond's army who were coming in a constant stream for work to be done on their harness. A lot of it he could delegate to the smiths and his less skilled armourers, but the finer pieces required the ability to alter, repair and retemper steel that was engraved, or embossed with intricate design.

"Take this piece of iron, for instance," he said, brandishing a pauldron. "The brother to this has been smashed and the wearer crippled in his shoulder, yet he insists on a replacement when the fool should retire to his home. You can see how the fluting goes. He has a scallop shell embossed upon it because his ancestor was a crusading knight and he must display it in his iron. There is hours of work in this alone and there is more of the same."

"Well I can tap out a new pauldron if you let me have this for the design," said Laurence, regarding the armour with a practised eye. "My lord, his grace the duke of York is not demanding so far as his armour is concerned, so I can find the time. I am sure we can come to some agreement over pricing the work done here at your forge?"

"Indeed we can," replied Martin with something of relief in his voice. Then, as if realising he had shown too much of desperation, he hardened his stance. "Of course, everything must come through this forge. There are extra expenses in a siege camp where supplies of charcoal and new iron must be brought in over hostile territory."

"It is always so," agreed Laurence, "but our lords must have their iron mended and we are the only ones here who can do that . . ." He let the sentence trail off.

Martin Boylan looked at him carefully and then, deciding they were fellows of a similar disposition, laughed and slapped him on the shoulder. "Then we are *confrères* are we not?"

"To be sure."

"Then let us seal our fraternity with a small drop of something to keep out the chill." The armourer led Laurence to the back of his forge. He had taken the trouble to construct if from stone, rather like that found in cottage walls, loosely stacked, but firm as a base. Over this was a timber frame covered with what looked like sailcloth. Though it was a rough construction yet it was more weatherproof than the tents and pavilions of the army. The furnaces were located just on the outside but the anvils and stake plates were placed under cover where the light was good but no rain could interfere with the work. The back of the forge was darker, but warm and Laurence noted a straw pallet bed where Boylan would sleep and noted, with some rearrangement, there might be room here for himself and Anna.

Whatever it was that Martin Boylan put into his cup, Laurence felt that a forge fire had been poured down his throat. Once his eyes had cleared of tears, Boylan poured some more and so they continued until he lost all sense of time. He was vaguely aware of the fall of evening and his need to get back to Anna, who was coming with the rest of the army, but somehow all this faded to nothingness as eternity opened up before him. Martin Boylan was, he discovered, a troubadour, or at least the Irish equivalent of one. He brought out a strange stringed instrument, something resembling a lute and began plucking it while singing in a language unintelligible to him. Laurence told him, fraternally as drunken men do, that he could not understand what the * * * he was singing of

250

and was there anything in his soul that might count as civilised song? Martin feigned upset, then grinned and sang an old song, *Ja nuls homs pres*, no man imprisoned. Originally written by King Richard the First of England, Martin sang it in *le langue d'oc*, or *Occitane*, the language of the first troubadours. It told of long imprisonment and the King's unhappiness as he waited for his ransom to be paid.

"I know all about waiting to be paid," lamented Laurence.

"As we all do - even the nobles wait upon a king's treasurer, but debt bears heaviest on those like us who have no rents they can call in to live upon."

"What is this we are drinking?" Laurence decided to ask at last.

"*Uisce beatha*," came the reply. "It is Gaelic and translates into English as *the water of life* and Latin as *aqua vitae*. The English cannot manage a civilised language so have started to call it whiskey, a bastard name."

"It has had a distinct influence on me, I must say," mumbled Laurence, his head decidedly muzzy. "I thought that *aqua vitae* was a medicine brewed only by monks and apothecaries?"

"Why do you think that monks keep to their monastery walls? Because after drinking they cannot walk far enough to get out."

"That is due to a surfeit of wine."

"Which applies to the Abbot only - the monks here brew *uisce beatha* from their barley beer. There is very little wine in Ireland, so we make do as best we can."

"I fear it will never become popular outside of Ireland," said Laurence.

"We keep it secret, although our neighbours in Scotland have discovered it."

"For medicinal purposes only I presume. Scotland has an affinity with France and the people there will appreciate the grape rather than the grain."

"If you say so."

"I do."

"Your lord is fortunate to be friendly with *Bellicosus*," said Martin. "If he were to go anywhere near the Pale, just to the north of here, his enterprise would be over."

"Bellicosus?"

"Oh, that is his name amongst us. It is due to the fierceness of his nature. Some style him *Vehiculus* because he is carried around on a litter, except in battle when he is placed upon a horse."

"I see," replied Laurence. "I am aware that the Pale is under the direct jurisdiction of the English king and so too is the earldom of Ormond, the domains of the Butler's and which borders the earldom of Desmond. I think our position here is precarious and when the Tudor sends help over from England, we will be in trouble – or is there something I do not understand?"

"You are correct, except matters in Ireland are rarely that simple. Though the Pale is under English domination, the people there are in a state of perpetual rebellion and must be kept in check. The English king demands high tribute, extorts money through charges for imports, exports, cartage and rents, in fact any coin that is not hidden ends up in the Tudor exchequer. There is scant enthusiasm by the people in the Pale for an attack on the earl of Desmond when he is besieging an English-held town. Having said that, the earl has come to terms with King Henry in the recent past and may yet do so again if it is politic to do so."

"Matters are not much different in England, so far as taxation and extortion by the Tudor is concerned. I have friends at home in Brittany who fled England because of it. Bishop Morton, Tudor's favourite, is in charge of finance and he simply assumes that if no coin can be found in your house, then you must have hidden it and concocts his own inventory whereupon he taxes you accordingly. Even if you pay what he demands in the first place, he assumes such enthusiasm means you must have more wealth hidden than you are declaring and raises the tax even higher."

Martin grimaced having clearly heard of matters in England too. "They call the process Morton's Fork, do they not? It stabs the English in their vitals. What makes matters worse all round is that the Tudor must raise an army to combat the claim of the duke of York, and that costs money."

"Tudor's right to the throne of England has been challenged constantly since he clambered upon it," said Laurence, his speech beginning to slur. "He has been, and is faced perpetually with military attack and rebellion. He must raise money for his army, having reduced the rights of the nobility to keep armed retinues of their own. His is the politics of fear and insecurity."

"He must fall eventually, I suppose," agreed Martin, "and it is that belief which keeps rebellion alive."

"And too the cause of the duke of York." Laurence slumped back against the wall of the forge, his head swimming with apprehension. He could not see a future here for Prince Richard and thought he might speak with Don Carlos again. His mind's eye saw the Spanish ship sailing away from Ireland with himself and Anna leaning over the rail, watching with relief the receding coast. Slowly his eyes closed and he began to snore stentorianly. Martin Boylan grinned and pushed him over to lie on his side, then covered him with a woollen blanket. He would be comfortable enough lying there for the rest of the night.

* * *

Laurence was well used to the sound of hammering, but the clamour that sounded within his skull was something rather more, as if he were possessed by demon smiths sent hot from Hell to torment him. If that were not bad enough, here was Anna, with a face of thunder who *would* persist in shouting at him. He clasped his hands to his ears as she railed at him. She had spent the night under a cart on a bed of straw that, according to her, would be kicked away by any respectable horse in stable. The cart had brought their chest, along with the possessions of some others in the duke of York's army and she was fortunate that she had the experience of camp life to stake a claim on her sleeping place before anyone else. He tried to explain that he had found a better place for them both in the forge, but that only served to increase her ire. He had left her to sleep under the stars while he was comfortably tucked up in a warm forge, besotted with drink.

"I had no idea how potent was the drink," he whispered, unable to raise his voice any louder.

"So you just had to go on swilling it to find out your limit." Anna was furious and upset. "I spent most of the night fending off leering Irish oafs who think a woman in a camp has but one purpose."

Laurence was uncomfortable at this news. He now had a feeling of guilt to contend with along with a sick head and stomach. It was this last organ that diverted Anna's wrath to be replaced by unsympathetic glowering as she watched while he vomited into a ditch by the side of the path.

"You had better come and deal with our chest before someone makes off with our belongings and your tools." She took his arm and steered him back the few yards along the path to where the carter had just finished depositing its load by the edge of the encampment. Already the owners of the other trunks were claiming their own and, no doubt something of Laurence and Anna's had they not turned up at that moment. Laurence slipped a coin to the carter and ordered him to take his chest to the forges. With some effort in his weakened state, he managed to lift Anna to seat her on the tail of the cart so she would not have to step through the mud and ordure of the camp. Somewhat mollified by this gesture she softened her features, though she refused to smile at him as they plodded along with him walking by the cart looking at her in dejection.

Martin Boylan was hardly human, thought Laurence as they came to the armourers' forges. The place was ringing with the strike of hammers upon iron and it was all he could do not to turn and run. Martin was beating at a breastplate as if he had never touched a drop of *uisce beatha* in his life.

His eyes leapt with light as he spied Anna. "Good mornin' yor ladyship," he cried, cheekily granting her an elevated title she did not own. He immediately began charming Anna out of her bad humour and she responded gaily, ignoring her husband and enjoying the blandishments of the Irishman. Laurence listened to the two of them exchanging pleasantries until he could endure their noisy chatter no more. Moreover, the sounds of the forge were boring into his skull.

"I must seek out the duke of York," he declared as firmly as he could. He needed to get away from the incessant clamour of the forges and his attendance upon the Prince was a good enough reason. "Martin has agreed we may rest in the forge while we are here."

"Surely, you are most welcome to share my abode," said Martin, smiling at Anna. "I will get your chest inside." He gestured to one of the forge labourers and ordered him to bring the chest from the cart.

"I shall not be a burden, master Boylan," she declared. "I have already noted there is sickness in the camp and I have tended to sick and wounded men ere now. There must be a place where the infirm are brought?"

"Indeed, yor ladyship," growled Martin with mock seriousness. "The physicians' tents are quite near. I shall escort you there myself."

"First, if you have some small beer for my husband? He is in sore need of something to restore him." Laurence's stomach heaved at the thought, but he did have a raging thirst and the water in camp would be death to drink.

"Water from the quenching barrels will revive him," responded Martin. "It's the iron in it I believe. The red iron boils it and you don't want to drink it hot, so we reserve some and cool it for

254

drinking." Laurence had used this remedy before in his own forge when the flux was upon him and he had come to no harm. Mother Malkin had taught him this and she even spooned water from the quenching barrels into the mouths of infants when they sickened. Joan had used the remedy on her own children. Quenching hot iron in it made water unpleasant and it was impossible to drink much of it.

"You are certain this is just water?" he asked, looking at Martin apprehensively. It was necessary to be certain what was actually in a quenching barrel – it was often not just water. There were several barrels in an armourers' forge filled with a variety of substances, typically urine and blood. Laurence had certain mixtures of his own that he used to get the finish to the iron he required.

"It is water, assuredly," laughed Martin. "I take it myself."

Laurence took a beaker and drained it in three gulps while Anna watched to ensure it stayed down. He grimaced and twisted his face with distaste, but after a few moments he did feel somewhat better.

Seeing Anna settled at the forge, Laurence tramped off towards the pavilions of the nobles. As he approached that of *Bellicosus*, where he assumed the Prince would be, John Watre, who was standing just outside hurried up to him. He was wearing full harness, though without a helm. His surcoat was in the blue and murrey of York with a single white rose decorating his left shoulder.

"Where have you been?" he snapped angrily. "His grace has asked for you to attend upon him and you were nowhere by." Laurence searched desperately for an excuse but merely managed a shrug. He would have to do better than that in front of the Prince. Watre bustled him past the guard at the entrance to the pavilion. The earl of Desmond was seated, as usual on a chair under a short canopy bearing the earl's device and with it, he noted, that of England. The duke of York stood beside him clad in his magnificent harness.

"Ah, master de la Halle," growled the Prince, "Here you are at last. We thought you fallen into a ditch. There are many between here and the town." Laurence got down on his knees in the rushes, which he noted were at least fresh, and looked up at Richard. Beside him *Bellicosus*, for Laurence was now unable to think of him by his formal title, eyed him with stern interest.

"Your grace," he began, his brain frantically groping for a suitable excuse. "I have been at the forges of the armourers here in the camp." Suddenly inspiration came to him. "I knew your grace would need my services ere long and I wanted to be sure the facility here was good enough."

"I wonder what you found there? Judging by your dishevelment I think you might have mistaken a sty for the forges."

Laurence thought it best not to comment. The Prince indicated for him to get to his feet.

"I have my squires to arm me, fortunately. It is not for myself that I have need of you now, but for my lord here, the earl of Desmond." Laurence shifted his attention to *Bellicosus*. My lord has a problem with his harness and I believe you have the skill to put him to rights."

"Whatever humble talents I have you can be assured of my best attention," he replied looking between the two, then facing the earl: "I am at your service, my lord."

The Prince turned to Desmond. "I shall get my men ready and send them off right away. Sir Anthony will see them aboard ship then return to us here. They are de LaLaing's men and should land around mid-morning." With that he left taking his entourage with him. Laurence wondered what was happening and looked to *Bellicosus* hoping for enlightenment. The earl ignored his unspoken question. He waved away all but one of his body squires leaving just the three of them in the pavilion.

"The duke of York tells me you are discreet in personal matters?"

"I hope so my lord."

"Hope! Are you not certain then?" snapped the earl irritably.

Laurence struggled to break through the fuzziness in his head. "I apologise if I failed to make myself clear," he replied hurriedly. "Anything of a private nature will be an inviolable secret between us, as if you were in the confessional with your chaplain."

"Yes, his grace the duke has recommended you. Apparently you were the one who arranged his escape from the Tower of London and his subsequent disguise at Tournai. You kept his secret well I am told."

"I had some small role in the business, though there were others involved too."

The earl scrutinised his face with fierce, probing eyes. "Then I can use your services for which you will be well paid, either in coin or, if you betray me, with the loss of your head."

"I am overly attached to my head, my lord, but my discretion would be assured in any case." Laurence felt a tight knot in his stomach that was something rather more than the remnants of the last evening's drinking bout.

The earl grabbed the golden cloth that covered his legs and threw it off revealing the deformity in his legs. Laurence was as used to the sight of physical deformity as any, but had something of a professional interest. Most men had some feature of their body they wished to be otherwise and his job was to enhance or conceal such deformity, as appropriate. Here, although clad in hose he could see that the earl had one leg a good three inches shorter than the other, while that other leg, though of average length was bowed and seemed twisted.

"Has my lord broken the limb at some time?" asked Laurence, careful not to make reference to the shorter one.

"As a youth in the joust," he replied. "The bonesetter was a clumsy fool and it was not until the limb was unwrapped after healing that the deformity was exposed. The louse never set another bone afterwards, except his skull, which I set for him on a spike over my gate."

"Is there much pain, my lord?"

"I can hardly bear to set my foot to the ground, but apart from an ache on damp days, it is bearable when I am seated. I have not asked you here as my physician. I have seen plenty of those and they are useless. No, what I want from you is harness to protect the legs. That which I have is no longer serviceable and makes me look odd."

Laurence stood back a little and studied the earl's problem. He had an idea for the twisted limb, but the short one was problematical.

"Can I see your old leg harness?" Desmond was already clad in his cuirass of breastplate and back plate.

The earl motioned to his squire who brought over the cuisse, poleyns and greaves of his harness. Laurence examined them. The workmanship was quite good, as he would expect for an earl would not engage an unskilled armourer. He noted that the iron matched closely the contours of the earl's legs, though some attempt had been made to crease the metal to deceive the eye, giving the impression of a straight limb, though this was unlikely to be very successful. Looking at the armour and then comparing it to the earl's leg he reckoned there had been some physical deterioration over time and the armour would no longer fit properly.

"My lord, I believe I can do something to clad your right leg comfortably. As for the left leg, the problem there is the armour must terminate at the foot, thus determining the limit of the iron and there is nothing I can provide that will alter that. I can shorten the tasset plate on your left side and that will give the impression of a longer limb?"

The earl tugged at his beard, thinking it over. "The length will not be noticeable much when I am horsed and your suggestion is sensible. You say you can do something to improve the appearance of my right leg?"

"Yes my lord. I must take some careful measurements, with your permission. I need some items from my work chest to do that."

"Then get to it, I have a fight to arrange today but you may attend me this evening. I will provide you with a pavilion of your own here by mine and a forge where you may work without hindrance." Laurence understood that what the earl meant was for him to work in private to preserve his dignity. He would not be able to disguise the nature of his work in the common forges.

"Thank you my lord."

The earl waved him away and turned to his squire. "Prepare my litter, there is work to be done."

As Laurence hurried towards the armourers' forges he met Anna hurrying towards him, alarm written in her face.

"What is it," he demanded, thinking someone had tried to molest her.

"Don Carlos," she gasped, a little out of breath. "He is ordered to take his ship along with another down river to Lombard's Wear, a landing just below the town. They are to land soldiers and attack the town."

"So that is what *Bellicosus* and the Prince had been planning, an assault on the town walls. Never fear, Don Carlos will not be expected to land with them, he will remain with his ship."

"Let us hope so," she replied. "He is our escape route should we need one."

"Hush you, for now we are rather better placed than before. I have secured us our own pavilion right next to that of *Bellicosus* and the duke of York. We must get our belongings together and my tools then bid adieu to Martin Boylan." He thought he detected a flicker of disappointment on Anna's face at this statement, reminding him he still had a thick head to provide him with an excuse to grunt with resentment.

* * *

The earl of Desmond had expressed disquiet when he discovered his new armourer had brought his wife with him. Laurence mollified him by pointing out that as the work he was doing was of a confidential nature, his wife's presence was an added security. She could help him with some tasks, such as working the bellows for his fire, meaning he would not have to ask for a servant from the camp who would likely comment on what he was doing. Laurence was watching the colour of a tasset plate in the fire for tempering while Anna slowly levered the bellows up and down according to his instructions. There were two of these arranged back-to-back and when one was blowing air, the other was filling. This arrangement provided an almost continuous draught of air under the charcoal and great care had to be taken not to get the fire too hot. It was tiring work, but Anna was coping bravely.

Both were subdued by the news from the army regarding the attack on the town by the men sent in the ships to Lombard's Wear. The Waterford citizens dispatched a force to oppose them and managed to kill or capture a large number of Prince Richard's Flemish mercenaries, mostly men under the authority of Roderigo de LaLaing. That was bad - a repeat of the fiasco at Deal beach. Men sent in support were bogged down in the ditches and moats in the land around the town and had to retire, leaving the mercenaries to the mercies of the townsmen. Even worse news followed. The men of Waterford had mounted heavy cannon atop the fortified tower that dominated the river approaches. They opened fire on the two ships and sank them, killing Don Carlos in the action. Thus, in one fell swoop they had lost a friend and their means of sailing away from Ireland. Mercenaries that had been captured were paraded - roped together through the town of Waterford, then beheaded and their heads set on spikes on the town walls, in full view for the attacker's benefit.

Laurence plunged the reddened tasset plate into the quenching barrel and momentarily disappeared in a cloud of steam. He examined it then passed it to Anna.

"You might rub that over with fine sand to get it bright," he said, his mind elsewhere. She took it from him and set to, glad for something with which to occupy herself. He hated having her do this work. Normally he would take on a boy to do it, but this job for the earl of Desmond was particular and it did provide them with good accommodation and status in the camp. Both of them had full bellies and warmth, which was more than could be said for the soldiers who slept under the cold stars, shivering at night even though it was early august.

"I shall offer this for a fitting today," he said, taking up the armour for *Bellicosus'* right leg. He turned the work around in his hands looking especially at the padding inside it. He had fashioned what appeared on the outside to be fairly normal leg armour, but inside were leather pouches stuffed with compressed wool. These were intended to support the leg where the limb curved so that the harness itself could be made to appear as a straight limb.

The earl of Desmond was delighted with his new leg armour. The iron comfortably supported his right leg and he found he could stand and bear his weight on it. The problem with his short left leg was partly solved by a device that Laurence had fashioned to fit under the sabaton at his foot, letting him stand straight. When mounted on a horse, he would have to remove it to get the foot into the stirrup. The earl still needed crutches under his arms to enable him to get around, but at least he could stand when he needed to display himself before his men.

The duke of York stood back from his ally and regarded the new leg armour.

"Excellent work, master de la Halle," he declared with a degree of enthusiasm that almost sounded as if he had done the work himself. "My lord Desmond stands straight of limb." The faces of the courtiers who had filed into the pavilion with the Prince beamed in agreement.

Bellicosus' face was a picture of delight. He stood upright and spread his arms wide to test his balance. After a few moments he began to sway and his squires hurriedly placed his crutches under his armpits. He set his face back to its habitual grimace, that being part habit and part natural belligerence.

"You have served me well, monsieur de la Halle," he growled, not quite curmudgeonly. He beckoned to one of his servants who handed him a leather purse. "Here, for your efforts." He handed the purse to Laurence who, having noted the weight, bowed his thanks to the earl. "Now let us get harness on our backs, then we can leave camp."

Laurence wondered what was going on. There had been plenty of activity around the earl's pavilion and he assumed there would be another assault on the town walls.

"I shall get into my harness, too," stated the duke of York. "Come, my lords, we must move quickly. Master armourer, I need you to come along with my company." The Prince took his leave of the earl of Desmond and left to go to his own pavilion. Laurence followed among the courtiers and managed to catch the eye of John Watre.

"Is there to be a fight?" he enquired.

"Not if we can get away in time," came the reply.

"Get away?"

That sounded as if a withdrawal was in the offing. He would have to get to Anna and ensure they had their belongings safely stowed in the baggage. He would settle up with Martin Boylan for the cost of the charcoal and iron he had purchased for Desmond's armour.

"Yes. We have word Sir John Poynings has mustered certain men of Ormond and the Butlers and is coming to the aid of Waterford. They are fewer than us but well armed with handguns and cannon. The earl of Desmond has ordered a strategic retreat rather than risk being caught between Waterford and Poyning's army."

"Are we to embark in our ships?"

"No, they have left us and have fled who knows where," lamented Watre. "Two more were sunk yesterday. They were down to six and their masters will not brook any further risk to their vessels."

" A vast reduction in the fifteen that sailed from Flanders," replied Laurence grimly, remembering Don Carlo's fears for his vessel, both now lost. "Shall we return to Flanders?" He asked this more in hope than with confidence. The enterprise of England had gone too far for them to return in ignominious disgrace. It would mean the end of all the hopes of York.

"Neither the duchess Margaret, nor the Emperor Maximilian will countenance that and we are far from finished, in fact, I believe the better part of our enterprise is before us." Was this false optimism, wondered Laurence? Watre was as fanatical in the Prince's cause as the duchess herself and seemed blind to the extent of the task they faced. Somewhere near a clarion sounded and men were running to form up in battle array. This would be a rearguard action, hopefully, to give the Prince and Desmond time to move away. A company of Gallowglass marched by, well disciplined and reasonably armed. Upon them would depend the quality of the resistance in the rearguard. All around, the pavilions of the nobles were coming down and men were bringing mules, horses, wagons and carts to pack away their goods and equipment.

"Where are we bound?" said Laurence anxiously. He felt something akin to panic rise in his breast, which he fought hard to suppress. Having Anna with him was concentrating his fears around her safety.

"Into Donegal and O'Donnell," came the reply.

"O'Donnell?"

"He is a firm adherent of our cause, being a thorn in the side of the English king by choice and habit. We shall reform at Donegal Castle and plan for our next move."

Laurence made some excuse regarding the stowage of the forge equipment and took his leave of Watre. There was now no chance of getting away by sea, though that was perhaps just as well. It was likely that those ships fleeing Waterford would be intercepted before reaching safe harbour in Flanders. He struggled through the mud towards the armourers' forges where he had taken Anna that morning, their pavilion near that of the earl of Desmond being one of the first to be dismantled. Boylan was there chivvying the forge labourers, smiths and armourers into getting their tools and portable equipment into a couple of heavy wagons. Anna was arguing with a churl who held a rope attached to a sturdy brown horse.

"Thank the saints you have finally appeared," she cried with obvious relief at the sight of him. This oaf is trying to cheat me into paying twice the market price for this nag."

"It be the price for such a fine animal. He is fit for a lord," exclaimed the churl. I can get more if I wait another day." This was true, Laurence knew only too well. Transport was at a premium and having come here by ship, he had been remiss in not getting them a horse before now.

"How much do you want for the nag," growled Laurence, eyeing the animal carefully. It was getting on in years but still had some useful life in it. It would bear some packs and let Anna ride it too, but they would have to place their chest in the armoury wagons and pay Boylan for the privilege.

Though he could hardly make out the meaning in the thick accent that passed for human speech that came from the churl, he did understand the figure he asked, which caused the scar on Laurence's cheek to whiten and the rest of his face to glow red with anger. He fought down his ire, realising he would have to remain calm if he were to get a better price. Anna placed her hands on her hips and glared fiercely at the man.

"Would you like me to settle a price?" offered Boylan, who had been watching them. He spoke to the man in some outlandish dialect particular to the peasants of the country. The churl seemed to become more deferential in his manner and Laurence gave Boylan a reluctant nod. A battle of wills ensued, with the churl becoming more hostile in the face of Boylan's remorseless bargaining. Finally they seemed to agree. Boylan turned to Laurence and mentioned an amount that, though still a heavy price, was considerably less than originally asked for. He opened his day purse, the other fuller one being hidden inside his doublet, and counted out the coin. The churl handed Boylan the rope attached to the bridle and with what sounded like a curse, stomped off.

"There you are, yor ladyship," said Boylan, handing Anna the rope. Anna smiled her thanks, patting the horse's neck while Laurence fumbled angrily with its drawstrings to close his depleted purse. "Your chest and tools are loaded with the rest," said Boylan cheerfully to the armourer before turning his attention again to Anna. "Let me help yor ladyship onto her horse," he offered. "There is no saddle, but throw over a couple of packs and you can settle yorself fine a'tween them."

"I will look to the stowage of my wife, master Boylan," snapped Laurence, the scar still a livid white in his red face. Boylan gave a gallant bow to them both and stood back.

"We move off within the hour. There is a hard road before us, but with good company, the miles will fall away." He gave another bow to Laurence and a more elegant one to Anna before returning to his task of breaking camp. Anna looked after him as he walked away, a fond smile at her lips.

"We must gather our things and make up some packs," he snapped at her impatiently. "There will be no finery about our shoulders away from here, so you had better wrap yourself in something suited to the road."

* * *

The castle at Donegal shone brilliantly in the September sunshine, its square keep washed over with white lime standing fine at the mouth of the River Eske and overlooking the bay. It had been a long and tiring march, across and up through the centre of Ireland, moving quickly to confuse their enemies. Laurence thanked the saints for leading them here. Bretons and French traded for many years with *Tir Chonaill*, the lands of the O'Donnell's. He had sent armour here from Brittany and earlier from Bristol, when he had his forge in England. Other merchants he knew traded in wine, fine cloths and other goods; all benefiting from the wealth of the region. The Spanish in particular fished the waters off the coast of *Tir Chonaill* and had license from Hugh O'Donnell to cure the herring they caught before shipping it onward.

The earl of Desmond had parted from them weeks ago and taken himself south to Kinsale where he was making plans for the construction of a castle. In the couple of days before they reached Donegal they had passed by fields cultivated with oats - there were cattle in the fields while the rivers and streams teemed with fish. Extensive woodlands abounded with a variety of game while the prosperous people of *Tir Chonaill* were assured plenty of fuel for their fires. The duke of York's followers were now but a few, perhaps a hundred or so, and the Prince ordered them to make camp about five miles from Donegal Castle so that they could get themselves into some sort of condition fit for greeting their greatest friend and supporter, Hugh O'Donnell. His prickers had found them some days ago and conveyed the Prince's greetings to their liege lord. On their way from Waterford, they had lingered at Galway, welcomed by Sean Burke, a virulent opponent of the Tudor's domination of Ireland. While there, they had word from Hugh O'Donnell informing the Prince that King James of Scotland would take up his cause against Tudor. O'Donnell, a friend of King James, would arrange for the Prince to get over the sea channel that separated Ireland and Scotland.

Anna and Laurence were discomfited by this plan. Their own idea had been to seek out a Breton ship at Galway, or even better now from Donegal and take passage for home. They had thought the Prince's advisers might even persuade him to get back to his aunt at Flanders, though she had made it clear defeat for his cause was not an option. Neither had Laurence quite shaken off his vision of the Prince in exile in Brittany, as Henry Tudor had been, which in his more reasonable moments he was forced to admit was the fancy of a perverse mind. In any case, Donegal was by far the best place from which to leave. The Prince, however, was determined to plough his destined course, declaring a king does not abandon his birthright when there is a very good chance of success. With the help of Scotland, he could raise another army and this time not one comprising mostly mercenaries, but Scots who had a long history when it came to invading England.

The small band made a brave show as they displayed themselves under the battlements of Donegal Castle. Less than twenty years old, the castle was in excellent condition, testifying to the wealth of its

264

lord, Hugh O'Donnell. A tall, rectangular limestone keep rose within the outer walls, having extensions to the upper corners that protruded beyond the walls where the castle guards could command a wide view of the castle grounds below.

Laurence had spent the previous evening getting the Prince's armour ready for his meeting with O'Donnell. Now, as they approached the outer bailey of the castle, the Prince rode in, resplendent in his brilliant harness. He wore his armet with visor removed and a livery collar of York was arranged around his shoulders. In front two bearers carried standards displaying the royal arms of England and the Sunne in Splendour, the badge of his father, King Edward the Fourth. Behind him rode Sir Anthony de la Forsse and Roderigo de LaLaing, John Watre rode behind them with the Prince's chaplain, William Lounde.

Laurence was some way back, in the middle of their procession, riding two abreast, his immediate companion being Edward Skelton, a yeoman adventurer who had been with the Prince since his first revelation at Cork. Laurence knew him vaguely from the court of King Richard the Third and it was no surprise to find him here attempting to restore the Yorkist fortunes. This morning, as they formed up in procession for the approach to Donegal, he had no alternative but to leave Anna with the baggage train. To his chagrin, Martin Boylan, who had decided to tag along with the Prince's followers after the retreat from Waterford, promised to take care of *her ladyship* until they arrived at their destination. For her part, Anna, pretending not to notice the dark expression on her husband's face, mischievously smiled her pleasure at Boylan's solicitude. They would be apart on the road a mere hour or so before they reached Donegal Castle, but he had mounted his horse with a grim visage and it was only when the castle came into sight that Skelton took it upon himself to break the silence between them.

"I expect we shall be well taken care of here," he ventured, leaning towards Laurence the better for him to hear. "O'Donnell lands are some of the richest in Ireland and resistant to the plundering of Henry Tudor."

"I have traded with the region," replied Laurence. "But as I understand it, we shall not remain here long."

"Our departure for Scotland, you mean? Let me tell you that King James the Fourth is a most cultured young man, as indeed is our own Prince Richard. The two are of an age and there has already been speculation that there might well be a marriage between our Prince and a lady of that land."

"Is that so?" said Laurence with some surprise.

"It is necessary a prince should marry and at twenty-one years of age he is overdue a bride. Letters have already passed between the Prince and the lady. It is certain there will be more of the same now we are here. Hugh O'Donnell is recently returned from the Scottish court."

"Who is she?" wondered Laurence.

"She is the lady Katherine Gordon, a cousin of King James."

"So that is why the Prince is so keen to get to Scotland," said Laurence jocularly, his black mood broken. "And here was I thinking it was part of his objective to gain a crown."

"To be sure, a king with a queen is more potent than a single prince," replied Skelton. "Look ahead - didn't I say we would receive a warm welcome?"

As Skelton spoke the Prince was already out of sight having passed through the gatehouse, which was decked with banners and pennants depicting the arms of O'Donnell and England. As they too entered the outer bailey they were greeted with the sight of colourful pavilions, soldiers and retainers in the O'Donnell livery, while castle servants hurried about the business of their master. They carried on, following after where the Prince had gone, towards the massive keep. Behind them the rest of their train was diverted towards the pavilions, which had been erected for their use while they were here. Laurence looked back to where the baggage wagons were being directed. He grimaced with annoyance as he realised he would have to go with the Prince into the keep while Anna remained with the others, including Martin Boylan. He resolved to send for her at the first opportunity.

Hugh O'Donnell, lord of Donegal and *Tir Chonaill* was a large man, thick and sturdy of body with a wide grin of bonhomie that made men believe camaraderie was his natural condition. He was clad in a rich red velvet houpelard trimmed with sable and topped by a black chapeau with red hangings. A short brown beard was neatly combed and curled, as was the moustache under a bulbous nose, traced with fine blue veins indicating a man who was fond of his cups. Beside him stood a matronly woman, red of hair and who had once been beautiful and still had enough of her youth to stir a man's blood. Her gown was pale green silk tricked out with pearls while her hennin had a drift of voile arranged to frame her face, giving her visage a softness that belied the hard steel glint she couldn't quite disguise in her brown eyes.

Laurence gasped as he looked around at the opulence in the Great Hall in the castle. This was the equal to any royal palace, though perhaps on a smaller scale. The lord's dais stood, not at one end but about two thirds of the way down the hall. This was because great stone fireplaces occupied both ends of the hall and now the year had turned into October they cheered the place with light and warmth. He remembered this was a fairly new construction and Hugh O'Donnell had made sure there were real fireplaces rather than the central brazier found in older fortresses and manor houses. The lord's seat on the dais was a long bench backed with a partition that was hung with silks and velvet cloths. In front was a table where the lord dined, behind which he dispensed justice or directed the management of his lands. Facing this, a minstrels' gallery had been constructed with stairs at both ends. There were three lutanists there now, gently strumming and plucking at their instruments, the melody carrying through the great oak beams of the roof. Fresh rushes sprinkled with fragrant herbs were strewed on the floor. Arras embroidered in the finest silk and tapestries of intricate design hung at the walls, obscuring the stone except for gaps where sconces held blazing torches or where windows were set into the thick walls.

The appearance of the duke of York before the lord and lady of Donegal, clad in harness to indicate the determination of his enterprise, seemed somewhat incongruous and after the first exchange of benevolences between the Prince and the lord of Donegal Castle, he asked if he could remove it and present himself in something more suitable to the sumptuous surroundings of the great hall. O'Donnell immediately had him shown to the chamber set aside for him and it was there Laurence was directed to help the Prince out of his harness and see to its stowage. Hopefully, once in his court dress, Richard of England would have no further need that day of his armourer and Laurence might be free to reclaim Anna from the clutches of the charming Boylan.

13 - The Light of Love

"Bring me paper, pen and ink," cried the duke of York excitedly. "I must send to my love, the lady Katherine." He was holding the letter he had been reading as if it were holy writ. His harness stood by on its frame, which Laurence had ordered to be brought into the Prince's chamber. There was to be a joust that day in the outer bailey of the castle and though the Prince would not take part, yet he must present himself before the people in martial array. The lady Nuah O'Donnell had requested the joust as a diversion for the Prince's followers who had been causing some trouble in the town. Hugh O'Donnell had dismissed this as youthful high spirits, but his wife had taken against the Prince and word had filtered down to Laurence via Anna, who had engaged in gossip with certain castle servants, that she would be rid of him. It was with delight that the lady Nuah received a letter for the Prince from the court at Scotland and passed it on, realising it would speed his way out of Ireland.

"I see the Prince is smitten," whispered Laurence to Roderigo de LaLaing, who was already clad in jousting harness and gravitated towards the armourer for an opinion on it. "Not surprising at his age. Has he had his belt removed yet, I wonder?"

"He is as lusty a lad as any you can find," grinned Roderigo. "As a noble contender for the throne of England, there has been no problem finding ladies ready to share his bed."

"Then the lady Katherine will need a determined chaperone, unless her father rejects the Prince's suit."

"George earl of Huntly – we should find him a man after our own hearts," said Roderigo. "He is known to be valiant in war and just as fierce in peace. Katherine is a daughter from his third marriage. He is a sturdy fighter, though his age will have slowed him somewhat – he must be over sixty years. It will be interesting to see what he makes of the duke of York." Laurence clamped his mouth shut rather than comment directly on this statement. Roderigo de LaLaing was himself a fighting knight and Laurence had pondered on his relationship with Prince Richard. Of course, Roderigo was under orders from the duchess of Burgundy, so perhaps he saw his role as protector. For sure, the Prince had shown no particular military skill. Prince Richard's jousting was confined to silver-tongued oratory at court where he excelled.

"Looking around here," ventured Laurence, directing his attention to the Prince surrounded by his courtly followers, "there is not much in the way of battle experience?"

"True, master armourer; there is just myself, Sir Anthony Forsse and, so I hear, you too who have actually been in a real battle. It is a concern. However, the Scottish king is one of us I believe, so I have great hopes for our cause in that land."

"But as for the immediate future, any couching of the lance is like to be between the sheets of the privy chamber rather than the lists."

"Yes," agreed Roderigo. "And in that our Richard will have the encouragement of King James, who is an adept in the bedchamber himself, and cares not who knows it. He is no stranger to scandal at his court, I can tell you."

Both men grinned lasciviously as they regarded the antics around Prince Richard, whose attendants were voluble in helping him compose a courtly love letter to his promised bride.

"Seeing as most of the work on the Prince's armour will be to wipe away any dust, kicked up by the horses in the field, there will be small business for you there. I ask that you attend on me in the joust," said Roderigo by his manner expecting no refusal. "I expect my harness to take a battering and thus be in need of repair before we move on. I would be in full fighting trim when we land in Scotland."

"It will be my pleasure, though I should tell you that Sir Anthony has also asked me to attend him. I am sure I can take care of you both." Roderigo glanced at him askance annoyed he would not have exclusive use, excepting Prince Richard, of the armourer's services. Laurence, too, had some concern in that respect. If it came to it he could invite Martin Boylan to help out. He cursed himself for considering allying himself with the Irish armourer, though depending on the work required on the harness of the two knights after the joust, hopefully he might not need his assistance at all.

"Then I shall strive not to take too many attaints lest my repairs become protracted," grumbled Roderigo.

At that moment Anna came over and Roderigo's attention was diverted as he made her a polite bow before withdrawing to join the Prince. She was in high spirits now she could dress herself in some decent clothes and it pleased Laurence that she now looked what she was, the wife of a prosperous artisan armourer to princes. She had managed to ingratiate herself with the younger ladies of the castle, those that served the countess, lady O'Donnell, though the senior among them kept her at a distance. Neither Anna nor her husband had noble rank, but he had instructed her to adopt the title Dame, which was a finer distinction than goodwife, or mistress. From now on she would be housed in a proper abode - a castle or manor house rather than endure the hardship involved in following an invasion army.

"What news, wife," he grunted.

"The ladies are all aflutter in the presence of our Prince," she chuckled gaily. "There will be a few sad faces when we leave here. The knowledge of his betrothal has not diminished their interest one whit."

"His betrothal? Has it gone that far?"

"Why yes," she responded brightly. "Apparently there has been a deal of letter-writing between the duchess of Burgundy and King James of Scotland regarding a bride for the duke of York."

"Strange the Prince has not mentioned it before?"

"It has been something of a secret until now. He first knew of it at Waterford where Desmond had been in communication with Margaret shortly after we landed at Youghall. Perhaps he hardly dared mention it in case all fell through? The duchess Margaret had previously tried to get him a bride from among the family of Maximilian. It seems that was one ambition too far."

"Yet Maximilian, the Holy Roman Emperor is unswerving in his support for Richard," mused Laurence. "I am reliably informed that Maximilian and the duchess of Burgundy are sending German and Flemish mercenaries to Scotland to help with the invasion of England."

"Such secrets. Matters of great import concerning the duke of York are going on all over England and Europe, even including the Holy Father at Rome. It is exciting, husband, but I still wonder if we would be better out of it?"

"But just think of our situation should the duke of York win his crown. Even if he fails, I have made contact with some of the most influential nobles in England and on the continent. Warfare and the making of arms is my family business. Peacetime jousts or open warfare; it all represents profit. Let the nobles fight each other - there has to be a winner and whoever that is will need my services first as victor then to hang on to their victory."

"But most of those who suffer in the conflict are innocent in all this," she said sadly. "How many widows and orphaned children will care who wins or loses, it will be the same to them."

"On the other hand there are stone masons to build fortifications, armourers to forge weapons, smiths and farriers to care for horses, cloth trades profiting from making banners and pavilions, makers of cannon and guns, arrows and all kinds of munitions. None of these are combatants yet all profit from war. Just as many might starve to death if there was no warfare, probably more, seeing as open war is spasmodic while preparing for it is more or less constant."

"These thoughts depress the spirit," said Anna disconsolately. "I wish we were back at our home in Brittany. I had begun to love it there even though it is not England."

"For the moment we are caught up in the affairs of Richard of England," he replied. "We should be safe in Scotland. It is where the English retire to when chased out of their own lands." He looked around to ensure there was nobody in earshot. "The same cannot be said for Ireland. There is no English Pale in Scotland neither does the English King claim it as his own domain, much as he would like to. How long do you think it will be before Poyning decides to attack Donegal? He has not the resources at the moment, but Irish lords, such as Desmond are prone to changing sides. The Tudor raises taxes in England to let him bribe for support in Ireland and he is desperate to get his hands on our Prince."

"The same goes for Scotland."

"Yes, but Scotland has strong ties with France, the auld alliance as they call it. Bribery there is, but it is not so potent as in Ireland. At this time King James despises Henry Tudor and would have him replaced, so would the main monarchies of Europe. The problem that seems to be emerging is that some of those who have met the Prince, while having no doubt of his Plantagenet blood, are doubtful whether he can win a crown and having won it, keep it."

Anna thought about this for a moment. "I suppose if this enterprise should fail then we simply sail away, taking our profit with us."

"Exactly so. It will be a simple matter to take ship from Scotland."

"Talking of profit, Martin has suggested you and he should pool your resources and make as much from the present situation while the conditions allow."

"He has spoken to you of this," he said with annoyance.

"It seemed a reasonable proposition. You cannot handle all the work that comes your way as well as your duties as the personal armourer to the Prince. There is a great opportunity here."

271

"I wonder what opportunity Martin Boylan is thinking of?" snarled Laurence.

"Why, good business is all he means. Is he not a fine armourer, like John Fisher? What would you have done without *him*? He is keeping your affairs in order at home, is he not?"

"John Fisher has a wife of his own," he snapped.

"What is your meaning?" she cried in anger.

"I know Boylan's sort. He is all charm and has learned to weave a spell about gullible women."

"Gullible women!" she gasped.

"It is common knowledge that women are drawn to a subtle tongue."

Anna stood back and glared at him. "Then why not fashion a subtle harness to fit me with," she cried. "You have the skill and it is not unknown for a jealous husband to confine his wife so."

"You seem to have little difficulty in realising my meaning, which tells me there is something in your head you dare not tell of."

Anna clasped her hands in frustration. The truth was that she had allowed Boylan's obvious endearments to flatter her and used him to torment her husband, who was constantly going off on his business while ignoring her. In her heart she knew he had little choice, but the opportunity for showing her chagrin had proved irresistible.

"I remind you, *monsieur*, that I came along to be with *you* rather than being left alone at home. If you doubt me now, how much worse would you feel should you have come back to me and discover I had struck up an innocent friendship with a local butcher? Would you beat me? Should you beat me now? You have the right."

Laurence began to feel the force of her argument. Truly she had refused to leave his side, electing to share the discomforts of ship and camp life. There had been no diminution in the urgency of their lovemaking, when the opportunity presented itself. In the few days they had been at Donegal castle they had a small closet to themselves. It had no door, only a blanket to screen them, nothing more than a gap between two buttresses really, but it was better than most had. Boylan slept in the forge and though there might be a warm place there, Laurence had managed to bribe the castellan into letting them have their own space.

"I find I cannot work with Boylan," he growled irritably rather than answer her direct questioning.

She softened her expression. "It would only be for the few days we remain here," she said placatingly. "Martin will not be coming into Scotland with us."

He brightened at this knowledge. It had seemed as if Boylan dogged his footsteps and now he realised the man would soon be history, then perhaps he could work with him. Moreover, with him close, he could keep an eye on his antics around Anna. He grunted and slouched away, reluctant to give ground and satisfied he had at least made his displeasure known.

* * *

Roderigo de LaLaing had been untrue to his promise of avoiding hard knocks in the joust. His harness was dented here and there, though none of his iron was broken, but the mount in the armet for his crest had come loose. Sir Anthony's harness was in much the same condition. Laurence would normally have kept the repair work to himself, but the Scottish king had sent ships, two of them riding now at anchor in Donegal Bay. None of the Prince's original ships had sailed around the coast of Ireland to reach them and so their numbers were much depleted. It was expected that they would need to display themselves in good order if they were to impress the Scottish court on their arrival and so Laurence had been forced to let Martin Boylan help him. He would be unable to carry out hot work on the harness aboard ship.

They sat together in the castle forge, hammering away at their respective pieces. Boylan set up a constant chatter with the other forge workers while Laurence affected aloofness. Anna kept herself away and occupied herself tending to those injured in the fury of the recent joust. There were the usual broken bones, dislocations and concussions to deal with. Monks who ran the castle infirmary resented the offices of a woman, but after the joust, the lady Nuah, had gone there herself and when she discovered Anna had the skill, took her along and commanded the monks to allow her to work there.

"'Tis almost worth taking an injury to have such as hor ladyship tend you," Boylan had said jocularly. Was the man deliberately setting out to annoy him or was he just insensitive? Anna had told him, as he had discovered for himself at Waterford, the Irishman fancied himself as a troubadour, though he was not noble enough to deserve the title, more of a jongleur, but it was the way of such to talk thus. It meant nothing, being merely a habit he had acquired by

273

way of his pretended calling. In any case, if he persisted in those remarks he might find his wish come true and end up with a broken pate. It was only the thought of Anna tending to him afterwards that caused Laurence to keep his temper.

"We are to take ship on the morrow," said Sir Anthony Forsse, who had come over to the forge to inspect his armour. "Is my harness restored?"

"It is, Sir Anthony," replied Laurence, "except for burnishing and that can be finished aboard ship."

"Then see to its stowage. I need to have it ready for when we go ashore in Scotland, and so does the duke of York. His grace is asking for you now."

Laurence bowed in acknowledgement as Sir Anthony turned away. Putting aside the piece he had been working on he called over one of the forge servants and ordered that Sir Anthony's armour and that of Roderigo de LaLaing, which Boylan had been working on, be packed in canvas ready for travel.

"I must go to the Prince," he informed Boylan. "I shall settle your account before we leave tomorrow." Whether or not Boylan detected something of a *double entendre* in his remark he could not tell. Only a cheery smile appeared in the Irishman's face.

Laurence entered the great hall where the Prince was standing among his and the castle courtiers, conversing with the lord of Donegal.

"Ah, here is our master armourer," declared O'Donnell. "I think my knights have put some business your way sirrah. Sir Anthony and Roderigo de LaLaing acquitted themselves nobly. Though outnumbered, they were not outclassed. As for the rest of my lord Richard's men," he chuckled with self-satisfaction, "we have unfortunately reduced their numbers by injury, though I expect his grace the King of Scotland and the duchess Margaret will soon provide more."

The duke of York smiled wryly at O'Donnell's remarks while the two knights mentioned stood stony faced. Laurence knew it was the way of nobles to boast the exploits of their own retainers. Glad of the chance to change the subject, the Prince beckoned Laurence forward to kneel at his feet.

"I must have my harness in the best of order when we reach Scotland," he declared. "My betrothed will be there to greet me and I would not have her think me a churl."

"She could hardly believe that, your grace, even if you appeared to her in rags," returned Laurence. "Your harness is in the peak of condition, showing off your puissance as befits a Christian knight and, dare I say - an ardent lover?"

"That is well, monsieur Laurence," he replied accepting as natural the armourer's flattery. "You will sail in my ship. My squires will arm me but I would have you there in case there are any problems." He indicated for the armourer to rise.

"As your grace wishes," said Laurence as he got to his feet. "My wife travels with me as you know. Seeing as the passage north around Ireland to Scotland should be little more than a full day she will fit in somewhere."

"Yes, I have had good report of her from the lady Nuah. She has salved the wounds of my men injured in the joust and some of them are recovered. I would have had fewer to take with me had it not been for her."

Laurence understood the concern behind the duke's words. Many of the German and Flemish mercenaries who set out from Flanders, along with hundreds of English had either been killed or had returned to Flanders after the siege of Waterford. He had heard that those captured earlier in the year at Deal beach had been executed as pirates, some of them hung on gallows erected by the sea at the low water mark. This was the usual punishment for piracy. Their senior captains had been taken to Canterbury and the Tower of London where they were beheaded and their heads set upon spikes in public view. Running scared, Henry Tudor was taking no chances with the followers of *Perkin Warbeck*. Laurence wondered if the Prince knew of this. It had come to him via camp gossip and was the kind of news the Prince's followers might keep from him. Now the Prince had but few men – Laurence counted somewhere around fifty, a paltry number for the retinue of a prospective king, but all of them fiercely loyal. His ships were those of the Scottish king, none of his own remaining to him. It would be hard to put on a brave and impressive show.

"I know you dislike Michael Boylan," said Anna tentatively as she placed her things into a trunk, "but he is a useful source of information." Laurence grunted his discontent while his curiosity caused him to keep his peace and wait for her to speak further. "For instance, he has told me that all Irish men, women, even children in England are being questioned by order of the Tudor to discover if any are traitors." They were in their tiny closet getting their things together ready to take ship.

"Our Prince has him well rattled then."

"It appears so. Tudor has no idea where we are. Lord Deputy Poyning is tramping all over Ireland looking for him but so far without success."

"It is a wild land and we, being a small band, are easy to hide and the Prince has many friends here," said Laurence while examining the edge of his sword. He was wiping the steel with an oiled cloth against the wet conditions on board ship.

"Or many who cannot stand the English king and in that they are not alone."

Laurence sheathed his sword and placed it by the trunk, then sat down on the lid in contemplation. "Sir Anthony has said that the Spanish monarchs want England to join the Holy League which is combating French ambition in Italy and our home of Brittany. King James of Scotland is using the situation in Europe to gain influence for himself. Henry Tudor cannot attack France while there is a threat to his border with Scotland. The whole of northern England has been commanded to array for an expected invasion."

"Is not there a scheme for the Spanish princess, Catherine to marry with Prince Arthur, the Tudor's son? Surely that will encourage Tudor to join with Spain against France?" said Anna sitting beside him.

"The whole situation in Europe is confused," replied Laurence. "Henry has offered his daughter Margaret as a possible bride for the French Dauphin, and even hinted that his son Arthur be betrothed to a Bourbon princess to discomfit Spain. The Spanish monarchs, Ferdinand and Isabella want Henry to join with them and the Holy Roman Emperor in the Holy Alliance to attack France, but Henry Tudor will not join them while Maximilian still supports our Prince. There is also the question of Burgundy. While the duchess is staunch in the cause of her nephew, duke Philip the Fair of Burgundy has diplomatically distanced himself from Prince Richard. Maximilian has pretended the same, yet he has refused to deny him as being any other than duke Richard of York, despite Tudor lies around the false persona of Perkin Warbeck."

Anna frowned as she considered this information. "I suppose it suits Spain to take the Tudor line regarding the identity of Prince Richard, but that can only be a matter of political expediency where the truth of his lineage is exchanged for diplomatic advantage. Perhaps his grace's cause is not so hopeless as we imagined?" she said. "In fact, he seems to be the axle around which great affairs are turning."

"He is so," agreed her husband. "And that can only be because the monarchs of Europe know he is the duke of York and rightful king of England. Yet I would wish the Prince to be more martial in his aspect," he lamented. "It is costing him the confidence of other Princes on the continent. Let us hope King James does not waver in his support. After all, Holy Scripture tells us: For if the trumpet give an uncertain sound, who shall prepare himself for the battle?"

* * *

Leaving Martin Boylan tapping away at iron in the forge of Donegal Castle gladdened the heart of Laurence the armourer, although he believed he had detected something of disquietude in the heart of his wife. Her face had not shown any particular depression in her spirit that might betray regret, but for a few minutes her quietness as the ship dropped its sails from the great spar at its mast made him imagine there was something more on her mind than the prospect of a rough passage to Scotland. He shrugged the thought off as the vessel began to move out across Donegal Bay and a rough passage it promised to be. The wind was strong and rising as they moved out towards the great ocean to head north around Ireland before turning to the east and the narrow passage between Ireland and the Scottish coast. The waves butted the ship's prow sending spray across the deck and already the sails were reefed in anticipation of a stiff blow. Laurence had noted before now how a sea voyage seemed to purge away the cares that dominated life on land. He supposed it was the vastness of the sea, bringing to mind the scale of mankind in eternity. They were at the mercy of the elements and though they sought to tame them, that would never be and if some sea God, once presumed defunct decided to rise from the depths, there was nothing to stop it happening and they might become lost, never to be seen again in this world.

In Brittany, tales had been told of a mad adventurer - a man named by the Spanish as Cristóbal Colón who, after trailing his ideas through the courts of Europe for years, had somehow persuaded the monarchs of Spain to equip him for a voyage across this very ocean believing he would eventually reach the Indes. He had even sent his brother Bartholomew to Henry Tudor in England, asking for his support but to no avail. Tudor was not the man to spend money on that kind of madness, particularly when his priority was to raise revenue to defend himself against a claimant to his throne. That was the call of the sea. It made men mad, confirmed by those who, compelled by raging thirst had tried to drink of it, only to die horribly. Colón set off in 1492 and returned more than a year later with tales of a fabulous land of gold. It was some comfort to think that this venture of the Prince's was not conceived of the sea, but of naked ambition. That were madness too, but one that was understood and could be used to the benefit of those not closely affected. Were he and Anna infected by this madness? They were close to Prince Richard that was true, but not as political allies, which might be their salvation; or were they adrift on a fathomless sea, sailing towards an unknown destination that might never be discovered before they drowned in its infinite depths?

They might have taken ship for Brittany from Donegal, and they had discussed it, but as Laurence pointed out, that would put them in bad with Hugh O'Donnell and he was a powerful lord and purchaser of armour. His writ extended to the continent of Europe. A word from him would deprive Laurence of much business. They had little choice but to continue on their reluctant course. On the other hand, James the Fourth of Scotland was a young king eager to make his mark on the world and he too needed arms, so perhaps fate was being kind to them after all.

It took two days of enduring wracks of storm and cold before they reached landfall. Once in Scottish waters the power of the wind might have lessened between the great towering headlands of the Clyde estuary, but it seemed they somehow funnelled the wind so that it tormented them the more. It was with some relief that Anna and Laurence caught sight of the castle of Dumbarton looming above the estuary, gaunt and grim, its mighty grey walls unlimed, and which seemed to rise as if growing out of the Basalt rock on which the castle stood. There was a landing below the castle where a group of soldiers and brightly dressed nobles stood ready to greet them as they came ashore. The banners of Patrick Hepburn, earl of Bothwell and Captain of Dumbarton Castle flew above the ramparts and towers. The earl of Bothwell was one of King James' closest supporters having taken his side in the rebellion that had removed his father, James the Third from the throne of Scotland.

Laurence recognised these banners. He had last seen them being hauled down at Berwick back in 1482 when the castle there held out to the last before the onslaught of duke Richard of Gloucester. When the castle finally fell, Berwick became an English possession and from what he had heard, King James wanted it back. This was one reason why he was supporting the duke of York, Prince Richard.

Remembrance of the scene in the great hall at Berwick Castle brought a lump to his throat as he recalled faces now lost who had been knighted there while duke Richard had promoted some further. The particular rank of banneret was reserved for those who had been in the actual battle and Richard of Gloucester had raised to banneret among others, James Tyrell along with Francis Lovell and Richard Ratcliffe. Of these only Sir James lived and he was now Captain of Calais having seemingly made his peace with Henry Tudor. A grimmer vision rose in the image of lord Thomas Stanley who had also fought there at that time alongside Richard of Gloucester, the future king he would later betray at Bosworth Field.

Once more Prince Richard would display himself and his retinue in martial array, harnessed cap a pie with a great white plume of feathers atop his helm streaming in the breeze. He had come as a soldier to conquer a kingdom with the help of the Scottish king and first impressions counted. Patrick Hepburn's men-at-arms formed up either side of the landing, providing the Prince with a guard of honour. Beyond the guard a small group of nobles stood clustered together the better to get sight of Richard as he came ashore. His banners went first displaying the arms of England and his father's Sunne in Splendour. Two trumpeters blew a fanfare as Richard appeared on deck and walked down the gangplank onto the stone quay. With him were John Watre, Sir Antony de la Forsse and Roderigo de LaLaing. By his side was his chaplain, to demonstrate that here was a Christian monarch come to claim his right by God's will. Following after came the rest of his depleted retinue dressed in their finest robes to give the illusion of royal authority. Laurence watched with Anna from the advantage of the poop deck, which gave them a commanding view of the ceremony.

"That is the earl of Boswell, I believe," said Laurence giving Anna a nudge. They watched as a man dressed in the finery of a nobleman stepped forward to greet his guest. Both swept each other an elegant bow and Laurence wondered at the protocols - if Richard of York were indeed considered seriously as a king, then the earl should be on his knees. However, this was not the place to argue such niceties and the young prince grasped the proffered arms of the old warrior in a fond and familiar embrace.

"The earl seems in a good mood," whispered Anna softly into his ear. There were others standing by and she did not want to include them in her conversation. "Strange, seeing as it was King

Edward, the prince's father who threw him out of Berwick town and made it part of England."

"Yes, but he put up a sturdy fight and was treated honourably afterwards by his grace of Gloucester. Besides, this is more diplomacy than a meeting of friends."

"At least the Prince looks the part of a soldier, thanks to you," declared Anna. "I wonder how long it will take for the earl of Bothwell to figure out the extent of his personal puissance?"

"It is but a short walk to the castle gate. He might make it across the bailey and up to the great hall where he will be found out, no doubt." Laurence smiled wryly.

"Oh, I think he might manage further than there," she replied with a giggle. "He is most charming and plays the part of a soldier to perfection . . ."

"As long as he doesn't draw his sword. Fortunately he has two with him who are fighting knights and they know how to deflect attention to themselves when appropriate. Patrick Hepburn will recognise them for what they are at first sight."

"It will be interesting to observe the earl's wife," said Anna. "She is another daughter of the earl of Huntly and step-sister to Katherine, the Prince's betrothed. No wonder the earl is so welcoming; he is probably under orders from his wife."

Laurence smiled at her. "Let us get ashore. I expect the Prince will call me to him once he has satisfied himself everyone has admired the quality of his harness and he can get into his court dress."

"I certainly cannot wait to get into mine," responded Anna gaily.

"Make the most of it, my dear," he replied. "We will not linger at Dumbarton when King James and a certain young lady await us at Stirling."

* * *

But they did linger at Dumbarton. Patrick Hepburn, 1st earl of Bothwell and his wife Margaret had arranged a banquet for the following day and would brook no excuse to avoid it, though the young lover was anxious to get to Stirling where his as yet unembraced betrothed was waiting. Anna had told Laurence there was something of guile in the attitude of Patrick Hepburn and his countess, which though of interest seemed not to have anything of the sinister about it, rather amusement. Laurence had spent most of the day with the knights Sir Anthony and Roderigo along with their counterparts in the castle garrison while Anna had been striking up acquaintance with the wife of the castle bailiff with whom they were quartered.

Lady Macrief was a stout and cheerful woman, aware of her status but not inclined to use it to subdue the wife of her artisan guest, as many would have done. She too seemed to be the custodian of a secret that somehow entertained her. Try as she might, Anna could not prise it out of her, rather her clumsy questioning merely served to increase her amusement. Having lived in a world of deceit, treachery and dissembling for so long, she wondered if they might find themselves taken up in a plot to destroy the Prince before he reached the safety of the Scottish court, yet nothing in the attitudes of the nobles and retainers within the castle was anything but benign. On the other hand, Scotland and England were long-time enemies and the auld alliance was with France. Also in the mix were the monarchies of Spain and Portugal, in fact the whole of Europe had an interest in what was happening in the cause of the duke of York. The enterprise of England could easily end here and Henry Tudor's purse might hold sway as well at Dumbarton as anywhere. What if he had promised the return of Berwick in exchange for the body of the duke of York? One thing she was certain of, the answer would come at the banquet that evening.

Laurence had dismissed his wife's fears having spent an amiable day discussing the relative advantages of one type of armour over another. He found the Scottish knights were interested in and well aware of the latest fashion and developments of armour ranging from the quality of steel to the best type of design suited for battle or the joust. He was careful to explain the relative merits between different suits of harness, knowing it might lead to some business coming his way. Patrick Hepburn himself had joined them and now, having drunk a fair quantity of wine, Laurence lay sleeping quietly on a mattress in a corner of a side chamber close to that of lady Macrief who was busy elsewhere, while Anna smoothed out the wrinkles in her dresses having extracted her best ones from their chest. Soon she would shake him back to life and get him to douse his head with cold water before dressing for the banquet.

The great hall of Dumbarton glowed in the light of blazing torches around the walls and the great log fires at each end of the vast hall. Laurence and Anna sat together by the end of one of the side tables nearest to the top table. The earl of Bothwell and Margaret were in their places with the duke of York on the earl's

281

right hand. Strangely there was a vacant seat between Prince Richard and Sir Anthony de la Forsse. Roderigo de LaLaing was seated beside lady O'Donnell engaged in bright chatter with her, entranced by her considerable beauty. The earl had chosen his wife well. Minstrels in the gallery above were playing a melody popular with the Scottish knights but unknown to the guests. It hardly mattered - few were listening as all were talking among themselves and overall was an air of bonhomie particularly among the castle retainers. They were wondering when the food would arrive and they could indulge themselves, seeing as they had eaten nothing but ship fare for some days. The earl of Bothwell waved to the minstrels' gallery causing them and the hall to fall silent. Surely now the food would be played in to begin the banquet? But no. A door opened and a troop of jongleurs capered into the hall. Strange? The entertainment usually began after the food was served. Laurence folded his arms over his growling stomach and leaned back impatiently. Anna frowned in consternation having not quite shaken off her previous anxiety.

The jongleurs were performing an acrobatic sequence that astounded the company. There were jugglers, contortionists and acrobats who leapt and bounded impossibly in the cleared space before the lord's table. One of them lit a torch from the candles at the earl's table and stroked the fire across his body before bending back and opening his mouth, quenching it in his throat. Bothwell turned his head and looked to the duke of York who sat enchanted by the entertainment, then returned his gaze to the performers with a pleased smile at his lips. Lady Margaret positively beamed with joy. The jongleurs kept this up for a few minutes until a veiled woman, clad in volumes of yellow silk entered and swirled in a lissom and capricious dance among them. By her form and the way she moved here was a young woman, her lithe form hardly disguised by the silken folds of her dress. She danced coyly with none of the abandon usually associated with jongleurs, yet there was a simple and virginal allure about her that had the prince in thrall. He leaned forward, eager not to miss anything of her dance while the earl of Bothwell watched him between narrowed eyes.

"Enough!" cried the earl suddenly, standing up. The dancer sank to the floor, her dress spread as yellow petals with her body a pert stamen at its centre. The jongleurs ran together into a line behind her then stepped back to face the earl. The hall fell to silence and nary a breath was drawn or exhaled. The earl turned to Prince Richard and bid him stand beside him. "Richard of England," he called above the heads of the gathering, "May I present the lady Katherine Gordon!"

A communal gasp filled the hall as the lady threw back her veil and lifted her head to present her beautiful face to her prince. Beautiful she was and the prince was frozen into the moment. She had volumes of red hair tied back by a rope of pearls under a brown hennin, her pale face flushed after her exertions enhancing the youthful bloom of her skin. As if under a spell of enchantment, which indeed he was, Prince Richard came from behind the table and approached his betrothed. Holding both arms out as he came to her, she arose and took his hands into hers.

"Bring the girl to her place here," called the earl, feigning stern authority. He pointed to the place left empty beside the prince, the purpose of its vacancy now clear. "We have waited too long and the meats will be cold ere we get them to our trenchers." Prince Richard, as if a man in a dream, let drop one hand and accompanied by thunderous acclaim from the court, led Katherine by the other to the reserved place by his side. "Strike up!" cried the earl to the minstrels' gallery, "and bring in the feast."

"So now we know what all the secrecy was for," breathed Anna with relief. "Lady Katherine must have been hidden in her chamber. She is as keen to meet her betrothed as our Prince. She must have planned this with her sister and being family, her father would have been easily persuaded to let her come to Dumbarton."

Laurence's gaze followed a steaming plate as it passed along the table and with his dagger poised, waited anxiously for his turn to spear some meat for them. "I will be interested to meet the earl of Huntly," he muttered. "Having a daughter married to the King of England is a triumph, but the duke of York has not obtained it yet." Finally the dish stopped near and he speared some tasty morsels placing them on Anna's trencher followed by more for himself.

"Yes, but he has several sons and daughters, including this daughter from his third wife and ex mistress Elizabeth Hey, so perhaps he thinks he can cast her to the fates and see what happens?" She had managed to extract this much from lady Macrief regarding Katherine's lineage.

"I would agree," said Laurence before stuffing some meat hungrily into his mouth. He chewed on it for a moment to reduce the bulk then continued: ". . . except the lady Katherine is very beautiful and a prize catch for any man. Huntly must have thought on that and the definite benefits from a safer wealthy match without taking a chance on our Prince."

"Then the hand of King James can be detected, I think," she said before popping meat into her mouth.

"Let there be no doubt. We are to travel on to Stirling soon. I expect there will be more surprises for us there."

The whole attention of those at the banquet was upon the betrothed couple who had taken to each other immediately. They made no move that was not commented upon but were themselves oblivious of everyone there. The entertainment of the jongleurs, the singing from the minstrels' gallery, except when a favourite song of Katherine's was sung, passed them by. Laurence gave Anna a nudge when the earl of Bothwell declared the revels over and folk began to seek their beds and pallets.

"I wonder if there will be a pattering of bare feet along draughty corridors this night," he jested nodding towards the young couple who looked as if they would take some prising apart. "Prince Richard is the image of his father and few women could resist King Edward as you know. This is a stem of that stock."

Anna snorted disdainfully. "Oh, I think lady Margaret will have some arrangement in place to prevent that," she replied. "She will not want her sister deflowered under her roof."

"Yet love might find a way, and they *are* betrothed - which brings me to our sleeping arrangements."

"We must behave ourselves. While I am quartered in the chamber of lady Macrief you must sleep outside along with the other servants to protect us." Laurence grumped at the thought of a pallet in a stone corridor, but at least he was inside the keep of the castle and not outside in a pavilion. The year had turned into November and Scotland was cold and bleak at best - this season was decidedly inclement. It was raining hard outside and he prayed to the Virgin that she might hold off the snowy season until they reached Stirling and the palace of King James the Fourth.

* * *

They were still a few miles from Stirling when they could see the castle in the distance, shining white upon its massive slab of rock. The weather had turned cold but mercifully clear, though there were louring clouds threatening to bear down from the north. The road along the valley of the Forth River was wide and well maintained approaching as it did a royal castle. Baggage wagons still managed to bog down now and then, but that was not unusual and they were easily freed from the mire. Laurence and Anna were riding together on palfreys donated to the Prince's followers by the earl of Bothwell on the orders of King James. Ahead they heard the sound of clarions and as they entered a wide expanse with trees all around they came upon the King of Scotland who was eager to meet with the duke of York, no doubt attracted too by the fair presence of his cousin Katherine riding by the Prince's side. Sir Anthony and Roderigo rode ahead of the prince along with his two standard bearers and they signalled the procession to halt then spaced themselves to reveal Prince Richard and the lady Katherine. Richard was clad in his full harness without a visor to his helmet while Katherine was wrapped in a crimson travelling cloak trimmed with sable, the hood pulled back to show her face.

The Scottish king came with banners flying, his immediate retinue galloping with him while others of his court, some of them ladies, followed after. From their place a few riders back Laurence and Anna could see the delight in the face of King James as he slowed, cantered up to the couple and reigned in. The duke of York jumped down from his horse and knelt in front of the king. James leaped agile as a buck from his saddle and pulled the prince to his feet before embracing him like a lost brother. He turned and waved to the lady Katherine then bowed gracefully while she, being mounted and her betrothed not having lifted her down, could only return the compliment by inclination of her head. Clearly the Scottish court was not a place of strict protocols, at least with regard to this company.

From where he sat atop his palfrey, Laurence examined curiously the king. He was clad in what looked like fine, hunting garments richly attired in a green velvet doublet under a red mantle trimmed with ermine. A black chapeau covered his head and this was decorated with multi-coloured jewels – rubies and emeralds set in mounts of gold. At his belt he wore a short arming sword and a dagger, both with jewelled hilts, clearly not fighting weapons. James was something short of six foot, trim of build, not scrawny but not heavy either. He was clean-shaven and his dark brown eyes were round and bright. By his manner in coming to them, Laurence had noted a superb horseman and he knew the king was an enthusiastic jouster. Judging by his body weight, the armourer wondered about his prowess in the lists. The king lacked the heavy upper torso of a champion jouster, though he might compensate with agility. Perhaps his courtiers and champion knights were gentle with him? He remembered King Richard the Third of England and he was even more spare of frame, yet there had been few who could withstand the fury of his onslaught in a straight fight. No doubt he would find out the true qualities of the Scottish king before long.

Prince Richard returned to his horse and leapt into the saddle, demonstrating that the weight of his harness was no obstacle. King James similarly mounted his horse and turned it to ride in between Richard and Katherine, the three of them chattering away gaily. His immediate household knights fell in behind him, pairing up with those in the prince's retinue to ride four abreast toward the castle of Stirling and James' royal seat.

"It seems that the two princes have taken to each other," said Anna as they fell in among the crowd of courtiers who had come with King James to meet the duke of York.

"Yes, they are of an age and similar of temperament, except . . ."

"What are you thinking?"

"King James has a warlike reputation and I wonder how our prince will compare when it comes to a battle. That is, after all, why we are here – to fight for the crown of England."

They entered Stirling castle by the north gate and Laurence was immediately struck by the amount of activity there. Massive fore works presented a formidable barrier to any that might approach the castle entrance. The outer bailey was almost an industry with, carpenters, masons, farriers and smiths working away at their trades, great stables for horses and the houses of the castle servants and their families. Others lived in the small town clustered at the foot of the massive rock on which the castle stood. The only way to the main gate was along an open passage with towering stone walls either side which would constrict and compress anyone attempting a mass attack at the gate, rendering them liable for annihilation by soldiers above in the massive bastions. Either side were separate walled pedestrian passages for everyday use. Today all was gaiety and the castle walls were alive with flags and banners while the brightly dressed courtiers that accompanied the king paraded through the gates and inside the walls. The saltire cross of Scotland was the most prominent along with the royal standard of England – somewhat incongruous smiled Laurence to himself as few Scots would be comfortable seeing that flying above the ramparts of Stirling castle.

The castle was a mixture of architectural styles, mainly French with some German and English influence here and there. The round towers had conical roofs and Laurence was reminded of le Château de l'Hermine at Vannes, and his home. This provoked a pang of homesickness, especially after he had sent orders for weapons and harness to John Fisher – work he had picked up from Hugh O'Donnell at Donegal. Hopefully he and Anna would be at Stirling castle for some time, at least over the coming winter when travel would be difficult and dangerous. It was an opportunity for him to write to John and exchange words. There were plenty of vessels plying between Scotland and the continent, even at this time of year.

King James led his honoured guests to a grand structure on the western side that looked as if it had only just been finished. The outer walls were bare stone, without the plaster and lime-wash that would complete it. A canopy of golden cloth was set before the doorway, the interior hung with coloured silks. Beyond, a flight of steps led upwards to the royal chambers above what appeared to be cellars and kitchens. A row of halberdiers in cuirass and sallets stood facing each other while the king and his guests walked between them and entered the building. Laurence remained outside, unsure as to how many would be invited inside. Of course, he would be allowed through, being the prince's armourer, but he had Anna with him and she with no certain place at the court of a king. He noted the vast internal ranges of the castle and to the southwest a chapel where he would go soon for a shriving. He had no particular sins with which to titillate the priest, but his soul was heavy with his treatment of Anna and her friendship with Boylan. He was still certain of the Irishman's dubious motives but recognised her mild flirtation was just a little amusement, a commodity not otherwise found in a war camp.

Holding back had a beneficial effect as it turned out. The king had ordered one of his retainers to find places within the castle for the duke of York's followers and he had appointed a courtier to see to their disposition. The more sycophantic followers had gone with the prince and as a consequence, lagging behind, though Laurence and Anna had not the pick of the best accommodation, yet they had some choice. When he stated he was the prince's armourer, they were taken to a place in the inner bailey where a series of chambers were set into the curtain wall. Happily they were given a single chamber that actually had a door and a window, open to the elements it was true, but provided with shutters to close off the outside world and its icy blasts. Not only that but it was beside a range of structures that, judging by the local sounds and smells, were clearly used for metalworking. Indeed, right next to them was what was clearly a forge, though unused at the moment. It seemed the armourer had been expected and properly accommodated. Leaving Anna to sweep out the dust from the chamber floor, he found the baggage wagons where they were being unloaded and paid a castle servant to take their trunk to her. For himself, fingering his reliquary, he took himself off to the previously espied chapel for his long-overdue shriving.

He returned from his shriving having been reassured by the priest that he had little fault, seeing that women were the daughters of the original temptress and inclined to sin as a consequence of their very sex. However, the priest, having particular care as to the extraction of penance and the necessity of paying for it, told him he had been lax in overseeing the discipline of his wife, knowing of her innate frailty and allowing her to succumb to it. As he emerged from the dim, smoky interior of the chapel, even though he had been absolved of the sin of jealousy, his purse, if not his heart, was somehow lighter.

It was some days later, after the welcoming banquet and festivities which the king had arranged for his cousin Katherine Gordon and her betrothed, Prince Richard, duke of York and by right of his Plantagenet blood, King of England that Laurence the armourer knelt, face raised in obeisance before the two monarchs. Acting in tandem, they smiled and indicated that he might stand.

"Master de la Halle," intoned King James, "his grace of York has been telling me of your adventures in the interest of his family and his blood."

"It has been my privilege, your grace," replied Laurence, brushing the residue of rushes from his knees.

"I remember tales of your former liege of England, King Richard who, though my dear cousin here has little good to say of him, nevertheless arranged for his safe conduct to Flanders. I understand you were the one to manage that?"

"Among others, your grace. I cannot claim it was all my doing."

"Yet you are here and the others are not."

"It appears so, your grace. Fate is a strange mistress. She poses and disposes as she will. I think his grace of York has many supporters in the world; he needs little of mine."

"I wonder if your self is something of a talisman?" James regarded him with a quizzical frown.

"I cannot think how that could be, your grace."

"Well, you are the only one here who has known him since childhood and you have proved your worth when it came to preserving his life. I believe you have something of a record when it comes to rescuing distressed nobles. Did you not discover the whereabouts of the lady Anne Neville, abducted and secreted away by my lord's other uncle, George duke of Clarence?"

"In that I had the help of my wife, without whom that enterprise would have failed."

"So I understand," replied the king, surprising Laurence with the extent of his intelligence. "Then there was your own son - abducted. You managed to find him too where anyone else would have failed. I think some magic was involved?"

"Put like that, your grace, it seems as if I have particular powers, but I can assure you, I do not."

"What cannot be disputed is that there is something about you that attracts whatever invisible elements there are in this world to give you aid."

"Your grace, I would never claim that!" Laurence was beginning to fear he might be charged with witchcraft. The king, who had been standing, seated himself in a chair in the hall where he had summoned Laurence to attend him. Other courtiers had been ordered to stand off so the two monarchs could converse privately with the armourer.

"Rest easy," said King James kindly, seeing distress in the armourer's face. "It is just that I have a particular job for you."

"I am at your service, your grace," he said with relief.

"Yes, I would ask you to make new harness for his grace of York."

"That would be my pleasure," replied Laurence, brightening at the thought of using his practical skills rather than being plunged into the dangerous subterfuges of the nobility. He was somewhat surprised because there was nothing wrong with Prince Richard's present harness. Perhaps the duke would joust after all and was to be given harness for that? Whatever work he was to do would attract a pretty penny; a king's harness never came cheap.

"You have an interest in the latest methods of metalworking, I believe?" King James took up a goblet of wine and sipped while looking at the armourer over its rim.
Prince Richard also took up his goblet and sat down in a chair conveniently placed beside that of the king. "Tell me - do you have a charm to reinforce the strength of the iron you make?"

"I use a prayer, your grace, to bless the iron before it is worn."

"That is not the same thing. It did not protect your last master, King Richard."

"King Richard was an anointed monarch, as you are too your grace and had his own arrangement with God which, I suppose, superseded any prayer I might have made over his armour. I would point out, your grace, that I was at Bosworth Field and the king's armour did not fail him, he lost his helm in a close fight and was thus fatally unprotected."

"A clever answer, master de la Halle, which I appreciate. It encourages me to believe you are the right man to craft his grace of York's new harness."

"You have my measurements," inserted Prince Richard. "and I look forward to my new harness. The making of it will keep you occupied until the spring, I think." The last statement gladdened Laurence's heart. Obviously there would be no fighting this year and well into the next. Both he and Anna were becoming weary of camp life and yearned for their home in Brittany. Their chamber was small, but it was their own while they remained here and they would eat in the king's own hall, as his other servants.

"Come, there are some men I wish you to meet," said King James, getting to his feet and placing the goblet on a side table. Duke Richard stood too, clearly intending to accompany the king and his armourer. "You will be working closely with them."

"My lord king," said Laurence with alarm. "I work alone. There is no need for any other except the usual forge labourers." He had his secrets and he was not about to give them away to another armourer. King James laughed and slapped him on the shoulder. He knew the close ways of artisan craftsmen.

"Fear not, master de la Halle, you shall not be required to disclose the secrets of your craft, rather you are about to acquire some new ones." Intrigued, Laurence fell into step with the two princes who made their way through the assembled courtiers and took the steps down to the inner bailey. At this point Prince Richard took his leave of them, seeing as the lady Katherine was close by. Her presence was deflecting his attention from everything else. Most knights would take far more interest in their harness than they would a lady, but here at court the women had more sway than was usual.

"Are you aware, master Laurence, that we cast our own guns here at Stirling?"

"I know you have great interest in such, your grace. There is a mighty cannon here that is larger than any other, so I have heard."

"Yes, Mons Meg is her name. I shall introduce you to her." They walked towards the furnaces and Laurence saw Anna standing at the door of their chamber, her face a picture of consternation, thinking her husband was bringing the king to call. Her relief was palpable as they passed her by and headed towards the forges. The buildings at this part of the castle were a mass of confusion, erected almost as temporary structures according to their uses rather than the ornate style found in all the other castle buildings. Some were stone, others brick with wattle and daub infill. All had tiled roofs rather than thatch, no doubt as a precaution against stray sparks. There were the usual sounds and smells, though Laurence thought he could detect rather more brimstone than usual.

"You recognise that I think?" said the king pointing to a stone structure where the open top was belching forth an oily grey smoke.

"A smelting furnace. Is that where you make the iron for your armament?"

"Not this particular one. There are others in the lower bailey for the more mundane work. This one has a particular purpose. Let me introduce you to master John Damian." As he spoke a spidery man in plain black robes came out of one of the stone buildings and knelt in front of the king. He wore a beard tied up in a net undoubtedly to keep it from interfering with whatever task he was working on. A simple black cap adorned his head and covered his ears. The king swiftly raised him, which the man seemed to expect. "Master Damian," he said pleasantly, switching into French. "This is master armourer, Laurence de la Halle. He is to craft new harness for his grace Richard of England and I would like you to instruct him in something of your art." John Damian frowned, trying to hide behind a bland mask what looked to be annoyance. Laurence understood, having had a similar experience himself with this king regarding the secrets of his own craft. Whatever Damian's art might turn out to be, in common with all men having craft lore to protect, he would not part with his arcane knowledge willingly. Damian's thin face had a grey pallor and there was an acrid whiff of the furnaces about him. His fingers were long and grimy, engrained with black, probably furnace ash and he brought to Laurence's mind the image of a distorted Cornelius Quirke, though this one was shorter with a strange look about him.

"If you would enter, your grace," he croaked in hoarse but courtly French, extending an arm and bowing to the king. They went into the building, which as soon as he entered Laurence recognised as the fume-laden laboratory of an alchemist. There was another closed furnace here belching yellow smoke and being tended by a boy while a short, plump fellow was mixing something in an iron pot over a fire.

"I wonder how familiar you are with the art of Alchemy?" asked the king.

"I know a little, your grace. Master George Ripley is an adeptus. He worked for King Edward the Fourth, as you might be aware, though he fell out of favour there. I visited him once in his laboratory at Westminster. He is at the court of the Tudor now, I believe." The king nodded in agreement.

"So you know of the four elements: earth, fire, air and water?"

"Indeed, all men do, I think they combine along with the *tria prima* - brimstone, quicksilver and salt."

"Ah yes," replied the king, "but what of the fifth element?"

"Grand magisterium – the philosopher's stone! It has proved illusive to mankind." Laurence noted how Damian stiffened, his eyes suddenly lighting with something a churchman might interpret as demonic, but not the king it seemed. James merely smiled superciliously.

"If you understand it as being an actual stone," said the king mysteriously. "Not an unreasonable idea seeing as it is the substance from which the other four elements devolve. However, consider the nature of quicksilver. It is pure and though not itself the fifth element, yet it is close. It can dissolve gold, silver and other metals."

"But not iron, your grace."

The king gave a cry of delight and clapped him on his back. "You have it, master Laurence. I hoped you would comprehend as much."

"It is not secret lore, sire. Quicksilver is contained in iron vessels, in fact, is that not one over there?" He pointed to a table where a variety of flasks and bowls were placed. One of these was an iron bowl where the silver gleam of mercury could be plainly seen. "And as for dissolving gold," he continued, "the process is used by gilders who dissolve gold in quicksilver before drawing with it on armour plate. By a method of their own, they heat the plate to drive off the quicksilver leaving the gold as a pattern on the iron."

"And iron, as you say, is not affected by the quicksilver; which brings me to my point – if iron is impervious to this one substance from which everything else on earth devolves, then it should be possible to build from it harness that protects the wearer from every possible harm!"

"I see that, your grace, and it has ever been my purpose."

"Except iron can be burst asunder in war, at least, iron made by conventional means – but what if the iron were rendered invulnerable by art?"

"Your grace has lost me," responded Laurence, uncertain as to where this conversation was going. Art was but another name for that which was forbidden. The king was coming close to blasphemy and Laurence was unsure as to how Holy Church would respond to the casual declarations of an anointed king. He resisted the impulse to cross himself and was contented by a surreptitious fingering of his reliquary.

"Then I ask monsieur John Damian to enlighten you," declared the king with a note of triumph in his voice." The alchemist, who had been almost dancing with anticipation, sprang to attention.

"You know, I think, that there are certain swords in the world having marvellous properties?" He hardly waited for a reply. Laurence opened his mouth but the alchemist jumped in before he could utter a single sound. "This should not surprise us. Steel is iron extracted from a single lump of stone, earth, and worked in fire and air before being quenched in water. It combines all the elements." Laurence could hardly argue with that. "Now iron can be broken, which is what would happen to a sword cast straight from the furnace, except this is not always so. The sword smith uses his secret lore to work and fashion the raw iron until it can take an edge and withstand the onslaught of lesser brands. There have been some swords that have rendered their owners invincible. I might mention the sword of the archangel Gabriel, and King David was given the sword of Goliath, who was slain magically, I should confess, by a stone of the earth, not a sword. Remember the two swords of King Arthur? The first one, which he drew from the stone, was broken, being worldly and it was the second, Excalibur that gave him his power."

"I know of these and others," said Laurence eager to display his knowledge. "There is Durundal, the indestructible sword possessed of the French knight Roland. That was one of three swords forged by Wayland the Smith, in England: the other two being Charlemagne's Joyeuse and Curtana of Ogier the Dane."

"Then you can see," cried Damian almost beside himself with enthusiasm, "that it must be possible to provide a suit of iron that renders the wearer invincible!"

Laurence gasped at the thought. "There is a deal of difference between the flexible concentrated steel of a sword and the iron of plate armour," he said incredulously.

"It is a question of form merely," replied Damian smugly.

"That will be your task here, master de la Halle," said King James, interrupting the alchemist. "I want you to make harness that will protect the duke of York from his enemies, come they hot from Hell. With the help of John Damian here, I am sure you will not disappoint me." With familiar bonhomie, the king clapped him on the back and grinned into his face. Laurence tried an enthusiastic smile, privately telling himself he and Anna must soon find a way of getting out of Stirling and back to Brittany with their skins intact, and hang the consequences for their future business.

14 - Forward Banners

The snows of winter confounded any idea of leaving before the spring of 1496. All roads to or away from Stirling were impassable. Though the river was navigable most of the time, even that froze over for several days at a time. King James, along with the duke of York and the lady Katherine had taken themselves to Edinburgh where there was some limited communication by sea with the continent of Europe. A letter had found its way to Laurence from John Fisher, acknowledging receipt of the orders for arms from Hugh O'Donnell. Business was brisk at Vannes and John had engaged the services of another armourer to help him. Other news, gathered from the men-at-arms of the castle confirmed that the earl of Surrey had called the men of the north of England to ready themselves for invasion from Scotland come the thaw. Laurence knew that Robert was an esquire in the service of the earl and his worse nightmare was that he would find himself with a Scottish army opposing another where his son was regarded as one of the enemy like Sohrab and Rustem.

"Just look at the state of this iron!" grumbled Laurence, showing the part-formed upper portion of a breastplate to Anna. He threw it down on the table in their chamber then sat down on a stool and stared at it morosely. She stood with her hands on her hips looking at it and gave a puzzled shrug.

"It looks like a lump of iron to me," she said helplessly.

"You describe it well, wife - a lump of iron. I have worked it three times now and it remains a lump of iron. It will never sustain a determined blow. Oh for some Milanese plate. I would have the job finished by now."

"Cannot you inform the king? He is a judge of good armour you say."

"He is that, but he has the idea of a magic harness fixed into his mind and it undermines logic. He believes John Damian has the knowledge to render it invincible and therefore expects it not to have the same appearance as conventional armour. That is what Damian has tried telling me and having the king's ear he brooks no contradiction." Laurence pushed the iron around the table. Cast from the blast furnace in the armoury, the iron contained certain substances added by the alchemist, which Damian supposed, would give the iron miraculous qualities. He had beaten it from the solid lump that had cooled after being poured from the furnace, then re-heated and beat it again to get any impurities out of it. Damian assured him there were none, but observing the multitude of sparks that came from the bloom under his hammer, he knew that was far from true. Sparks were particles of stone or fuel remaining in the iron after casting, and removed by repeated beating with hammers. Nevertheless, he persevered and finally, after much reheating and beating, he had a plate of pure iron ready for cutting and forming to shape. The problem was he had tried, but could not get it to harden, or at least harden sufficiently to sustain a blow in battle. It had been long and hard work. Normally he would begin with plate already cast and worked in the furnaces of Milan or Munich, not a lump straight from the blast. The quality of the iron had been rendered too poor ever to make good armour by whatever Damian had added to it.

"I wonder why the king does not order similar harness for himself?" said Anna.

"I must admit that has puzzled me, too," he replied. "Perhaps he doesn't really believe it will be effective?"

"Another answer could be that he doubts the duke of York's puissance and is providing him with magical protection to compensate."

Laurence thought about it for a moment. "You know, I think that might be so," he said at length. "Certainly, Prince Richard's side performed badly in the joust we had a few days after our arrival and if it had not been for Sir Anthony de la Forsse coming to his aid, he would have been unhorsed. King James saw that and made his own judgment as to his fighting quality."

"Yes, I think the Prince only joined in the joust to impress lady Katherine and she, being blinded by love, saw but a very Galahad. Tales of the legendary King Arthur abound here; even the jousting field is called the Round Table."

"He will need more than enchanted iron to protect him in battle against an English army," grumbled Laurence. "If the harness fails in combat it will reflect badly on me. My best hope is he will be surrounded and protected by the king's household knights and thus never have to take or exchange blows."

"Shall it be left in the white similar to his present harness, or blued as the king's armour?" asked Anna.

"In the white of polished steel and therein lies another problem," the armourer sighed lugubriously. "I have tried to polish a piece and it compares badly with Milanese plate. Strange if, as I suspect Damian has put gold or silver into the mix."

"Cannot you decorate it to disguise the dullness?" she suggested.

"I will have to think of something I suppose. I wonder if I can persuade the king to let me blacken it? That might be a solution. One thing is, it works under the hammer very well so perhaps embossing will help. If only the king were here at Stirling. I need to talk with him, and Damian is never away from the forge, interfering in everything I do." He picked up the piece he had brought with him and took it outside. Soon came the roaring sound of a furnace accompanied by the creaking of bellows as Laurence heated the iron plate. She could hear him giving instructions to the boy who worked the bellows followed thereafter by a spate of hammering.

She began to reflect on the strange alchemist and necromancer, John Damian. Italian by birth, his name in that language was Giovanni Damiano de Falcucci, though here in the castle he spoke mainly French thus the servants called him the French Leech. Another of his titles was Abbot of Tungland, at Galloway. His purpose at Stirling was as a physician and, among other things to make the quintessence, the fifth element - a substance essential for converting base metal to gold and also preserving life. Anna thought the fellow mad. He showed the signs of madness, though eccentricity was also an indicator of a great intellect. She had been told that Damian claimed he could fly as a bird! Madness was common in certain trades such as gilding and alchemy. In both these, the strange substance *argentum vivum*, or quicksilver was extensively used and she supposed that being in regular contact with a magical substance would set anyone's mind on a course not understood by common folk. Here at Stirling the king had paid for regular deliveries of quicksilver, along with gold and silver plate to be consumed in the experiments he and John Damian carried out. It was said they were near to changing base metal into gold. Certainly King James was in great need of gold to pay for his planned invasion of England. Maybe this was one way of getting it without putting himself into debt. She had no idea if the gold with which her husband was being paid for his work on the prince's harness was enchanted or the real thing, but so long as it was finding its way into Laurence's purse, and didn't rust like iron, why worry?

* * *

297

The Court returned to Stirling Castle just after Christmas for the wedding of Richard, duke of York and lady Katherine Gordon. King James had been generous with his gifts to the couple, paying for the duke's horses and his retinue of around two hundred followers. There was to be a joust in the field of the Round Table after the wedding, which was to be solemnised at the Abbey of St. Mary of Stirling at Cambuskenneth, built on the Abbey Craig just over the river from the castle. Laurence had been busy finishing the Prince's new harness. He had managed to talk the King into letting him cover the white armour in dark red damask. Anna had discovered from one of the ladies she had befriended that this was the king's favourite colour. Laurence, surprising himself with his guile, pointed out that in the tales of knights in the French Book, and that other written by Sir Thomas Mallory set around King Arthur, was described harness of different hues. In particular there was the tale of Gawain and the Green Knight, much favoured by James. John Damian, who seemed at last to understand something of the unsatisfactory appearance of the white, or plain iron, while still declaring its superior quality and admitting no defects, lent his support, telling the king the damask would have no detrimental effect regarding the necromantic power underneath it.

Laurence and Anna stood in one of the darkest recesses of the Abbey while the Abbot blessed the marriage of Prince Richard and his bride. In virginal white, the two young people knelt before the altar and exchanged their eternal vows, pledging themselves to each other forever. The Augustinian monks of the Abbey stood in their ranks dressed in white habits with black cloaks and pointed hoods, chanting prayers to bless the union. Afterwards the procession wound its way back along St. Mary's Wynd, the road between the Abbey and the castle, for the wedding feast. They made a colourful show parading where the wynd had been swept clear of the snow that was drifting around them, the large flakes in fancy awarding heavenly blessings. The bright clothes of the courtiers stood out in the snowy landscape, as if embroidered on a ground of bleached cloth as they approached the great lime-washed walls of the fortress, hung for the moment with brilliant banners and pennants, which once the procession was inside the castle walls would be withdrawn to preserve them from the weather.

"King James has taken a fancy to that lady, I think," said Laurence, leaning sideways to speak discreetly into Anna's ear. The wedding feast was in full flood in the great hall and wine was flowing freely. The king had his arm around the waist of a lady who was not in the least perturbed by his attention.

"She is one of his conquests, lady Margaret Drummond. I believe she is but one of several reasons why they cannot get the king to consent to a marriage. He thinks it will spoil his fun."

"There is no reason why that should be," he returned without thinking.

"Really! And has marriage not spoiled your fun?" snapped Anna, not quite with amusement. Laurence spluttered into his wine cup suddenly realising his *faux pas*. In a second he recovered his wits: "I meant with kings, my love, not mere mortals as we. A king marries to beget a royal heir and may not have much choice in a bride. We chose each other freely, which makes all the difference." She sniffed and tossed her head.

"The duke of York and lady Katherine have chosen each other for love, it would appear." They looked to where the couple were chatting together closely, he selecting sweetmeats from the table for her and popping them into her mouth.

"The Prince's expectations were not very great until the day in 1491 when he revealed himself at Cork. He would have seen women as common men do and had expected to pay court to a lady of his own fancy rather than have one chosen for him."

"Lady Katherine was chosen for him." Anna gave him one of her knowing smiles.

"He is a child of Fortune and favoured by Her, at least so far. I hope it will continue so."

Suddenly there was a fanfare of clarions from the minstrels' gallery at the far end of the hall opposite the king's table. The company fell silent wondering what was to happen. An announcement by the king? James released lady Drummond and sat back in his seat, clearly in expectation of something. Suddenly there was a loud bang and a sulphurous cloud of smoke shot up into the air before a door half way down the hall. Men leaped to their feet and looked to their daggers, having no other weapons in the hall. Women screamed in fear, believing they were about to be attacked even though the castle was shut and guarded. As the smoke began to clear a figure could be discerned, short of stature and stout, an imp from Hell? Some crossed themselves in anticipation of some malign visitation from the nether regions, including Laurence until he recognised the figure emerging from the smoke and burst out laughing. Those around looked at him wildly, thinking he had gone mad while Anna thought she would have to lead him off to somewhere quiet. Then everyone joined in Laurence's laughter. Bowing with mock dignity to the assembly was a ludicrous figure attired in the cap and bells of a jester.

"It's Jolly John," gasped Laurence. Anna looked puzzled. Here was a jester to be sure, but how did Laurence know his name? "I remember him from the court of King Richard - he was the king's jester." Jolly John began his capers, skipping about the hall, occasionally leaning against a servant or a guard in mock exhaustion at his antics. He was a dwarf, with a face that might in a dungeon provoke fear but here merely induced mirth. He worked his crowd, leering into the faces of the most beautiful ladies, pretending to court them while standing behind their men folk making fun of them in dumb show until they turned to look and then he would fawn most deprecatingly. He leapt onto the platform where the king sat with the duke of York and his bride beside him. The jester bowed to them then, fluttering his eyes forlornly at lady Katherine, squeezed himself in to sit between the two newlyweds and ignoring Richard, smiled lovingly into the face of his bride. He slid a hand inside his doublet and began squeezing something. Slowly a lump appeared at his groin, swelling to impossible proportions expanding his codpiece. The hall was in uproar as he got up and, bowing to the lady and lewdly indicating the way to the couple's sleeping quarters, solemnly and to enthusiastic applause, marched out of the hall, his inflated codpiece to the fore.

"I remember having to put up with certain lewd comments from John and Gurden Fisher the night we were married," murmured Anna to Laurence, "but I would have locked you out of our room if you had arranged that spectacle."

"It is the custom, the bedding of the bride and groom," he replied with a grin, "and the ladies here are delighted." Anna looked around and sure enough the women were beside themselves with glee while the men guffawed uproariously, no less the king himself along with lady Drummond, who they noticed, patted the king's codpiece fondly. Richard and Katherine were laughing a little self-consciously, but not in any way displaying anger. Anna's face remained frozen, which he thought curious as she had been a tavern bawd when he first met her and would have remained so had he not taken her away from her stepfather at Nottingham.

All the more curious then, when they accidentally met up the next day with Jolly John. The jester was in plain brown doublet and hose under a bright yellow cloak and sitting by the fire in one of the forges where he had come for warmth.

"A cold place this Scotland," he grumbled when he saw the armourer and his wife approach. Anna's face was icy as the compressed snow in the foundry yard while Laurence's lit up in the expectation of a jest. He was to be disappointed. The jester pulled the woollen cloak closer around his shoulders and shivered.

"Come to our chamber," invited Laurence. "We have a brazier there and I am about to have a charcoal fire brought in from my forge to warm us. You would be most welcome." Anna glared at him but kept her lips tightly drawn.

"Is John Damian about?" he asked.

"He is in his laboratory," replied Laurence hoping the jester would not ask him along too.

Jolly John, his demeanour belying his soubriquet got to his feet. "You work with him, I know. Do you have any *aqua vitae?* Damian makes plenty but keeps it close to himself and the king."

"The ultimate restorative? I have none but I do have some of the first distilling, which though it has no magical properties, yet stimulates and warms the blood." Laurence had sneaked away some of the elixir, conspiring with Damian's assistant, Caldwell whom he had caught one day siphoning some off for himself. The price of his silence had been the gift of some of it. The making of quintessence or *aqua vitae* was simply the distillation process repeated over and over again using good wine as its base. The armourer understood the logic of this, after all, it was the repeated working of raw iron that produced fine steel, so why not with liquor? Damian distilled large quantities of wine, although the number of repeat distillations necessary to produce the fabulous fifth element, *aqua vitae* seemed to be greater than that possible, seeing as the liquor reduced in quantity each time it was distilled. It simply ran out before the thousand or so distillations to produce the quintessence could be achieved - a situation exacerbated by Caldwell's frequent siphoning in the early stages.

A few minutes later Jolly John sat with Anna and Laurence around the brazier in their chamber, where the hot charcoals soon warmed the place. Laurence had opened the top section of the window shutters to let out the haze while keeping most of the heat inside. All three had pots containing the essence, which they sipped carefully, letting the fiery liquid warm them from the inside. He had brought some charcoals and a small bellows with which, every now and again he blew air into the fire.

"I remember you at the court of King Richard – Christmas it was," said Laurence.

John grinned and his intrinsically ugly features brightened somewhat. "Ah, yes, King Richard. Those were good days. I served his brother, too; Edward – ever a jolly fellow yet his liking for the ladies was his most grievous fault."

"Really?" gasped Anna. "I should have thought you would have approved of that, being a lewd fellow yourself."

The jester looked at her coolly. "Indeed, dame Anna, I can see why you should think that and usually I would not disabuse a lady's opinion except it seems you disapprove of my frolics?"

"They are not to my taste, sir, that is all," she replied.

"Nor mine," responded the jester surprisingly. "It is all an act and now, as I am getting into my twilight years one that becomes more of a routine than festival. It is tedious to me. We are all trapped in our cases – the knight must always fight even when his bones would be better resting by his fire, and the minstrel must affect passion long after his ability to prosecute the amours he sings of have passed. You refer, no doubt to my performance at the wedding feast of our Prince and the lady Katherine?" Anna nodded, realising here was a man not quite as he seemed. "Would it surprise you to know I spent much of the following morning at prayer in the chapel just over from here?"

"I had not thought on it, sir."

"Yes, my entertainment extends into the confessional where the priest invariably asks for a detailed description of all the lewdness I display before the nobles. The only difference is the king pays me for my performance at court, while I must pay the priest upon repentance of it."

Anna felt a wave of sympathy wash over her for the little man and she too would have to be shriven for her hasty judgement of him. The world was a hostile place for everyone; how much more so to a man born a dwarf and thus often subject to persecution. Jolly John had earned a place in palace and hall for himself in spite of his size and unfortunate physiognomy. He was right when he described entrapment. Didn't everyone fawn and scrape to their betters, even though their betters were largely undeserving of such servitude?

"If I have misjudged you, I repent of it," she said sincerely. Anna too was feeling the effects of the essence and it was making her doleful.

Laurence wriggled uncomfortably as he listened to them. Until now, he had merely regarded the jester as a figure of fun who through his mimicry and dumb show ridiculed the nobility in the only way that was acceptable. He little thought that the man had tender feelings of his own, inviting him to their chamber expecting but a few hours of mirth.

"Think nothing of it, dame Anna," replied John, raising his pot and taking a sip.

Laurence decided the subject needed to be changed and besides, the jester might have an interesting opinion, his trade being the comic interpretation of political events. "What think you of the duke of York and his quest for the crown of England?"

"Now there is an example of what we have just been saying," came the reply. "Prince Richard is caught in a tighter trap than any of us. We can find a means of escape, he cannot. Even I, entrapped as I am in this case," he gestured to his body, "have found something of a way clear. There is no way for him other than the path he is on, or poverty in exile."

"Because of his birth?" said Anna. "He could have chosen to remain as Peter Osbeck, not Perkin Warbeck as the Tudor insists on naming him and no one the wiser."

"Perhaps, though while alive he would still be a threat to the Tudor and so constantly threatened with assassination. Remember, Henry Tudor has always known there is a Plantagenet prince in the world other than the earl of Warwick who is close confined in the Tower of London. The Prince did indeed, at first, attempt to preserve his anonymity but was persuaded by others to show himself. Once he revealed himself as the duke of York, then there was no going back. For one thing the whole nobility of Europe now know his true identity, not just Tudor. You can be sure it will have been checked and monarchs have particular means of discovering the truth of someone's lineage that is beyond the powers of the rest of us. King James here in Scotland knows Richard of York is a true prince of the blood – monarchs are obsessed by it and would never for a moment support a usurper – that is something only lesser nobles and common people do for purposes of their own. Lambert Simnal was an example of that. King Henry Tudor is keeping that impostor by the heels as a mere device to cast doubt on our Prince. It can only work on common folk – princes know better."

"But it is the common folk who must rise to his banner," said Laurence pointedly.

"Exactly, which is why the Tudor has Lambert Simnal close by him, or whatever creature of Tudor's is pretending to be him. The duke of York's former identity as Peter Osbeck is now turned against him letting the Tudor claim he is but another impostor."

"I am fully aware of his true identity," Laurence declared. "After all, I was the one who got him free of the Tower and into Flanders. There are others, too – Sir James Tyrell for one and he will have confided his secrets to others, I am sure."

"Sir James has made his peace with the Tudor and remains silent on the matter, I believe. His brother Thomas is with our cause and there are many others in a like case."

Laurence reached for the stone bottle containing the elixir and topped up the jester's cup. "It sounds as if you have some idea that the Tudor still has Yorkist sympathisers about him?"

"It comes with my trade," replied John with a crafty grin. "There are many who would have the Prince on the throne of England. People let things out in the course of a jest, thinking me but a simple-minded fellow. How do you think I have managed to get invited to the courts of high nobles and monarchs? I have my uses just as you do as an armourer to the same."

Laurence was somewhat shocked by this revelation. He had regarded the jester to be, as he put it, simple-minded merely because he acted the fool and looked the part, while in reality he was highly intelligent. At once, when comparing the jester's case to his own, he realised just how valuable a spy he would make. Both men, by their trade, were close to the highest nobles, here and in other lands.

"I see I have surprised you?" said John. Laurence gave a shrug of agreement. "Then let me surprise you some more – It was not a casual meeting between us at the forge, though your kind invitation in asking me to join you here in your own chamber was a bonus." John turned his attention to Anna. "And your rather virtuous attitude to my courtly frolics, dame Anna encouraged me greatly."

"I fear I might have been rude," she said demurely. "What encouragement could you find in that?"

"It denotes how by your character you can be trusted. Of course, I know your story along with that of master de la Halle. I am in the service of her grace the duchess of Burgundy and my task is to look to Prince Richard's continued existence. The Tudor has his spies here too and danger lurks all around."

"Danger?" gasped Laurence. "To Prince Richard?"

"Yes," replied the jester, "and now to his spouse the duchess Katherine."

"How can the lady Katherine be a threat?" asked Anna, her eyes wide in consternation.

"By becoming pregnant," said John bluntly.

Anna and Laurence fell silent at this statement, both suddenly realising the full implications of the Prince's marriage. A child would be yet another heir to the English throne and a direct threat to the future of Henry Tudor's own progeny. For a king with a manic drive to build a new royal dynasty, not to mention his mother, this would be intolerable.

"You might not be aware, but there has been an attempt to poison the Tudor," continued the jester. "It came to nothing except it both frightened him, not unusually, and put ideas into his head."

"That is interesting," said Laurence, his voice laden with curiosity. "What happened?"

"A Spaniard named Bernard de Vignolles, an agent of a certain personage you do not need to know, has confessed at Rouen to promoting an attempt intending the deaths of Henry Tudor and his family, including his mother."

"Ha," snorted Laurence, "Margaret Beaufort, lady Stanley, the Devil's dam – that were bound to fail. She has ghostly protection."

"That seems so; were it not for her malign influence her son would be plunged to perdition ere now. That fate awaits him yet, but for the present we must look to the safety of the Prince and his duchess."

"What was the nature of this plot?" queried Laurence.

"It is a strange and largely laughable tale, but what is behind it must be taken seriously. It involves an astrologer, John Disant, and a deadly ointment. Originally, Disant was to come to England personally to do the job, but de Vignolles decided he could arrange it himself. He obtained a box from Disant containing the poisoned ointment with the intention of bringing it to London. The mixture was so foul, however, and stank so abominably that he considered it bound to be detected, so he threw it away and replaced it with a counterfeit substance he obtained from an apothecary. The idea was to smear the poison on a doorway that the king and his family were known to use. Apparently this would drive them, their guards and anyone else contaminated to attack one other and do each other to death. He delivered the box with the ointment to Father John Kendal, Prior of the Order of St. John of Jerusalem in England. He has long been a supporter of our Prince as you might know and is now near the court of the Tudor secretly working in our interest. Kendal was to organise the actual deposition of the poison."

"I do know of him," replied Laurence. "He has a similar name to another John Kendall who was killed with King Richard at

Bosworth. But I am intrigued to know what happened when the poison was used."

"It never was used and remember, it was counterfeit anyway, though at that time John Kendal did not know it. He only knew the story of the original substance and considered the ointment too deadly to use safely, so he disposed of it. King Henry knows only of de Vignolles' confession and is unaware of Kendal's part in the plot."

"And you believe the Tudor will attempt to dispose of the duke of York and his bride in a similar way?"

"Poison, or some other means of assassination, is an obvious and cheap solution so far as he is concerned and not without precedent. Certain Scottish nobles have ever shown themselves amenable to accepting English gold, or even lordly titles for reward, a trait King Edward the First exploited."

Laurence stood in silent contemplation for a few moments. "How am I to help in all this? I am expert in making armour against weapons but there is no armour that will protect from poison. Is that the purpose of the enchanted harness I have been asked to make?"

"Not really – enchanted harness would not do for lady Katherine. Apart from vigilance, you can do little more; however, as for dame Anna . . .?"

"Me!" she cried.

"Yes, I have a command from the king that you attend upon the duchess Katherine as one of her ladies."

"But I cannot. I am not noble." Anna swigged the rest of the essence in her cup and spluttered as its fire coursed down her throat.

"That is so, dame Anna, but you have certain qualities that the duchess will be in need of: your healing arts."

"Is she sick?" Anna responded with alarm.

"No, but it is suspected she is pregnant."

"Pregnant – she was just a bride yesterday!"

"Well, you know how it is," said John with a wry grin. "The two have not been apart since their meeting at Dumbarton and the king is not careful of a lady's chastity so there has been little in the way of supervision since then."

"Even so, are you sure? They have been together less than two months." Anna was incredulous.

"Her maids have said so and they have been watching for her courses. In any case, you will be there as a sort of wise woman rather than a lady's maid, looking to her general health so it matters not if she be pregnant or no. If she is not now I have no doubt she soon will be. You are commanded to attend upon the King after the bell for nones."

Laurence and Anna exchanged worried glances. He was aware that the Prince might be in mortal danger and as his armourer it was possible he might happen to be close by his side should there be an attempt on his life. He was ready for that and felt he could handle himself well enough in a desperate situation – but Anna? That was a different matter and if there were poison around the duchess Katherine, it was likely his wife would come in contact with it too.

"We can hardly turn down a royal command," he lamented, gazing at Anna with a worried frown creasing his face.

"let us not concern ourselves unduly, husband," she replied, suppressing her own feelings of dread. "There are many proofs against poison, should that be attempted." She thought it prudent not to mention the idea that had immediately sprung to her mind, that the best test for poison was trying food and drink on someone else before the intended victim tasted any. He was thinking along similar, but more brutal lines - the possibility of armed attack where assassins would not want to leave witnesses alive.

The jester regarded them with a puzzled frown. "Most would be overjoyed to be moving closer into the royal household," he said curiously. "There are those at court who would slit their best friend's throat for such advantage."

"We are somewhat taken aback, that is all," said Laurence not wanting his and Anna's reticence reported to King James. They had been looking to finding an excuse to leave for their home in Brittany come the spring thaw and now the prospect had receded again. It was as if some malign fate was sitting in the shoulder of their sail.

* * *

The highland chieftain's along with their clansmen had come at the command of their king for the wappenshaw. Always eager to gather for an attack on England, they were streaming in to the environs of Stirling, thus placing a great burden on the resources of the local people and, because he had called them, the straightened purse of King James. The summer weather was indifferent and it rained regularly. Underfoot the ground was soft and there would be problems moving the heavy cannon and baggage trains. These had already set off, moving them closer to the border ready for when the army marched into England. Mercenaries arrived by sea from

Flanders, sent by the duchess Margaret and the Holy Roman Emperor.

While at Edinburgh the duke of York had addressed an assembly of Scottish nobles. The supposed purpose was to establish his true identity as a royal Plantagenet prince. In fact everyone knew his provenance; Scottish nobles had excellent intelligence, having friends in Europe and France in particular. The Prince's address had been given by way of an official introduction to the aristocracy of Scotland and a counter to the falsehoods of the King of England.

King James intended Richard's address also as a rallying cry to arms in the cause of a friend and fellow monarch. Naturally, there were those who interpreted this enthusiastically as an excuse to invade England legitimately rather than as bandits, which was the usual case. Others in Scotland wanted no part in the scheme while some were ambiguous in their support. King James, however, was popular, with a reputation not dissimilar to that which King Richard the Third of England had enjoyed. He too won support among his people with firm but fair government.

The king had returned to Stirling to ready his army for the invasion of England. One of those reluctant in the Prince's cause was George Gordon, earl of Huntly who stood with Laurence the armourer in the outer bailey of Stirling castle watching the incoming of the clan chiefs for the wappenshaw, or weapon showing, the ancient ceremony of a call to arms. Although he was the father of Katherine, queen of England in waiting, his demeanour displayed little of the delight the potential prospects of his daughter should have given him. He was a big man getting on in years and one who would not admit he was getting too old to fight. His hair was red with threads of grey, as was his short, cropped beard trimmed neatly and squared off below a long weathered face. He was dressed in full mail hauberk covered with a red surcoat belted at his waist where a dagger was attached by a scabbard with another scabbard vacant, the sword it usually contained being in the hands of his squire while the earl trained with a wooden baton at the pell. A warrior by birth and inclination, a few minutes before he had been exercising his sword arm against one of the pells provided for the purpose in the bailey and runnels of sweat ran down his face.

"No need for plate iron - the pell never fights back," he growled, as close to a jest as he was ever likely to come. He handed the heavy wooden baton he had been using to his squire who exchanged it for his lighter sword. He found the scabbard and slipped his sword smoothly home. "They tell be the harness you have made for my son-in-law is enchanted." He guffawed derisively. Laurence, anxious that the earl should not consider his work trivial answered plainly.

"You must ask master Damian about enchantment," he said coolly. "The iron is not that which I would have chosen, my lord." The earl scrutinised his face.

"I am relieved to hear it," he said after a few moments. "There is some work I require." He patted his ample stomach. "You can see why I practise in mail rather than my plate. I am somewhat constricted in it – fine for show but not agile enough for battle." The earl was a fond trencherman it would appear, and the evidence was in front of him.

"I understand, my lord. A common problem easily resolved. I am at your service." Laurence swept him a low bow.

"Your wife, dame de la Halle, she attends my daughter." It was a statement that Laurence decided deserved an inclination of the head in courtly acknowledgement.

"She has that honour, my lord."

"Yes, she also has some skill with simples and potions. My daughter sent her to me the other day because I had a mild ague and the potion she made for me gave some relief – more so than the poison concocted by that Damian fellow, a supposed physician. I hope he is more successful in his spells for fending off the enemy from Prince Richard."

"I am not encouraged to think so," replied Laurence. "A ring of men in good plain iron around him will serve better, I think."

"Not his own puissance then?"

"The duke of York will acquit himself well enough, I hope." Surely, he thought, the earl did not expect him to voice his doubts as to the fighting quality of a royal prince.

The earl of Huntly smiled, nodded and patted the armourer's arm. "I see we understand our Prince well enough." Laurence kept his mouth firmly shut.

"Your wife – she is expert at curing ills, but can she counteract the effects of poison?"

"It depends on the poison used, I suppose. She can make up purges and suchlike, but if a poison is not in the gut, something that has been eaten or drunk, then I think other skills than hers might be needed."

"I suppose you mean a priest – well, that is a last resort in my experience. You know my daughter is pregnant, eight months gone?"

"Indeed, my wife keeps me informed on her grace's progress – happily she carries well I am told."

"She does." The earl stood with a far away look in his eyes, as if trying to divine future events.

"Have you consulted an astrologer?" asked Laurence, thinking it the most sensible thing to do. In fact, he might do that himself to see what the future held and how soon he and Anna could get out of this business with the Prince.

"Yes, there are several here who advise the king, but I can get no clear response when I ask about the future regarding Katherine and the duke of York."

"We can only trust to God and Holy Church," said Laurence fingering his reliquary. "Priests do not favour the advice of astrologers, perhaps with good reason."

"Then let us get the fighting underway. In the end a strong arm can carve its own fortune and confound a whole pack of necromancers. Attend upon me this evening before I go into the hall with the king. I shall have my harness sent to me and you can look it over."

* * *

Water splashed all around as Laurence and Anna stood close together in the tub of water heated on the forge fires and brought into their chamber by one of the labourers. They were standing, enjoying a bathtub together before attending upon the court that evening.

"Why is it that some parts of my anatomy appear to be attracting more attention than the rest?" chuckled Anna, flicking soap into her husband's face.

"I am responding to your initiative in that respect," he returned. "There is one particular part of me that is squeaky clean."

"I had hoped that the sweat we had worked up before we took to our bath would be entirely purged," said Anna.

"Hope was the last that thing that Pandora found in her box," he responded gaily.

She reached down and filled a clay pot, the contents of which she poured over his head. "That should be cold except it would chill me too – so be thankful and calm yourself. We are not in the first flush of youth."

"Ah, but I feel as though I am when I stand thus with you," he replied curving a hand around her waist and pulling her to him. "I am an armourer and know how to forge a ready spear."

"And I am an armourer's wife and know when it is appropriate to quench a hot brand to preserve its temper."

"But steel is tempered all the finer for constant reworking," he returned, stepping from the tub and lending his arm as she followed.

"Your wit defeats me, *monsieur*," she whispered. "But let us hurry, we have little time to prepare for the court."

Afterwards they lay together, getting back their breath. Laurence had seen little of Anna for some days and he wanted to speak to her about the goings on around the court, except their rare chance of intimacy had diverted his purpose.

She told him of the common gossip. "Henry Tudor is claiming he has found the Prince's true parents, the Osbecks of Tournai."

Laurence considered this in the light of what he knew had actually occurred. "Richard had indeed lived with them as a child in obscurity," he said. "It is simple for Tudor to make out they are his real parents. Few others than the monarchs of Europe have the resources to confound it. Tudor well knows that a convincing tale, irrespective of its veracity, can be used diplomatically by those monarchs, as well as himself, to distance themselves from the Prince should changing circumstances demand it of them. That is what he works towards."

"The French had offered to persuade King James to hand the duke of York over to the Tudor. This was but a ploy on their part, of course. The French, being eternally duplicitous, as we know, have separately offered King James 100.000 crowns for the Prince, who would be taken into exile in France. There he will become a pawn in the international game and forever a threat to Henry Tudor."

"Which alone should convince the waverer's that here we have a true prince, and worth a king's ransom at that!"

"Just so," said Anna firmly. "Impostors are habitually dupes who fool no one and are used merely as a temporary rallying point for some nefarious purpose or other. Lambert Simnal was one and easily detected. Charles of France would never make such an offer for a mere impostor, no matter how superficially convincing he might be. The pity for us is that King James has repudiated the French offer and is intent on winning the Prince's crown for him," she lamented, " which means we must remain here. Of course King James expects there will be benefits for Scotland with an English king in debt to him both financially and morally. The town of

Berwick is worth more to James than any amount of gold the French king might offer."

"Especially if John Damian triumphs with his experiments, and conjures it from base metal," replied Laurence speculatively.

"Humph, when he recovers," said Anna with a wry smile at her lips.

"Yes, a broken thigh does restrict a man," said Laurence sagely. "It serves him right, though. Flying is best left to the birds - and the angels."

"I have always suspected the man is mad. To leap from the walls of Stirling Castle with a bunch of feathers strapped to your arms is hardly the action of a sane man. He is lucky only his thigh was broken."

"Unless he has been siphoning off the quintessence and imbibing of it. That would make sense as he probably thought its magical properties would bear him aloft." He thought on this idea for a moment. "Perhaps it worked after a fashion? After all, another man would have been killed."

"Then he can think some more on it as he lays upon his bed. The duchess Katherine has offered to send me to tend his injury but he will not hear of it. King James has tended him personally and he reckons the ministrations of a king superior to those of a wise woman."

Laurence chuckled at the thought of Damian's broken thigh being set by James. "King James counts the skills of a physician among his considerable accomplishments," he declared, "and no doubt is delighted to practise on his fellow alchemist. Perhaps he anticipates a day when he might need to call on John Damian to minister to him and is getting his revenge in early. What does the duchess Katherine think will happen?" he asked as he tugged on his breeches while returning the conversation to the politics of the court.

Anna pulled a shift over her head and ran her hand over a rich gown lying on the bed. King James had paid for it saying she must be decently attired to attend upon the duchess. "She is besotted by her prince and, it must be said, he with her. Her father, though, is uneasy and has questioned the duke of York relentlessly. He is sure of the Prince's lineage but rather less of his chances in winning the English crown, yet he is tempted by the idea of having a daughter as Queen of England. I think there might have been some parental interference with their amours else."

"I have spoken to the earl of Huntly and he gave me the impression he has small regard for his son-in-law." He drew a clean linen shirt over his head.

"The earl is a soldier," said Anna, "and expects a monarch, particularly a potential one, to have martial accomplishments. Even Richard's most loyal followers credit him with but little in that respect. He is a courtier and excels at the battleground which is the court."

Laurence nodded in agreement. "His personal valour is untested so the coming war will give him the opportunity to determine his fitness to rule a kingdom," he said struggling into his hose. "In any case, King James has all the military prowess needed to win through without the duke of York drawing his sword, other than to wave it about his head afterwards."

"Your hose has either shrunk or you are getting weightier," noted Anna with wifely concern.

"It fits perfectly," he responded stubbornly while taking up his doublet. "Help me tie this – I cannot reach around my back." Anna fussed with the ties of his hose to the doublet. Both could call on a servant to help them dress, but their recent intimacy had demanded privacy, as did their present conversation. "King James is to deliver a proclamation this evening. The year advances and if we do not make a move on England soon, the season will turn against us and I do not mean just the weather."

Anna put on her gown and turned her back for her husband to fasten the ties.

"If I draw these any tighter you will like to be pinched to death," he joked in response to her remarks about his weight. She sniffed and wriggled like a young girl, declining to comment. True, her waist was somewhat thicker since they had been at Stirling Castle, but she remained in his mind's eye the young woman he had first seen at a low tavern in Nottingham. He gave her bottom a fond squeeze before turning her around and kissing her.

"I must go," she whispered softly, tugging fondly at his beard. "The duchess will be ready to enter the hall soon and I must be with her before then in case she feels unwell. There is already some spite directed at me by her ladies, especially the woman brought in to tend to her birthing. Fortunately the duchess favours us, you as her Prince's armourer and I as her special attendant, charged with caring for her well-being."

"And I must attend upon the duke of York, especially now there is an army to get on the move."

* * *

Laurence knelt in front of an image of Saint Triduana located above her relics interred below the altar of her shrine. The church at Restalrig, near Edinburgh, had been built under the patronage of James the Third, the present King's father. Beside it a few yards away was an older chapel known as St. Triduana's Aisle. He had been here once before, in 1482 with his own patron King Richard the Third while he was still the duke of Gloucester. It was just after Berwick-upon-Tweed had fallen. Gloucester had camped briefly at Restalrig though just the chapel had been there at the time, the present church being built five years later.

King James the Fourth of Scotland was at prayer with the duke of York in his royal chapel, St. Triduana's Aisle. The two kings prayed alone except for their confessors, none of their followers permitted to intrude. James was known to be wearing a celice, an iron chain he fastened around his waist as a penance for the death of his father at the battle of Sauchieburn. The son had never forgiven himself for supporting the rebellion that had cost his father his life, even though he had no hand in it himself, yet he wore the celice from Lent to Easter having an extra link forged and attached each year. Now contemplating battle, he had taken to wearing it for the duration of the campaign.

Beside Laurence in the parish church, a man in ragged robes lay spread out and face down on the cold stone of the church floor, a scrap of cloth around his head obscuring his eyes. Laurence had met him at the church door, leaning on a staff and hoping that a priest would come to assist him. Unfortunately the priests were all gathered close to the adjacent chapel waiting for the king to come out and had no time for a beggar, so Laurence took him by the arm and led him to the saint.

Triduana was a Holy Woman who had come to Scotland from Greece in the 4th century and settled at Restalrig. Being a great beauty, she attracted the interest of a local Pictish king named Nechtan. To spurn his determined advances, she tore out her own eyes and gave them to him. When she died she was buried here where the church now stood. Ever since, those with eye disorders came to her shrine at Restalrig for a cure and Laurence heard she had the power to heal the blind.

Having spoken to the man beside him as they entered the church, he discovered he had been a gunner, blinded when testing gunpowder.

Laurence was not surprised at this. He had witnessed the testing of the black powder, sensibly from a safe distance. It involved heaping a small quantity of powder on a white paper in the centre of a stout table, then the gunner would turn his back while reaching behind with a glowing taper hoping to ignite it. The condition of the paper afterwards told something of the state of the mix, a combination of saltpetre, brimstone and charcoal. Often he would attempt to observe the flash by covering one eye with his hand to note the strength of the reaction. If tempted thus, then one or even both eyes could be lost or damaged. It was common to find at least one gunner in a king's army with an eye covered over by a leather patch.

After making his own devotions to the Holy Virgin, and before getting up from his knees, he asked that Triduana intercede for the unfortunate gunner beside him. The fellow showed no signs of movement and he considered he would probably have to lie there for some time if he was waiting for a miracle to restore his sight. He made the sign of the cross over him and left him there in peace.

September sun, warm and bright brought out the colours in the liveries of the knights and nobles assembling ready for the invasion. Here were men from Germany, France and Flanders to augment the forces raised by King James himself. The bright escutcheon of Scotland with its single rampant red lion on a yellow ground fluttered beside that of York, a White Rose, the badge repeated in the murrey and blue surcoats of the Prince's followers. King James had bought great quantities of crimson and other coloured cloths along with gold and silver thread for embroidery so that his army would enter England resplendent as any army in Christendom. Laurence, too, had been one recipient of the king's largesse – his purse was richer by over twenty pounds, payment for the duke of York's harness. To Richard, duke of York he had given a greater sum, thirty-six pounds and paid for his horses and a carriage to take him in state to the battle.

The heavy guns of the king's army had gone before, but the wagons with powder and shot were being assembled in the meadows around Rastalrig. Included were transports containing food, weapons, equipment for smiths, farriers, miners and carpenters – all the skills needed to prosecute a determined war. There too were the tents of the Scottish army - highlanders come down from

315

their mountains and uplands at the bidding of their clan chieftains, eager to fight the English. Laurence worried at their lack of discipline. These brutal men fought hard and well but were almost naked, having little or no actual armour. Time and again English armies, with superior discipline, managed great slaughter against them, and yet they came back for more. Not far from here, an ill disciplined English army under Edward the Second had been thoroughly routed at the Bannock burn, within sight of this very castle of Stirling and no Scot would forget that. Scottish nobles, men-at-arms fully harnessed and in fighting trim would provide the vanguard and the main driving force. Bannock burn proved the English could be beaten and with this young King, cultured, educated and a fine fighting soldier they had a match for any English general. In the next few days, all these, along with the retinue of Richard the Fourth of England would move south to cross the border at Caustrim, known to the English as Coldstream and the location of the ford across the River Tweed.

15 – Cry Havoc!

George, earl of Huntly was beaming from ear to ear. He was a seasoned campaigner and glad to be in this army with his king and also his son-in-law, relieved the latter at last was readying for battle. Duke Richard stood in the pavilion of King James while a squire fussed around him, fastening to his pourpoint the last pieces of his leg armour. Laurence was there too, surveying the new harness with a critical eye and noting with satisfaction the way in which the brilliant red damask, embroidered with golden thread to display the three leopards of England, covered the breastplate and masked the true nature of the iron underneath. Of course, only the experienced eye of an armourer would be so critical of the iron, but the earl of Huntley hadn't been fooled and neither, he suspected, had King James. Presumably the King had more confidence in John Damian's arcane alchemic craft than Huntly and Laurence. It was only the cuirass that was made of the enchanted iron so, hopefully, his enemies would confine themselves to beating him about the head where his armet and visor was of good Milanese steel. His leg harness, too, was of the same, forged in the workshops of Milan and crafted by Laurence to fit the Prince to perfection.

King James was already in full harness and raised a golden goblet filled with wine to his friend. The Prince was about to respond in like manner, reaching for a goblet proffered by an attendant when a herald bustled into the pavilion. He went straight to King James and falling to his knees, looked up into his face.

"Your prickers have returned, your grace and Sir Kenneth Pierce would speak with you."

"Send him to us," responded the King. "Now we shall have news of where we might make our first strike," he announced breezily. The herald got to his feet and bowed himself out of the presence to be replaced by a man-at-arms, the forenamed Sir Kenneth Pierce. The knight made his obeisance to the King and glanced nervously at the Prince.

"Sire, the news is not good. I have managed to find some local English nobles and though claiming some sympathy with the cause of the duke of York, yet none of them are willing to join us in arms. Not only that but the whole populace hereabouts is hostile. The people have fled their farms, hidden their livestock and mewed themselves up in whatever fortifications and towers they can find for defence."

"Is that so," snarled King James. "Well we have the means of bringing them down. My gunners will be glad of the practice."

"Your grace - James," cried Prince Richard, "They are my people and are not to be treated so. They do not know me yet. As soon as I show myself to them they will rally to my banners."

Sir Kenneth shuffled his feet uncomfortably and looked at King James, his face showing hopelessness. "If I may speak freely, your grace?"

"You may, Sir Kenneth," replied the King. "We are not Henry Tudor that you must weigh your words before you speak."

"It is the Scots army they fear, your grace, and not without reason. We have raided these lands for years, as they have ours, and little love is lost between us. The duke of York might be their rightful king, but accompanied as he is, not only by we Scots, but with French, German and Flemish soldiers, they will not come to his aid while he is allied thus."

"Nonsense!" cried the Prince. He turned in desperation to James. "My cause is not presented properly, that is all. Place me at the head of your host, your grace." Sir Anthony de la Forsse and Roderigo de LaLaing moved in close behind the Prince as if reinforcing his intent. John Watre was there too, coming faithfully to his side. Patrick Hepburn, earl of Bothwell pushed himself forward eagerly and stood beside King James, unspeaking but alive with interest at the argument.

"My lord king," responded Sir Kenneth, "there is already incidents of burnings and rapine in the countryside. I fear it is too late to bring the English who abide in these regions to our service, nor possible for long to restrain your highlanders who see rich plunder all around and no effective support from English rebels, as promised."

King James strode up and down within the confines of his pavilion for a few moments, considering his next move and impatiently scattering his servants. Presently he came to a decision.

"My friend," he said to Richard, "You are right. We shall ride together at the head of our host to show the people our common cause. Pre-emptive actions of our own shall be punished and full restitution given for any damage done providing the people of England come to the aid of their true king. If not, we shall cry havoc, and advance into England until your throne is won."

Laurence thought this last speech of James' nothing more than bravado. He could hardly imagine this army getting far into England without the support of the people there. Latest reports had been of a great muster of arms ordered by the Tudor and now heading towards them out of Newcastle led by lord Latimer. Lord Thomas Howard, the earl of Suffolk, was at York raising levees for an attack to oppose Scotland. This last report worried Laurence the most because he knew Robert would be there in the household guard of Suffolk. Again his heart was leaden as he contemplated the thought of being on the opposing side, facing Howard and his own son.

Richard of York and King James of Scotland mounted their war-horses and gathered their household knights around them. While on the march Laurence would remain within easy distance of Richard, but should there be a battle, then he would retire to the baggage with the other armourers. Taking no chances, he was clad in a leather brigandine over a mail hauberk while his helmet was a barbute. This latter piece he had made at the castle forge of Stirling castle to replace the one he lost fighting for another king on the Redemore plain twelve years ago. Steering clear of any idea of using enchanted iron, he contented himself with good Milanese steel and his usual prayers to St Barbara, trusting in the protection of heaven rather than that invented by the likes of John Damian. A murrey and blue tabard over his harness proclaimed him a member of the Prince's entourage. His weapons were a short arming sword and a murderer – a long-bladed dagger.

The banners of Scotland and England moved up and the cavalcade started into the countryside, the army following. Looking around, Laurence noted the close formations of the Flemish, German and French mercenaries in contrast to the ill disciplined straggle of the Scots. Everywhere they marched the country was bare of people and livestock. Where they came across a farm, while sheep or cattle had been driven off and hidden, the barns were filled with recently harvested wheat, barley and hay. Highlanders were finding carts and filling them with these, ignoring their king's pronouncement regarding plunder, and sending them back to Scotland and their own homes. They understood their king as well as he them, neither taking seriously his words. Mercenaries took no part in this plunder. They had no farms and homesteads in the land to take the produce to. Their hopes were pinned on the sacking of a town where there would be rich pickings in the houses of rich merchants and churches. They passed by a fortified tower that had been attacked where wood had been stacked against the door and ignited. The fire and smoke killed some of the inhabitants who had taken refuge there and the rest were butchered as they tried to get out, men women and children.

After a few hours a halt was called while the King surveyed the land and received reports from his prickers as to the whereabouts of any possible English army. Laurence urged his horse through the press around the two generals in order to try and discover what he could of the King's next orders. Duke Richard was angrily haranguing the earl of Bothwell, who was never far from the king's side. Everyone understood this was the Prince's way of getting at the king indirectly, it being an offence to James' dignity to face him outright. Bothwell's features were red with anger, realising he could not respond as he would wish in front of the king. Other Scottish nobles came by him in tacit support. It seemed to Laurence that the duke of York counted little with these men who were only here at the command of their king. The earl of Huntly was but one of the Scottish nobles who displayed concern in his features for both James and Richard. Before leaving Stirling, Jolly John, who had a close ear by every door at court, had informed him that Bothwell had tried to dissuade King James from invading England, believing it would bring an English army down on them in righteous indignation from Henry Tudor. King James, though, stood resolute in the Prince's cause and could not be deflected from his chosen path.

The King gave the command to press forward further into England. His army was spread out over a wide area and difficult to bring to order, though James seemed unconcerned. Laurence supposed he could afford to be lax seeing as there was no immediate danger from an English army. Reports were coming in of pillage and rape. At one point they passed through the remains of a hamlet where the houses and barns had been razed to the ground. Dead bodies of men, women, children and babies lay between the houses and at the remnants of doorways where the stubborn inhabitants, believing their Tudor king would protect them, had refused to abandon their property. Laurence, who was hardened to the dreadful effects of war turned off that part of his brain which generated pity, an old soldiers trick, or at least one practised by those with a conscience. He closed off the sight of one grey-haired old man, his throat cut, sprawled out and reaching towards an infant that had been killed by a sword thrust, or some such. By the attitude of the bodies, the babe had been torn from the old man's grasp before being thrown down as garbage. A man of middle years was hanging from a tree while a naked woman lay on the ground beneath, her legs splayed having been raped then butchered. Perhaps they had been suspected of hoarding money or valuables and this was the tragic result of their interrogation?

As night drew on, it brought some temporary respite to the country folk of England, while the King ordered his army to camp. They feasted well. The cooks got their fires going and began roasting the meat brought in by those soldiers who had found where livestock was hidden. Duke Richard of York discovered he had no appetite. The sights he had seen that day sickened one who, until now, had no experience of war. His education had been centred on the gallantry of knights who fought each other according to the code of chivalry, where women were elevated and championed, not raped and butchered. He had enjoyed the pageantry of the joust and admired the skills of the brilliantly accoutred knights as they showed off their skills in combating each other as equals. He had not imagined how these noble skills, so particularly learned, would be used thus. Of course he knew that there was carnage in a battle, but that was where men were armed and ready for the fight. These were his own defenceless people whom he had come to save from the tyranny of the Tudor, not cause them to be struck down, robbed and slaughtered. Animals slain in the hunt were respected more than these, his subjects.

"You savour too much of a tender conscience, my lord," said King James to the Prince while selecting a morsel from the platters before him. "You will have to deal with harder matters than these when you are King of England." They were sitting together at a long table in James' pavilion along with a few favoured nobles from the retinues of both men. The insides were hung with brightly embroidered tapestries, the king's favourite ones brought with him on campaign. His cooks were heaping the table with viands and sweetmeats as if in a royal castle rather than a draughty and capacious pavilion along the bleak borderlands of England. The duke of York pushed with his dagger point at the meat he had cut somewhat despondently from a beef.

"It was the sight of slaughtered babes that brought me most grief," he murmured. "I suppose it is the thought of Katherine being with child. There was one woman, clearly pregnant who . . ." His voice began to collapse and he choked at the recollection of what must have been the sight of the opened belly of some female.

"Put the thought from you," advised King James placing a gentle hand upon his arm. "You cannot rule for individuals, except in your court, and even then you must detach yourself from ideas of pity. As for the present, you are not responsible for this war. Remember the unworthy Tudor has usurped the crown of England. It is he who must stand before God at the last and answer for it."

"But I am the one whose cause has brought about this present carnage. I cannot think that God would thank me for it, even after victory when I am proved to be chosen by Him and an anointed king."

Laurence, sitting at a lower table and just within earshot, pondered upon the last statement of the Prince's. He knew that, if Richard were intended by God to become king then nothing would prevent it, the anointing of a king being the embodiment of God's Will. Let the duke of York fail in his adventure then it could be argued the responsibility for these dead souls would rest on him and his followers. Fear for his own soul came upon him - the sooner he could get away from this the better. If, however, he were to be one of those who had helped a rightful king to his throne, then by this rule, his own passage through purgatory would be swift indeed?

But there was, lurking in the back of his mind, the fact of the charge of bastardy, which had deprived the Prince and his brother of the English throne and promoted the legitimate king, Richard the Third to the Crown. Though Prince Richard still had a better claim than the Tudor, yet like his it was not entirely a true one and only God could decide upon it. If, as the priests said, God were on the side of humanity, then which of these would he choose? Was there, in the mind of God, a better purpose for one rather than the other? Both were weak men, needing the might of others to promote them, yet the Tudor was ruthless enough to manipulate events while the tender conscience of the duke of York was being carried along on the tide of those same events, rendering him a child to Fortune with no identifiable means of control. That was no bar to the purpose of God, but what of King Richard the Third? He had fallen when there was no doubt he was a full blood prince? Whom would God choose now - bastard one, or bastard two? Isn't it the meek that are to inherit the earth?

Laurence, having no access to the eternal mind, decided he should be off to his bed. He would forgo a visit to a priest, feeling that his present thoughts would confound the theology of a saint. He was quartered in a nearby pavilion with the duke of York's main followers and it was John Watre who turned up exactly at the same time for them to enter the tent together.

Master de la Halle, good greeting."

Laurence responded in like manner. Watre was a short, rotund man with a neatly trimmed beard and dark brown hair under a black chapeau. He was richly attired, as all the Prince's followers, dressed by the munificence of the King of Scotland.

"You have a particular aspect about you which tells me you are thinking too much," said Watre jocularly but with a perspicacious aspect to his eyes. Laurence looked upon him, carefully weighing what he might reply in response. Watre was close to the Prince as his skin, though only those who had been with the campaign for some time would notice that. He kept himself in the background but always within speaking distance.

"I am troubled," Laurence replied. "I believe I am not alone in that."

"Indeed no, but troubles lead to thoughts and thoughts might lead us astray."

"You are too obscure for me, sir," replied Laurence. "I am a plain man."

"And all the more honest in your opinions for that, I hope? May we walk together for a while?" He cast a cautious eye over the guards who stood laconically beside the pavilion. Laurence nodded and they strolled off through the camp together. "Tell me, what do you know of the earl of Bothwell?" asked Watre casually.

Patrick Hepburn – only what everyone else knows. I do remember he fought hard to hold Berwick-upon-Tweed against the army of the late King Edward. It was Richard of Gloucester who commanded then, though Thomas Stanley was the one who finally took the town. I was with Gloucester at Edinburgh, but we returned to Berwick afterwards where certain knighthoods were handed out, but I had no sight of the earl at that time. I have no idea where he was being held."

"Then you will understand Bothwell has little love for the Plantagenets?"

"He was the perfect host to the Prince at Dumbarton," replied Laurence.

"He would be," mused Watre stroking his beard. "I know of the charge given to you by the duchess of Burgundy, to keep close to the Prince. Now your wife is doing the same for the duchess of York, lady Katherine. Both of you have proved your worth – believe me, had you shown any inclination to betray the Prince, I would have discovered it." Laurence was taken aback and offended by this remark.

"I have been intimately involved with the affairs of the House of York for too long to consider changing my loyalties. Besides, I am under threat of death from the Tudor and before you think I might be looking to overturn that by spying for him, let me tell you I could never rest easy under a pardon from him, even in the unlikely event he would grant one." An image of Henry Tudor trembling at the sight of the armourer bearing down on him at Bosworth Field flashed into his mind. He had witnessed his abject cowardice and there was no way Tudor shame would let him live should he fall into his clutches.

"You misunderstand me," said Watre placatingly. "I intended no offence, it is just that we are wrapped in intrigue. There are agents of the Tudor all around and though King James has his spies, so too the duchess of Burgundy, yet it is the Tudor spies here we must be wary of."

"Then there is something particular you wish to convey to me?" he said, recalling that Jolly John had already identified himself as a spy for the duchess Margaret.

Watre nodded and stopped, looking around to ensure no listeners were near. "It is necessary that you know the earl of Bothwell is dealing secretly with the Tudor."

"Ah, that comes as no surprise. There is not a Scottish noble I would trust in this venture of ours. They have a history of dissembling between their own sovereignty and the English Crown. It was that which destroyed King James' father and the reason his son wears a celise as penance for letting himself be carried along on a tide of intrigue."

"Yes, and the Tudor is working on several others. It is not difficult. Many here, though loyal to King James, have no enthusiasm for invading England to win a crown for an English Prince. Others are always looking to advance their personal wealth and power and see no advantage to themselves in fighting for the Prince's cause. Bothwell has been stirring discontent among these. The King can deal with that by stamping his authority on them, but this is a camp full of armed men and anything might happen." Watre raised a quizzical eyebrow and looked him in the face.

"Murder, you think?"

"Aye, murder. It would solve a lot of problems for the Tudor."

"Vigilance then."

"Yes. I have ordered a close guard around the pavilion of the duke of York. His companions there with him are a minimum of trusted men. In cases such as this, high numbers are dangerous."

"Julius Caesar was murdered by a few of his close compatriots, was he not?"

"True, but they were patricians who stood to gain by his death. Those with our Prince may only gain when he wins his crown."

"A lordship and a sufficiently large bribe might change someone's mind?"

"If we continue thinking like this we shall confound ourselves," said Watre impatiently. "These are high stakes and there is always risk. Let us take turns about the camp through the night. That will keep the guard awake at least."

Jolly John had already alerted Laurence to the same problem, though the main concern there was for lady Katherine and the child she carries. Watre had disturbed Laurence's own concerns regarding the possibility of an armed assault on them. It was all very well protecting the duke of York here in camp, but what about Katherine and Anna? Jolly John was vigilant back at Edinburgh to be sure, but he was not a soldier. What if they were attacked with the King away invading England? The two men parted, Watre agreeing to take the first patrol while Laurence would take the second in the hours before dawn.

Fitful fires flickered and the smoke of smouldering embers drifted among the pavilions of the nobles. Stretching out in the country around, the red glow of similar fires punctuated the camp of the army. Outside the pavilions of the King and the duke of York torches were kept ablaze throughout the hours of darkness. It was by constant attention upon these that ensured the guard was wakeful. As Laurence appeared out of the night the guard jumped to attention and pointed their halberds towards him in silent challenge. They could not call out for fear of disturbing the repose of the nobles within the pavilions. As he came into the circle of light they recognised him and came to attention. He gave them a brief nod and walked off again, wandering the camp in the vicinity of the Prince. There were the usual sounds of men coughing or snoring. Occasionally there would be a bad-tempered exchange of curses as someone disturbed another's sleep. The laughter and ribaldry in those tents where the camp women were situated had died down in the darkest hours and all he could hear was the slapping of flags and banners and the rustling of leaves caused by the light breeze in the trees and bushes by the camp. Clouds obscured the sky but there were ragged holes in them here and there which let the moon light the countryside for a few moments, like a mother peeking into a nursery before quietly closing the door on her sleeping infants.

The night was when goblins and demons, sprites and fairies were naturally abroad and he hated standing watch at these times. There were strange goings on in pasture, wood and forest at night and Christian folk took care to get inside somewhere and lock their doors until dawn, when the forces of darkness would retire to those hollows and caves and subterranean caverns which they inhabited during the day. His ears were tuned to every sound and twitched continuously. He stood quietly, fingering the reliquary around his neck for Holy protection, not wanting to draw to himself any unwanted attention. Just then he thought he heard the sound of movement. It was something solid, not a spirit, an animal of some kind. There were badgers around here, which were nocturnal creatures and earlier one had frightened him almost out of his skin by snuffling in some nearby bushes before a casual glimmer of moonlight revealed what it was. He froze to the spot, hardly daring to draw breath.

He saw a shadow in the low scrub that grew here and there. It flitted silently across to another bush to be followed by more shadows. There were about eight, he thought and prowling thus towards the place where the Prince was sleeping it was obvious what they were about. To shout a warning prematurely would merely cause them to turn on him before fleeing into the night. Better to wait and see if there were any more in reserve. When they were closer to the Prince's pavilion, he would shout to the guard and rush upon them in the rear hoping that in the confusion they would not think him to be alone. When it became apparent there were no more of them, he bent double and stalked after them, his hand on his sword ready to draw it, hardly daring to do so just yet in case the sound of steel being withdrawn from its scabbard would give him away. Thankfully he had put on his brigandine. He had thought to leave it off due to its weight but he heard Anna's voice in his head telling him to keep out of trouble so he obediently put it on before his patrol.

Hers too was the voice that told him he was in danger, a feeling of dread that told him to make a final check to see if there were more attackers coming behind. He looked back just in time to dodge the charge of a shadowy figure. The man had the spike of a rondel in his raised hand, clearly intent on using the heavy pommel to break Laurence's skull. The sudden movement of the armourer caught him off guard as he swung the weapon, stumbling while Laurence tripped him, sending him crashing to the ground. As the man tried to scrabble to his feet, Laurence had his murderer in hand

and slashed at the man's neck. Slicing through the blood vessel there, he felt a warm splash of blood on his hand while the man cried out, clutching his neck in vain.

Ahead, he saw the others turn to look back. "To arms! to arms!" cried Laurence. "We are attacked!" Two of the men crouched and spread out, clearly intent on bringing him down while the others rushed the Prince's pavilion. He drew his sword and waited for them to come to him, his sword in his right hand and the already blooded murderer in his left. Already he could hear shouts from the camp and the clash of arms. There were but two guards at the entrance to the Prince's pavilion and if they were overwhelmed the six remaining killers could be in there, do the job and be gone before the rest of the guard was raised. Was it curiosity in heaven that the moon found passage between the clouds to illuminate the scene? Suddenly he could see them clearly, hardened soldiers by the look of them dressed in black leather for silence. Each had falchions, heavy swords with a single cutting edge, useful for hacking down an enemy and, along with the short blades in their left hands, a deadly combination ideal for murder. A falchion was a butcher's weapon intended to cleave through flesh and bone, requiring not much finesse in its application other than a strong arm and a brutal mind. A man might recover from a stab wound, but a body and head carved by a falchion guaranteed death.

His own weapons were of little use, a light arming sword and dagger. He would find it hard to fend off a blow by the heavier blade and there were two of them manoeuvring to attack from both sides at once. His only chance was to keep away from their blades until someone came to help him. Nearby were the remnants of one of the cook's fires from the evening before. Embers smouldered among ashes where an iron tripod over had a great cauldron hanging from it. One of the men was between him and the fire. He lunged at the man who, as expected easily swept his blade aside, though the weight of his swing let Laurence leap and grapple him close. This prevented him using the falchion but not his smaller blade. He instinctively jabbed at Laurence's body while raising his arm intent on beating down on the armourer's unprotected head with the pommel of the sword. He felt the smaller blade slide off the iron plates of his brigandine then jabbed with his own blade before leaping away and getting at the cauldron.

The man grasped at his side where Laurence had managed to nick him. Being clad in leather with no metal armour to betray his casual approach to the camp, at least these men had some vulnerability. His fellow had run forward when Laurence grappled his partner intending on slitting his throat from behind but now the two were bunched together. Jumping into the ashes of the fire, Laurence grasped the tripod, overturned it and hurled it at them, the great iron pot bouncing towards them with a hollow ring. The two jumped out of the way and rushed him. He kicked the still glowing embers of the fire into their faces, keeping them at bay until the fire had all been disposed of. He stood now in a circle of stones. Shouts from the camp stopped them in their tracks. They had no idea how their fellows had done and the increasing bellowing told them they had best be away. Laurence, seeing them hesitate, leapt out of the ring of stones, thrusting at one, his sword point finding a target and driving home into his chest. The fellow clutched at the wound as Laurence pulled his blade free only to have it knocked from his grasp by the other felon.

This one was the fellow he had already wounded, and he was mad as hell seeing their clear advantage diminished and his companion wounded to death. He advanced on Laurence swinging the falchion from side to side, his face twisted into an insane snarl. The armourer realised he could not back away as fast as the man could advance upon him and so must be hacked to pieces. The only defence was to turn and run towards the camp, hoping someone would come to his assistance. As he turned he managed but a few steps before a blow struck his back. He felt the blade bite into his flesh and stumbled over a rut in the ground twisting as he fell onto his back, faintly in some vain hope that he might somehow fend off his attacker with just his dagger. The fellow stood over him grinning and hefting the falchion, wasting time in contemplation of his victory. It was a fatal mistake. Suddenly he seemed to sprout bristles, which were in fact crossbow bolts, three of them. He arched his back and dropped his weapons before collapsing to the ground, writhing there before expiring.

Laurence tried to clamber to his feet but found the best he could do was crawl on all fours. Someone came and grabbing him under his arms, lifted him to his feet. He stood there, swaying, knowing he was injured but not the extent of it. Two soldiers in murrey and blue supported him and half dragged him to the physician's tent. On the way he passed the laid out bodies of the attackers. The features of John Watre swam into view.

"The duke of York?" he managed to pant.

"Safe, thanks to you, master de la Halle. We had armed men sleeping within the Prince's pavilion but had it not been for your timely shout, Richard would have been murdered before they could get to their feet."

Groaning with the pain in his back they took him off to the physician. He remembered that John Damian was not with the army, being laid up with a broken thigh. Hopefully whoever would treat him might rely on something more than astrological prediction.

* * *

It was King James who tended his wound. James prided himself in his healing art and Laurence was now high in his favour. The falchion blow had been deflected by the iron of his brigandine but managed to find a way between the individual plates to slice into his flesh.

"It is a nasty cut, Laurie," said the king cheerfully, "but you will mend. I have packed the wound and bound it so you can sit a horse. If it were not for your protection it would have been into your rib cage."

They set off just after dawn, looking for plunder, there being no English army to contend with. The loss of blood was not so severe that he was unable to rise, though the pain in his back meant he needed the office of a mounting block to get on his horse. Furthermore, there would be no more wearing of mail before he healed and he felt vulnerable in doublet and hose under a mantle, riding in the company of steel-clad men-at-arms. He could have chosen a place in a wagon with the baggage, but he spurned that idea, succumbing to a feeling of pride having fought off the Prince's killers and preferring to keep close to him as if he were in any condition to repeat the performance.

They came upon a small, fortified house with a few poor dwellings around it. Again the marauding Scots attacked with fire and sword, having no regard for the lives of the people there. The duke of York was visibly distressed, commanding his own men to stop the carnage. Anthony de la Forsse looked helplessly about him wondering how he could possibly comply with the Prince's order, seeing as these were James' soldiers. The king was out with his forward scouts and came back just as the house was ablaze and the inhabitants crying for mercy as they ran out and being cut down. Richard pulled up his horse beside James.

"Your grace, stop them," he shouted in what was becoming a familiar cry. "Stop this slaughter. These are innocents!" James set his face and scowled at his friend.

"Innocent are they," he growled in reply. "These . . ." He waved his arm over the scene, "have spurned your crown. None in these regions have come to you; had they done so we would have been further on in our quest and with greater chance of success. Then they would be safe in their homes under the protection of their true king. They are little better than rebels." James, his face registering something akin to contempt, hauled at the reins of his horse to pull away and galloped off with his men. Richard sat rigid in his saddle, aghast at what he was seeing, his face blanched and horrified. Laurence thought it would be better if the Prince put his visor down rather than betray to his men the un-kingly emotions and paroxysms of grief that were chasing across his features.

"I would rather spurn a crown than win it at such a cost," he screamed vainly at the distant and unhearing James. He too pulled the head of his horse around, but rather than go after James, to the confusion and distress of his followers, he galloped off back the way the army had come – back towards Scotland. His entourage had no choice but to follow him and it was a desultory convoy that made its way through a desolate land, heading towards the ford at the River Tweed. Laurence looked back as they left and noticed a lone knight sitting upright in his saddle, watching them as they rode away. He recognised the livery of the earl of Huntly, Katherine's father who was witnessing the dashing of his family's hopes. Laurence could hardly imagine what he was feeling now.

They were back at Coldstream just four days after they so bravely left the town. During the ride Laurence had chance to gather his own thoughts. At first he had been shocked and despondent, along with the rest in the Prince's company. It was not long, however, before he began to feel a certain relief. The duke of York was eager to get back to his very pregnant duchess and where she was, so too was Anna. Laurence wondered if the duke's love-sick yearning for his wife might have had more influence with him than the killing of his subjects? As for his own concerns, if the kind of assault that he had foiled in the army camp was replicated upon Katherine, then he feared for the safety of her and her women. From what he had witnessed these last few days, he understood only too well that the tender condition of a pregnant woman was no bar to her murder. He shared these thoughts with John Watre after they had forded the Tweed.

"I have mentioned the earl of Bothwell as a spy for Henry Tudor," said Watre matter-of-factly. "There is little chance of the earl plotting against the life of the lady Katherine, but that is not to say there are no others less delicate of conscience. Combine that with greed, or simply a penurious purse and you have the potential for bribery and murder. We now know the extent to which the Tudor is working against the duke of York. His lady is a logical victim too, particularly as she carries his grace's child."

"I wonder why King James has not arrested the earl of Bothwell for conspiring with Tudor?"

"Ah, you see, the King makes use of him, and Bothwell is not working against James, but our own Prince. If he were to arrest Bothwell then others with less integrity towards the Scottish crown would fill the void and have a free hand. It is a delicate balancing act."

Laurence understood that perfectly. "King Richard the Third did much the same when he was combating Tudor wiles," he replied. "He kept lord Thomas Stanley close at court even though the man was dubious in his loyalty. All would have been well had he won the battle of Bosworth, but afterwards the rumours he let to fly so freely were thus unresolved and have been used to blacken his name since. Many believe that he murdered his nephews, though we have one of them here with us, alive and well. Of course, Henry Tudor knows this as do the monarchs of Europe, but the common people of England don't."

"A tale of bloody murder will always triumph over a mundane but truthful explanation," said Watre shaking his head sagely.

Laurence bit on his tongue. Watre, being close to the Prince, was not one with whom to extend this conversation to its logical conclusion. While the Tudor government was afloat on a raft of corruption and lies, the only practical way to sink it was in battle, discourse being futile. For that a challenger must have a martial disposition, which, it seemed, was not a characteristic of the duke of York. Of course, the Prince had not yet been in a battle and he might, for all anyone knew, acquit himself well; but judging by what Laurence had seen in their recent wanderings, and particularly the previous few days, that was unlikely.

At Coldstream they had word that the lady Katherine was at the royal castle of Edinburgh for the birth of her child. A few days later they rode, one would think in triumph, into the courtyard there. The duke of York flung himself from his saddle and ran up the steps and into the royal apartments where his duchess was in labour. He was stopped at the chamber door by a bevy of ladies all intent on keeping him out while the mysterious performance of birth was under way. Laurence decided to take himself off to the great hall, seeing that Anna was fully occupied in the birthing chamber, though he did manage to send word to her that he was here in the castle.

The great hall was packed with the usual courtiers, though the best fighting knights were away with the king who was still plundering the borderlands of England. Laurence sought out one of the scribes and asked for paper, pen and ink so he could write to John Fisher. He was fretting for his home at Vannes and though Anna was not so attached to Brittany, yet he knew she was eager to be away. His back was paining him and he wondered if the wound might fester. A friendly clerk showed him to a desk by a window and he spent an hour or so carefully scribing a letter enquiring of the business.

He was just sanding the paper when Jolly John found him. The jester, having by advantage of his trade found a friend who could supply him with a fine wine, led him off to his own small chamber. It was close to the kitchen and may have been a store cupboard, but it was comfortable enough for one person and better than a pallet in the great hall. Its chief advantage was privacy, though John kept the door open in case a casual listener felt the desire to put an ear to it. They sat on two stools, sipping at wine John had supplied from his secret source.

"The king will return to Scotland soon, never fear," said the jester tapping his nose.

"I suppose he can do little else now he has no duke of York on hand to rally the English to his banner."

"Another fiasco," sighed John. "Yet the king will not abandon a fellow prince in distress. The whole episode goes to show how to hold a kingdom rather than win one."

"Your meaning?" asked Laurence.

"Henry Tudor holds back, making no attempt to aid his own people along the border with Scotland, content to let King James beat himself out, wasting money and resources while building righteous opprobrium in the English against the duke of York. Contrast that with the attitude of his grace Richard. Here we have one contender compassionately abandoning a war because of the depredations on his own people, while the other uses the same to strengthen his own hold. You have to admit – Henry Tudor knows how to be a king, even though he has no royal blood."

"So even if King James and Richard of York were to rally the people and win the Crown of England, Richard would soon be relieved of it."

"That is probably so. Running from war is not in itself serious in a monarch when it is sensible to do so. Henry Tudor ran away before the battle of Bosworth and had to be brought back. His generals, mainly the earl of Oxford, his equivalent of King James won that for him. However, he first ran for fear of losing his own blood. He has never balked at the sight of others losing theirs in his cause, as the present situation attests."

Laurence was forced to agree; yet there was another element to be considered. "Let us hope that the child, when it comes, is a male. Having a son and heir might toughen his resolve."

"Or that of the duchess Katherine," chuckled the jester. "If she were ever to become queen then we might have another Margaret of Anjou on our hands or a Margaret Beaufort?"

"Heaven forbid," responded Laurence with horror, crossing himself rapidly several times. "Surely the God of Battles would not be that perverse?"

* * *

"This wound is healing well," muttered Anna as she probed gently at Laurence's back. He winced and gritted his teeth while she cleaned it. "King James did a good job on you, as well he might – getting you into a fight yet again."

"The King had nothing to do with it," he responded. "I was simply taking my turn to watch the Prince's pavilion. How was I to know he would be attacked?"

"Well then, why mount a guard at all unless you expected something of that sort? Once again, in a camp of thousands, you are the one to get himself in the fore at the only place that is attacked." He winced again and decided he better keep his mouth shut until she had finished torturing him. Her response had been accompanied by a more vigorous rubbing as testimony to her temper. "I see you have presented your right side to the blow," she went on. "Just as the scar on your face. Perhaps you are leaving the left side of your body plain, as blank spaces in a book of hours to leave room for scribing souvenirs of your next campaign?"

"I hope to return to our home soon," he replied between clenched teeth. "I cannot think there will be another foray into England from Scotland. We would be away ere now had it not been for your attendance upon the duchess Katherine."

He felt the tension in her silence at this remark. She gently patted the wound and applied some ointment of her own devising then, binding a dressing in place, handed him a clean linen shirt. They were in their own chamber near to the castle forges in the lower bailey of the castle. It was a cold, bleak place here on the castle rock above the city and the season was, once more, turning towards winter.

"The duchess has taken to me, and keeps me close to her and the child," said Anna laconically. "And I am fond of her, yet I would be away if I could. I am commanded by King James to keep by her. Your skirmish with the Tudor's murderers has unsettled him."

"There is small chance now of a violent attack on her or the child. The duke of York is ever in attendance upon them and he has enough followers around him to protect them."

"The child too, the baby Richard has his own servants, all paid for by King James," she grunted disapprovingly. "There is one in particular, dame Ramsey who has charge of the nursery. We cannot abide each other. It stems from when the duchess, having the child sickness upon her was given relief by one of my remedies. She mostly spurned the concoctions of dame Ramsey after that."

"Dame Ramsey, yes, she has a face that would fright a gargoyle. I wonder that the child can sleep peacefully having her leering over him."

"He doesn't," Anna replied, "except when I take him up, or when he is clamped to a teat of his wet nurse, and that is another matter of contention between us."

Laurence thought on her words, particularly her ability at quietening the infant. "You have not conceived another child since Philip was born," he said tenderly. "And it is not for want of trying. We know there is no problem between us. I wonder you had no children with Barrat Thorne and Cornelius was not that old he could not provide you with one either?"

She sat down on a stool and stared morosely at the earth of the floor. "I have no idea why it is so," she sighed. "I did have some trouble delivering Philip, but many have fared much worse and gone on to carry more babes. I must confess tending to Katherine's babe has depressed my spirits and awoken a longing I thought had gone."

"It is God's will and we do have Philip. How many women have a numerous brood only to lose them to plague or some other disease? Again he shut off the visions of war so recently witnessed and the sight of slaughtered infants. At least you are spared the grief of losing a child. We have at least one blessing in our son." His thoughts turned to his lost children, two daughters lying with their mother at Gloucester. His constant worry was Robert, his only surviving son with Joan. Reports were that the earl of Surrey was bringing a large force to the borders ready to invade Scotland come the spring and Robert would almost certainly be there with him. Whatever happened, he was determined to be away before then. He shook himself free of such dark musings. "Let us not think on it, we have other work to occupy us."

He pulled on his shirt and looked around for his doublet. "Now the king is returned I hear the Tudor is amassing a great force to invade Scotland. King James scoffs but must be worried, in fact, I know he is because the work at the forges here at Edinburgh has increased and the armoury is being checked to ensure the weapons there are in fighting condition."

"While the duke of York holds his own court as if oblivious to the trouble he has caused." Anna flapped her arms in frustration. "Katherine tells me he talks of going into England again, but from Ireland this time. I could not go through all that again."

"Nor I," agreed her husband. "If that is his plan then he will have to go without us. There are other armourers who can serve him. I know not how he expects to recruit an army large enough to take on the Tudor in his own territory."

"Katherine talks of exile in Spain. Sir Anthony de la Forsse is Spanish and he has probably put the idea into her head. Richard has written to Sir Anthony's father, Bernard de la Forsse exploring that scheme though I get the impression Richard is all for winning his crown, not spending the rest of his life in exile. Sir Anthony has left with a letter for Spain and I wonder if he will bother to return?"

"Sir Bernard was useful at the courts of kings Edward the Fourth and Richard the Third, as I remember," said Laurence, stroking his beard. "He had Yorkist sympathies then and acted as a kind of trading partner between England and Spain with a little spying on the side. He has filled a similar role for Henry Tudor too. Recently, he has kept himself prudently at home in Fuentarabia, no doubt due to the involvement of his son Anthony in the affairs of the duke of York. As for supporting our Prince now, well, that is another matter. Reports of duke Richard's recent squeamish departure from King James in England have spread and he has done himself no good by it."

"Roderigo de LaLaing has been given a generous gift of money by King James, I hear," said Anna. "He said his farewells to Richard the other day before leaving for Flanders and the duchess Margaret. He didn't say, but I think he will cut his losses and not return here."

"And still King James has not abandoned the duke of York," marvelled Laurence.

"In that respect he is like the late King Richard; he will not abandon his loyalty lightly." They both nodded quietly in agreement.

Laurence took himself off to the armoury forges where he engaged in some particularly fine embossing work for the helm of one of King James' retainers. Engrossed in his work, he hardly noticed the approach of a soldier in the livery of King James.

"Am I addressing master de la Halle?" he asked quietly.

"I am he," responded Laurence.

"Henry Patton – gunner in the service of King James." The fellow made a short bow by way of greeting. "I have come to ask if you would kindly spare a few moments to speak to my father. He has something he wishes to say to you."

"Your father – do I know him?"

"He tells me you will know him. Other than that he will not disclose what he wishes to talk to you of."

"Then why didn't he come to me himself?"

"He would, but there is some difficulty there, he is blind."

Laurence frowned at this, then remembered the blind gunner at Rastalrig. Was this the same? The last he had seen of him he lay prostrate on the floor of St. Triduana's Aisle. Letting his curiosity get the better of him, he put his work aside and went off with the gunner.

"Were you with the army on its recent raid into England?" he asked.

"I was and had my father with me. He told me it was you who helped him out at the shrine of St Triduana. I would like to thank you for that." They walked through the castle down to the outer bailey where the round stone structure of the St. Barbe was situated well away from the main walls to limit damage in the event of an explosion there.

"We have a common benefactress in Saint Barbera, do we not?" said Laurence conversationally. "She is patron of artillery men and armourers."

"Yes, my father prayed to her too, though a priest told him of St Triduana and it is as if he has found a new wife. Saint Barbara is divorced since his sight was lost. He prays now to Triduana constantly."

They reached the powder store and pushed the wooden door open on its leather hinges. The doorway was the only means of providing interior light, no flame permitted there, not that it mattered to the blind gunner who was its keeper. Barrels of the black powder were stacked around the walls of the round building and there were sacks of the raw material - brimstone, charcoal and saltpetre. A stout oak table occupied the middle of the chamber on top of which were copper measuring scoops and a stone pestle and mortar. The blind man was seated on a barrel, his head inclined as he listened for the familiar footsteps of his son and those of the other with him. He was dressed in the scrappy rags he wore the last time Laurence had seen him, with the dirty bandage still obscuring his eyes. He had a small pile of powder in front of him, which he had been tasting. This was one way of telling its quality.

Laurence stood before the blind gunner. "Laurence de la Halle, at your service, master Patton," he said politely. "You wish to speak with me?" Henry Patton went and stood beside his father, he too curious as to what the old man wanted to say.

"Henry, check the door. Be there any by?" Henry went to the door and looked about outside.

"None near, father." He went back to his place by the old man.

"Your lady, she tends the lady Katherine I think?"

"She does, with several others," replied Laurence, wondering what this could be about; nothing to do with powder and shot that was certain.

"And dame Segwen Ramsay, what of her?" *The gargoyle, thought Laurence.*

"She has charge of the nursery chamber."

"But has nothing to do with purchasing vittles for the feeding of the bairn?"

"I hardly think so. That is the responsibility of the castle cook. Besides the child is still being suckled by a wet nurse."

Old man Patton tugged at the wisp of grey beard that decorated his chin. "Can you get word to your woman?"

"Of course, she is not a prisoner here."

"She is a cunning woman, I hear tell."

Laurence disliked the term. It reminded him of Mother Malkin and though he had eventually come around to accepting *her* as a Christian woman, in a sort of way, he balked at applying the term to Anna, yet he was forced to agree that is what she had become. Strangely the revelation gave him a peculiar frisson - a small rebellion against the doctrine of Holy Church. Resisting the temptation to cross himself he returned his attention to Old Patton.

"She has healing skill, but not I fear that which can restore sight to the blind."

Old Patton cackled at this, waving his hands about dismissively. "That is not my meaning, good master," he chuckled. Suddenly he became serious again and beckoned Laurence closer. His son leaned over to hear him speak. "Tell her dame Ramsey has obtained a quantity of ergot."

"Ergot! The swelling below a horse's fetlock?" said Laurence.

"No, not that, another ergot. Never mind, she will know. Tell her dame Ramsey has some. She will know what to do." The old man chuckled at their ignorance. Henry Patton and Laurence looked at each other, both puzzled as to what this mystery could be.

"I was at the grain barn yester e' en. Ask your woman why dame Ramsey would pay for a sack of rye that should be thrown out. Just tell her - ergot!"

"Rest assured, master Patton, I shall, if only to define your meaning."

"It may come to nothing and I would not have it said I am the one to bring trouble upon the king. Just tell her; tell dame Anna - ergot."

"The old man hears things as he wanders around the castle that he shouldn't," said Henry Patton as they left the St Barbe. "He gets away with it, being blind. One of these days he will be found out and whipped, or worse. He is useful at the St Barbe, measuring and tasting powder for quality while ensuring it is properly preserved. He was a fine gunner once and there are few with his experience, but without sight what is the use of a gunner? He does find out that which he would be better off not knowing. Mention what he has told you to your lady. I think you might find he has chosen her for a reason. The old fool will lose his head one of these days so be careful nobody hears you in case it is something she would be better off not knowing."

* * *

"Ergot?" breathed Anna, her brow creased in a puzzled frown. "Of course I know what ergot is. I have some from the apothecary I use in the town. It was one of Cornelius' staple medicines." They were in the great hall where the Prince and his duchess were engaged in casual banter with their followers.

"Then what was old Patton twittering on about if it is merely a medicine?" Laurence asked her.

"That depends on how it is used. Duchess Katherine was given some after she gave birth to control bleeding. As it happened, dame Ramsey let me minister to the duchess for once. That is not much of a risk and I know the correct dose. There were certainly no ill effects other than a few hallucinations, which is expected. There is nothing suspicious in either I or dame Ramsey having ergot among our simples and cures." She looked around for somewhere away from prying eyes and ears and moved to a side of the room where the walls were bare of arras.

"That was three moons since and the duchess is thriving," said Laurence, shaking his head.

"Rye, you say? Old Patton said that dame Ramsey has bought some bad rye – now that is curious."

"Yes, I would expect the castle bakers to buy in any grain they want for bread," replied Laurence. "It is below dame Ramsey's dignity, surely?"

"You don't understand," responded Anna. She placed herself in a window seat. The stone sides prevented anyone coming close to listen in, especially with Laurence standing facing her. "Ergot is a malady of grain, usually rye, but also barley and wheat. It is a deadly poison especially if it be ground into flour. Bread made of it causes the sickness known as St. Anthony's Fire and often results in agonising death. That is why Old Patton said the grain was for throwing away."

"I know certain grain is known to poison folk," said Laurence, a sudden wave of apprehension sweeping over him. "But I had no idea what causes it."

"It could be dame Ramsey wanted it to make up a potion of her own. We must be careful not to read too much into this. Yet it is strange that she would want to do so when the extract is easily available from an apothecary." Anna clasped her hands in her lap and stared hard at the floor. "Duchess Katherine is fully recovered from the birth and has no further need of the remedy."

"What if she eats bread made from the flour?" Laurence let the thought lie there for a moment. "The duke of York could be poisoned at the same time."

"That is a possibility, but the cause would be immediately apparent. The sickness and its symptoms are well known. There are more, subtler poisons than bread infected with ergot, and with ergot the source of it could be easily traced."

"And the child is fed milk by his wet nurse, so he is safe."

Anna's head shot up at this. "But he is due to be weaned and the first solid food he will be given is bread soaked in warm milk!"

"Could it be he is in danger? The woman would be found out, surely?"

"The effect of ergot on an infant would be fatal for sure, yet a babe might die of any manner of sickness. It is common and there would be nothing to say there had been foul play. He would develop a fever then die in great distress, unable to tell us what is wrong."

"But if it were shown to be ergot poisoning, who was it that is known to have administered it to the mother?"

"Surely not," gasped Anna, her hand flying to her mouth and her face pale with fear.

They both realised it was only too possible that, with the help of Old Patton, they had uncovered a plot by dame Ramsey to dispose of a royal prince while placing the blame on a rival in the nursery, thus diverting suspicion from the real murderer. Laurence paced the floor in front of the window where Anna sat, her head in her hands.

"What do you know of this woman, dame Ramsey?" he demanded.

"Only that she is an unmarried sister of one of the bastard sons of the king's father, James the Third."

"Then her loyalties are probably ambiguous and, in any case, we are dealing with the son of the duke of York, so she need not think herself bound to the cause of an English prince."

"That is only too true," lamented Anna. "But then, who can actually be trusted here? You have already discovered the earl of Bothwell is looking into the Tudor's purse."

"Duchess Katherine is of true Scottish blood, which must count for something," he added more in hope than certainty. "Her father will not want his grandson poisoned."

"Where the chink of English gold can be heard," muttered Anna, "all men can be bought and Scotland has a long history of that."

Laurence considered the way in which the murderous scheme could be prosecuted. "If the poisoned rye grain is to be ground to flour and baked into bread, either dame Ramsey has a baker's oven in her chamber or she must get someone who has an oven to bake the bread for her."

"And that can only be the castle bakery!"

Anna found her husband in the castle forge later that day towards evening. She had gone to the kitchens and found the baker, a man with the appropriate name of Thomas Barley.

"Master Barley is instructed to bake a special bread for the weaning of the infant. Dame Ramsey has provided the flour. She has explained the flour is sanctified with a blessing from the prince's own chaplain so he needs must keep it separate from any other. It will be among the first bake of the morning and tomorrow begins the weaning of the child."

"Will he not notice it is infected with ergot?" asked Laurence.

"No, not now it is milled. It appears no different to clean flour." Anna suddenly became subdued and looked at him with darkness in her eyes. "There is something more."

"What is it?" said Laurence, becoming alarmed.

"Dame Ramsey has put me in charge of weaning the babe."

"Then our suspicions must be correct. She intends to revenge herself upon you while distancing herself from blame."

"Fortunately, we have knowledge of her plan and so the babe will be safe," she stated. "I only have to throw away the contaminated bread and exchange it for another."

"Leaving dame Ramsey with the belief the babe is blessed by God when he remains healthy." He grinned ruefully.

"It is impossible she has thought up such a dire scheme completely alone," considered Anna. "There will thus be another attempt and next time there may be no Patton to give warning."

"I think we both must go to the duchess Katherine and tell her what we have discovered. That will put her on her guard, and duke Richard too."

"Then ask for a private audience with them, husband. I fear that dame Ramsey might be alerted if I approach the duchess."

The duke of York and duchess Katherine were in their privy chambers listening to the delicate sound of a lutanist along with John Watre and another of the duke's long-time followers, Rowland Robinson. Katherine had the babe close by, in the arms of dame Ramsey. The child was awake and fractious, though lulled into a low gurgling by the song of the lutanist. Laurence was admitted immediately, the duke believing he had something new to show him regarding his armour. Anna was sitting quietly with the other ladies attendant upon Katherine, pretending she knew nothing of her husband's business with the royal couple. He knelt and made obeisance to them. Being raised and with a bow to the duchess, he addressed the duke.

"May I speak to you privately, your grace, and with you too my lady?" Katherine showed mild surprise, thinking that the armourer could have nothing to say that would be of interest to her. "It is a matter of great urgency to you both."

John Watre and Rowland Robinson exchanged glances and turned towards Laurence with a look of annoyance on their faces. If the matter were indeed urgent, then they would know of it too.

"You may speak freely here," intoned the duke. "We have only our closest friends with us."

"That is so, your grace," snapped John Watre while Robinson nodded in agreement. "Whatever master de la Halle has to say can be safely said to us also."

Laurence felt the tension in the ladies who had stopped their chatter and were listening intently. One of them waved impatiently to the lutanist who stopped playing. The sharp features of dame Ramsey had impacted upon his senses when he first entered the chamber and she, having heard his request, turned her habitual malign gaze upon him. Of course, she could have no idea that she was the reason for Laurence's attendance. The babe began to whimper now that the music had stopped.

"It is a personal matter, your grace," he tried. "If I may speak to you and her grace alone?" The duke frowned at him. The request was indeed peculiar.

"There are no secrets here, master armourer – speak out!" This was an unfortunate trait of the duke's character, speaking freely while surrounded by eyes and ears that might have dubious loyalties.

"I may not, your grace. What I have to say is for you and her grace to hear alone."

"Then away with you," the duke responded angrily. "I will not be argued with."

Laurence resisted the considerable temptation to look towards Anna, though he could feel her eyes upon him as he struggled to get his way.

"One moment," interrupted Katherine, placing a gentle hand on the duke's arm. He at once relaxed, his anger subsiding. "You say this concerns me also?"

"It does, your grace."

"I confess myself intrigued. It is not usual for my husband's armourer to wish to speak with me." She turned to the duke. "I think we must grant master de la Halle his request."

"Then let us hope what you have to say will be worthwhile," responded the duke. "Clear the chamber all," he commanded and waved a hand towards the door. It was a sullen crowd that shuffled reluctantly away, the ladies muttering and gathering around Anna, believing she might know her husband's purpose. She, of course, would plead ignorance. Dame Ramsey was the last away, the tiny babe bundled in her arms and howling lustily.

"I think I shall have you on your knees while you speak, master de la Halle," said the duke haughtily. It was his way of displaying annoyance. Katherine merely leaned towards him, her beautiful face a picture of curiosity.

Laurence sank to his knees and looked directly up at them. He told them of what Old Patton had discovered, the plot with the poisoned bread flour and dame Ramsey's part. Duke Richard's face had disgust and fury written large in his features, getting angrier by the moment. Katherine was horrified, her hand at her mouth and wide eyed with fear for her child.

"My babe Richard is with dame Ramsey at this minute," declared Katherine jumping to her feet, her voice trembling with horror.

"Never fear for the babe, your grace," said Laurence comfortingly. "My wife is close by and there is no danger to the child yet. The weaning has not begun, I believe?"

"No, not until the morn."

"The woman shall hang within the hour," snarled the duke.

"Wait a moment, my dear," said Katherine, her eyes alight with fear and her mouth turned down with disgust. "There is another way. Let us not leap to conclusions. You say the flour for the weaning bread is blessed by Holy Church?"

"That is what dame Ramsey has told the baker. It is her way of reserving the bread for the purpose of the weaning."

"Then we shall let God decide upon the issue." Katherine began pacing the floor. Duke Richard opened his mouth to speak but was waved impatiently into silence. With matters such as this, when her child was in danger, it was the woman who had all authority and it would be a brave husband to wrest it from her. In the interim, the duke raised Laurence to his feet. The duchess stopped her pacing and fixed him with a cold stare.

"You say dame Anna is to go to the bakery in the morn for the weaning bread?" she snapped.

"That is what she has been told to do by dame Ramsey, yes your grace. But she will not bring the poisoned bread; that will be thrown away."

"No! Tell her to wrap the weaning bread in a cloth and bring it secretly to me. As for the weaning, I shall attend upon that myself. Just make sure the bread is from the ordinary castle supply."

"It shall be done, your grace."

"And speak of this to no one, except dame Anna of course."

Duke Richard stood open mouthed, wondering what his wife was about. As Laurence begged leave to go, he waved him away and sat down gazing at her. He would speak to her alone.

* * *

"Now we are more than ever stuck in the company of the duke and duchess of York," reflected Laurence. "His grace can do without me as his armourer, but duchess Katherine will have none but you tend upon her babe."

On the day following Laurence's revelation of the poison plot, the duchess had come into the nursery declaring her intention of beginning the weaning of her babe. This was unusual, though Anna reported a crafty gleam in the eyes of dame Ramsey. Having the mother poison her own child would indeed bring down great wrath on the perpetrator and if it were shown to be Anna then she, and her husband too, would suffer for it. That would remove two faithful watchers from the person of the duke and his wife.

After the weaning, where Katherine had ordered bread soaked in milk from Anna and fed it to her babe, the duchess and her ladies sat at table to eat together. Strange as this was, the women thought it the special circumstances that had brought the duchess into the nursery. Normally the child would be taken to where she was. Katherine ordered a meal of bread and cheese, cheerfully serving her ladies herself and distributing bread to each of them in turn. Dame Ramsey declared her appetite was not as it should be, but the duchess insisted that while the cheese might be left, all the bread should be eaten before it went stale and was wasted. There was small beer to wash it down with.

Later that day, dame Ramsey was taken with a severe fever and her limbs became inflamed and painful. As she worsened it was said she cried "judgement!" constantly and asked for a priest. The priest came and heard her confession. Afterwards he hurried away, greatly troubled and looked neither right nor left but scurried into the chapel by the great hall and remained there in prayer for many hours. Dame Ramsey died in agony the next day. Those who saw her during her last hours described how her face was a picture of terror. St. Anthony's Fire was, indeed, a dreadful sickness.

16 - Aeturnum Vale

"They have transferred allegiance from King Henry the Seventh to King Richard the Fourth!" announced Laurence, bouncing into the chamber he and Anna shared at Craigmillar Castle. "That is how his name is announced in Cornwall."

The two of them had moved here with the duke of York and duchess Katherine, it being more comfortable and Katherine had not unreasonably developed mistrust of the inhabitants at Edinburgh Castle. Just three miles from Edinburgh, Craigmillar was a favourite residence of King James and convenient for communication with the other castle in the city. Anna, of course, had to stay close to Katherine and the royal babe but they had been given a decent chamber with a fireplace, which was just as well. They were both eager to get back to Brittany and would be gone by now had it not been for Anna's nursery duty by the command of King James. At least they were comfortable and Laurence had ensconced himself in the castle forge where he was doing work for Scottish and rebel English men-at-arms and being well paid for it especially now King James, too had begun to use him."

"What news, husband?"

"The Cornish rebels in England - they are defeated at Blackheath but not beaten in their own lands. They want rid of the Tudor, not just his taxes but they need a potential king to lead them. If there is anywhere in England where duke Richard will find a welcome it is Cornwall. He is all fired up with the prospect of getting his crown at last."

"For sure, the people of Cornwall have been in a state of rebellion for some years. Agents of the Tudor have to journey with an armed escort when they go there."

"It is good news for King James, too," continued Laurence. "There is no chance of the expected invasion by an English army into Scotland while rebellion is rife in the southern counties. It is not just Cornwall that would like to see the back of Tudor."

"What a relief," said Anna. "I know how worried you are about serving an army in opposition to another where your son is a squire to the earl of Surrey."

Both were familiar with the latest news from England. Henry Tudor had been gathering a large army along the borders where there had already been punitive raids into King James' territory. The

English invasion had now been delayed by an earlier rebellion by the men of Cornwall who had gathered others on a march towards London. Men came to their banners from around Bristol, Wells, Bath and the southern counties. Their numbers were thought to have been up to forty-thousand. The plan had been to first capture the city of Bristol, but the mayor fortified the place and so, rather than get bogged down there, the rebels marched on to London. The ill-equipped rebels were confronted at Blackheath and beaten by the army of Henry Tudor who had been fortunate in that his more powerful nobles responded to his defence, having no desire to depose him and start up again the dynastic wars.

"It is said the rebels would release Edward, the earl of Warwick from the Tower of London and proclaim him king," said Laurence, stroking his beard while he pondered on the situation. "I suppose that now they have been dispersed our own Prince becomes another option. Cornwall remains in a state of extreme agitation. Tudor reprisals are already causing more dissent. The man's a fool not to appease them, preferring hangings, torture and dispossession of property, spreading terror to force obedience to the crown."

"He is only too aware of the tenuous hold he has upon his throne. The world is not short of Plantagenet claimants," replied Anna. "Apart from the earl of Warwick there are the de la Poles."

"You think so, well one of them, Edmund de la Pole, another turncoat now the earl of Suffolk is one who helped Tudor defeat the rebels."

"To think it was his brother, John, earl of Lincoln, killed at the battle of Stoke during the Lambert Simnal fiasco who was King Richard's heir." Anna tossed her head in disgust. "High treason is the dominating attribute in these times. Is there no fidelity in anyone?"

Laurence gave one of his familiar dismissive shrugs. "There be two other de la Pole brothers, William and Richard, the latter is in exile and opposed to the Tudor. That is why Edmund has not prospered under the Tudor in spite of his declared support for his crown. Perchance he believes his help in dispersing the Cornish rebels will bring reward."

"More to the point," reflected Anna, " I wonder what this means for us?"

"I shall not go with the duke of York into England," responded her husband with conviction. "I am done with such folly and I doubt the duke will prosper there any better than he did in his first attempt. I remember Deal beach too well and unlike Scotland, there will be no King James to support him. The Cornish rebels have been defeated once already and I cannot see how having a blood prince in command of them will prevent a repeat, even less seeing as duke Richard is hardly a blooded general. The only two men who could command an army, Sir Anthony de la Forsse and Roderigo de LaLaing are no longer with him. You are tied to the duchess Katherine. I cannot see her going to war alongside her husband, the situation being dubious and her with a babe to consider."

"She is devoted to her husband none the less," replied Anna. "Katherine is a woman faithful to the man she loves and her babe by him, a splinter of their stock. Then there is the tradition of her blood, a noblewoman of Scotland. She has a broader vision than common folk."

"Margaret Beaufort," said Laurence pointedly. "A woman who shaped her son's future in spite of himself."

"And we have proof of how the duchess Katherine can move to protect her son."

"I wonder how these new developments will affect her in that respect?" pondered Laurence.

"She is very much in love with her husband and blind to his lack of martial fervour. As you say, the sensible thing for her would be to remain behind here in Scotland while he takes himself into Cornwall."

"I believe we shall discover something for ourselves. King James has called the duke and duchess of York to Edinburgh to discuss the matter and I am to go there too. I suppose you will remain here at Craigmillar with the babe."

Anna scowled fiercely at him. "Just be certain you don't involve yourself in any more madness. The time is come when we must depart from the Prince's enterprise. If he manages to win his crown he will not forget us, I am sure and we can go safely into England once more. If his cause fails, and we both believe it will, then we need to be safely out of the way in Brittany."

"Yes, wife, I think you say aright. I shall dress him in good steel where I can, he clings to his enchanted iron yet, and God be with him afterwards. He will have no further need of me then."

* * *

To their joint surprise, Katherine commanded Anna to attend upon her at Edinburgh. The babe Richard was left in the care of her ladies at Craigmillar Castle. As soon as they passed the guard at the gate, a retainer in the livery of King James came to them and conducted them to the royal chambers. James was in a side chamber to the great hall, along with duke Richard and duchess Katherine. Unusually the chamber was clear of courtiers, even servants. The king raised them as they made obeisance and bid everyone seat themselves on stools placed at a round table. There were five candles ablaze on the table, the only source of light. It was cool in the chamber, despite there being no windows to the outside and the early June weather having turned warm. The seating arrangement around the table had all the hallmarks of a conspiracy, where they could lean forward and talk quietly together will small chance of being overheard. Even in a castle with walls as thick as those of Edinburgh there was no guarantee someone would not find a way of listening in. Laurence noted that there was a single stool remaining empty between him and the king and wondered if there should be another there?

"It has been decided that his grace of York will take ship for Ireland and from there to England where he is assured of armed support," said King James, suppressing his usual regal tone. "Once with his subjects in Cornwall, we shall mount an invasion from Scotland to catch the Tudor between our two forces."

"An ambitious plan, your grace," said Laurence, a worried frown creasing his brows.

"We consider it has a better chance of success than invading solely from Scotland where we have the whole of England to fight through," replied the king. "We have seen how the northern English mistrust our aims, but in Cornwall duke Richard is assured a welcome. He has, after all, been invited there to lead them."

Laurence felt there was something wrong here. If King James was actually contemplating a full-scale invasion on two fronts it would require the presence of his fighting nobles at least to plan it. Yet there was a good deal of preparation already. He knew that from the increase in work already being carried out in the castle forges here at Edinburgh and at Stirling. No doubt there would be the ringing of hammers on iron in other castles of Scotland too. Several men-at-arms had approached him with enquiries for the making or enhancement of their harness. Why then, was there but the five of them here?

"I must tell you, my lord king," spoke Laurence tremulously, "that it had been our intention to return to our home in Brittany. My business there has been too long neglected."

"Yes, duchess Katherine informs me she has spoken to dame Anna who has expressed a desire to quit our land of Scotland."

At that moment there came a knocking on the stout oak door. King James raised his head: "Enter!" he shouted.

The door opened to reveal the dwarfish shape of Jolly John." The jester entered the chamber and carefully closed the door behind him before kneeling to the king. James raised him immediately.

"Come and join us, master John," ordered James. "Your seat is ready here beside us. The jester came over and clambered clumsily onto the vacant stool between the king and Laurence.

"Duchess Katherine is determined to accompany the duke of York in his endeavour," said King James when all had settled themselves again. Laurence and Anna looked at each other, their eyes displaying a combination of surprise and confusion. Laurence turned his attention to the duke.

"Surely, your grace will not permit this," he gasped. "Think on the danger to lady Katherine. First is a difficult sea voyage with constant threat of attack and there is no place of sanctuary on a ship; then, after landing, who knows what will happen when the duke's army meets with the Tudor."

"The babe Richard!" exclaimed Anna unable to keep silent in what was to her an intimidating royal assembly. "He will be left here at the mercy of Tudor agents. He has already had one narrow escape."

"Just so. Dame Anna," replied Katherine, smiling at the woman she had come to trust implicitly with the care of her child. "Which is why my babe must stay by me." She turned her head towards the duke of York for support.

"We are aware of the dangers," said the duke. "It is precisely the risk of an attack on the duchess Katherine that has decided us. If she remains in Scotland, she and my son are ever at risk and I not able to secure them. Indeed, a threat to their lives might be used against me. They are in less peril of their lives surrounded by loyal supporters of my cause than in a royal castle, begging your pardon, your grace." Richard gave a nod to James who gestured his open-handed understanding of the position. "A royal castle that is peopled by hundreds where just one determined murderer may find a way to infiltrate. The example of dame Ramsey is proof of that."

Laurence, who was seated opposite Anna noted his wife's deep concern. Sickness was churning his stomach as he began to ponder on the reason she was here. No doubt Katherine would want Anna to accompany her with the child. Somehow he had to prevent that, yet for the moment he could not think how without incurring the severe displeasure of King James and the duke of York. Jolly John seemed to understand what was going through his mind and put a firm hand on his arm, conveying reassurance and patience.

King James continued where he had left off. "I confess I too have severe concerns and am most reluctant to agree to the duchess Katherine accompanying the duke of York; however, there is a kingdom to be won and that cannot be achieved without risk. It is the duty of monarchs to put the ordering of a kingdom before personal advantage. In this case there is as much risk to lady Katherine and the child in staying here as going with her husband. Therefore, we shall agree to the proposal and make provision of ships to convey them."

Laurence and Anna exchanged worried glances, She too had now realised the likelihood that she might be part of the expedition. It was strange to hear King James declare Scotland unsafe for Katherine and her child. Was this a tacit admission that his royal protection of the pair would be insufficient to secure their safety? That was something royal pride would never normally admit. The thought passed through Laurence's mind that the king was eager to get his friend out of Scotland so he could concentrate on the diplomatic pressures that his conflict with England had provoked internationally. The devious and unpopular Spanish ambassador, Pedro de Ayala, had already tried to get James to rid himself of York with a promise of exile in Spain. There had been no safe conduct attached to this request and James rightly suspected the malign hand of Henry Tudor behind it. The plan had been to entice York to Ireland from where he would take passage to Spain. Ferdinand and Isabella of Spain had duplicitously offered the hand in marriage of Catherine of Aragon to James, even though she was not available, being promised to Arthur Tudor, should he fall in with the scheme. This deception on their part, being merely a ruse to get the duke of York out of Scotland, had annoyed King James who now had no desire to acquiesce to any Spanish request. It was plain that the person of the duke of York was confounding international politics and the monarchs of Europe wanted a resolution to the problem he was causing, irrespective of his royal blood. King James was no less discomfited than any of them, but his pride and loyalty to a fellow monarch stayed his hand.

"You Laurie, and dame Anna will go along with my cousin of York and the duchess Katherine as far as Ayr," instructed King James. "You will take your leave of them there. They will take ship for Ireland, though not to a place of de Ayala's choosing, and from there to Cornwall in England. A passage for yourselves back to Brittany afterwards will easily be arranged. Indeed, I have Breton masters in charge of two of the three vessels I am providing for my coz. Ships from Brittany call at Ayr regularly."

Laurence was puzzled and relieved at the same time. What was the point of accompanying the York's to Ayr only to watch them sail away?

"Before then, I have one last task for you, Laurie." Laurence wondered what the reaction would be if he addressed the king as Jamie, but prudently pushed the temptation aside. The King of Scots was an amiable monarch, but there were limits beyond which it was unsafe to go. "You will assist master John, here, who has come up with the plan." The king leaned forward conspiratorially and the others followed suit, eager to know the king's mind.

* * *

A full moon shining within a field of brilliant stars lit the road down by Holyrood Park, throwing black shadows in the wagon ruts where traffic between Edinburgh and Craigmillar plied its frequent course. In between the ruts the ground was churned by the heavy hoofs of ox and horse and by the smaller but more numerous prints of sheep. Two men, one tall and well built the other dwarfish and short of leg picked their way along the better parts of the way on the approach to Duddingston where the sheep slaughterhouses were located. As they reached the shambles the dwarf put his hand out in a silent command to halt their progress. The shambles were a confused huddle of dark hovels clustered along one side of the road while on the other was an alehouse. Behind the hovels could be heard occasional animal movement where the moonlight illuminated the wooly backs of the sheep held there ready for slaughter.

Laurence and Jolly John silently stood unmoving and waited. Presently there was the creaking of a gate from behind one of the hovels while a shadow detached itself from the blackness and approached. A foul churl, a gabergunzie in Scotland, came to them and passed his gaze from Laurence to rest on the jester. John waved his hand impatiently and the fellow led them towards the alehouse. He stank abominably and Laurence hoped they would not have to remain in his company too long. They approached down a path furnished with what looked to be white stones, but which felt peculiar under foot. The sign above the alehouse door was a sheep

352

skull complete with curled ram's horn. The gabergunzie led them around the back of the alehouse and knocked gently on a small door no more than four feet high. After a moment the door opened a little and someone within could be sensed examining them. John pushed the gabergunzie out of the way to let whoever was inside get a look at him. This must have satisfied the inhabitant because the door was opened and a shadowy figure could be seen lurching towards the interior of the place. John passed a few coins to the gabergunzie who melted away into the darkness. He led the armourer through the door without having to stoop, unlike Laurence who, in spite of ducking low still managed to bang his head on the lintel.

The inhabitant could be seen working a bellows to get a fire to life that had been smouldering in a grate. Throwing on a few sticks a blaze was soon away causing the people and objects in the room to throw shadows against the dingy walls. Laurence presumed this was the alehouse keeper, indeed the fellow was typical of his type. He had a thick mat of unruly red hair that extended down the sides of his face to join forces with a formidable beard. His face was scarlet and his eyes could just be seen reflected in the firelight under thick, bushy brows. He was brawny and Laurence guessed he would need plenty of muscle to keep some sort of order in the place when it was full.

"Mmadadh-ruadh?" asked Jolly John. He had informed Laurence that this was the man's soubriquet, being Gaelic for red fox.

"Aye," came the monosyllabic reply.

"You have the goods?"

The "fox" nodded and slouched off through a door covered by a curtain. Soon they heard the sound of an argument and female voices, one in anger the other clearly distressed.

"This is an ill favoured place," whispered Laurence.

"It serves the men of the shambles and their women well enough," John replied. "Yonder is the place where the sheep are butchered for the city supply. The only parts they cannot sell are the heads. You walked over a path made up of sheep skulls as you came. Nothing is wasted. They boil the heads and serve them up to the poor folk hereabouts, hence the name of the alehouse – the Sheep Heid."

The tumult behind the curtain died down except for a low sobbing and the "fox" re-appeared with a bundle of rags. John made to take hold but the man stepped back possessively. John took out a purse and tossed it up and down, letting the man's greedy eyes follow it as if mesmerised.

"Let me see the goods first," he demanded. The man stood still, watching suspiciously and holding the bundle firmly while John unwrapped it and peered inside the rags. Satisfied, John handed the purse over and took up the bundle. The "fox" tipped the contents out onto a low table, his eyes shining at the gleam of gold and silver coin reflected in the firelight.

"Let us get back to Edinburgh," said Jolly John. Laurence opened his mouth to speak but was silenced by John squeezing his arm.

The "fox" bowed them to the door deprecatingly, a direct contrast to his former demeanour. Once outside they hurried down the white path of skulls and turned into the road.

"Why did you tell him we were bound for Edinburgh?" questioned Laurence. "We are on the road to Craigmillar Castle."

"That fellow is not named Mmadadh-ruadh for nothing," came the reply. "It is likely there will be men on the road to Edinburgh waiting for us. He might not want this bundle back but if there is a chance we have other coin between us, he will try for it."

"And we could hardly have brought armed men to guard us in our mission."

"Precisely. Now, keep your eyes open and your sword arm ready. We cannot rest easy until we are safe inside Craigmillar."

* * *

The journey to Ayr had been difficult, the terrain between there and Edinburgh being wild and desolate in many places. King James insisted on accompanying his friend and his fair cousin Katherine, and because Laurence and Anna were travelling in such company, they were at least well provisioned. Laurence had obtained a horse and cart for the transportation of his tools along with his and Anna's clothes. For Anna, these were precious indeed, some were her own, others the gift of the lady Katherine and some made up from cloths purchased and given her by King James himself. Privately they had noted that nothing had come from the duke of York, not entirely surprising seeing as he was a pensioner of King James. Laurence knew that the duke had managed to run up debts in spite of the generous pension that James had allowed him during the time he had been in Scotland, even unto the present. It had been the king who had paid for the duke's harness, as well as work he had asked

Laurence to do on his own iron and that of his men-at-arms. He felt with satisfaction the heavy money belt he wore and the weight of the coin in his purse hanging from his belt. At least he and Anna would be returning to their home with something to show for their adventures. She was somewhere ahead with the duchess Katherine in charge of the child, a duty she was soon to relinquish.

There were nearly five hundred in the cavalcade that wound its way into the town. Richard of York had around one hundred and fifty followers with him, all paid for by King James while Katherine had but a few women to serve her and her baby's needs. If any in that company were worried what the future would bring, it was not evident in the air of festival that dominated the talk of the courtiers and chatter of the women. Of course, the bulk of these would return to Edinburgh with the king after he had said his farewells to the duke and his wife. Observing the Scots laughing and joking together, Laurence wondered if it was not the product of relief that their king would at last be rid of a great burden. Jolly John was there, capering among them adding to their mirth.

It was late in the afternoon when Laurence trundled his cart into Ayr. His first task was to find safe lodging for his tools and their chattels, which were firmly locked inside a pair of great chests. He found a grain warehouse and paid the proprietor to lock his belongings securely inside until he was ready to take ship. That might be a few days yet. First they would attend upon duke Richard and his duchess until they embarked on their voyage of destiny.

He found Anna at the inn, which the king had commandeered for duke Richard and Katherine. Jolly John was there too, never far from the duchess. Anna had a chamber strictly to herself with the babe, Katherine having declared she felt the child in danger until free of the shore and surrounded only by her own people. Even her women were barred from entering. The only other persons permitted to go near Anna were Laurence and Jolly John, the latter being a point of contention with Katherine's women. They were outraged that the dwarfish jester be allowed near the heir to the duke of York in preference to themselves.

Laurence felt the hostile stares of the servant women as he knocked on the door to Anna's chamber. Jolly John opened the door and, sticking his head around the door leered at those gathered outside. Seeing Laurence he stepped back to let him enter, then pushed the door firmly but quietly shut. Putting his finger to his lips, he feigned to tiptoe in comical dumb show to the crib where Anna was looking down with maternal care on her charge. She joined

Laurence in laughter at the antics of the jester who couldn't help but entertain them, the three sharing as they did a great secret. Laurence kissed his wife, having seen little of her during the journey from Craigmillar Castle where she set off with Katherine and the child.

The chamber was lit by candles of the finest beeswax, having no windows and the fire not needed, this being the early days of July in the year fourteen ninety-seven. The babe in the crib was sleeping contentedly having recently been fed, when an infant cry came to them from a far corner where there was a second crib. Anna hurried over and reaching down, took up a tiny babe, which immediately began gurgling happily upon seeing her face. She brought the babe over to the candlelight.

"Which one is this," said Laurence, tugging at the wrap that covered the child's head. "Ah, I see now."

"Yes, they are easy to tell apart," chuckled the jester as he too looked up at the babe. "One with red hair, the other fair."

"Just as duke Richard and duchess Katherine. We must be careful to remember which is which."

Anna sat down on a chair and cradled the babe in her arms. "I thing lady Katherine will have no problem with that."

"And no man can tell who has never before seen the babe; they are few and none in England."

"I weep for the poor mother," sighed Anna. "It is a hard thing to part with a child you have carried for a term."

"Do not concern yourself," put in Jolly John. "Her babe will have a better chance in life than had it remained with its true mother. I hazard it would be dead anyway within a month or two. Most of those born in that place die before they reach their first year."

"Which may still be the case if Henry Tudor has his way," snorted Laurence.

"Thankfully both boys are healthy," said Anna.

"Though but one of them baptised into Holy Church," intoned Laurence sanctimoniously. "It will be suspicious if the lady Katherine tries to baptise anew one that is already known to be baptised."

"We must hope that condition is remedied in time," mused Anna. "As for now, the child is cast adrift, a very Moses resting in the hand's of a foster mother, which we must hope will keep him safe."

"Or else caught and killed while unbaptised, cast forever into Limbo?"

"Which is where he will join the company of his fellows, or perhaps the souls of heathens," said John. "Let us not dwell on that which we cannot control and work towards what we can actually achieve in this world."

Anna raised her gaze from the babe and fixed it determinedly on the two men. "Everything might work out, and the matter of the babes properly resolved. We are presumptuous in believing the cause of Richard the Fourth of England will fail."

"You are right, dame Anna," agreed Jolly John, clapping his hands and skipping a little dance of joy. "Let us no more brood on disaster and death, but on the hope of life. That is what you have in your arms, is it not?" The three of them gathered around Anna to gaze on the babe. The child's eyes seemed to flick between them, settling at last on the grotesquely twisted features of Jolly John, upon which it smiled and began to chuckle happily. Anna looked up at her husband whose brow was creased in a frown, puzzled at the babe's preference for the ugly features of the jester. He still tended to judge people according to appearance, much as he had with Mother Malkin. She made a silent prayer of thanks when, seeing a kind of understanding soften his features, he showed her he was slowly coming to repent of such folly.

* * *

The gathering on the quay at Ayr the following day was a strange combination of festival and doleful leave-taking. The Scottish nobles there with King James were ecstatic at the departure of the duke of York while those in the duke's retinue were somewhat subdued. A *berfois* had been erected on the quay where King James sat in regal splendour surrounded by his nobles. Richard, duke of York and his duchess Katherine knelt before him, looking up into his face to receive his blessings on their enterprise. Behind them a ship was tied to the quay, its seamen standing on the deck rails and clinging to the rigging the better to observe the colour and splendour of the scene. The royal flag of England flew from its masthead under which was the banner of the white rose. Further out in the harbour another two vessels waited having already on board the remainder of the duke's followers; those not in immediate attendance upon him. All the ships had been provided and provisioned by King James.

Duke Richard was clad in his new harness. The cuirass needed no surcoat as the triple leopards of England were embroidered in

357

gold on the bright red ground. He was bare-headed, his fair hair blowing untidily by the breeze coming off the sea.

Katherine had a brown hennin over her red hair, which tumbled down and was tied here and there with yellow silken threads. A wispy veil was thrown back to reveal the loveliness of her face. She was clad in a gown of warm tawny wool over which was a black travelling cloak of the same material. Her kinsman, King James, had gifted these garments to her. John Damian stood beside the king, having come there in his capacity as Abbot of Tungland to confer the blessing of Holy Church on the couple. A company of monks stood to one side, intoning a solemn and harmonious *te deum laudamas* while Abbot Damian pronounced upon the young couple.

Kneeling in a group behind their prince was John Watre, Rowland Robinson and several more of those who would advise the duke when he reached England. Laurence and Anna were there too, though they would not embark with the rest. Katherine's father, the earl of Huntly had stayed at Edinburgh, sternly disapproving of her decision to go with her Prince. Looking around, they noticed there was a distinct lack of anyone with real experience of battle, and no nobles of note to impress those English whom they expected to flock to the banner of King Richard the Fourth. The two men with most martial credence, Sir Anthony de la Forsse and Roderigo de LaLaing had left Scotland never to return.

Presently the king indicated the farewell ceremony was at an end. Richard took Katherine by the hand and led her to the ship where planking had been provided for them to step easily aboard. Those friends and courtiers who were to remain in Scotland lined up to say their farewells. While this was taking place, Anna went off into the tavern to return shortly with a tiny bundle in her arms and accompanied by Jolly John. Laurence, Anna and the jester approached the duke and duchess, these being the last to say their farewells. Anna handed the bundle to the jester while she and Laurence knelt before the royal couple. Richard indicated they should rise.

"My good armourer, master Laurence de la Halle," said Richard in a regal tone, "as you see I am wearing the harness you have made for me and with the added protection given it by John Damian, will serve me well I have no doubt."

"It is my dearest wish that your grace never has need of its protection," replied Laurence, hoping the prince would not detect the double meaning in his words. "That is, your household knights should keep your enemies away from your person in battle."

"Which is my hope, too," interjected the duchess Katherine. Richard acknowledged her words with an elegant bow to her. "And now, dame Anna," continued the duchess, speaking in a loud clear voice for everyone to hear, "I cannot thank you enough for the service you have rendered us in keeping safe our precious babe." Anna dipped her a curtsey and blushed, unable to speak for fear of bursting into tears. Katherine had a slim gold chain around her neck with a single pendant pearl. She took this and handed it to Anna. "Please take this gift as a token of my most profound gratitude. When his grace the duke has removed the Tudor from his undeserved throne we shall invite you and your family to our English court as our most honoured guests. Until then, God keep safe you, your husband and those you care for."

"My thanks are to you your grace for allowing me to serve in your cause," whispered Anna, perceiving the deeper meaning behind Katherine's words. "We wish you Godspeed and the protection of the holy Virgin on the child."

The duchess turned her attention to Jolly John. The jester was standing clad not in motley but in plain brown hose and a black leather doublet. He stepped forward and handed the bundle containing the babe to Katherine who took it from him and looked down upon it. She tenderly drew back the cloth from the child's face and freed its arms, which it waved and reached out to her. She raised her head and gave a most profound sigh before fixing upon Anna an agitated expression, which those present might have interpreted as anguish rather than maternal joy. Just for a moment her eyes flicked towards the tavern by the quay where Anna had nursed the babe. If there were any there who wondered at this, Laurence, who was discreetly gazing around him could not detect it.

Laurence and Anna stepped back as the duke and duchess spoke a few final words to the jester, who then came and stood beside them, watching as the couple walked to the ship accompanied by King James. The three talked quietly together for a while then, with a great show of bonhomie, Richard and Katherine, with the babe in her arms, entered the ship leaving James on the quay. The tide being at the flood, this was the sign for the mariners to pull in the planking and untie the vessel from the dock. Soon the great sail dropped and slowly the vessel drew away. Out in the harbour the other two vessels dropped their sails and before long a white crest was showing at their bows.

They watched as the ships gathered way and the figures on deck grew smaller with distance. Soon the great mizzen sails were hoisted. That on the royal vessel was raised and filling with wind, obscured as if drawing a veil the last sight of Richard the Fourth of England and his queen who were on their way to claim a kingdom.

Epilogue - Vannes 1500

Chatter in *Le Rose Brave* was all of local matters, corn prices, the availability of fish and meat in the markets, the price of fine cloth, gold and silver, spices, the cost of cheeses and bread. The only stable commodity was the price of wine and so long as that remained comfortable, the denizens of the tavern would continue to come here to berate the cost of the rest. Few were interested in the doings of the English king or the state of that country whose monarch had spent much of his young life as a refugee in Brittany, a country that in these latter years had itself seen much change of sovereignty. Not so le Patron John Fisher, nor the armourer Laurence de la Halle and their respective spouses. John Fisher and Laurence had finished their work at the forge for the day and were relaxing with their wives along with Philip, fresh out of England with news. They were sitting in their reserved corner where they habitually huddled together whenever anything of a clandestine nature was being discussed.

For Laurence and Anna, the intrigues of the latter years had been relegated to the dream world of nostalgia now they were safe at home with no further prospects of adventure to halt their gradual decline into the twilight of their years. Yet the past had them still in its grip. Robert was building a prosperous life for himself in Tudor England and now had some land granted to him along with a small independent income, won by the strength of his arm in the service of the duke of Norfolk, Thomas Howard, newly restored to his father's defunct title by a monarch grateful for his martial services. They must call him Sir Robert de la Halle now he had been raised to the status of a knight by his master. He had his eye upon a young lady, the daughter of a mercer in the city of Norwich and whose hand would come to him along with a considerable dowry. Laurence had some regret that the wedding would be in England and he, being still on the long list of subversives that Henry Tudor would like to see stretched out on the rack, could not attend.

Yet here was Philip. His son with Anna had carved out for himself a fair living in England working as a physician. Philip's visits to Brittany were frequent, he having a love for the country and no less his mother who lived here happily with her husband Laurence the armourer. His education and his establishment as a physician had been paid for by Cornelius and also his father

Laurence. Doctor de la Halle's fashionable popularity in London meant he no longer needed to rely on his parent's support, rather he had the means to invest his money in whatever venture took his fancy. Philip had grown into a handsome man, well favoured by the female patients who flocked to his chambers, or commanded his presence in the expectation of a cure for whatever ailed them. The fact that their infirmity tended to concern a fluttering heart meant he was never short of patients, though most were, unfortunately, married. This last condition was the source of much distress to his mother who despaired he would ever settle down and produce grandchildren for her. Philip, on the other hand, was biding his time and sampling the delights of fashionable London rather than tying himself down.

He was here now, telling them of the fate of duke Richard of York, whom they could never think of as Perkin Warbeck, the counterfeit name originally given him to hide his true identity and afterwards being applied to obscure it.

"They ruined his face so the people could not compare his features to those of his father, King Edward," he informed them lugubriously. "They would have been hard put to do so anyway, judging by his physical condition. I think they had tortured him before displaying him in public."

"What news of the lady Katherine?" asked Anna tremulously.

"She resides at the Tudor court. The king has taken something of a fancy to her, though she has not encouraged him in any way. He has taken her into his wardship and may dispose of her hand in marriage now her husband is dead, but I hear he is not too ready to let her go. I think he fears she will find her way back to Scotland and thus be free to stir up trouble for him."

"And her child – what of him?"

"The child," mused Philip. "He was taken from her soon after she was captured. Rumour has it he is being brought up by a couple somewhere in Wales, but who knows?" Philip gave a shrug and turned down the corners of his mouth. "Strangely, the lady Katherine Gordon, she has reverted to her maiden name, seems not too upset at the loss of her child. Perhaps she is content he still lives, or believes he does?"

Anna and Laurence resisted the urge to exchange glances lest the others suspect there was some secret they were not sharing with them.

"I suppose she could hardly remain at the Tudor court with the name Katherine Plantagenet," said Anna.

"Nor call herself widow Warbeck either," intoned Laurence.

"I would like to see the face of the Tudor queen, Elizabeth, when Katherine is in sight of her husband," grinned Gurden mischievously while reaching for a pitcher and replenishing the wine in their cups.

"If you ask me," inserted John Fisher, "the lady is better off a widow rather than be shackled to Warbeck, or the duke of York as you all insist on naming him." John knew the true story but could not embrace the cause of the duke seeing as it had taken his friends away for two years. It had been a struggle for him and Gurden here in Brittany without the native support of Laurence.

"I must agree with you," replied Philip. "I mean, there he was with a great army at his back, men who were relying on him for leadership and what does he do? He takes himself off at dead of night leaving them to face a Tudor army or get away as best they might."

"Yes, with no generals to support his backbone as Tudor had, there was never much hope for his enterprise," declared Laurence. "It was a business conceived by a combination of false hope on his part and desperation in the people of Cornwall."

"Which Cornwall has suffered for ever since," said John. "He might have been of royal blood, but that alone does not make a king, not in these days."

"When he ran he must have known his wife would be left without any protection and would be taken by the Tudor," said Gurden in agreement with the opinion of her husband.

"Well that is not without precedent, you know," put in Laurence. "When I first joined with King Edward's army in Flanders, his queen was in sanctuary at Westminster Abbey, having been abandoned when he fled England. Before him, his father Richard also fled and left his wife Cecily along with two of her boys, George and Richard."

"Ah yes," replied John, "but in both cases they fully intended to return and fight. *Peterkin* simply ran having never fought a battle in his life and with no determined intention of doing so."

"At the end he capitulated and denied he was the true blood prince Richard of York, the son of King Edward," said Gurden, her tone tinged with disgust. "He even signed a confession stating he was Perkin Warbeck of Tournai."

"Yes, I think Tudor must have a scriptorium dedicated solely to writing forged confessions," put in Laurence. "I suppose it was Richard's propensity for running away that brought him to his death. The pity of it is, due to the machinations of the Tudor, he brought the earl of Warwick to his along with him."

Philip, who had been there when the two men were hanged, ventured his opinion. "It was obviously a contrivance of the Tudor to put them near each other in the Tower of London then arrange for them to escape together. That was all the excuse he needed to accuse them of high treason. They were too easily recaptured. Afterwards, conviction and a death sentence was a foregone conclusion."

"Then the story of the murder of two princes in the Tower of London, fabricated by Tudor, or his mother against King Richard, is become a kind of prophecy but with Henry Tudor as the true murderer," mused Laurence. "Tudor has indeed ordered the judicial murder of the duke of York and the earl of Warwick, both princes of better blood than he. In the case of Warwick, by blood he was the rightful King of England."

"I am tired of this talk," grumbled Anna. "The lives of monarchs and nobles are no longer of interest to me. They deserve their respective fates whatever the intrinsic justice of a particular cause might be; they expect the common people to pay with their lives for it and no thought of reward for the survivors."

"Well, that is not strictly true in our case," replied Laurence. "There has been a considerable amount of business for us since my return to Vannes. It is known I made harness for the duke of York, King James the Fourth of Scotland, King Richard the Third and others of the English nobility. Our Prince might have died as Perkin Warbeck but the monarchs and nobles of Europe know who he really was in spite of Tudor lies. They might be relieved politically he is gone, but my status as having been his armourer, and sharing in his travels has never been higher."

"And you brought back from your adventures a son to carry on your craft," stated Gurden, fixing him with a penetrating stare.

"Dickon? Yes, he is never away from the forge, except when his mother takes him for his lesson."

"To prevent him becoming cut or burned, both of which he has suffered recently," grumbled Anna.

She felt a tremor of apprehension whenever Gurden mentioned the boy. Gurden Fisher had never quite accepted the explanation that the lad had been conceived and born in Scotland, wondering why a pregnancy had not been announced during the relevant nine months of correspondence between Laurence and her husband John. She had tried to get Anna to discuss the matter, hinting whether she might have had a clandestine relationship with a man of lighter complexion than her black-haired husband. The child was fair, as Anna herself, but with no similarities of features with either of his supposed parents. Laurence, however, seemed content with the boy and Gurden failed to detect any kind of mistrust in him regarding the felicity of his wife. Having led a difficult life before being rescued from death by Laurence and her subsequent marriage with John Fisher, Gurden had developed a certain perspicacity for sensing the true relationships between men and women. She knew there was some mystery regarding the lad and if she were privy to it, would be dragged on a hurdle and burned at the stake before betraying her friends. Nevertheless, she understood certain secrets were best left as they were, for the sake and safety of loved ones.

At that moment a crowd of gamins scampered into the tavern. At their head was a small boy, not quite four years old dressed in a coarse woollen cloak and brandishing a wooden sword and shield. His hair was long and fair and already he was big for his age. He was not allowed to mingle with the patrons in the main room but knew where to find his parents in their reserved corner.

"Hello Dickon," said Philip familiarly. He was actually his brother but the age gap meant he was regarded almost as an uncle. "That is a fine sword you have."

"It is a practice sword," declared the boy striking at one of the wooden posts in the room.

"Stop that at once!" barked Anna. "This is no place to practice swordplay." She was not happy to see him playing so. Dickon had asked his father to make him a steel sword, which Laurence might have done except Anna dissuaded him. He got around her interdict by explaining to the boy that knights practised with wooden batons rather than real swords.

Anna could see Gurden regarding the boy with her usual fondness and wondered if she was pondering yet on the question of his paternity. The gamins who accompanied him were the beneficiaries of Gurden's largesse, as she would habitually find a few scraps for them all from her kitchen, which is probably why they were here now. They were the children of local tradesmen and like feral animals always on the search for food.

Laurence grinned at the boys, proud to see his son as the leader in their games.

"I see you have your soldiers with you, sirrah," he chuckled.

"Yes father, these are my men," piped up Dickon dramatically.

"And are you, then, their captain?"

The lad drew himself to his fullest height, slapped the sword against his shield, then, spreading his legs for balance, raised his sword arm and brandished it upwards.

"No father, not their captain - they have made me their King!"

END

Author's Notes

Henry Tudor – It is often said that Henry Tudor's was the first "modern" government. It had all the attributes found today in England's parliamentary system. He was the first to introduce stealth taxation and gave his tax gatherers almost unlimited licence to assess and collect money for a variety of reasons that had no benefit in return to the people. His was a morbid desire to come up with new and bizarre methods of taking to himself the earned wealth of the country, while promoting and enriching a few self-seeking nobles, providing they gave him absolute obedience. Duplicitous, renowned for manipulating the laws of England for his own benefit, a man who would break his word in an instant, his roots seem to have been set down in Europe. Many favoured by his court were contacts made while in exile: French or Breton, himself having little or no empathy with the English people living under the burden of his regime. After his death, his son soon bankrupted the treasury and then made the people pay for his profligacy. It would seem the modern denizens of the Westminster Village here in England had their nascence in his reign. Truly the Tudor's were the first modern politicians.

Battle of Bosworth – conventionally it was William Stanley who came to the rescue of Henry Tudor at Bosworth, simply because this was what he told Henry after the battle. While it was true both Stanley brothers were duplicitous with a calculating eye on the main chance, it has been too easy to accept this version of events, even though, militarily, it is implausible. For one thing, William commanded his men to charge into the fray after letting King Richard with just his household knights ride safely past his considerable force. Then, after the Tudor standard had fallen he orders his men to charge. He could not possibly have known at that point whether or not Henry Tudor had been killed. Then there are his men – they were there by command of their properly anointed king, Richard III, and to order them in a moment to commit treason would at the very least provoke confusion in their ranks. On the other hand an order to charge to the defence of King Richard would have been instantly obeyed – as Englishmen that is what they were there for. Opposing them were a few rebellious English, headed by a man they hardly knew, with the bulk of his invading army being Swiss and Breton mercenaries with Welsh rebels in support. I believe the Stanley's, particularly Lord Thomas Stanley, held back because of the impossibility of treasonably ordering their soldiers to attack fellow Englishmen for the sake of a usurper and a foreign invader. It seems the dubious reputation of William Stanley preceded his charge and Richard's household knights believing they were being attacked, turned to face what they thought was a real threat. In other words, William Stanley's action was a military blunder that diverted attention away from the Tudor allowing the king to be isolated and subsequently killed. Afterwards, King Richard being dead, William Stanley obviously claimed to have been coming to Tudor's rescue, a convenient version nobody has thought to challenge since.

Perkin Warbeck – Landed at Whitesand Bay in Cornwall early in September fourteen ninety-seven and raised his banner at Penzance shortly afterwards. Large numbers, up to eight thousand, flocked to his standard. The Sheriff of Cornwall was despatched to attack Richard's camp at Bodmin, but when in sight of it, his men defected to the prince. The earl of Devon tried to stop him and he too was forced to retreat to Exeter. The duke then attacked Exeter and laid siege, but this proved costly in men and time. Marching to Taunton, he began to lose men through desertion. Faced with a superior Tudor army and his leadership skills virtually non-existent his men gradually drifted back to their homes. Finally, realising his cause was hopeless, the duke of York with a handful of loyal followers fled his camp at night. Finally he sought sanctuary at the Abbey of Beaulieu where, upon a promise of pardon from Henry Tudor, he gave himself up. From this moment Henry Tudor began a propaganda campaign claiming the duke was an impostor and no true Plantagenet. While this was accepted by some of the common people, the question of his true identity with many, including the monarchs of Europe still persisted.

As a boy at Tournai, should Richard of York have been discovered by Tudor agents and questioned as to his identity, he would have been given a credible and traceable cover persona to conceal it. Thus he would have been able to "prove" he was actually Perkin Warbeck, a boatman's son to confound any pursuit. Thus, all Henry Tudor had to do to confuse these two identities was to reverse the process, expose the original cover story and "prove" the prince was actually Perkin the boatman's son. Seeing as the original cover story was intact and deliberately constructed to prove a false identity, it could equally be used to confirm it. Henry was simply using the original deceit to confirm his own. Once a false persona has been positively established for you, it is impossible to convincingly prove that you are, in fact, who you say you are! Never did the monarchies of fifteenth century Europe convincingly repudiate Richard of York's (Perkin Warbeck's) claim to the English throne. Some, James the Fourth of Scotland, the Holy Roman Emperor Maximilian, even Ferdinand and Isabella of Spain believed his claim even after his execution.

Henry Tudor had him at court for a few months, unable to dispose of him due to his considerable credence with the monarchies of Europe. He made sure there was no contact with the Queen, who was, of course, his sister and who could confirm his true identity. If she could have convincingly repudiated his identity as her brother, it is unthinkable that Henry Tudor would overlook such a propaganda coup. Later he imprisoned him in the Tower of London deliberately close to the earl of Warwick, son of George duke of Clarence, a brother of Edward IV, who had been incarcerated there since 1485.

They hatched a plot to escape together, were caught and brought to a contrived trial for high treason. York was displayed and humiliated in public and forced, after torture, to sign a confession stating he had no claim to the English throne. A traitor's death by hanging, drawing and quartering was prescribed but due to the weight of public opinion, there still being residual doubt that Perkin Warbeck was indeed an impostor, and the earl of Warwick being of royal blood, the sentence was commuted to a simple hanging. The two were hanged together at Tyburn on the twenty-third of November, fourteen ninety-nine; thus Henry Tudor had judicially murdered two Princes: the earl of Warwick, the rightful King of England and Richard duke of York who though illegitimate still had a better claim than Tudor.

Modern historians tend to dismiss Perkin as a fraud, but this has more to do with current literary fashion and the demands of a publisher than a desire to tell the truth of his identity. I would rather, as previous historians have done, give credence to the fifteenth century opinions of those powerful monarchs who had the means of discovering the truth and who could and did interview York personally. It is impossible to draw exact conclusions five hundred years later, by referring to contemporary Tudor records, documents and confessions that are highly suspect and of dubious provenance. It seems to me the apparent rejection of Richard of York by his contemporaries was due to his obvious unfitness to be a monarch rather than his being a fraud, though this charge was a convenient diplomatic excuse for some to distance themselves from him.

Katherine Gordon - was kept close at the Tudor court, Henry being captivated by her beauty. Later, after a period of eleven years, she would remarry by permission of the then monarch, Henry VIII. She went on to have a daughter with a third husband and when he died, married a fourth. She died in fifteen thirty-seven and is buried at Fyfield, Berkshire. As for her child with the duke of York - there is no record of their having had one, merely rumours of one, possibly two. There is a speculative account in Holinshed of Tudor's soldiers pursuing her to St. Michael's Mount lest she took sanctuary there and gave birth to a son. This seems to suggest there was a pregnancy at some time emanating from her marriage to the duke of York. Obviously Henry Tudor would not have allowed her child with York to be acknowledged and let it live. He did go to extraordinary lengths to try to discover if there was somewhere in the land a child of "Perkin's". Did Katherine persuade him to put the babe out to anonymous foster parents in a bid to save it? Whatever the case, the lack of a record does not mean there was never a child at all. After his execution, there is no record of her ever speaking of her first husband and when she died her will mentions her three subsequent husbands but not the first, Richard of York.

King James the Fourth of Scotland and John Damian – James was a highly cultured monarch. He spoke several languages, was something of a physician and experimented with alchemy. John Damian maintained a furnace at Stirling Castle to extract what was thought to be the wonderful "fifth element", Grand Magisterium or the Philosopher's Stone. I have brought his attendance at Stirling forward a few years for the sake of this story. He is recorded as being there from the year fifteen hundred. The mention of his attempt at flying from the ramparts of Stirling Castle is true, though the production of enchanted iron is entirely fictional. James attacked across the border with England to coincide with the invasion by Richard in Cornwall but this was badly coordinated and Prince Richard's subsequent defeat and capture put an end to it. In the year fifteen-three, He married Margaret Tudor, a daughter of Henry the Seventh. He did invade England again in fifteen-thirteen, when he challenged Henry the Eight's army under the earl of Suffolk, but lost at Flodden Field where he was killed along with huge numbers of his men. He shares with King Richard III the unfortunate distinction of being the last king to die in battle, King Richard III being the last English Monarch and King James IV the last British monarch.

Upton cum Chalvey Church - Dedicated to Saint Laurence and over 900 years old, this is the place where the poet Thomas Grey penned his famous elegy: In A Country Churchyard. Readers familiar with this poem will recognise references to it in the story. The building became derelict but was restored in the nineteenth century. The description in this book is how it would have looked in the fifteenth century.

Sheep Heid - This is reputedly the oldest pub in Scotland, dating from the fourteenth century and still survives at Edinburgh. It gets its name as described in this book, though the cuisine today is rather more palatable than in the fifteenth century.

Jolly John – was court jester to King Edward IV and King Richard III. Later he is recorded at the court of King James IV of Scotland. My creation of his persona here is fictional though the idea for making him a dwarf comes from another court jester, Jeffrey Hudson who was granted the title the Royal Dwarf by King Charles I of England. Hudson fought in the English Civil War on the Royalist side. Court Jesters were cast aside during the Cromwell years and not reinstated at the Restoration of Charles II.

Laurence the Armourer – There is a record of an armourer of this name being employed by King James IV of Scotland to make armour for the duke of York for which he was paid. This is the only mention of him and who he was or where he came from is otherwise unknown. I made him a Breton because this suited the invention of the stories in the three books of his exploits. Whoever he was I hope I have given him a new life in these stories.

Glossary of Arms and Armour

This story is told through the eyes of Laurence de la Halle, a Breton armourer. Because the terms used to describe medieval arms and armour may be unfamiliar to some readers, this glossary, arranged alphabetically, will explain those that are used in the book.

Armet á rondelle – a later development of the bascinet having a round form and favoured by Milanese armourers.

Arming nails – the modern term is rivet.

Aventail – mail that is attached to a helmet and draped over the shoulders to protect the neck of the wearer.

Barding – armour for horses.

Barbute – a visorless helmet for protecting the head. It was open at the eyes with a slit down the front. Italian in design after the ancient Greek model, it was rare in England.

Bascinet – a helmet with a pointed skull, worn with a visor. Old fashioned in the 15th century and largely superseded by the sallet.

Bevor – also called a gorget it provided protection for the neck, made of plate and extending up over the chin. This would be worn as a pair with a helmet, usually a sallet.

Brigandine – a leather coat fitted inside with metal plates to form effective body protection.

Cap à Pied – the term used to describe full harness (from head to foot).

Caparison – the colourful cloth covering of an armoured horse.

Chamfron – armour fitted to the face of a horse and connected to the criniere.

Chapel de fer - an iron domed helmet with a broad rim worn by common soldiers.

Courser – a horse bred to run.

Couter – metal protection shaped around the elbow (see lames, rerebrace and vambrace).

Criniere (or crinnet) – a series of lames formed and fitted to protect the neck of a horse.

Croupiere (or crupper) – armour that protects the hindquarters of a horse.

Cuirass – This is a term that describes a set of upper body armour comprising breastplate and back plate.

Cuirboille – leather boiled and then moulded into a hard plate as a means of providing protection.

Cuisse – Armour for protecting the thigh.

Falchion – A heavy sword with a single edge, sometimes called a curtal axe.

Faulds – articulated plates similar to lames for protecting the hips. Attached to the bottom of the breastplate and the backplate (cuirass).

Gardebrace – a plate that covers over a pauldron to give additional armoured protection to the shoulder and breast. Usually fitted on the left side as this is where a lance is most likely to strike in the joust.

Gambeson – a padded coat worn under armour to protect the wearer from bruising. Also worn by archers and others of low rank as a protection against penetration by arrows.

Gauntlet – a leather glove covered with armoured finger and hand protection.

Gatlings – the finger joints of a gauntlet.

Halberd – similar to the pole axe except longer with a spike at the base.

Harness – the term for full armour worn by a man at arms and used when referring to this.

Haubergeon – a mail shirt to protect the body and extending to the thigh.

Hauberk – similar to haubergeon but completely covering the body including the arms and legs.

Jupon – a quilted jacket to which armour is tied.

Lames – strips of formed metal over and under joints at the elbow (couter) and at the knee (poleyn). Also used in the flexible neck armour (criniere) for horses. They are made to pivot so that the joint can move.

Lance – the immediate henchmen of a noble lord who ride with him and support him in battle. A typical lance comprises men-at-arms, perhaps a few archers and squires to tend the horses and additional arms. A lance would vary in form and size according to the status and wealth of the lord.

Latten – the old name for brass.

Mail – links of metal formed into a body shape according to where it was being worn. Often worn under plate armour where a gap might offer an entry point. The term comes from the French for chain: *maille*, thus *chain-mail* is incorrect, being a tautology.

Pauldron – articulated plates that cover over the shoulder.

Pike – spear-like weapon typically eighteen feet long used as a defence against cavalry. French pikemen were used at Redemere (Battle of Bosworth) along with halberdiers to defend Henry Tudor from the onslaught of King Richard.

Pole Axe – similar to the halberd. It comprised an axe having a single blade on one side and a hammer, or spike on the other. There would also be a spearhead on the end for thrusting at an enemy. Usually fitted to an extended shaft for use on foot, though mounted knights sometimes carried a shorter version.

Poleyn – metal protection shaped over the knee (see lames). Usually fitted with wings for extra protection of the joint.

Prickers – armed scouts that ranged around the countryside to report back on the location, position and the strength of an enemy.

Prod -   the "bow" of a crossbow.

Quarrel – the missile fired by a crossbow; also known as a bolt.

Rerebrace – armour for the upper arm.

Rondel (1) – a round plate typically fitted over the front of the shoulder joint (pauldron) to protect the armpit. Usually embossed, ornate and embellished with latten or chased with a pattern. Also fitted to the chamfron of a warhorse with a spike fitted to the centre.

Rondel (2) – a round spiked dagger with a haft and heavy round pommel. It was used to force entry between armour joints, visors, etc, while the heavy pommel was a useful club. It also let the soldier strike hard with the palm of his hand to drive the point home. This might have been one of the weapons used to kill King Richard.

Rouncey – a horse chosen for stamina and speed, much favoured in the middle ages for scouting work and for hunting.

Sallet – a helmet with curved edges sweeping to the tail.

Stake (arming) – a shaped metal device with a post that fits into a Stake Plate. The armourer selects the shape relevant to the profile of the piece he is working on, which he then hammers over it into the shape he requires.

Stake Plate – a heavy iron plate with various shaped holes into which is fitted a stake.

Sumptuary Law – laws that set down the kind of clothing allowed according to rank. For instance, only princes of royal blood could trim their clothes with ermine.

Tassets – The plates suspended from the faulds to provide additional leg protection above the cuisses.

Vambrace – armour to protect the forearm.

War Axe – a shortened version of the halberd with a curved blade backed by a hammer or a spike. This was a weapon capable of killing or disabling a fully armoured knight.

White Armour – armour in the white - this term refers to plain steel harness and not the actual colour.

Author's Web Site: www.quoadultra.net

The Laurence the Armourer Trilogy:

On Summer Seas
A Wilderness of Sea
The Roaring Tide

14817621R00208

Printed in Great Britain
by Amazon.co.uk, Ltd.,
Marston Gate.